The Invisible Economy

A profile of Britain's invisible exports

David Liston, OBE, MA, FRSA, FSS, CIEx
Visiting Professor, European Business School
Honorary Education Adviser, British Overseas Trade Board

Professor Nigel Reeves, OBE, MA, DPhil, FIL, FRSA, CIEx
Head of the Department of Linguistics and International Studies
Dean of Faculty of Human Studies, University of Surrey

The Institute of Export

Pitman

PITMAN PUBLISHING
128 Long Acre, London WC2E 9AN
and
THE INSTITUTE OF EXPORT
64 Clifton Street, London
EC2A 4HB

First published in Great Britain 1988

British Library Cataloguing in Publication Data

Liston, David J. (David Joel), *1914–*
   The invisible economy: a
   profile of Britain's invisible exports.
   1. Great Britain. invisible exports
   I. Title   Ii. Reeves, Nigel
   382.1'7

ISBN 0 273 02704 2

Printed and bound in Great Britain at The Bath Press, Avon

We have had considerable help in specialised fields from Peter McGregor, Julian Arkell, Derek Honeygold, Mike Rimmington, Susan Moore, Liz Anstis and Lorraine Watkins-Mathys. In producing the text we were greatly assisted by the Project Administrator, Joan Miller, and by Rosemarie Harris of Surrey University.

Contents

Foreword by The Earl of Limerick KBE vii
Authors' Preface and Acknowledgements ix
Structure and Summary of the Book xii

Introduction xviii

PART I: Setting the scene – domestic and international context of world trade

1 The economic framework – a changing profile 3
2 Trade liberalisation, development and protectionism 23

PART II: The international service industries: sectoral studies

A: Finance, insurance, markets and exchanges

3 International banking and capital markets: transformations in the world of finance 47
4 Financial services: underpinning world trade 83
5 Markets and exchanges, old and new 114

B: Transport, communications, travel and tourism

6 By land, sea and air – international transport and telecommunications 139
7 Tourism, hotels and leisure-related industries 170

C: Consultancies and trade in knowledge

8 Construction, engineering and design 196
9 Trade in knowledge, experience and specialist skills 225

PART III: The education and training dimension

10 The cerebral revolution – challenge to education worldwide 265
11 Post-school education in the UK: vocational, professional and management 286

PART IV: Issues, challenges and conclusions

12   Some major issues: invisibles and a balanced economy   319
     Conclusions   348

Appendices

Appendix 1   Organisations, institutes, companies, etc. consulted by the
               authors   357

Appendix 2   Glossary of abbreviations   361

Index   365

Foreword

When most people talk about this country's overseas trade balance, they are generally referring only to the balance of trade in goods. It is a curious fact that even economic commentators, in reviewing Britain's trade performance, generally do so solely in terms of visible goods. It is even odder that a sector of the economy which provides nearly one half of the country's foreign earnings and has consistently produced a balance of payments surplus for nearly 200 years, largely does so unnoticed by the general public. The missing elements? The service industries and their invisible exports.

The term 'invisible exports' is hardly a recent innovation. It has been traced back to Sir Robert Giffen who used it in a paper to the Royal Statistical Society in 1882. Put simply it relates to anything which can be sold to a non-resident which you cannot drop on your toe. Thus the 'invisibles' embrace not only straightforward services like banking or insurance transactions conducted for foreigners, but also their spending in the UK as tourists or businessmen, their use of British ships and aircraft, and the fees and commissions paid to British intermediaries or consultants. Little was known about the contribution of invisible exports to the British economy until the publication in 1967 of the report by the original Committee on Invisible Exports entitled 'Britain's Invisible Earnings'. Perhaps it was more than coincidence that I made my maiden speech in the House of Lords during the debate on that report.

Much has happened in the intervening twenty years. Britain has always been heavily dependent on external trade and invisible trade has equally been of vital importance to us. What has changed recently is the composition of the income from visible trade. As the manufacturing capability of the newly industrialised countries has grown, so Britain's surplus on trade in manufactured goods has declined, to the extent that there has been a deficit in our balance of trade in manufactures since 1983. On the other hand, the exploration for hydrocarbons in our home waters was greatly stimulated by the oil shock from 1973, and in 1982 for the first time we had a surplus as net exporters of oil and gas. Given the fall in oil prices and the fact that the oil and gas fields have a finite life, variously estimated between 25 to 30 years, the importance of a growing income from the services sector is apparent.

This work by David Liston and Nigel Reeves is much to be welcomed as the first attempt in twenty years to give an overview of Britain's service industries in all their diversity. I feel some affinity with its origin, for it was at the launch of the authors' previous work *Business Studies, Languages and Overseas Trade* that a chance suggestion of mine sent them into invisible waters.

The moves towards the creation of a single European Market by the end of 1992 and the current negotiations within GATT on the liberalisation of international trade in services demonstrate the need for Britain to have a clear strategy for the education of its workforce to face the challenges of the next twenty years. This well set-out and readable book charts the way forward. I commend it to all who have our national prosperity at heart.

Authors' Preface
and Acknowledgements

The coverage of this book is very wide and its subject matter intricate and varied. It makes no claims to be a work of theoretical research, nor does it attempt simplistic solutions in areas which are of their very nature complex.

The objectives of the authors are indeed, quite modest. The book aims simply to present a perspective through which a vitally important part of the economy, Invisible Exports and the International Tradeable Services, may be seen as a whole and through which the prospects, difficulties and challenges of the future, particularly in terms of human skills and resources, can be most easily comprehended in the totality of their component parts.

The viewpoint of the book is that of British overseas trade. Its context is, however, international, reflecting the degree to which industry and commerce in the United Kingdom, in common with its major competitors, operates in almost all its major aspects on a world scene of increasing mutual interdependence.

Our information has been gathered from many sources. They include national and international statistics, though with due allowance for the many statistical imperfections which abound in this field; reports and commentaries from government departments at home and abroad; from worldwide government sponsored institutions; from economic, social, industrial and educational organisations; from a selective study of literature—books, monographs, seminars, journals and the specialist and general press; and finally from the many personal discussions (more than 100 in number) through which we have been able to explore the personal views, hopes and forebodings of individual firms, organisations, academic and professional establishments, Chambers of Commerce and Trade Associations.

Clearly, in the course of our work we have incurred many obligations and we owe many debts of gratitude. In the notes and references at the end of each chapter we have sought to acknowledge, though without overloading the text, the main sources of our material. We are conscious that in many cases our references are far from adequate to do justice to the long hours of most fruitful discussion which we were privileged to have with senior officials, businessmen and academics, whose knowledge and experience cover many countries of the world and almost every continent. Very sadly, however, from considerations simply of space and balance, a great deal of material, particularly from the academic world, has had necessarily to be excluded. It is, of course, also to be emphasised that whilst many have contributed to our story, the views expressed are the sole responsibility of the authors.

In a work like this, it is perhaps invidious to single out individuals for special mention. We must, however, say a special thank-you to our sponsors whose very generous contributions financed our research, travel and administrative expenses. They include the British Overseas Trade Board, Clearing and Merchant Banks, the Wincott Foundation, Professional Institutes, the London Chamber of Commerce and Industry Examinations Board and academic establishments.

We were particularly fortunate in the constitution of our Editorial Advisory Board who monitored our progress regularly as a Board and whose individual members responded magnificently to our many calls on their time and experience. Again, individual mention is invidious but we would be wrong not to give special thanks to Alistair Hunter for his quiet work on our behalf as Under-Secretary at the Department of Trade and Industry; to William Clarke who, as Director-General of the British Invisible Export Council, saw us on our way initially and who pointed out in his own trenchant fashion some early failures in our findings; to Richard Mason, Executive Director of the BIEC, who was a tower of strength throughout in guiding us through what were perhaps the most complex areas of our work; and to Dr. Tom Soper of Barclays Bank for having placed at our disposal, his unique knowledge of developments at the European Community, both in the UK and in Brussels and who, in addition, helped us greatly in our studies of the British overseas education.

The full list of sponsors and the members of the Editorial Advisory Board is given on page iii.

We owe very special thanks to the Alexander von Humboldt Foundation in the Federal Republic of Germany which, in appointing Professor Reeves as a Research Fellow at the University of Hamburg, offered him a unique opportunity to study in Germany, over a six-month period, many aspects of our work; to the German Academic Exchange for a shorter, but very welcome supplementary grant; and to the University of Surrey both for their financial contribution and for the granting of sabbatical leave to Professor Reeves.

Similarly, we owe a special debt to the European Business School and to their Director, Peter Coen, who in addition to financial contributions have made available to us, free of charge, their premises and administrative resources throughout our work—a priceless facility to the authors as well as to our hard-pressed Project Administrator.

Finally, we also thank our co-publishers, the Institute of Export, for their help in launching the project and for their continued association with the Editorial Board; and Pitman Publishing for involving themselves with the project to a quite unusual extent. Both Ian Pringle, Managing Director, and Simon Lake, Business Management Publisher, have served as members of the Editorial Board and we are grateful for them both for their constant assistance and reassurance. Howard Bailey, the Managing Editor, faced as he was with a moving target, has shown quite exemplary skill in applying his editorial talents to coping with the many modifications to the text made inevitable by the fast-moving developments in almost every aspect of our work. We also thank Professor Peter Buckley, Professor of Managerial Economics at Bradford University, for having read the text in draft on behalf of the publishers and the authors and for his most useful comments.

One final word of warning. We have tried to give wider coverage than in any previous study, but there are omissions. What we offer is a profile rather than exhaustive account. We have been concerned in the main with international tradeable services and therefore have not covered capital investment overseas. No direct attention is paid to advertising as an invisible export, if only because we were unable to lay our hands on the necessary basic statistics. Marketing and marketing research are touched on but not examined in detail, and mostly in the context of corporate consultancies and trade in knowledge. Finally, our approach to retailing is confined to specific channels such as the duty-free outlets in airports and purchases by overseas tourists.

Even within the areas which are covered in the text there are in every case specialists who know a great deal more about their particular subject than we do. We can only hope that during the processes of reading, consultation and discussion we have been able to grasp the essentials of the individual sectors and in our treatment have done justice to the subjects themselves and fulfilled the broad intentions of our work.

We have spoken more than once of 'moving targets' and the rapidly changing state of this field of operations. In some vital aspects we have incorporated changes that have occurred almost as the text passed to the presses. In general, however, the termination date for our material should be regarded as December 1987.

Structure and Summary of the Book

The book consists of an introduction and twelve chapters, divided into four parts. Each chapter is followed by a list of sources and references. Appendices 1 and 2 give respectively a list of organisations, institutions etc. consulted during work on the book and a glossary of abbreviations. The book concludes with a general index of contents.

Part I comprises chapters 1 and 2. Each is by way of being a scene-setting chapter for the text as a whole.

Chapter 1 outlines the broad economic trends within which the UK trade in invisible exports operates. It is derived from a selective analysis of national and international statistics disaggregated not only to throw light on some major changes in the UK economy from the 1960s, but also to place the developments in the international service industries into a broader economic context. It highlights a growing reliance in the UK balance of payments on invisible surpluses to offset visible trade deficits.

Chapter 2 gives an account of the major, and often conflicting, political, commercial and social factors which bear upon world trade in both visibles and invisibles. It describes some of the major international organisations such as the OECD, GATT and UNCTAD which are charged with the responsibility for keeping under review trade barriers, both tariff and non-tariff, and with seeking trade liberalisation and development. It points to the growing mood of trade protectionism in many countries of the world, particularly the USA, and by contrast to the pending negotiations which could lead to the service industries falling for the first time wholly or in part under the auspices of GATT. The final section of this chapter turns to the major resolution by the European Community to achieve a single free internal market by 1992.

Neither of the scene-setting chapters aims at a degree of statistical detail inappropriate to its purpose or to the nature of its material. Comparative international statistics on invisible exports are something of a technical minefield. The flow of information tends to be slow and uncertain, leading to adjustments both on a monthly and yearly basis. The figures are particularly susceptible to fluctuations in exchange rates. Nor is there in certain cases any common method of collecting the data adopted by government and industry or trade associations. The inter-pretation of statistics is often, therefore, a matter of judgement rather than precise measurement. Their value is in determining orders of magnitude, in identifying trends and, in particular sectors, in highlight-ing areas of growth and decline.

Part II of the book is directed to an analysis of the many individual industries and activities that contribute to the UK invisible exports. It has seven chapters divided into three main divisions – finance, insur-ance and markets; communications, travel and tourism; and trade in consultancies, intellectual property and specialist skills.

The first division (**Chapters 3, 4 and 5**) looks at the diverse world of the City, capital markets, international banking, insurance, accounting and related services; corporate consultancies, finance and shipping infor-mation services; and the many City markets in metals, commodities, foreign exchange and futures, and freight. The emphasis is on present-ing the radical reorganisation and technological transformation that the City is undergoing, and on London's competitive position as an historic leader in these fields.

The second division of Part II has two chapters, concerned respec-tively (in **Chapter 6**) with communications by land, sea and air and with telecommunications, and (in **Chapter 7**) with the movement of people in the British travel and tourist industries.

Chapter 6 points to the considerable changes which are under way following the continuing depression in the world shipping industry; the prospect of substantial liberalisation of land and air transport services within the European Community; and rapid technological change in all these areas of communication, but particularly in the transfer of information through telecommunication systems.

Chapter 7 is concerned with the movement of people in the context of both work and leisure. It presents a profile of the British tourist industry, its economic and employment dimensions and its future prospects. A large-scale commitment to education and training, in this field of substantial employment and rapid staff turnover, characterises the industry and a major part of the chapter is devoted to the discharge of these commitments.

The final division of Part II (**Chapters 8 and 9**) tackles the diverse but most innovative of international tradeable services and consultancies, the transfer of knowledge and the international trade in intellectual property and the creative arts.

Chapter 8 concentrates on the activities of UK civil engineers, archi-tects, surveyors and designers and other specialists in overseas engi-neering and construction. It draws attention to the changes that are occurring in the political and social context of overseas infrastructural development; and the competition and pressures to which British project consultancies are increasingly exposed. It emphasises, in particular, the new patterns of organisation and financial arrangements that have urgently to be considered by British consultants in conjunction with construction companies and finance houses.

Chapter 9 concentrates on the performance and competitiveness of Britain's knowledge-based services together with the legal environments in which they will operate in the UK following the enactment of the Copyright, Design and Patent Bill of 1987. It discusses income from overseas students and educational consultancies, health care, legal services, the sale of know-how through patents, licences and copyrights; and overseas earnings from royalties on books, television, films, music and computer software.

Part III (Chapters 10 and 11) addresses the problem of human resources in the conduct of international trade and services.

Chapter 10 places the creation of resources in the widest context of schooling and education in the light of the changing demand for personal skills and expertise, as well as of the whole process of the technological and what the authors term the 'cerebral' revolution. The emphasis is international, embracing both the worldwide studies of the International Labour Office in Geneva and more detailed critiques of progress in France, Germany and Japan. The chapter deals finally with the British scene, with particular reference to the Education Reform Act of 1988.

Chapter 11 examines in some detail post-school education and training in the UK. It describes a range of recent initiatives in vocational training sponsored by government departments and organisations, by trade associations and chambers of commerce, by academic institutions, and by private enterprise. The chapter then concentrates on those professional institutes and associations which are of particular relevance to invisible exports and the service industries. Their common aim is to produce from their large membership an adequate reservoir of young people, mostly of graduate status and all of them possessed of up-to-date and relevant qualifications for the world of work in which they will engage.

This leads, naturally, to a discussion at the end of the chapter on management education which the authors see as the culminating point in the total process of education and training for the new generation of leaders in British industry and commerce.

Part IV. Chapter 12 brings together a number of issues which have arisen in the previous chapters of the book. These are:

1 Manufacturing versus services. The authors question the validity of a distinction between alternative forms of economy. They consider the term 'post industrial' misleading for the type of knowledge-led economy on which the UK, in common with other developed nations, has embarked; and strongly maintain the continuing interdependence of manufacturing and services.

2 **Employment and people.** Emphasis is less on the numbers of jobs than on the skills and attitudes required to fill them adequately. The sectoral situation will remain uneven with financial, leisure and knowledge-based services as the major elements of growth, but with transportation (particularly shipping) faced with continuing decline.

Technological developments in international screen trading are likely to extend the number of centres for financial services beyond London, confirming the significance of Edinburgh, and certain off-shore islands such as the Channel Islands and the Isle of Man and extending to new centres such as Poole.

It sees as a major hope for the future the long tradition of professional education which has been developed within individual professional institutes, in some cases for more than a century. The requirement now is for more broadly based school curricula; a higher level of achieve-ment among the average and below average in the schools; more attention to adult and vocational training, in which a number of initiatives have been launched in recent years; and a closer and more sharply focused alignment of professional and management education for which the framework has already started to emerge.

3 **International competition.** This is treated in two parts – knowledge-based services and the financial sector.

The knowledge-based services make special demands on higher education, and progress in both teaching and research has inevitably been affected by cut-backs in public expenditure. The income from overseas students has been sharply affected by adverse policies in fees and grants.

One further point is made. As knowledge becomes more sophisticated and specialised, it becomes increasingly beyond the scope of any single nation to remain in the vanguard over the entire spectrum of relevant technology. The European Community, particularly in view of 1992, offers a unique opportunity for the pooling of knowledge and for joint programmes of research and development.

Within the financial sector we have assessed the financial centres of New York, Tokyo, Zurich, Frankfurt and Paris. It is concluded that the position of London as the world's financial centre is very strong indeed, not least because of the deregulation of the London markets in 1986 and the continuing restrictions on ranges of business activity contained in legislations in New York, Tokyo and Frankfurt. Other factors in favour of London include the convenience of the time-zones, the strength of the eurocurrency markets and the large number of foreign finance houses and securities organisations established in London in recent years.

4 Liberalisation and the stability of the world's financial system. The maximum liberalisation of world trade is accepted as a desirable objective, particularly in view of the extended range of the current round of GATT negotiations. The fears of over-exposure of the less developed nations, however, as expressed through UNCTAD are considered as very real and need to be taken very seriously.

This section concludes with the effect of the destabilisation of the world's financial systems through the removal of the bulkheads of containment as a result of rapid liberalisation and deregulation, together with the breathtaking speed of communication.

In the final analysis, it is concluded there is a tight-rope to be walked between completely free liberalised trade, with markets open to all, and the overall balance of each individual national economy. The situation in the UK is particularly precarious in view of the ever narrowing base of British industry.

It emphasises once again the need to build for the future on the twin strengths of manufacturing on the one hand, and a large diversity of professional, financial and commercial services on the other.

The **Conclusions** consider the competitiveness of Britain's international service industries as the country moves decisively, in what we have called the cerebral revolution, to a knowledge-based and information-intensive economy.

Four trends have been identified as major influences on these industries; fundamental technological change, deregulation and liberalisation of the markets, intensifying international competition and the emphasis on information and knowledge transfer. Together they are seen to form the constituent characteristics of the cerebral revolution.

Strength is found in those historically established service industries most affected by this revolution, particularly the financial sector, and most encouragingly in the new international service industries, corporate consultancy, television and entertainment products, computing software, telecommunications and global information services.

That is not to say there are no vulnerabilities. The greatest, affecting almost all the service industries, is the volatility of exchange rates, itself a reflection of what is probably, at present, an inherently unstable global monetary system.

Moves to stabilise the system are identified as a priority and a key to a successful future. They include the assumption by the European Community of the world's leading monetary role, the reinforcement of the European Monetary System by membership of sterling and the adoption of the ECU as a key world trading currency.

The second priority, of especial significance for the UK, is a new emphasis on the value of education – a substantial improvement in the standard of general education of the lower and middle achievement groups in schools, a broader and larger entry to higher education, and the fusion of initiatives for continuing management education with the tradition of professional training in the service industries.

Above all, it is imperative that the UK's international service industries seize the opportunity of 1992 to widen their activities in a free home market of 320 million people. In 1973 British manufacturing failed to make such advances (though 1992 will offer a possible second chance). The service industries discussed in this book have to a significant extent not yet enjoyed that opportunity. It would be tragic if they were to fail in this endeavour.

Introduction

There are few industrial or commercial activities in any country of the world that have enjoyed an annual peace-time trading surplus for over 200 years. Yet this is the remarkable achievement of the United Kingdom's invisible exports. Until 1983 that record had been shared by the traditional heart of the British economy, manufacturing industry. By the end of 1987, however, historical surpluses in manufacturing had been transformed into a record deficit at the annual rate of some £14 billion. Despite the continued contribution of North Sea oil exports (but at substantially lower prices than in the early 1980s) the deficit for all visible trade remained just under £10 billion. Invisible exports, on the other hand, showed a 1987 surplus of more than £5.4 billion [1].

It is not only in the balance of payments that the UK's invisible exports have such a vital and increasingly important role to play. In employ-ment, too, there has been a dramatic shift, dating back to the 1950s, away from jobs in primary and secondary industry, chiefly from agricul-ture, mining and manufacturing, into the services sector. Over two-thirds of Britain's employed now work in this sector. Of course, the services sector ranges very widely indeed over activities as diverse as cleaning, security services, hairdressing and retailing, through to inter-national financial services, air transport and tourism and many more. Not all these services are internationally tradeable, except perhaps very indirectly. They may not be services that can normally be sold to customers based overseas or visiting from overseas, thus constituting an export. But the British Invisible Exports Council has, nonetheless, calculated that well over 40 per cent of UK employment can be attributed to the tradeable service industries, while fewer than 25 per cent remain in manufacturing [2].

International service industries are, then, critically important in the welfare of the UK economy. Nor is Britain alone in its growing dependence on these industries and their contribution to exports. This reliance is shared by several other OECD countries, including the UK's greatest challenger in much of the sector, the United States. Profound international concern at the chronic trade deficit of the United States and at the stock market crash of autumn 1987 add to the urgency for a review of the UK's invisible exporting activities.

This book undertakes that review. It looks at the full range of the UK's international service industries, their nature, the changes occurring within them, their exposure to international competition, their strengths and vulnerabilities, and human resources available to them in the UK.

What are invisible exports?

A useful working account of invisible exports is given by the British Invisible Exports Council, a body backed by the UK Government whose task is to monitor and to promote British invisible exports. It was established some twenty years ago as the National Committee on Invisible Exports and has operated under its present name since 1983.

Invisible exports as defined by the Council include foreign export earnings, (whether in foreign currency or in sterling) from a range of internationally tradeable services. These include banking, insurance and the activities of the 'City', encompassing The Stock Exchange and international securities trading, currency and commodity markets and financial, professional and information services. Invisibles also comprise very large earnings from tourism, hotels, catering and leisure-related industries; from transportation by air, sea and land including shipping, airlines and telecommunications; and from many aspects of overseas consultancy such as management, accounting, environmental health care, educational and legal services. Overseas earnings arise also from various activities in engineering and construction, including the management of overseas projects. There is, in addition, a significant contribution from the transfer of 'Intellectual Property' such as licences, patents, copyrights and franchises, as well as from royalties from books, TV, films and entertainment.

There is, finally, the income derived from overseas investment, a source of income which showed a substantial rise in the earlier 1980s as the UK oil surpluses were invested abroad. While it has not been our concern to plot the specific sources of this income, the management on the international markets of much indirect British investment overseas in the form of securities is an important service contributing to the UK's invisible export balance.

Through this range of activities, it is estimated by the BIEC that private British sector invisibles generated in 1986, for example, gross foreign earnings of nearly £73 billion with a net *surplus* of nearly £12 billion. (The corresponding figures for visible trade were £73 billion gross and a net *deficit* of £8.8 billion). Government transfers such as contributions to the European Community and support for the British Army on the Rhine reduce the private invisibles surplus (which surpassed the £12 billion mark in 1987) to net national surpluses of the order we have already quoted (over £5 billion).

Invisible exports in a world setting

This record of stability and growth in the UK's invisible exports does not emerge from some compact or sheltered area of trade, nor from activities which are shielded in any way from the full impact of worldwide political, technological, industrial and social developments. On the contrary, invisible exports combine a variety of commercial and service activities, each one of which is compelled to fight for its life in an environment of intensive international competition.

The historical place of the UK in the world's financial markets (at or near the top of the league) is now challenged not only by their long-established rivals and competitors in the USA and on the Continent of Europe, but also through the rapid emergence of fast-moving capital markets in the Far East and especially Japan.

Traditional services such as banking and stockbroking are still working through a massive structural and technical revolution, which has already shattered long-standing patterns of operation and professional practice in the markets. Specialist services such as construction and engineering consultancy face growing competition from the newly industrialised countries in the Far East and Latin America. The United States, Canada and Australia are ever more successful in Britain's traditional educational service markets.

Tourism and travel, a considerable growth area, contend with fluctuating exchange rates and with the deterrent effect of factors as unrelated as international terrorism and nuclear pollution. Transportation by sea, land and air has suffered very severely from a combination of commercial and political factors which are outside the direct control of the UK's national industries, including a world-wide shipping recession. Finally, the newer and perhaps most promising of services – computing, telecommunications and the media – rely almost entirely for their continued growth on the sheer creative skill of British engineers, designers, authors, playwrights, musicians and media specialists.

It is under these challenging and complex circumstances that the UK has increasingly looked to invisible exports and the trade in services to remedy the sombre figures elsewhere in the balance of payments. True, manufacturing in the UK was more buoyant in 1987 than at any time since 1973, growing at an annual rate of 6.5 per cent. It is a rate that outstripped any other member of the European Community. Moreover, non-oil exports grew by 10.8 per cent from 1986 to 1987. But the hunger for imports continued to surge, growing by 10.9 per cent.

The temptation, therefore, has been to seek excessive consolation from these invisible revenues and, in some circles, even to maintain that the UK is already well set to replace a manufacturing-based economy with one which is largely dependent on invisible exports and the UK's domestic and international service industries.

Objectives and approach

The objective of this book is to take a closer look at the particular elements in the internationally tradeable service industries on which these hopes are based and to see how well founded they are. This book looks at the full range of the UK's international service industries, their nature, the changes occurring within them, their exposure to international competition, their strengths and vulnerabilities, and the human resources available to them in the UK.

While the economic circumstances and fortunes of these many diverse activities vary, we have identified in the majority of cases four broad trends decisively affecting their future:

1 fundamental technological change, largely induced by advances in computer technology and telecommunications;
2 a worldwide move towards the deregulation of service markets and the international liberalisation of trade in services;
3 intensifying international competition;
4 an increasing and decisive emphasis on information and knowledge transfer as the basis of internationally tradeable services.

These trends call for new technical skills and for fresh, more flexible professional and management attitudes. Remaining competitive places greater demands than ever before on the human resources available to the service industries and to individual enterprises.

Few explanatory stones were left unturned in the quest to discover why Britain performed relatively weakly in manufacturing over the past quarter century. One major recent explanation has been the inappropriate nature of the British educational system. Industry Year 1986 was inspired by the view that the most fundamental cause of the British 'malaise' was the existence of an anti-industrial culture. Remedies are being applied by Government to schools and higher education alike with the over-riding objective of inculcating a positive view of enterprise and wealth-creation. The speed and weight of change is unprecedented since the Education Act of 1944, and significantly 1988 saw the most important legislative Act in the educational sphere since then.

It is for these reasons that we devote, unusually perhaps, considerable space to an examination of school systems in some other major competing countries and of the UK's professional and management education provision in the main international service areas. For we conclude that education is a vital long-term factor in maintaining the excellence not only of manufacturing but also of the service industries. Increasingly, invisible trade is based on the transfer of information and knowledge. Success is dependent on the supply of people of the calibre and training to cope with this change, a change we have called the cerebral revolution.

References

1   Balance of payments statistics from *The Current Account of the United Kingdom Balance of Payments*, Department of Trade and Industry, (DTI) and Central Statistical Office (CSO), January 1988.

2   Statistics from British Invisible Exports Council (BIEC) and Employment Gazette in BIEC, *Annual Report and Accounts 1986/87*, London, 1987, p. 36.

PART I

Setting the scene – the domestic and international context of world trade

1 The economic framework – a changing profile

Towards 'deindustrialisation'? – the aberrant British economy

When in 1959, Harold Macmillan was misquoted by the Press as having told the nation, 'You've never had it so good', (it was in fact a mild warning to car workers – *you've* never had it so good) his words still broadly reflected the state of the British economy. Admittedly, Britain could no longer lay claim to the 34 per cent of world visible trade that she had possessed at the beginning of the century and before two world wars. Nevertheless, she still possessed some 18 per cent – no mean achievement considering the unrelenting rise of the industrial power of the United States, the recovery of other West European nations and the transformation of West Germany's fortunes in her economic miracle. But the speed and magnitude of Britain's post-war return to prosperity was rapidly being overtaken by other industrialised economies and today we can see that the performance of the late 1940s and early 1950s only marked a temporary respite in a continued secular decline.

By 1986 that share in world trade had fallen to some 8 per cent, comparable to that of Italy which had commenced the century with a mere 2 per cent. From Figure 1.1 it is evident that the countries that have replaced Britain as the world's leading manufacturers, the United States apart, are Japan and West Germany. The Federal Republic in location, size of population, and technical and educational development might have been expected to follow a similar course to that of Britain, but this was far from the case.

Some statistics demonstrate the point. In 1950 the gross national product per head in Britain was marginally below that of two European countries spared the travails of the Second World War, Switzerland and Sweden, but was marginally ahead of most other European countries, including quite markedly, West Germany. Figure 1.2 shows how the situation (in Gross *Domestic* Product) developed. In 1960 the UK held seventh rank in Europe and was higher than Canada. By 1984 her position had dipped to tenth in Europe and was below Canada, Australia and Japan as well as the United States.

Of course, Macmillan's words were still true. Britain had never had it so good and, while the manufacturing economy continued to grow

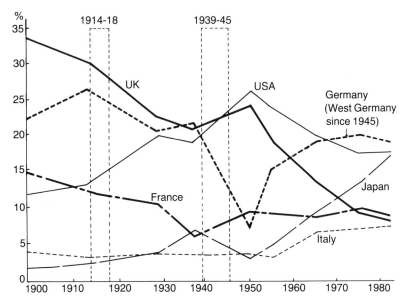

Figure 1.1 Proportions of world exports of manufactured goods; long-term trends. (Source: Barclays Review November 1983)

through the 1960s and into the late 1970s, the rate of growth was substantially below that of her neighbours. Then, with the second 1978–79 oil shock, inflation rates shot up well beyond 20 per cent. The Conservative Government attempted to throttle this with record high interest rates, matched fatefully for Britain's fragile manufacturing sector with an astonishing recovery of the pound sterling in its exchange rate with the key currencies, the dollar, the Deutschmark and the franc, a recovery determined not only by the Government's anti-inflationary monetary policy but also by the market's view of the pound as a petro-currency. The combination of world recession, domestic monetary constraint and a high exchange rate produced an absolute fall in manufacturing output (*see* Table 1.1) experienced by only one other OECD country, Norway, which had similarly suffered from finding itself in possession of an over-valued petro-currency.

What was particularly worrying was that Britain's decline in manufacturing was not restricted to a small number of large but old-fashioned industrial sectors. On the contrary, a 1985 CBI investigation showed that poor performance compared with the rest of OECD countries extended across the entire range of manufacturing. By 1982 in seven out of twenty-three sectors the UK performed worst of all, while in all but three it was never more than fourth from bottom. In clothing (eighth from bottom) and footwear (fifth from bottom), which have been considered most at risk, performance was, ironically, marginally better.

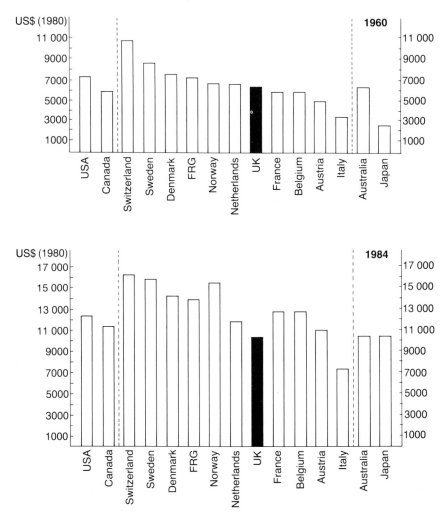

Figure 1.2 Per capita real GDP (1980 US $). (Source: Wharton World Economic Service)

As the CBI wryly commented, 'with twenty-one countries in the OECD and twenty-three sectors in the list, a median country could expect to outperform others in 242 country sectors. The UK outperforms in a mere thirty-six.' [1].

Critics of the Conservative Government point to the cruel combination of massive rises in energy cost, exceptionally high interest rates and an arbitrarily strong pound as the principal causes of the 'collapse' as the CBI termed it. But, as we have seen, these factors exacerbated the condition of an already vulnerable manufacturing economy, which, from the time of Harold Wilson's devaluation in 1967, had relied heavily

Table 1.1 Indices of manufacturing production for selected OECD countries 1983 (1975 = 100)

Country	Manufacturing production
Canada	113
USA	131
Japan	147
Austria	125
Belgium	116
Denmark	127
France	112
Germany	114
Italy	117
Netherlands	115
Norway	95
Sweden	101
Switzerland	105
UK	92

Source: CBI, OECD

on falls in the value of sterling in order to remain competitive. We should, however, consider two other frequently cited causes. They are: poor productivity and low investment. Table 1.2 shows clearly a striking juxtaposition in the case of the UK, of slow economic growth rates in the twelve-year period 1970–82, sluggish productivity, high inflation, and soaring earnings, resulting in steep increases in unit labour costs. The only country of the seven shown to come close to Britain was Italy, which could show high higher productivity increases and far higher economic growth.

We have then a picture of a country that would seem to be compelled to overprice goods in an attempt to recover constantly and fast rising labour costs not matched by increased output.

Turning to investment, we find in the 1979–83 period positive dis-investment in British manufacturing. The average percentage fall when we compare 1979 with 1983 across sectors was 41 per cent. In metals it was a staggering 63 per cent, in mechanical engineering 54 per cent, construction 49 per cent, vehicles 44 per cent. Even electrical engineering suffered a 19 per cent fall and chemicals 46 per cent [2]. But again, it has to be stated, that grave as this was, it was not an altogether new phenomenon. Investment in British industry had been chronically low [3], reflecting, in a vicious circle, the relatively unattractive return on capital. In real terms since 1963 that had hardly ever exceeded 8 per cent per annum and was generally about 6–7 per cent, peaking in 1972 and 1977 [4]. Capital formation per employee in manufacturing was in 1965 half that of France and some 30 per cent of that of the USA. By 1970

Table 1.2   Selected performance indicators for industrialised countries, 1970–1982

	Real GNP	Consumer prices	Industrial production	Labour productivity[b]	Hourly earnings[c]	Unit labour costs[d]	Unemployment as % of total labour force 1970	Unemployment as % of total labour force 1982
				Annual rates[a] of change of				
UK	1.3[e]	17.5	0.8	3.0	22.9	17.7	3.1	12.5
USA	2.8	9.0	2.6	3.4	8.8	5.3	4.8	9.5
Canada	3.3	9.8	2.4	3.4	12.3	8.7	5.8	10.9
Japan	5.0	9.0	3.6	6.3	12.3	6.4	1.1	2.4
France	3.1[e]	11.9	2.3	5.2	18.6	10.8	2.5	8.0
Germany	2.4	5.1	1.6	4.2	7.5	3.6	0.6	6.1
Italy	2.8[e]	22.5	2.8	5.1	35.9	26.0	3.4	8.9

Notes: (a.) Compound, from regression trend line. (b.) Output per person-hour in manufacturing, seasonally adjusted. (c.) Manufacturing in national currency. (d.) Seasonally adjusted in national currency. (e.) GDP.
Source: Meyer F.V. (ed), *Prospects for Recovery in the British Economy*, Croom Helm, London (1985)

these ratios were worsening and by 1975 the only marginal improvements were in relation to the US and Japan from a very low level.

In 1983, for the first time since the Industrial Revolution, the UK imported more manufactured goods in value than she exported. This historic and baleful event was, of course, connected with the drastic fall in output after 1979, but more disturbingly it was also the reflection of a long-term trend that had accelerated. It was hardly a failure to export – Britain has consistently exported larger proportions of her national product than Japan or even West Germany. Rather it was the result of the growing import penetration of the domestic market. By 1984 nearly 30 per cent of the overall deficit with the EC was accounted for by motor vehicles, and 10 per cent by textiles, for example [5]. Figure 1.3. illustrates the widening gap between imports and exports in volume

Table 1.3   Gross fixed capital formation per head employed in manufacturing

	1965	1970	1975
UK	460	604	1006
France	905	1439	2682
Germany	—	—	1707 (1974)
Italy	367	751	1469 (1974)
Japan	760	1317	1768
USA	1675	2145	2947

Source: Pollard, The Wasting of the British Economy,
Croom Helm, London (1982), p. 348

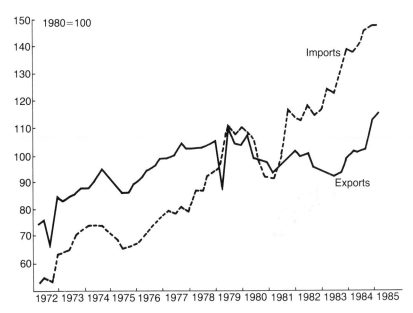

Figure 1.3 UK exports and imports of manufactures by volume. (Source: Monthly Review of External Trade Statistics) (*Crown copyright. Reproduced by permission of the Controller. HMSO*)

terms. In 1986 the gap in value terms was £4.9 billion for finished manufactures together with a deficit of £578 million in semi-manufactured goods. The overall deficit for visible trade including oil was £8.5 billion in 1986 and continued to rise in 1987, according to Central Statistical Office figures, to £9.8 billion, while the deficit on manufactures soared to £9.2 billion, and on semi-manufactures to £3 billion.

The relative decline of manufacturing's contribution to the economy, known in the literature as 'deindustrialisation' [6], is a rather misleading term, since it could suggest a deliberate strategy to reduce manufacturing industry. Naturally, it has aroused a great deal of attention, the more so since it was a phenomenon apparently already observed in the United States before the late 1970s. There, too, traditional heavy and extractive industries were in historical decline as newly emerging industrialised countries were able to produce low technology goods and basic manufactures more cheaply. Indeed, the diminution of steel-making, mining and shipbuilding since the 1970s is common to all advanced industrialised countries. The other convergent feature of economic change in such states in this last quarter of the twentieth century is the move to the service industries as the largest national source of employment. Here, too, Britain was no exception. It was to describe these phenomena that the term 'post-industrial' was coined, indicating what was regarded as a secular shift into a new evolutionary stage for mature industrial economies [7].

Whatever the merits of these analyses, they cannot mask one major point in which the UK is divergent from other modern economies; nowhere else, except in Norway, was the change in employment pattern away from manufacturing also accompanied by an absolute fall in overall manufacturing output.

In the USA 'deindustrialisation' has been accompanied by a rise in the absolute contribution of industry to the gross product, if not in terms relative to the growing contribution of the service industries. Industrial expansion has also continued in West Germany and Japan and, although Japan has shown markedly faster growth, both have in common an unabated increase in their visible trade surpluses (to the point where it is argued, particularly in the USA, that they are endangering world trading stability).

There are, however, now positive signs in the UK of recovery from the traumatic early 1980s. UK manufacturing output has increased yearly since 1982. By the end of 1987 it had surpassed its output levels of eight years before (but had still not reached those of 1974). Industry now is more productive. There is much greater awareness of the need to introduce new, competitive technologies. Historically entrenched working practices are changing – sometimes in savage confrontation as we have witnessed in the newspaper printing industry. Yet the resultant rise in UK productivity still fails to match that of the major competitors as Figure 1.4 shows.

Unemployment has been falling steadily. By 1987 some 2.9 million were without a job compared to 3.4 million in 1985. But even modestly

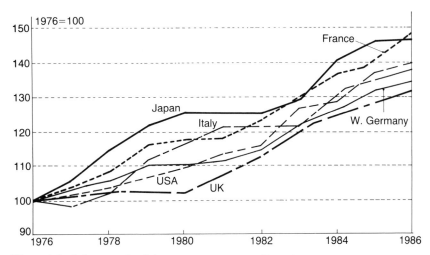

Figure 1.4 Labour productivity: output per person/hour in manufacturing. (Source: NIESR – Financial Times)

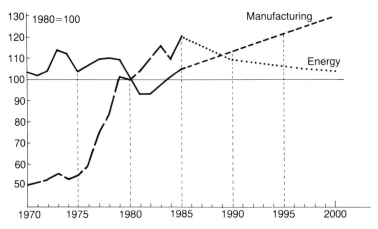

Figure 1.5 Output in the production industries. (Source: NIESR; UK National Accounts (Blue Book) 1986: (*a*) 1970–85 actual, (*b*) 1985–2000 forecast.

optimistic forecasts of consistent growth at levels not so far below the British performance of the 1960s make it, in the words of one authority, 'questionable whether (the increase) would enable the manufacturing industries to raise their exports in the next decade to a degree sufficient to close the trade gap that would inescapably develop in line with the falling oil export revenues' [8].

For, even if we assume a sustained growth of manufacturing output of $1\frac{3}{4}$ per cent per annum until the end of this century, this will do little more than offset in output terms the fall in oil production. For this to make up the loss in oil's contribution to the balance of payments, all that new output would have to be exported or substituted for imports, an optimistic scenario if the economy as a whole grows and thus draws in further imports (*see* Figure 1.5).

This means that the service industries in the UK must shoulder a great burden, and since the UK, unlike the USA, is essentially an international trading nation, it places an awesome responsibility on those service industries whose products can be sold to overseas customers. It is to the rising fortunes of these industries that we now turn.

The rise of the service industries as employers and sources of production

So diverse is the nature of service industries that scholars have had considerable difficulty in defining the common element that justifies considering them as a single major economic category. Essentially they are those industries, processes and sources of employment that are not involved directly in the manufacturing of goods. Yet manufactured goods could not be sold in a modern society without the support of services – for the provision of capital, for research and product development, for marketing, distributing and retailing. An activity least apparently associated with manufacturing, leisure, relies, however, on the construction industries for its location and buildings, and the food industry for much of its catering.

As manufacturing grew in volume and complexity of process and product while markets expanded in size and geographical coverage throughout this century, it was inevitable that the contribution of services to national economies would grow. This is as true of domestic trade as it is of international trade, whose volume has grown prodigiously after the setbacks of the Second World War. The sophistication of consumer economies requires a growing multiplicity of services. As these services themselves become more sophisticated, the trend continues among manufacturers not to carry out such work in-house but to subcontract it out to the specialists. That was invariably the case with banking and insurance and usually advertising, but it now extends to market research, transportation, consultancies of all kinds, security, cleaning and catering. Thus it is not surprising that the share of services in the UK GDP by value had risen from some 44 per cent in 1955 (48 per cent by volume) to 50.5 per cent in 1983 (50.3 per cent by volume). The pattern has been broadly similar in other advanced industrial countries and in some is still more pronounced. The share of GDP by value in the United States in 1953 was, as in the UK, 44 per cent; by 1983 it was 54 per cent. Even countries of such manufacturing strength as Japan and Germany have followed the same pattern: in Japan the 1954 figure of 43 per cent had risen to 54 per cent in 1982; in West Germany the change was also some 10 per cent upwards from the lower 1964 base of 39.6 per cent [9].

The nature of the change is further illuminated if we look at some individual sectors. In 1976, agriculture, forestry and fishing contributed 2.9 per cent of UK GDP. By 1986 it had fallen to 1.8 per cent. Construction declined from 6.5 per cent to 6.2 per cent, and manufacturing from 28.3 per cent to 24.3 per cent. Distribution, hotels and catering over the same ten-year period rose from 12.4 per cent to 14.0 per cent and banking, finance and business services from 10.8 per cent to 15.8 per cent. This latter striking rise was to a small extent offset in the services area as a whole by a stagnation in communications (2.8 per cent to 2.7 per cent) and a fall in transport, 5.5 per cent to 4.5 per cent [10].

The shift in employment that has accompanied this change is still more striking. Manufacturing processes have had to become more efficient, and increasingly capital-intensive. Indeed, were it not for significant changes created by computers and computer networks, the growth in employment in service activities would have been even more marked. But many services, which, in the final analysis, are more or less tailor-made for the individual client, remain and will continue to remain more labour-intensive than manufacturing. Thus the share of services in UK employment rose from 42.5 per cent in 1954 to nearly 64 per cent in 1983 and in the United States from 49.5 per cent in 1953 to 66.7 per cent in 1983. A similar trend is also observable in West Germany (37.4 per cent to 48 per cent) and in Italy, for example, (36 per cent to 50 per cent), though the total share in employment is still lower than in the UK and US. This is not because German or Italian manufacturing productivity is lower but may reflect a greater in-house retention of services for manufacturing.

Probably the most exhaustive investigation of employment trends in the UK yet conducted was concluded by the Institute of Manpower Studies in 1986 [11]. Based on 3000 questionnaires and interviews with 450 employers covering half the British work-force, it found that by 1985 two-thirds of all those in work were active in the service industries. The largest sector with some six million jobs was the distributive, finance and business sector, while leisure at some 2.7 million came third after public services. Manufacturing and agriculture together only made up one-third of the remaining total. But, still more significant for this study are perhaps the trends in employment for the next five years and within those forecasts the uneven prospects for the various service sectors. Agriculture and production industries are expected to lose a further 8 per cent of their total or 665 000 jobs by 1990, with half of that accounted for by service elements subcontracted out. Within the services sector the distributive, finance and business sector could provide 400 000 more jobs, building on an existing increase of 680 000 from 1979–85. Leading this rapidly expanding sector in both output and employment are banking and business services. In output banking has increased at 6.5 per cent per year over the period and business services at 8.9 per cent while employment has risen at a rate of an annual 10.9 per cent. The leisure sector in the survey included not only the hotel and catering industries but cleaning services, recreation and cultural services, repairs of goods and vehicles and research and development.

In 1985 the hotel and catering industry is estimated, in this report, to have employed 1 041 000, with an annual growth rate of 1.8 per cent per annum since 1979. More than one hundred thousand new jobs have been created in this sector during the six years to 1986, reflecting the growth of tourism and the general trend towards eating out and buying fast food. With the notable exception of cleaning services (the most vigorously expanding sector of all) the other areas were static or declining; however, the forecasts for the following five years look forward to a continuing impressive growth in tourism, provided that American visits hold up. In all some 200 000 new jobs could be created by 1990, mostly in favour of female, part-time and young employees.

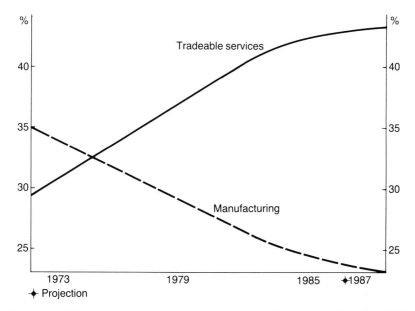

Figure 1.6   UK employment: manufacturing and tradeable services. (Source: BIEC)

And what of those services that are specifically tradeable at an international level? This is of course notoriously difficult to calculate because tourist facilities cater for the domestic and foreign customer simultaneously while retail shops and personal services such as hair-dressing anywhere in the country may serve foreign visitors. By 1984 some 40 per cent of all employment was in the tradeable services sector compared to 26 per cent in manufacturing. The significance of this is still greater when we compare the long-term trend: in 1973 manufacturing still employed substantially more people than tradeable services. Though the trend slowed down significantly in the mid-1980s, the disparity had grown to 43 per cent for services in 1986 (with the same projected for 1987) and 24 per cent for manufacturing (and the same projected for 1987) [12].

One area which is specifically concerned with international invisible trade and has been measured is City banking employment. From 1980 to 1985 the number of foreign banks in London grew from 403 to 463, creating 12 000 new jobs or a phenomenal 20 per cent of all new banking employment [13].

Invisible earnings and the balance of payments

Employment alone could, then, demonstrate the key importance of the international services sector for the national economy. But when we come to the balance of payments we see that the contribution of these industries and of earnings from overseas investments is substantial. The British Invisible Exports Council has calculated that the surplus for the entire private sector in 1986 was £12 billion, substantially more than the oil surplus (£4 billion) and more than offsetting the visible trade deficit of £8.5 billion. By 1987 it could, however, no longer match the deficit. While invisibles in the private sector showed a net surplus of 5.4 billion, the manufactures deficit had, as we saw above, reached some £14 billion.

Figure 1.7 illustrates vividly the transformation in the relative roles of the productive and service sectors in contributing to the UK balance of payments in this decade.

Twenty years before, in 1965, according to government statistics the private sector surplus had been only £873 million. Although these figures are not adjusted for inflation the improvement is remarkable. Two principal and interrelated areas can be identified as the sources of this change – investment income which has risen ten times and financial services whose net earnings have soared from £346 million in 1966 to £8.4 billion in 1986 (both sets of figures in unadjusted values) [14].

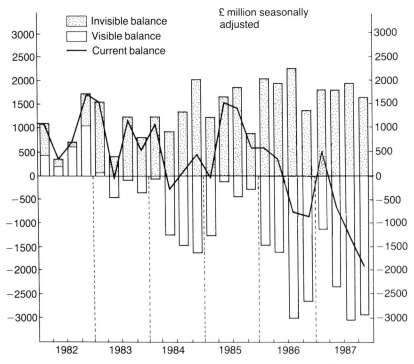

Figure 1.7 Balance of payments. (Source: Economic Trends) (*Crown copyright. Reproduced by permission of the Controller, HMSO*)

The performance of the individual sectors

The financial institutions and the City

The performance of the individual service industries is, however, uneven. By far the largest source of net earnings is the financial sector with a surplus in 1986 of some £9.4 billion. Table 1.4 gives a break-down of what the individual financial services and related City institutions earned.

Particularly evident in Table 1.4 is the success of insurance companies, which includes both earnings on insurance transactions themselves and investment income from abroad. Banking makes up a very substantial contribution of £2.3 billion net, ranking second to insurance. Indeed, as can be clearly seen from this table, an impressive range of service trading activities plays its part, revealing the breadth of Britain's financial institutions and their successful involvement in overseas trade. With the notable exception of the major Scottish insurance and investment houses, the activities in this list largely operate from the City of London. In fact the City is the largest single source of net foreign earnings for the United Kingdom. When we further consider that Britain's net overseas annual investment soared from £8.6 billion in 1976, to £110 billion in 1986, that in 1986 a total of some £146 billion net was invested by UK residents in overseas securities and some £91 billion in direct investments, and that the bulk of both types of investment was probably looked after by City advisers, we see the remarkable strength and

Table 1.4   UK financial institutions – net earnings overseas in 1986

	£ million
Insurance	4260
Banking	2295
Pension funds	638
Securities dealers	552
Export houses	350
Other brokerage	248
Commodity traders	223
Baltic Exchange	221
Investment trusts	188
Unit trusts	175
Stock Exchange	152
Leasing	50
Lloyd's Register of Shipping	24
TOTAL	9376

Source: CSO Pink Book, 1987

significance of the City. And these investments themselves contributed net earnings from abroad totalling £5.6 billion in 1986 [14].

Transport and tourism

This encouraging performance must, however, be contrasted to a grave decline in the shipping account. The UK share of the world fleet (itself diminishing from the mid-1970s) fell from 11.3 per cent in 1968 to under 2 per cent at the end of 1986, and the balance of the sea transport account plunged into increasing deficit from 1981, flattening out in 1985 at minus £1.16 billion and recovering a little to a deficit of £937 million in 1986. This rapidly deteriorating performance has been described as catastrophic in some political circles, for not only does the diminished size of the merchant fleet involve a serious weakening of the British strategic shipping reserve in a time of emergency (as for example when the Falklands crisis erupted in 1983) but the balance of payments figures continue to give credit to all UK-owned vessels even when they fly a non-UK flag.

Nor has land transport performed well in recent years. Until 1981 it had enjoyed a series of modest surpluses. But since then, reflecting the growing strength of imports which are largely brought to the UK by overseas hauliers, the balance slipped to a deficit of some £178 million in 1986, nonetheless a marginally better achievement than in 1985 [14].

This rather bleak picture is not offset by civil aviation. This sector had long earned surpluses, peaking at £347 million in 1981. But since then the surpluses have declined and in 1986 turned into a major deficit of £449 million. While passenger income for UK airlines was almost exactly balanced by overseas airlines passengers income from the UK, freight on imports and disbursements by the airlines abroad substantially exceeded domestic receipts [14].

The largest gross earner of foreign income in this field is travel and tourism, which in 1986 earned some £4 billion. Its significance is above all, as we have seen, its major and growing contribution to employment. When we consider it in the context of the balance of payments, tourism appears in a slightly different light, for despite its impressive foreign earnings, the British succeeded since 1981, and with the exception of 1985, in spending still more overseas on leisure travel than the domestic tourism industry could earn in the UK.

The vulnerability of this sector lies in part in its heavy dependence on the exchange rate. Thus in the early 1980s the value of the pound rose in relation to the dollar and the European currencies. A favourable swing in the opposite direction triggered by the fall in oil prices and affecting the pound as a petro-currency reversed that trend in 1985, however, producing the first surplus on the tourism account in five years. Unfortunately, from 1986, further factors detrimental to a sustained surplus emerged – a weak dollar which made travel to Europe substantially more expensive for Americans, compounded by their fears of terrorism and radioactive contamination from the Soviet nuclear power station disaster of late April 1986.

Consultancy, communications, media and education

This far from exhausts the rich and surprising variety of British international service industries, however. Services, after all, accompany the entire economic process. So far we have looked at earnings from those services that assist financially in the purchase of plant and in the manufacture of the goods, that arrange for trade in raw materials and transport both them and the finished product to their destination. And we have glanced at those leisure services that refresh the weary worker. But production also requires research, know-how and an efficient physical infrastructure. Advice on civil engineering projects, on production processes themselves and assistance in the development of products constitutes an area of internationally tradeable expertise where the UK is a major net exporter. While construction projects require initial surveying, entire planning processes from the decision to build through to the administration of the new organisation, many also need advice on construction management techniques and finance. Beyond this, all transactions are regulated by contracts between the business partners which require the services of legal experts. In all these areas of consultancy the UK is active, as can be seen from Table 1.5.

The five-year pattern of earning in consultancy is (with the notable exception of legal services) in marked contrast to that of financial services. There, trends were characterised by accelerated growth in the 1980–85 period. Here, growth has flattened significantly, and indeed consultancy engineers and surveyors both show a fall in net earnings from 1984–85, while consultancy engineers experienced a further sharp

Table 1.5   Net income of UK consultancy firms (£m)

Year	Total	Consultancy Engineers	Process Engineers	Solicitors Barristers	Management Economic Consultants	Surveys etc
1975	386	136	170	19	61	–
1980	923	423	263	61	34	142
1984	1281	577	319	120	48	217
1985	1262	562	282	155	53	210
1986	1216	508	250	190	54	213

Source: CSO Pink Book, 1987

fall in 1985–86. This reflected the drop in business emanating from OPEC countries, previously anxious to build up their communication networks and social service infrastructure.

There remain four areas contributing to a positive balance in invisible exports that are statistically recorded. They are the private expenditure of foreign nationals resident in the UK of which the most important are students. In 1986 overseas students spent, it is calculated, some £631 million, the equivalent of one-third of the Government's expenditure on universities through the University Grants Committee. But in inflation-adjusted prices that contribution has hardly grown since 1980 when the so-called full economic fees were imposed.

Other areas that yield net earnings are the sale of films and television rights, licences and patents, royalties and advertising. Indeed, apart from the United States, the UK is the only country in the world that earns more than it pays for licences, patents and rights, as a category. And specifically in the film and television field, net earnings have more than doubled from 1982 to 1985 (£67 million to £147 million), though in 1986 the surplus fell back disappointingly to £90 million.

In concluding this sketch of the trading performance of British invisible exports we may record the negative joint balances of Britain's telecommunications and postal services (only one surplus in twelve years) and a very sad feature, the repeated deficit of £400 to £500 million per annum in services supporting Britain's North Sea oil and gas industries, largely reflecting the price of expertise purchased from the United States. It must, however, be added that the statistics for the telecommunications industry are contested by the industry which regards itself to be in surplus. We should repeat the caveat stressed in our Introduction, that the statistics in the international services area are not satisfactory and should be used to express orders of magnitude and trends.

Table 1.6   United Kingdom private sector invisible earnings 1986.

Main UK gross invisible earners

	£ million
Banking	36 041
Tourism	5 419
Insurance	4 316
Shipping	3 339
Civil aviation	2 922
Royalties etc.	2 800
Consultancy	1 216

Source: BIEC

*Table 1.7   United Kingdom private
sector invisible earnings 1986.
Main UK net invisible earners*

	£ million
Insurance	4 260
Banking	2 295
Other financial services	2 281
Consultancy	1 216

Major sectors in net deficit

	£ million
Civil aviation	449
Tourism	646
Shipping	937

Source: BIEC

Tables 1.6 and 1.7 summarise the topography of British invisible exports, the first showing the major gross earners of foreign currency, the second the major net earners and identifying the areas of major net deficit.

Britain's invisible earnings – the international challenge

Invisible earnings are of inestimable value to the welfare of people living in the UK. In their most vigorous areas they are world leaders. Tourism enables UK residents to travel the world without becoming a drain on national trading resources. Their responsibility for supporting the balance of payments increases by the year. Their role in swelling employment is vital to the country's well-being.

It was all the more alarming, therefore, to hear in 1985 from the Bank of England that Britain was losing its share of world trade in invisibles at the same rate as it had already been losing its share of world exports of manufactures. The UK's total share of trade in manufactures, the Bank stated, had fallen from 9.6 per cent in 1968 to 6.29 per cent in 1983; its share in the export of services has fallen from 11.9 per cent to 7.3 per cent, this despite a good increase in travel (from 4.8 per cent to 6.1 per cent) [15]. This is an observation of grave implications. It would point to the beginning of a long-term historical decline in services, parallel to that in visible trade, though occurring rather later in time. Examining the competition from overseas, and the new challenges which that and other changes present, is a major theme for our studies of the individual sectors. But first we need briefly to consider in global context the significance of the Bank of England's view.

Certainly there is further evidence to support it. If we look at trends in national receipts from world invisibles trade, we find that the UK's receipts (in non-fixed prices) have increased fivefold since 1969. But, and this is perhaps surprising, the annual growth has (as with productive industry) been slower than in every other EC country. Indeed, Belgium and Luxembourg have increased their invisible receipts nearly fourteenfold, France tenfold, the Netherlands over sevenfold and West Germany more than sixfold. Japan's receipts have soared by a factor of $13\frac{1}{2}$ [16]. In total value of these receipts the UK has slipped from second place in the world in 1969 to third, behind the USA and France.

Despite the marked shift in the UK's GNP towards services production, invisibles trade receipts as a proportion have grown substantially more and faster elsewhere. In the UK their contribution rose from 8.4 per cent to 12.3 per cent (1969–84), but in Belgium and Luxembourg it was a remarkable increase from 8.9 per cent to 41.9 per cent, in France from 4.0 per cent to 12 per cent, in Germany from 3.3 per cent to 6.4 per cent and in Japan from 1.6 per cent to 3.0 per cent [17].

But, as the British Invisible Exports Council has vigorously riposted, the strength of the UK remains in the relative absence of import penetration in key major areas and in its world ranking in net income. The Council argues that it was inevitable that the UK share of world trade in services would fall as other economies became wealthier and more sophisticated. In total net earnings the UK is second only behind the USA and in financial services, consultancies and professional services and entertainment the UK has been first in the world in three of the last five years. In the value of international banking transactions Britain is firmly ahead with a 25 per cent share compared with the US's 15 per cent. These, then are great strengths.

But no nation can afford to be complacent. One must look to the future to see if the new challenges can be met by having the right people, the right technology and the right strategies. In some tradeable service areas the UK is no longer a net earner and the position is slipping. Shipping has to be quoted as a major example. Indeed, as the Bank of England conceded, the growing deficit in shipping alone has a significant impact on the statistics. The British capacity for maintaining her position in the most successful sectors will depend on the rate of advance of new rivals, especially Japan, and on the success of the deregulation of the markets in continuing London's emergence as the world's premier financial centre.

In summary, two great elements will play their part.

One of those elements is the preparedness and the preparation of the people who will be meeting the new technological and market challenges. How will the new needs by met by education? What must be changed *now*, in order for us to meet the new environment of trade in services in the 1990s? Chapters 10 and 11 draw together the diverse threads from the sectors and review what the challenges mean for the UK educational and training systems.

The other element concerns the systems within which trade in services operates. In all areas old regulatory systems are being replaced, dismantled or are simply disintegrating. The dangers of liberalised and deregulated systems, whether these dangers take the form of insider trading in the securities sector, of volatility on the international and domestic stock markets, or, in a far-removed sector, the scramble for acquisitions in the deregulated UK airline industry and consequent emergence of mega-carriers are plain to see. We shall look at these momentous changes and their consequences in the following chapters.

But what has already occurred is the exciting prospect of the liberalisation of the market in services in the whole European Economic Community. The progress of the European Commission, OECD and GATT in achieving the goal of liberalisation is plotted in the next chapter. These are matters of enormous importance for the UK, and none more so than the proposal to complete the internal market of the European Community by 1992. It is in the EC that the UK has her natural extended domestic market, the largest capitalist market in the world. And beyond that again comes the question of freedom of *world* trade in services and the extension of the GATT to services. We turn to this now as a conclusion to our review of the changing economic framework in which UK international services are operating.

Notes and references

1   'The future of manufacturing industry in the medium term', CBI, London, 1985, (unpublished report).

2   As above, CBI report, based on Central Statistical Office statistics.

3   *The Growth in the Imbalance of Trade in Manufactured Goods between the UK and Existing and Prospective Members of the EEC*, House of Commons, Second Report from the Trade and Industry Committee, 1983–84, pp. xii, 47, 139 (= Commons Report).

4   *Bank of England Quarterly Bulletin*, June 1983, quoted in Meyer F. V. (ed) *The Prospects for Recovery in the British Economy*, Croom Helm, London, 1985, p. 116.

5   Commons Report, pp. xviii, 81, 154.

6   *See*, for example, Ajit Singh, 'UK industry and the world economy: a case for deindustrialisation?' *Cambridge Journal of Economics*, 1, 1977, pp. 113–36. Frank Blackaby (ed), *Deindustrialisation*, Heinemann, London, 1979; 'Deindustrialisation: restructuring the economy', *The Annals of the American Academy of Political and Social Science*, special edition, (ed.) Gene F. Summers, September 1984.

7 The classic work was Daniel Bell, *The Coming of Post-Industrial Society*, Heinemann, London, 1979.

8 George F. Ray, 'The changing structure of the UK economy', *National Institute Economic Review*, November 1986, pp. 82–88.

9 'Services in the UK economy', *Bank of England Quarterly Bulletin*, 25, 3 September 1985, p. 408.

10 *United Kingdom National Accounts 1987*, Central Statistical Office, 1987 (= The 'Blue Book').

11 Amin Rajan and Richard Pearson (eds) *UK Occupation and Employment Trends to 1990. An Employer-based Study of the Trends and their Underlying Causes*, Butterworth, London, 1986.

12 British Invisible Exports Council, *Annual Report and Accounts 1986–87*, London, 1987, p. 36 (1987 figures projection by the Employment Gazette).

13 *The Banker*, November 1985.

14 Statistics derived from *United Kingdom Balance of Payments*. The CSO 'Pink Book', HMSO 1987.

15 'Services in the UK economy', *see* ref. 9.

16 *World Invisible Trade*, British Invisible Exports Council, July 1986. Tables 2a and 3, pp. 9, 11.

17 As ref. 16, Table 4b, p. 13.

2 Trade liberalisation, development, and protectionism

The aftermath of the Second World War

There threatened in the immediate post-war period a position of near anarchy in world trade, as the older economies, many of them still plagued by wartime devastations, sought to protect their position against threats which they saw arising from every side.

At the same time, the newly industrialised and developing countries of the Far East were beginning their rapid entry into the major markets of the West, backed by a fast-growing skilled labour force, low production costs and a diverse range of international subsidies. Then in the 1970s oil prices rocketed in response to influences, both political and economic, from the major oil-producing countries of the Middle East. Finally, a very large number of countries – weak, friendless and often desperately poor – felt themselves left out altogether, as other countries, either better positioned or simply commercially more acute, helped themselves to the rich pickings which seemed scattered all around.

World responses

It was in fact the very magnitude and complexity of these problems that determined the initial world responses in the late 1940s. It was clear that urgent action was called for, which of necessity would be multilateral and under international auspices. At the same time, greater parity of negotiating strength had to be contrived, possibly through regional and interest groupings. On the other hand, proper allowance needed to be made for the legitimate established interests of the older trading nations, and a realistic timetable evolved to ease the way for the complex and often painful transition from the older-style protected markets for goods and services to newer concepts of liberalised trade. The objective was to secure the free movement of goods, unfettered international development of such services as banking, insurance, and capital and currency movements, and for the cross-frontier flow of scientific, technical and commercial information.

These were daunting tasks for the statemen of the post-war world, and for their economic, industrial and technical advisers. Nor is it surprising that even now, well into the fifth decade since the War, so much still remains to be done – and so much, too, to be undone. For liberalisation, even within the limits now visualised, calls for the clearing away of a multitude of deeply entrenched barriers to trade, some of which, particularly in agriculture, date back nearly two hundred years, whilst others are themselves products of post-war bargaining and negotiations.

Moreover, it calls for a recognition that the concept of liberalisation itself can be (or be thought to be) constraining and, indeed, damaging unless set in the total world context. Liberalisation, therefore, must itself be used as the instrument of trade development and expansion, not simply by freeing the flow of trade within specific industry groups and regional areas, but by opening up new trade opportunities for all the nations of the world on terms which can reasonably be related to their resources and capacity to compete.

It is this balance between trade liberalisation, development and protection of legitimate national self-interest that constitutes the basic target of current international trade negotiations.

Trade barriers

Trade barriers themselves go by many names – embargoes, restrictions, quotas, preferences, agreements, arrangements and tariffs. Behind them is the more subtle and infinitely more dangerous network of non-tariff obstacles to trade, both financial and technical, and inspired as often as not by motives of national self-interest, economic prudence, and sometimes by sheer political and commercial opportunism.

For all that, remarkable progress has been made over the years, particularly in the institutional approach to multilateral debate, and in the techniques for negotiation, agreement, execution and supervision. Many of the mechanisms involved, it is true, have been slanted in the first instance towards matters of politics and economics. But the spread of worldwide economic recession, accompanied by volatile exchange rates, trade imbalances and mounting unemployment during the early 1980s, all ensured that international trade figured with increased prominence and urgency at the negotiating tables.

The results, if not magnificent, have certainly been substantial. Many of the detailed negotiations, it is true, have been concerned with tariff and many other barriers to visible goods and with the general financial substructures of international trade. But there has also been a great deal of painstaking work on the liberalisation of current invisible operations, of services, and of capital movements; and there is every indication that the detailed bargaining in the years that lie immediately ahead will take place within a conceptual framework and with clarified codes of practice which have taken years to evolve and which now at last seem to have opened the way to realistic business discussions on a very wide front indeed.

It is time, therefore, to look in more detail at a few of the individual institutions whose activities lie at the heart of these particular areas of multilateral trade negotiations and discussions – the Organisation for Economic Co-operation and Development (OEEC/OECD); the General Agreement on Tariffs and Trade (GATT); the United Nations Conference on Trade and Development (UNCTAD); and (in a rather different way) the European Economic Community (EEC/EC).

All these institutions date from the period following the Second World War, at a time when international trade was severely hampered not only by high tariffs and quantitative restrictions on the import of goods but also by extensive limitations on the convertibility of national currency. It was a time of large scale resort to bilateral and 'most favoured nation' agreements, covering both the import of goods and services and modes of payment. The total effect on the flow of international trade, whilst undoubtedly accompanied by benefits to the participants to individual bilateral and regional agreements, was highly discriminatory and in many directions constraining. It was in the reduction, and eventual removal, of these constraints that these organisations found their essential purpose.

OEEC

The Organisation for European Economic Co-operation (OEEC), the predecessor to OECD, was established in 1947 as a condition of the Marshall Plan. It aimed to secure orderly economic restitution of the industrial substructure of the West, through the administration and distribution of the Marshall Aid funds (totalling $13 billion).

With seventeen member states, all of them from Europe, and with the USA and Canada as Associate Members, the OEEC registered its first success in the European Payments Agreement of 1948 and 1949 and the setting up of the European Payments Union in August 1950. The aim was to free payments between member countries from the constraints of bilateral agreements. The result was to commit members to a full multilateral payments system with, however, reservations sufficiently flexible to meet balance-of-payment difficulties in individual countries.

It was during this same period that the concept of trade liberalisation gained its first momentum. It found expression in the 'Code of Liberalisation of Trade', a code approved by the OEEC Council in 1950 which imposed on member countries the obligation to remove or to reduce quantitative restrictions on the import of goods ('visible' imports) by percentages sometimes as high as 75. The code in turn was extended in

1951 to include services and other invisible operations within the general field of current international trade.

These basic codes were worked on and refined during the 1950s. At the same time work proceeded, although at a much slower rate, on the liberalisation of capital movements, and a limited code was introduced in this area in 1959.

OECD/OCDE (Organisation for Economic Co-operation and Development)

When the OECD was formed in October 1961, the OEEC itself came to an end. Its main purpose and objectives, however, were built into an OECD Convention, whereby members agreed 'to pursue their efforts to reduce or abolish obstacles to the exchange of goods and services, and current payment, and maintain and extend the liberalisation of capital movements'. With the United States, Canada and Spain now incorporated as full founder members, and with Yugoslavia (the sole representative of Eastern Europe) retaining its special relationship, the OECD became from the start a very powerful instrument indeed for developing the total concept of trade liberalisation. Its main area of interest continued as before:

1 Classification and codification of the main sectoral areas of international trade.
2 Harmonisation and publication of international statistics on trade, industry and economics.
3. Interpretation of economic and financial trends.
4. The complementing and reinforcement of other institutions concerned with trade liberalisation (notably GATT/UNCTAD) as well as other agencies of the United Nations; the European Economic Community and other Area organisations; the International Monetary Fund; the International Labour Office and other International Research Institutes.

The OECD Codes of Practice

The OECD was progressively strengthened by the addition of new members – Japan (1964), Finland (1969), Australia (1971), and New Zealand (1973). Moreover, the work of its predecessor body was brought to fruition by the adoption in December 1961 of the twin codes of Liberalisation of Current Invisible Operations and of Capital Movements – codes which since then have formed the conceptual and factual base for negotiations and agreements, and which are now in the process of a major updating in preparation for the next round of negotiations on tariff and trade.

The new drafts

Draft codes for Liberalisation of both Current Invisible Operations and of Capital Movements were completed and circulated in 1986. An explanatory brochure on the Codes was distributed in March 1987. At the same time and as a background to these documents, the Secretariat released for general circulation a broad commentary on the 'Elements of a Conceptual Framework for Trade in Services'. It also issued separate monographs covering particular areas of the field such as banking, insurance, and audio-visual works, as well as (in June 1987) the 'General Introduction to the OECD Code of Liberalisation'.

Although it is true, as we have seen, that work on codification of invisibles and financial services dates back to the days of the OEEC, the almost simultaneous publication of so much analytical and factual material has a very special significance. It means that a new and, hopefully, decisive stage has now been reached in attempts to codify and harmonise the world trade in services, so that governments can get down to the serious business of item-by-item bargaining against a background of agreed principles and practices.

It is to be noted, too, that the original OEEC codes, however obscure and subject to evasion, had from the start a statutory status for the OEEC's subscribing members; and to this extent the successor body OECD, whilst primarily a research monitoring and servicing body, inherited statutory responsibility for formulating the framework of international trade practice.

Each code consists of a schedule of undertakings of the signatory countries. This is followed by a detailed list of the activities and transactions covered by the code, and a very substantial annex listing the reservations of individual countries for discussion and negotiation.

The value of these documents lies not only in identifying barriers but also in mapping the great diversity of the total trade in services, as becomes obvious when we list the sectors that they treat.

Code 1 – Current invisible operations

1   *Servicing operations* in businesses and industries such as repair, assembly and processing of work under contract.
2   *Foreign trade* including commissions and brokerage; dealings in commodities and foreign exchange; customs clearance, duties and fees.
3   *Transportation*: maritime, road, and air, including both passenger and freight; harbour services; ship repair; warehousing, storage and transit charges.
4   *Insurance*: personal, institutional and freight insurance and re-insurance; condition and costs for establishing branches and agencies of foreign insurers.

5   *Films*: export, import, distribution and use for private and public exhibition and for TV.
6   *Profits* from business; dividends and share in profits; interest and rent.
7   *Travel and tourism*.
8   *Personal income and expenditure*: pensions, maintenance payments; immigrant remittances; upkeep and repair of private property abroad.
9   *Public income and expenditure*: taxes; transfers due by governments to non-residents; costs of official representation abroad and contributions to international organisations; settlements for public transport and postal and telephone services; consular receipts.
10 *General*: advertising and professional services; registration of patents and trade marks; expenses in overseas courts including fines and damages.

In a number of sectors updating work is well advanced, notably in banking, insurance (a particularly complex field), in tourism and travel and in audio-visual work.

Where the existing Code already contains liberalised obligations such as transport, construction, and engineering services and advertising and professional services, the aim of updating will be to strengthen existing obligations and eliminate or weaken escape clauses. Certain high technology areas, such as information, computer and communication services, are not covered by current liberalisation codes – gaps which the updating will aim to fill.

Code 2 – Liberalisation of capital movements

Banking, finance and financial services are, of course, the concern of both Codes on Invisible Operations and on Capital Movements. The latter Code is extremely complex, covering as it does the main areas of economic policy and finance. It is also highly sensitive politically. Its main classifications are as follows:

1   *Placing and liquidation* of direct investments.
2   *Admission of securities* to capital markets.
3   *Buying and selling* of securities, short-term Treasury Bills and other short-term securities normally dealt with in the money market.
4   *Real estate*: building, purchase and selling.
5   *Credits* directly linked to international commercial transactions or with rendering of international services.
6   *Financial credits and loans*.
7   *Personal capital movements*.
8   *Physical movement of capital assets*.
9   *Disposal* of non-resident-owned blocked funds.

Progress of up-dating

It is perhaps enough to say that the draft Code as presented already incorporates one hundred and thirty-nine Council Acts on Liberalisation of Capital Movements. The Acts cover obligations, procedures, definitions and reservations. It would be foolhardy to maintain that all, or indeed any, of these issues are yet resolved beyond debate and they will certainly continue to feature for many years in the process of updating and regulating. It falls now to the appropriate committees of the concerned bodies, most notably OECD, GATT, UNCTAD and the European Community, to make progress in the mammoth task of repairing omissions, disharmonies and divergences, to translate resounding declarations on liberalisation into worthwhile practice, and generally to clear a way through what in almost every direction appears still to be an almost impenetrable jungle.

General Agreement on Tariffs and Trade (GATT)

The GATT has a number of factors which distinguish it from OECD.

1   As an agency of the United Nations, GATT has ninety-four full members and a further thirty countries which are associated with it in some particular field of negotiations.
2   It is therefore not subject, at least in the same degree, to the charge of exclusivity levelled at OECD whose members (with one or two exceptions) come from the wealthier trading nations of the world. This has not prevented, however, the establishment of a separate organisation (UNCTAD) as a forum for trade development, with particular reference to the worries and concerns of the developing and poorer nations.
3   Unlike OECD, whose function is primarily research, servicing, codification and statistics, GATT is a decision-making and negotiating body whose decisions are, in theory at least, binding upon its members. It is true, however, that its large and disparate membership, its many regional product and interest groupings, and the huge number of items within its purview make the process of decision-making in GATT both protracted and costly. A cycle of some five years is, therefore, considered the norm in a GATT negotiating round.

GATT operations and tariff reform

Tariffs have been GATT's traditional and most successful field of activity – indeed the tariff is the only instrument of protection allowed by the General Agreement. There have been seven rounds of tariff negotiations, from the Geneva Round of 1947 to the Tokyo Round of 1973–79.

As a result of these successive rounds of negotiations, tariffs have been reduced on thousands of industrial and agricultural products, affecting trade to the value of some $300 billion. The weighted average duty for industrial products in nine principal markets has fallen from 7 per cent to 4.7 per cent – a reduction of some 33 per cent.

The result of these negotiations has been to reduce the relevance of tariff protection on a very large number of products in a large number of countries, although there are still some major exceptions.

Fibres and textiles, for instance, have been subject to a special 'temporary' arrangement (three times renewed) which both in its basic concept and in its execution is felt by some countries not only to run counter to the principles of GATT, but to be positively damaging to it.

Similarly, the workings of the Common Agricultural Policy (CAP) of the European Commission has been thought (although the issue has been very strongly contended) to be alien both in spirit and in practice to a general international agreement on tariffs and trade. Moreover, as we have seen, services in general have been subject to revision outside the GATT field of operations.

It is a sad reflection on international commercial realities that, with the decreasing significance of tariff levels as factors in world trade, GATT has found itself drawn more and more into the scrutiny of non-tariff barriers erected by member nations as an alternative route to direct trade protection and promotion.

UNCTAD

In the aftermath of the Second World War it is not perhaps surprising that the first priority was felt to be the restructuring of the shattered economies of the industrialised countries of western Europe, if only because they and they alone possessed the skills and resources on which to build a new industrial infrastructure for the world as a whole.

We have seen, therefore, that the administration of the Marshall Aid funds fell solely to the OEEC and in turn to the OECD. The OECD, consisting as it did of seventeen nations, was a body of very considerable economic power and muscle. In turn the development and growth of GATT, with its successive rounds of tariff negotiation since 1947, sought to ensure that tariff reform and policy was discussed in as wide a context as possible, both in the products brought under review and in national coverage.

But there were many countries of the world which felt that these instruments of international consultation, particularly OECD, were necessarily loaded in favour of the most highly developed countries. In the early 1960s, therefore, following several years of discussion, a separate body with its own secretariat was set up by the United Nations

General Assembly specifically designed to foster and co-ordinate activities on behalf of the developing countries.

This new body, the United Nations Conference on Trade and Development (UNCTAD), which now has twenty-five years history behind it, may have achieved only a small fraction of the hopes and ambitions of its founding states. However, it has certainly established itself as a focus for discussion and for pressure; and through such countries as India, Brazil, Taiwan and South Korea, has ensured that the voice of the newly-industrialising countries of the world, if not always heeded, was at least heard, particularly at the four-yearly UNCTAD rounds, the last of which (UNCTAD 7) was held in 1987.

The issues are familiar; they include the changing structure of employment in manufacturing and services, a subject of great interest also to the International Labour Office (ILO), protectionism and non-tariff barriers, and the world debt crisis.

UNCTAD is indeed an important element in the North–South dialogue concerned with significant and long-term issues and fighting on behalf of its less privileged members with considerable courage and tenacity and, in spite of frustration, with some success.

GATT and the service industries – the Uruguay Round

In Autumn 1986 at a meeting in Punta del Este (Uruguay) the contracting parties of GATT committed themselves to what they have described as the most complex and ambitious programme of negotiation ever undertaken by the Organisation. The declaration following the meeting is in two parts.

Part I launches a new round (the 'Uruguay Round') of tariff negotiations and provides for the standstill and roll-back of trade restrictions and distortive measures under which governments undertake not to increase existing levels of protection and to phase out their existing breaches of GATT disciplines.

Part II launches a set of negotiations on the trade in services – negotiations which are not to be placed within the legal framework of GATT (at least for the time being) but which are expected to follow GATT practices and procedures. The Uruguay Round is to extend over four years. GATT had previously confined its work to trade in agriculture and in visible products. A great deal of the conceptual framework for its approach to services and to finance has, as we have seen, been clarified by the OECD and embodied in its code of 1961 and the draft codes for 1986. In addition many of its negotiations in visible trade involved considerations of the services and financial back-up of the individual products under review. For all that, many aspects of the new exercises will launch the GATT Secretariat and the participants into waters which are largely uncharted.

Negotiations on the trade in services; objectives, ambitions and limitations

The aims of the negotiations are ambitious. Their object as stated by GATT (Focus 41, October 1986), 'to establish a multilateral framework of principles and rules for trade in services (including elaboration of possible disciplines for individual sectors) with a view to expansion of such trade under conditions of transparency and progressive liberalisation and as a means of promoting economic growth of all trading partners ... such framework shall respect the policy objectives of national laws and regulations applying to services and shall take into account the work of relevant international organisations'.

The objectives are beyond reproach. In addressing them, however, the negotiators will find themselves confronted with a wide variety of economic, political and social issues, including the interrelationship of services, manufacturing and investment. In all of them, both they and their technical advisers will find themselves up against the inadequacy of the raw data on which they will have to work.

In an early meeting of the Working Group of Negotiations on Services, the Chairman of the Group, Mr Felipe Jaramillo, reported that discussions of the Group had centred around the five elements set out in the initial phase of negotiations. He noted that differing degrees of emphasis had been placed on the importance, for the commencement of the negotiating process, of arriving at an agreed definition of trade in services and of a comprehensive data base. Considerable discussion had taken place on the availability and adequacy of statistics on trade and production of services and on the efforts that could be made to seek improvements that would further the negotiating objectives in this area.

With respect to the broad concepts upon which principles and rules for trade in services might be based, there had been a discussion of the significance and relevance of concepts such as transparency, non-discrimination, mutual advantage and national treatment, among others. Mr Jaramillo said that the Group had addressed itself to the possible relationship between existing international disciplines and arrangements and the multilateral framework on services. Suggestions had also been made as to how perceived barriers to trade in services might be examined.

It is clear that the work of the Group will be determined to a considerable extent by their success in coping with their source material, particularly the origins and quality of their basic statistics. In the main, these derive from the national accounts and from official statistics of payments, supplemented by sectorally specific information collected by government agencies and/or the private sector. The technical difficulties in using this type of data are manifold. They include problems of definitions and of harmonisation, as well as variations in reporting sources, and in frequency, speed and modes of collection. Research work of a very high quality is already taking place in this area, notably at Ann Arbor University in Michigan, OECD in Paris and the Trade Policy Research Centre in London. In the UK also the Council for Invisible Exports has been of invaluable help both in aggregating the statistics and in applying them to individual sectors. BIEC themselves, however, would be the first to point out that many of the statistics, even in areas of the greatest economic significance (such as the calculation of gross and net surpluses in banking and movement of securities) have been subject in the past to major divergences of definition and interpretation.

Moreover, as the work grows in significance so, too, have the statistical ambitions. There is talk, for instance, of constructing a global data base to provide much-needed information on the magnitudes and composition of services in the world economy. It is aimed, too, to link data on services with comparable data on goods; and in this way to develop a comprehensive picture of the different components of inter-national transactions in both goods and services, and in turn to make it possible to analyse the significant interrelationships between the two.

Measurements through tariffs and agreements

These are legitimate objectives of the professional economists and statisticians, although sadly we may still be light-years away from the types of precise calculation for which they continue to strive. Tariffs negotiated under GATT auspices do, of course, give a starting point, in so far as tariffs are at least visible and quantifiable. So also do bilateral and multilateral agreements such as the Multifibre Arrangement for Textiles and Clothing; and other forms of volume-based agreements such as 'orderly marketing arrangements' and 'voluntary export restraints' – a number of which were designed to skirt around the GATT rules. These arrangements, distortive and undesirable as they may be, do at least insert a quantitative element into the volume calculation of world trade in the goods involved. However, even the trade in goods which falls entirely within the GATT system is itself often subject to special arrangements as well as to barriers and controls which, as often as not, are unquantifiable and which are, moreover, frequently negoti-ated under conditions of diplomatic obscurity and duress.

Non-tariff barriers

Until very recently, the most obvious area for non-tariff barriers was the trade in goods and manufactures. Latterly, however, events have occurred of a whole new order of magnitude affecting many aspects of world trade both in goods and in services. They include the growth of world debt, notably in developing countries in Latin America and in

Asia, and the growing groundswell of protectionism in the USA following the weakening of the American economy and the fall in value of the dollar. There has also been the rapid advance of Japan in world markets and its huge trade surplus, and the increase in unemployment, particularly perhaps in Europe and the USA but also in other countries of the world.

It is non-tariff, non-quantifiable barriers to trade which have the greatest impact on services. The field is alive with restraints, distortions and evasions. Their total effect in such fields as insurance, shipping and construction is certainly very large indeed and often quite devastating. It is these barriers and protective devices which lie at the heart of the forthcoming rounds of GATT negotiations on the liberalisation of trade in current invisible operations and capital movements.

It is, of course, not surprising that services should not only be particularly susceptible to political pressures, but also well adapted to protectionist restrictions and restraints outside the normal range of trade negotiations. For central to most service activity lies money – the most sensitive commodity of every national economy. Successful trade in services (as we shall see in the individual sectoral studies) depends upon professional skills, commercial acumen, experience and tradition. The ultimate key to competition in international markets lies, however, in money, particularly in exchange rates, loans and credits, availability of liquid resources and freedom of capital movements.

Many of these pressure points, it is true, have been eased by the introduction of floating exchange rates, the progressive abolition of exchange controls by leading industrial nations, codes of practice such as those of the OECD, and regional agreements as in the EC. There still remains, however, ample scope for individual government and para-government influence, both in general and in particular situations. These include the manipulation of 'hard' and 'soft' loans, extended credit, changes in interest rates, subsidies, exchange rates and taxation, all of which can be made responsive to political and economic situations. Results of this influence are in the main, non-quantifiable, and of their very nature they are beyond the scope of any precise calculation. They can be exercised through a variety of bodies – clearing or commercial banks, finance houses, chambers of commerce, export houses, para-governmental commercial agencies and (mostly in the background) the treasury and finance ministers of the government involved.

The micro-chip and the semiconductor war between the USA and Japan, which was wrongly thought to have been settled by an agreement in 1986, is of particular significance both because of its implications for Europe in terms of diversion of trade and because it involves barriers in high-tech areas as well as in the traditional areas of the 'smoke-stack' industries, agriculture and primary products. These new areas will certainly involve software as well as hardware and, indeed, the whole field of transfer of high technology information, impinging in turn on the American embargo of trade in these areas with the Soviet Union and Eastern Europe. It is difficult to see where the pressures will end, bearing in mind the high sensitivity in these matters of both Senate and Congress in the USA.

Banking, too, presents a frightening network of obstacles to the creation of a more open framework of trade in services, not least because the principles of bilateral reciprocity, particularly strong in banking, run directly counter to the concept of political openness behind the thinking of both OECD and GATT. This is sharply illustrated in the conflict between the major financial centres of Europe and Japan over areas of business activity to be opened to their respective banks and investment houses.

In transport 'flags of convenience' have for many years been vehicles of evasion both of tax liabilities and the more stringent national laws on condition of employment, rates of pay and health and safety. More recently, particularly in the Gulf, re-flagging has been an important instrument for defence and national protection.

Air transport, particularly in Europe, has been subject to conventions, charters and bilateral agreements covering routes, fares and schedules which have sharply restricted opportunities for private or even national airlines to optimise their commercial operations.

The European, and especially the German, insurance industry must face determined attacks by British and Dutch insurers to break wide open a market which has been one of the most restricted in the world as barriers are removed within the European Community. Telecommunications, films and publications all demand urgent attention if liberalisation is to have real meaning, not least on the question of licences, patents, copyrights and counterfeit.

Major and long-term construction contracts are all too often negotiated in most dubious circumstances and certainly constitute an area where the 'transparency' of international negotiating practices needs as soon as possible to clear away the fog of international suspicion and distrust.

The European Community – towards a free market for services in Europe

No doubt the Uruguay Round will continue to see all these arguments rehearsed over years – and probably into the subsequent Round. And there are essential dangers in liberalising on such a scale as represented by GATT because of the vast disparity between economies and national interests across the North-South divide. Here destabilisation – or at the very least an unfair advantage to the service giants such as the US, the UK, France and Japan in relation to the developing countries – is a real possibility and a very real concern of UNCTAD. That can hardly be said, however, of the world's largest internal market outside India and The People's Republic of China, the European Community. After thirty years of existence (and admittedly expansion) the basic principle underlying the Community, the formation of a single trade unit without internal barriers, is only now being realised in a complex and frequently painful process of rhetoric, negotiation, legislation and even litigation. Nothing bears more eloquent testimony to the deep-rooted passions and vital interests that seem threatened by free trade in services in this, *l'Europe des patries*, than the debates accompanying the campaign by the European Commission to complete the *Internal Market* by 1992.

The European Community, (or Common Market as it used to be known in the UK), shares one central tenet of faith with GATT – the belief in free trade. But there the similarity ends for, while GATT's membership extends across economies of all kinds and conditions and has the relatively modest (though no less difficult) ambition of gradually reducing tariffs, the Community is restricted to a group of industrialised nations clustered in a single geographic region. Moreover, it had as its original motivating force not free trade for its own sake, but political union. The establishment of a single internal market without tariffs or barriers was seen as the means not the end. The full inclusion of trade in services in the Internal Market programme is a brave move and stems from a logic internal to the Community and not from GATT. Indeed, in a sense the EC might be seen to breach GATT, since the absence of internal tariffs, most obvious in agricultural products (which are also prodigiously subsidised to the point of commercial nonsense), is accompanied by a common external tariff barrier applicable to all members of GATT except those in the Community itself. The principle of trading throughout the GATT network on the 'most favoured nation' (MFN) basis could be seen to be permanently contravened – unless one regards the Community as a single GATT member, or alternatively as falling within Article I of GATT which provides for customs' unions and free trade areas which conform to certain conditions.

However, it was the effective contravention of the common market principle *within* the Community that led in 1985 to a vigorous revival of the European ideal. Until the late 1970s there had been steady progress in expanding membership and eliminating what were visible barriers to visible trade. But with the recession following the second oil shock, individual members began propping up indigenous manufacturing industries with subsidies, and far from moving towards reducing obstacles to free trade in services erected new ones (such as strict exchange controls in France and Italy) in order to shore up their currencies, utilising the so-called Safeguard Clause of the Treaty (Article 108) to ensure that the letter of the law was not contravened. The catalyst to change, the White Paper issued by the Commission and presented to the European Council of Ministers in Milan in June 1985, condemned this contraction of the Market as 'disgraceful'. The European Council had been disturbed by the signs of retrogression as long ago as 1982 in Copenhagen and had repeated its intent to move forward twice in 1984 and again in March 1985. Not since the heady days of the Treaty of Rome had such rousing words been heard emanating from the Commission Headquarters at the Rond-Point Schuman in Brussels. And behind those words is an unmistakable political rallying cry:

'Europe stands at the crossroads. We either go ahead – with resolution and determination – or we drop back into mediocrity. We can now either resolve to complete the integration of the economies of Europe; or, through a lack of political will, to face the immense problems involved, we can simply allow Europe to develop into no more than a free trade area.

The difference is crucial. A well-developed free trade area offers significant advantages: it is something much better than that which existed before the Treaty of Rome; better even than that which exists today. But it would fail and fail dismally to release the energies of the people of Europe; it would fail to deploy Europe's immense economic resources to the maximum advantage; and it would fail to satisfy the aspirations of the people of Europe ...

Just as the Customs Union had to precede Economic Integration, so Economic Integration has to precede European Unity. '(*Completing the Internal Market*. Commission White Paper June 1985)

The policy was to move forward on three fronts. Firstly, the removal of physical barriers, particularly in the areas of frontier controls (on goods and persons), import quotas, health regulations and restrictions on transport. Secondly, the removal of technical barriers. This included not only agreement on common technical standards (through mutual recognition rather than harmonisation) but free movement for labour and the professions, establishing a common market for services, freeing the movement of capital, and promoting a common system of protection for intellectual and industrial property. The third front was the removal of fiscal barriers, meaning, in particular, progress towards a common level of indirect taxes and a similar approach to their application. (This could mean for example the imposition of VAT in the UK on foodstuffs.) The date set for the achievement of this remarkably far-reaching programme is December 31st 1992.

Officials at the Commission are convinced that, despite the stormy weather experienced by some of the central measures, the timetable can still be held. And indeed, substantial progress has been made. But nor can the urgency to press forward be ignored, for here is the West's largest trading bloc with a population of 320 millions, and half of that trade occurring within the bloc itself, yet with 16 millions unemployed, and clear signs that technologically, scientifically and industrially Europe could gradually and fatefully fall behind Japan and the United States. The greatest area of potential growth in employment and the infrastructure on which industrial advances can be made is the services sector, the spearhead of the second front opened by the Commission.

The most important advance has been the final ratification and implementation in 1987 of the *Single European Act*. This Act is directly designed to help bring about a complete Internal Community Market, aims to reduce regional and national economic and social disparities and adds to the EC Treaty new sections on research and technological collaboration and on the protection of the environment. It also strengthens, as the monetary basis for the Community, the European Currency Unit (ECU) and the European Monetary System (EMS), (the agreement on fixed parity bands between the currencies of member states). The UK does not belong to the EMS. The Single Act is effectively the legislative embodiment of the Commission's 1985 White Paper, and incorporates in the Treaty, for the first time, the objective of completing the Internal Market by 1992. The most immediate impact on free trade in services results from a change in Community procedures, whereby most Commission proposals referring to the Internal Market no longer need unanimity in the Council of Ministers in order to become binding decisions. A so-called 'qualified majority' will be needed with member states possessing block votes related to their size. Fascinating and varied alignments of interest may be foreseen as a result. At the same time the European Parliament's 'Opinion' is given further formal weight, though no veto. However, the veto may still exist in a convention known as the Luxembourg Compromise, whereby any member state can block a Council decision if it cuts across what it claims to be a vital national interest. In the past Ministers had invoked the Compromise 18 times – but civil servants had deployed it more than 200 times!

White Paper proposals for the completion of the Internal Market by 1992 which had been agreed in Council by 1987 and affect the service sector include:

1 a common procedure for publishing the accounts of banks, ending the need for branches in other member states to publish separate accounts;
2 mutual recognition of procedures for stock exchange listings of securities;
3 the liberalisation of trade involving long-term commercial credits, transactions in unlisted securities and the admission of securities to the capital markets of other member states;
4 agreement on cross-border non-life and credit insurance;

5 substantial agreement on the liberalisation of maritime transport so that companies are free to supply services between member states and other countries;

6 an increase in multilateral licence quotas for road haulage within the Community.

Important recommendations have also been adopted to achieve common guarantees on deposit levels by banks across the Community and on acceptable levels of debt exposure ('Recommendations on Deposit Guarantee Schemes and Large Exposure'), backed by a proposal before the European Parliament on a common definition of what constitutes banks' own funds (e.g. for the purpose of calculating capital adequacy ratios). A 1987 Commission proposal that credit, payment and cash cards should adopt the same technical system (e.g. magnetic strip or micro-chip) and that terminals across the Community whether in banks or retail outlets should be standardised has far-reaching implications reinforcing all these movements towards a free European financial system. For, if Europeans can freely use credit cards or obtain cash by instant account debiting (EFTPOS – *see* Chapter 4) anywhere in the Community, the unimpeded movement of finance will have been largely achieved.

In broadcasting, a 1986 Directive introduced common specifications for satellite technology and common standards in information technology and telecommunications. Another called for a co-ordinated introduction of digital mobile telephones across the Community, culminating in a thirteen country agreement in May 1987 (*see* p. 163).

This detail illustrates, however, the sheer complexity of the task. Certainly substantial progress is being made, especially in the financial sector. By May 1987, for example, the Commission's Vice-President, Lord Cockfield, was able to state in his progress report on the implementation of the White Paper that 60 per cent of all measures had been put before the Council. And while the Report accused the Parliament of being slow in reaching opinions on the Council proposals, it highlighted the serious failure to reach agreement at Council level in some key international service areas. Such delays in completing the Internal Market affect the future of significant sections of the British services industries and we shall, therefore, look at the obstacles in greater detail in the appropriate sector chapters. Here an outline may suffice.

Since the dark days of the recession there has been an almost universal move towards liberalising trade in financial services and in capital. Indeed, in this field, the Commission has fallen in line with a trend rather than provoked it, except in the area of exchange controls. Among the topics that remain to be settled is the freedom to sell mortgages across borders. The problem here lies in differing national laws governing freehold. The Commission hoped to see agreement by

1988. It is a proposal of considerable significance for a home-owning economy like the United Kingdom with its powerful building society system and involvement of the High Street banks in the mortgage market.

A proposal for common standards in issuing prospectuses for bond issues has also met great resistance, not least from the British side where it is feared that small issues (not previously requiring a full prospectus) will be impeded. Indeed, some go so far as to see in this a threat to the efficient functioning of the Eurobond market, fearing that extra restrictions might drive it away from its European centres in London and Luxembourg.

Land transport did not initially make the progress that was hoped for, although an initial increase of 27 per cent in the licence quotas for cross-border haulage was accepted for 1987. In June 1988 Council, however, did agree to scrapping quotas altogether by 1993. But agreement was not reached on allowing firms to sell haulage facilities for transport within other member states (or 'cabotage'), as opposed to the carriage of goods across borders. No decision was adopted on maritime cabotage (i.e. the transport of goods by sea within an external member state by a shipper from another Community state). Hopes that inland waterways might also be opened up to free trade in transport remain. But perhaps the most frustrating at the time was the temporary blockage by Spain on 30 June 1987 of the Air Transport Package. This will eventually result in more competitive policies in fare pricing, in more liberal quotas for sharing passenger capacity on European routes that are at present underused, and in permission for more than one airline from a single country to operate the same route ('multiple designation'). It is a package that, while not completely deregulating the European airline system, will over three years have introduced a substantially more liberal system. Spain blocked it, arguing that Britain was using land at Gibraltar Airport that had not been ceded to her by the Treaty of Utrecht of 13 July 1713. Nevertheless, agreement was finally reached in November 1987 between Britain and Spain. The Air Transport Package was able to proceed.

Finally – and perhaps most contentious of all – there was the ambiguous outcome of the European Court of Justice's judgment on freedom in cross-border (non-life) insurance. This followed litigation in 1986 by the Commission against the Federal Republic of Germany for preventing foreign insurers from supplying insurance to a German resident unless they had an independent establishment in Germany itself and equally for prohibiting a broker from selling such an insurance to a German resident (the only exempt area being in the insurance of vehicles involved in international transport). Furthermore, the Commission also proceeded against Germany, France, Denmark and Ireland for prohibiting insurers from other members states not established in their territory from leading co-insurance transactions. While the Commission's case was unequivocally upheld in the co-insurance cases, it was only given qualified support in the major case against the Federal Republic. This lack of clarity and decisiveness prevented the Commission from immediately proceeding with its Directive on non-life insurance. In turn further Directives planned to extend freedom of trade in insurance to the life and motor sectors were delayed.

None of these disputed areas is irrelevant to the interests of British service industries, except perhaps the rulings on freedom to ply trade on European inland waterways. British Airways, the haulage industry, the British insurance institutions all stand to benefit from the completion of the European market in services. The Community is already the UK's largest market for manufactures, taking a half of export production. The further opening up of the services market by 1992 would give a substantial impetus to the British international service sector and, if progress can simultaneously be achieved in GATT during the Uruguay Round, the opportunities could be prodigious. Of crucial importance is to what extent members of the Community, and on the global scale, members of GATT and UNCTAD, continue to regard key measures of liberalisation in the services as an infringement of their national sovereignty, and a threat to their interests and trade development.

Notes and References

We have been greatly assisted throughout our work in this chapter by Mr Richard Mason, Chief Executive of the British Invisible Exports Council, and by Mr Julian Arkell, Consultant to the Council.

The basic statistical reference work is the CSO 'Pink Book' on Balance of Payments (1987 edition).

The most relevant material for services and invisible exports is contained in sections 3 to 6 of the Pink Book and tables. All figures are subject to periodic revision and require careful handling with particular reference to the explanatory notes.

General References

Invisible Trade in the World Economy 1972–85, BIEC, 1987.

Trade in Services, Open Markets and the Uruguay Round Negotiations – papers of Conference organised by Trade Policy Research Centre and others, London July 1987. (*See* in particular paper 1 delivered by Brian Hindley on 'Issues in the negotiations of a general framework of rules for trade in services').

Systemic Issues in the International Trade and Monetary Fields – Current Trends and Policies in the World Economy, Chapter 2 – UN Survey 1986.

Report on Markets for UK Invisible Exports – prepared for BIEC by Graham Bannock and Partners, August 1987.

Sampson and Snape, 'Identifying the Issues in Trade in Services', *Quarterly Journal of Economic Affairs*, Vol 8, No 2, Blackwell, 1985.

Coping with Global Interdependence, an interesting overview by Sylvia Ostrey, Department of External Affairs, Canada, December 1985.

1   OEEC

An account of the historical background to the OEEC was published in 1987 by the ESU in London as part of the 40th anniversary celebrations and entitled *From the Ashes – The Marshall Plan and the Reconstruction of Europe.*

2   OECD

We owe much to personal conversations at OECD in Paris and particularly to Mr John Drew, Head of the UK Delegation. The following publications of OECD are referred to in the text:

Introduction to the OECD Codes of Liberalisation.
Code of Liberalisation of Current Invisible Operations.
Code of Liberalisation of Capital Movements.
Elements of a Conceptual Framework for Trade in Services.

All the above were issued by OECD in Paris in 1986–87.

See also comments by Brian Hindley (cited above) and monographs on the relevance of the OECD conceptual framework in various contexts, including their relevance to consultancy services by Arkell and Harrison, London, May 1987.

There is also a valuable summary of the OECD instruments dealing with aspects of foreign enterprise, the scope of each instrument and the relationship between them (DAFFE/172/SF/85120; September 1985).

A general history and guide to the OECD was published through the Secretary General in September 1985.

3   GATT

We were privileged to discuss the issues involved with Ambassador Jaramillo, Chairman of the GATT negotiating committee on the liberalisation of services.

Much of the information about GATT has been collected through personal conversations and, again, the help of the British Commission throughout has been invaluable.

Full details of the discussions leading to the Uruguay Round and the agreed objectives and the negotiations framework are contained in the GATT *Focus* Nos. 42–47, 1986–87, published by GATT information services in Geneva.

A publication by the GATT Secretariat (June 1987), *Work in other international organisations on data and trade in services*, illustrates very clearly the nature and extent of the statistical difficulties.

4 UNCTAD

We have benefited greatly from personal discussions with Mr Richard Kronen-macher and Mr Murray Gibbs of the UNCTAD Secretariat.

A major report of the UNCTAD Secretariat, *Revitalising Development, Growth and International Trade: Assessment and Policy Options*, was published in Geneva in July 1987, in preparation for the provisional agenda for the VIIth session. The final Act of Session VII was issued in Geneva in August 1987 and contains details of the final Act and Resolution and other actions by the conference at its VIIth session.

A paper by P. S. Randhawa, First-secretary of the permanent commission of India to UN and delivered to a seminar in New York in 1987, contains a clear statement of the worries of the less developed nations over the general concepts of liberalisation and development.

5 European Community

The two basic papers are:

(i) *Completing the Internal Market*. White Paper from the Commission to the European Council, Com (85) 310 final, Brussel, 1985.
(ii) 'Second report from the Commission to the Council and the European Parliament on the implementation of the Commission's White Paper on completing the internal market' (Com. (87) 203 final – 11 May 1987).

See also 'The European Community: 1986 Review and 1987 Prospects', prepared by the Belmont European Community Law Office, Brussels, 1987.

Other interesting papers are:

'Europe could play an ace: The new payment cards', Com. (86), 754 final, Brussels, 12 January 1987.

'Looking forward to 1992', statement by Mr Frederick Ost, Spokesman of the Federal Republic of Germany, January 1988.

The international service industries:
sectoral studies

A: Finance, insurance, markets and
exchanges

3 International banking and capital markets – transformations in the world of finance

The global shift from compartmentalisation to competition

Money is as life-giving to business as water is to the human being. Without it there can be no growth of industry and commerce. But, like water, money has to be circulated efficiently and cleanly through a system of storage and supply [1]. If it gets out of control or becomes contaminated it can wreak appalling damage. Indeed, in the very language of finance we speak of cash flows, of pools and liquidity, while in more common parlance we may say that a source of money has dried up or that someone has spent money like water. Analogies are not a substitute for technical accuracy, but in this case the metaphor highlights the theme of this chapter – and some of the problems to be examined at the close of the book.

The forms such damage can take are manifold – hyper-inflation in Germany in the early 1920s destroyed the currency and with it a whole population's monetary savings. Dramatic as was this collapse, it was at least contained within a single national system. When the major New York banks failed in their efforts to shore up an inflated stock market in 1929, not only did over one-third of the United States' commercial banks have to close – the notorious Wall Street Crash infected the whole of the world economy, bringing in its wake the chronic unemployment of the 1930s. Precisely because money and capital interpenetrate whole industrial systems, loss of credibility in either the currency or the market value of industrial stock is perhaps the greatest threat to any economy. And that interpenetration extends to different domains of finance. A complex, yet classic, example occurred in 1985 in the United States. Two government security traders, ESM Securities in Florida and Bevill Bresler & Schulman in New Jersey, failed. Their failure led to massive losses by a number of loans and savings institutions, or 'thrifts', in Ohio and Maryland which had undertaken unsecured repurchasing agreements with the securities traders. The thrifts consequently suffered a run on their deposits from worried customers, which in its turn caused one of the thrifts to default on over $1 billion in mortgages and mortgage-backed securities. And at the end of the chain, this brought heavy losses to mortgage insurance firms [2]. But the most spectacular and disturbing example of world stock market and stock market-currency market contagion was the Crash of Autumn 1987 which took place during the writing of this book. We look at this and its implications in the last chapter.

Yet this is not the only type of contagion that can spread through a financial system. Like water money can also be corrosive. The shameful utilisation of confidential information about a company's imminent plans for an acquisition or a merger to make massive personal capital gains – or insider dealing as it is known – severely shook both New York and London in 1986 and 1987.

It is in the knowledge of these possibilities, that governments and the finance industry itself throughout the era of evolving capitalism moved through prolonged phases of regulation and control designed to limit damage to the economy through compartmentalisation of financial activities, constructing as it were bulkheads to prevent damage to one area capsizing the entire structure. Perhaps the most influential legislation designed to prevent inherent instability in the system was the American Glass-Steagall Act of 1933, which is still in force and bans US commercial banks from undertaking investment banking and trading in securities. This legislation was effectively re-enacted in post-war Japan with the establishment of the similar Article 65 of the Japanese Securities and Exchange Law. The lines of demarcation in Japan between the securities houses, the long-term credit banks, the trust banks and the city banks are rigid.

In Britain compartmentalisation has historically been enforced only in part by legislation. It was also established by self-imposed rules within the industry. The charter granted by Parliament to the Bank of England in 1694 already reflected the view that a commercial bank's assets should be capable of ready liquidation to meet the possible demands of its depositors. Investment in securities or property has traditionally been regarded as outside the domain of British commercial banks whose business has, almost until this decade, been very largely short-term, or at most medium-term lending, together with providing a national clearing service for customers' payments. In the post-war years this self-defined role was reinforced by Treasury controls on the volume of permitted lending and in the 1970s by the so-called Corset, which required banks to make special deposits with the Bank of England free of interest and in proportion to their liabilities.

Medium-term and long-term corporate lending remained the province of the merchant banks whose origins had lain in financing overseas trade through the acceptance of foreign merchants' bills of exchange. The London merchant banks came to world prominence towards the end of the last century both as direct lenders and as intermediaries in raising capital for major infrastructure work such as building ports and railways in Britain and throughout the world. It was their activities above all that had made London the world's financial centre before the First World War. But what is important in the present context is that the merchant banks did not encroach upon the traditional domains of the clearing banks, or vice versa until the 1960s at the earliest.

Compartmentalisation was equally evident, and particularly in the City of London, in the securities trade. Merchant banks have long specialised in floating capital issues for corporate clients on The Stock Exchange and for most of this century they have also managed the portfolios of private clients, but it was not possible for them directly to trade in securities. This was done through the system of brokers and jobbers in the Stock Exchange. Acting on behalf of a client in buying or selling stock and buying and selling on your own account had been regarded as properly separate occupations even as early as the late seventeenth century [3]. The dealers or 'jobbers' made the market in government and corporate stock, while the brokers, acting for their clients, disposed of or purchased it through them. True, the distinction was not statutorily imposed, even in the nineteenth century, though both a Stock Exchange Committee reporting in 1847 during the financial crisis following the end of Railway Mania, and the Royal Commission on the London Stock Exchange in 1878 make it clear that in practice the two functions were largely carried out by different people – and in their view quite rightly so [4]. But in 1908 the Exchange's Committee for General Purposes brought in new rules, prohibiting 'dual capacity' (or acting as both a broker and a dealer), calling on Exchange members to declare which capacity they served and disallowing jobbers from dealing with non-members. In short, jobbers could only make their markets through the intermediation of the brokers, who alone could transact business with outsiders. In 1912 to prevent jobbers from creating dummy broking businesses or coming to 'friendly' arrangements with brokers, minimum commissions were imposed irrespective of the size of transaction. This was in contradiction to the free trade climate that had prevailed throughout the preceding century when there was no requirement to adhere to any scale of commissions. Despite resistance in the provinces to the removal of competition through fixed commissions, and indeed the absence of any imposition of single capacity upon exchanges outside London, the new restrictive system was to stay in place, dominating the British securities trade until October 1986.

This system was further reinforced by measures to regulate the number of jobbers and brokers who could be members of the Stock Exchange. From as early as 1904 new members had to be nominated by two existing members and pay a substantial premium for the privilege. Since their total number was restricted by custom, it became common practice to purchase a nomination from a retiring member or from the estate of a deceased member. Still more significant was the restriction on any outside interest's stake in a member firm to 10 per cent and a prohibition on any member firm having a non-member director. Together these regulations blocked external financial institutions from having any major direct influence on the Exchange and at the same time held down the potential capital base of the members. And within this closely regulated structure, there was an area of further restriction. Jobbing in gilt-edged (or government) stock (which accounted in 1981–83 for an average £186 billion annual turnover compared with £42 billion turnover for equities) [5] was in the hands of six jobbers only. Of these only two were successful in making markets in substantial amounts of stock, Ackroyd Smithers and Wedd Durlacher.

Yet the only financial institutions in Britain whose range of business was defined and restricted by national *law* were the building societies. For over a century the building societies were confined to lending based on mortgages for the purpose of purchasing property. Furthermore, they were heavily and predominantly reliant for their funds on the savings deposits of individual shareholders, with borrowing on the wholesale money markets restricted to 5 per cent of total liabilities unless permission was obtained from the Registrar of Friendly Societies. Indeed they were supervised in all their business operations by the Registrar's Office while their scope for independence of business judge-ment was further constrained by their voluntary membership of a cartel that fixed the current interest rates paid by the mortgage-holders. Thus there was little effective competition between building societies and the commercial banks except in attracting retail deposits – and that did not become critical until the 1970s. For while building societies' deposits rose dramatically from 5 per cent of personal investment in the UK in 1957 to 18 per cent by 1981, bank deposits remained stable at around 20 per cent [6].

But compartmentalisation was not confined to domestic financial systems such as that of the UK. On the contrary, in the immediate wake of the Second World War the international financial scene was dom-inated by controls over the free movement of currency and capital. Sterling controls were put in place as a temporary war measure in 1939. They were confirmed in 1947 and in 1965 even strengthened with the introduction of the 25 per cent surrender of the dollar premium, effectively a tax on the dollar proceeds from the sale of overseas equities [7]. The purpose of the measures was to prevent the outflow of investment from a weakened economy, holding down balance of payment deficits and supporting the value of the pound. This was all the more necessary following another wartime measure, the 1944 Agree-ment signed by the major Western powers at Bretton Woods to peg their currencies to a specific dollar price. The parities, which were jealously guarded, could only be changed in consultation with the IMF. It was a costly and cumbersome process involving central banks in frequent currency defence operations.

Beyond these regulatory bulkheads, taxation acted as a further line of defence, both within domestic systems and as a discouragement to trade in capital between the systems. Sometimes taxes operated in an arbitrary fashion, favouring for example a particular form of savings through specialised institutions to the competitive detriment of others. The tax advantages in Britain in the 1960s and 1970s of saving through life insurance policies and for pension provisions as opposed to equity investment substantially strengthened insurance companies and institutions managing pension funds to the detriment of National Savings. Building societies, which paid tax directly and thus made net interest payments, also benefited substantially as we saw. But such shifts did little more than alter the balance of power within a national system. Domestic withholding taxes on overseas investments in securities were an almost universal feature in the 1960s and 1970s. The USA, UK, West Germany, France, the Netherlands, Japan all had such taxes, reducing the attraction of investing in foreign stock markets and thus slowing down international capital flows. Foreign issues in domestic markets were similarly discouraged by regulations such as the American Interest Equalisation Tax of 1963.

Clearly, the purpose of these lines of defence went beyond the control of money during the economic turmoil of the post-war years. They extended into deliberate protection of domestic markets and economies, and into the prevention of competition both between domestic financial institutions and internationally. The common prohibition, even among the members of the European Economic Community, of foreign banks lead-managing foreign bond issues, let alone domestic issues, was symptomatic of this protectionism. For, as we saw in the last chapter, while progress in the Community towards free trade in manufactures was reasonably rapid, free trade in services is still far from a reality.

But the cushioning effects of compartmentalisation both within the national systems and without were not to be entirely beneficial. We have observed the distortions in savings patterns created in the UK.

Investment in equities through heavy taxation on profits, was unattractive. For top UK tax payers, for example, ten-year pension contributions gave a tax privilege of plus 250 per cent; investment in equities a tax penalty of minus 154 per cent [8].

The corporate sterling market at The Stock Exchange was stagnant from 1972 onwards. The majority of stockbroking companies and the jobbing firms were, thanks to The Stock Exchange's single capacity system (which was accompanied by tight rules on capital participation and membership) woefully undercapitalised by US standards [9]. Nor had our merchant banks built up their capital at the rate of their US rivals, despite a great extension of their services into leasing and

factoring, insurance broking and underwriting, and unit trust management during the late 60s and early 70s [10]. Indeed the key to
understanding why change had to come – and come so dramatically –
was competition. Despite compartmentalisation and protectionism the
regulated financial world of the 1930s and still more of the post-war
years was breaking up under the competitive pressure of the financial
institutions engaged in the international money trade. And that competitive pressure was possible for a number of powerful reasons:

Firstly, despite all the bulkheads, it had not been possible to contain
the world's money within the nationally and internationally designated
channels and pools.

Secondly, the very existence of the regulations had challenged institutions into devising methods for by-passing them.

Thirdly, there came the upset in the balance of the global economy
wrought by the oil shocks (and especially that of 1973–74).

Fourthly, there was the startling development of information technology and matching this transformation, the internationalisation of the
world's securities markets and a rapid trend towards disintermedi-
ation, (or cutting out the intermediation of banks in asset transactions).

They were factors which in combination would almost certainly have
proved overwhelming. But the speed with which they were allowed to
impact upon the UK system was determined by a series of actions
initiated by government and in particular the Conservative Government
under Margaret Thatcher. The result has been a financial revolution in
the United Kingdom which, within the space of a few years, swept aside
the containing structures of a century or more, radically altering the
nature of the industry, its international prospects and the challenges
facing the people who work in it.

The emergence of the euromarkets

By the end of the Second World War the most powerful economy in the
world was that of the United States. It knew no rival at that time, so it
was inevitable that the dollar should replace sterling as the world's
trading currency. Marshall Aid was the major factor in restoring health
to Europe's shattered economies and the aid came in the form of the US
dollar. Restrictions on currency convertibility prevented the commercial
exploitation of the billions of dollars in Europe while low interest rates in
the USA (enforced by Regulation Q) discouraged return flows, a
tendency reinforced by the 1963 Interest Equalisation Tax (IET). In 1958
sterling had been made freely convertible into other currencies for
overseas residents. London had the tradition of being a world financial
centre, irrespective of the setbacks to Britain's relative economic standing and the weakness of the domestic currency. The IET, supplemented

further by the 1965 Voluntary Foreign Credit Restraint Program which limited the amount of foreign loans that US banks could make from American-based offices, made borrowing in an off-shore dollar market in Europe highly attractive. At the same time British banks, which were restricted by a squeeze imposed in 1957 on using sterling for financing Third World country trade, began to turn to these 'off-shore dollars'. These Eurodollars (or dollars held by companies or individuals resident outside the US) rapidly formed the basis of an expanding deposits and loans market. While British banks became pre-eminent in this business, the most unlikely players joined, such as the Moscow Narodny Bank, which found it useful to offer its dollars to a market outside the USSR. The Eurocurrency market is almost entirely a short-term, inter-bank market (that is, based on large loans made between banks for as little time as overnight and now extends beyond dollars and sterling to all the major hard currencies, or for up to a year). It has been calculated that at least a third of the world market is on the books of London banks and that the bulk of global dealing goes through the City.

Related to the Eurocurrency trade but distinct from it, there also rapidly emerged the Eurobond market. These were bonds, issued in a Eurocurrency, offering individual companies a medium to long-term source of finance not readily available to them in their domestic markets or in the Eurocurrency market since it was largely confined to short-term, inter-bank loans. The inventor of the Eurobond, the form that the Euromarket first embraced, was Sir Siegmund Warburg, chairman of S. G. Warburg & Co., who issued in 1963 a $15 million six-year bond for the Italian Autostrade Company. And, although growth in the market was slow for the first year or so, the potential was enormous. Yet Warburgs, Hambros, and Strauss Turnbull, who had seen that potential, were unable to persuade any London jobbers to embark upon market making. Hemmed in by exchange controls and, unlike their foreign competition, unable to approach customers directly because of the single capacity system, London jobbers did not find Eurobonds very attractive at that time. US financial institutions, on the other hand, saw their opportunity. In 1968 President Johnson insisted that US companies raise money for foreign operations overseas. The Eurobond market took off. It grew from $17.4 billion in 1966 to $575 billion in 1980 and by 1985 had exceeded a thousand billion. [11]

Drawn by the emergent Eurocurrency and Eurobond markets, foreign banking and securities houses, and especially those from the US, began to flock to London. In 1967 114 foreign banks were represented directly in London. This had grown to 300 ten years later and in 1986 had reached 400 [12]. The dominant players were soon White Weld & Co. of the USA (which was eventually to become part of the Crédit Suisse-First Boston), the Union Bank of Switzerland, the Swiss Bank Corporation, Deutsche Bank, Morgan Guaranty – and utilising expertise derived from the other major off-shore banking centre in Europe – Kredietbank of Luxembourg. For it was a development that was not solely centred on London. On the contrary, in the early days Paris seemed an alternative centre, as did Amsterdam. But it was the growing strength of the German banks coupled with heavy minimum deposit restrictions with the Federal Bank, restrictive credit to capital ratios and a ban on interest payment to foreign Deutschmark depositors that led to these banks setting up in an off-shore oasis right beside their border, Luxembourg. Yet despite these challenges London had by the 1980s established itself as Europe's leading Eurobond market. In 1986 the market recorded a $3,500 billion trading volume. Of this some three-quarters passed through firms based in London.

From floating exchange rates to the abolition of exchange controls

However spectacular the emergence of the Eurobond market, it would not in itself have been sufficient to transform the compartmentalisation of *domestic* banking and capital markets. But it was far from the only factor at work altering the balance of the world's money stocks and upsetting the post-war order. In 1967 Britain's relatively poor economic performance, and in particular her balance of payment problems, led to the devaluation of sterling. Yet Britain's problems were only a small part of a global shift in economic power to which the fixed exchange rate system was not suited. The pressure on the dollar as the reference currency was great and it, too, had to be devalued under the Smithsonian Agreement in December 1971, while upward pressure on the Deutschmark as the currency of an emergent world economic force was similarly irresistible. The Bretton Woods Agreement was abandoned in 1971 and was succeeded after a series of devaluations by the floating rates of exchange.

Volatility was then massively fuelled by the quadrupling of oil prices in 1973–74. The entire basis of the industrial economies of the West was shaken as their prime energy source, once cheaper than any other fuel, became a substantial drain on the balance of payments. Almost overnight the OPEC countries were awash with dollars that could not be absorbed within their own economies. The money returned to London and New York, particularly, for investment. The depressed Western economies could not use capital on this scale despite a recovery in 1977–78, while the entire situation was severely exacerbated by a further massive rise in the price of oil in 1979. The British and American and West European banks found their solution to the recycling problem in syndicated loans to Third World countries. By 1979 such loans, of which the lion's share went to Latin America, were growing at a rate of nearly

30 per cent annually [13]. And as a concomitant to this shift in the pattern of the world's economy, inflation rose in the 1970s to levels unprecedented in advanced industrial countries since the 1920s.

But disconcerting as all these factors were, in practice they gave an enormous boost to the internationalisation of banking. For not only could individual countries' high surpluses and deficits not be balanced without the intermediation of banks, the excessive rates of inflation were a challenge to the creation of new financial techniques designed to hedge against risk and exposure [14].

This helps to explain why the new Conservative Government of the UK finally abolished exchange controls in 1979, freeing the flow of capital at a time when caution might have seemed to dictate the reintroduction of stricter controls. For behind this decision there was more than the ideological mistrust of the Conservatives of any control that restricted market forces. Another major reason was Britain's own build-up of surpluses as she became an oil producer of world format and as the value of that oil rose dramatically. But beyond either of those reasons was a recognition that, if the City was to remain Europe's principal financial centre, the unfettered movement of foreign exchange and capital in and out of the UK was essential [15]. The result, as we noted in the opening chapters, was rapidly to make Britain the world's second largest exporter of capital after Japan and to give the global movement towards the internationalisation of finance a further decisive thrust forward.

Thus for a variety of reasons the dams and bulkheads that had been built over the years to contain the flows of money internationally had been significantly breached. The availability of off-shore dollars and the growth of a sophisticated market in bonds based on these dollars, and subsequently other currencies, provided an alternative to domestic financing. The old order was further shaken by the sudden and almost stupendous liquidity of the oil-producing countries, including latterly the UK. The fourth ingredient in this heady brew was a revolution in the supply of information, made possible by the silicon chip breakthrough in computer technology.

The new technology

Money will flow as fast as information can guide it. The very origins of the London Stock Exchange in the coffee houses of the City and the establishment of a recognised Exchange in Threadneedle Street in 1773, was to enable the latest information to be passed directly between those in the know. Indeed, it was precisely because London was becoming the heart of the world's shipping network in the late eighteenth century that Lloyd's Insurance and Shipping Information Services or Register also emerged there. Thus the origins of both the dealing floor in The Stock Exchange and the Room at Lloyd's was to facilitate the transmission of the latest information, enabling immediate judgements to be made on the market value of stock or advisability of writing insurance.

The invention of the telegraph and then the telephone already enabled trade in capital and currency to assume new international dimensions by the turn of the century. The telex in the 1960s was a further development in the same direction, providing, like the telegram, written evidence of communication, arriving directly at the business partner's premises. These methods of transacting business were essentially restricted to two partners at a time. The advent of the computer, and especially the micro-computer, swept aside such restrictions. (We look at the significance of these advances for financial information services, specifically, in the next chapter.)

The first major breakthrough for banking was the creation of the automatic cash dispenser, later refined as the automated teller machine (ATM) enabling the customer to obtain cash and order other banking services 24 hours a day. The pioneers of the ATM were Citicorp which, under the leadership of Walter Wriston, saw electronic banking as a method of offering banking services from a single banking corporation across the whole of the US notwithstanding the restrictions on interstate banking imposed by the McFadden Act of 1927 [16]. The implications for retail banking of microchip technology go far beyond the circumvention of normal banking hours. The clearing of payments which used to be done physically by the transfer of cheques is already being supplemented for payments over £10 000 by a system known as Clearing House Automated Payments System or CHAPS. Eventually all British clearing will be achieved electronically. But beyond that facility it will mean that financial institutions such as building societies will also be able effectively to become clearing banks, blurring the distinction between their functions in the retail market. The ATM, for example, already enables building society shareholders to obtain cash 24 hours a day. But with the advent of EFTPOS (Electronic Funds Transfer at Point of Sale) it becomes possible for customers to transact quite sophisticated payments and fund transfers from stores or even, as has already occurred in Finland, Sweden and France, direct from home using a personal computer and a telephone, or even just a telephone that links to a computer. The eventual result will almost certainly be a substantial revision of the clearing banks' branch system. Branches are expensive to maintain and expensive in labour. How often does a bank customer actually need to seek face-to-face advice from a manager? Routine salary credits, payments and balance information could all be handled by EFTPOS or a new generation of ATMs, such as the interactive video system introduced by Lloyd's Bank.

However, it is the international scene which is our special concern. In this context the impending transformation of the retail banking world will be still more significant once foreign banks based in a national capital like London try to break into the solid domain of the High Street banks through the installation of ATMs, say in major shops, estate agencies or insurance offices – or even when they try crossing national borders, a prospect not so fantastic when you consider the European Commission's objective of a totally free trade area in services by 1992, which we discussed in the last chapter.

But the area in which the impact of new technology has already been greatest is in international securities dealing. The essential differences between the older forms of international communication via telephone, telex, and even the latest – telefax (the electronic transmission of photocopied documents) – and the new computerised screen trading, is that the older forms were all restricted to communication between two people. The power of the computer enables markets to be made and constantly updated on the screen, thus replacing the throng on the Exchange Floor with a live international network in the market-makers' own office. The way things had to go in London were dramatically foreshadowed in the United States with the creation of a screen trading exchange in non-Stock Exchange listed stock in 1971. Over the counter (or OTC) trading in this unlisted stock had become so popular by the later 1960s (because of the higher returns) that it became virtually impossible to conduct an orderly market over the telephone and telex. The NASDAQ system, developed by the National Association of Securities Dealers, showed on a three-level screen average prices for all OTC stocks, allowed dealers to see bids and offer quotes themselves and enabled market-makers to put in prices on the top level. NASDAQ proved immensely popular. By 1985 it had 120 000 terminals, its volume of share dealing had reached $200 billion and it was the third largest stock exchange in the world.

This startling development was matched in the foreign exchange markets by screen information services, such as Telerate, Reuters, Topic, Datastream, which enabled dealers not only to see the very latest prices but to input their own information into the systems. In 1981 Reuters introduced their Monitor Dealer Service based on the screen information enhanced with a high-speed telex-type system linking the dealers in the market. They have since matched this with an equities dealing system acquiring and linking in with the US Instinet (Institutional Networks Corporation) established by Merrill Lynch and others in 1969 for trading bulk shares from the US and overseas. The system now extends to options on stocks and currencies traded on the Chicago Board Options Exchange (CBOE). We look in further detail at international financial information services in the next chapter.

Internationalisation, securitisation and disintermediation

It was inevitable that the possibility of trading electronically across the world instantaneously should profoundly alter the existing systems. The new technology opened up the opportunity to trade in securities (including those not even listed on the world's official exchanges) without resort to a dealing floor and completely outside the established structure. Trade, particularly in currencies, could be effected across borders 24 hours a day. Global dealing became a reality. The massive current account surpluses of the UK in the early 1980s and with still greater yearly consistency those of Japan and the Federal Republic gave the impetus. The business was there. Huge international funds were available for immediate investment. And with ageing populations and a falling total labour force the pressure on pension funds in all the major Western countries to diversify their investments across economies and maximise their growth was growing apace. As the surplus countries sought new investment outlets, the unprecedented United States current account and budget deficits sucked in massive sums, largely through US Treasury Bond issues. The major purchasers were the Japanese; by 1985 Japanese banks had replaced US banks as the world's largest international lenders [17].

This highly dynamic process has brought new players, and in particular the giant Japanese banks and securities houses, into the global trading scene. American banks, still restricted in the scope of their activities domestically by the Glass-Steagal and McFadden Acts, have similarly gone for expansion abroad. Yet by 1987, thanks to the fall in the value of the dollar in relation to the yen, Japanese banks (measured by their assets) came to dominate the world's top bank league. The Dai-Ichi Kangyo Bank, Fuji Bank, Sumitomo Bank, Mitsubishi Bank and Sanwa Bank occupied the first five places. Citicorp, formerly the world's largest bank in asset terms was sixth and followed by two further Japanese banks, Norinchukin and the Industrial Bank of Japan. While the French bank, Crédit Agricole climbed to eighth position (it had, however, been first in 1980), Banque Nationale de Paris fell from sixth in 1985 to tenth and Crédit Lyonnais from tenth to twelfth, sandwiched between two further banks from Japan, Tokai Bank and Mitsui Bank. The next largest European bank was Deutsche Bank in fourteenth place. For the UK, National Westminster Bank fell to seventeenth place (twelfth in 1985), Barclays to eighteenth (sixteenth in 1985, ninth in 1980) and Midland to thirty-fourth from twentieth position. [18]

This decisive shift towards an internationalisation of the world's banking and capital markets scene has of course intensified competition between financial institutions of all kinds. In the UK during the 1970s the banks became increasingly aggressive in their search for business. The OPEC surpluses compelled them to look for new investment openings. Perhaps the most fateful (and in this the UK banks followed the same route as others in the US and elsewhere) was the ready supply in the late 1970s and early 1980s of syndicated (or bank group) loans to developing countries which, as we saw, grew at prodigious rates at the beginning of the decade. The interest rates that had to be charged as a result of the Reagan Administration keeping the dollar interest rate abnormally high, together with the artificially high value of the dollar itself, put terrible pressure on the young industrial economies of Latin America. The subsequent slide in the mid-1980s of the dollar's value was, most unfortunately for countries such as Mexico, Venezuela and Peru, accompanied by a fall in oil prices almost to pre-1974 prices in real terms. It became impossible for a whole series of Latin American countries to service their debts, let alone repay capital. Only through the greatest ingenuity, patience and continued preparedness of the banks to renegotiate has it been possible to prevent wholescale defaulting by means of various rescheduling schemes. Though the major UK banks have since strengthened their position, a default by a country such as Brazil or Mexico would still cause the severest disruption, not just to the balance sheet of the individual banks but to the world's entire banking system. The Mexican crisis of 1983 was the first warning of the disaster that can result from the internationalisation of the world's banking. For while it is true that the banks in the UK and abroad have built up contingency reserves to soften the blow of any default, interest rates have been so high that the totals owed today exceed those in 1982, while even the most cautious banks, Barclays and Natwest in 1987, still had a 50 per cent exposure on debts of £2.5 billion and £2 billion respectively. Midland, with an exposure of $4.6 billion, had provisions for only 21.3 per cent [19]. And Citicorp, despite a dramatic addition of $3 billion to its debt provision in May 1987, still had provisions for only 25 per cent for its outstanding sovereign debt [20].

In the UK itself, the same years saw banks rapidly evolving their expertise in liability management, and with the stagnation of the British Stock Market in the 1970s, a substantial increase in banks' term lending to companies. UK bank intermediation grew – in 1963 loans had accounted for 42 per cent of gross corporate debt. By 1983 it had risen to 75 per cent! [21]

Yet circumstances were changing. The Latin American debt was, and still remains despite cautiously confident statements, a millstone. A transformation that was itself in part an attempt to circumvent the lending role of the banks was ironically to come partly to their aid – securitisation. Securitisation is the name given to the move among corporations and indeed local government, sovereign states, and supranational bodies away from raising money through direct loans, usually from banks, to issuing financial paper.

For long-term borrowing the Eurobond issue, which can be today in almost any hard currency and not necessarily dollars, has become a major source of finance. Bond offerings net of repayments (and effective reissues) ran in 1986 at a rate of $170 billion, $40 billion more even than in 1985. In 1983 (in gross figures) the value of dollar denominated Eurobonds stood at some $39 billion. By 1986 this had soared to $121 billion. Yet the growth in Euro DM issues and still more so Euroyen issues has been still more spectacular. Standing at $4 billion (DM) and $0.2 billion (Yen) in 1983, these had accelerated to a value of $18.9 billion for the Deutschmark and $18.8 billion for the yen three years later.

International bank loans declined from some $60 billion to £32 billion in the same period, a graphic illustration of this, the so-called disintermediation process. Part of this reflects the policy of banks themselves as they try to sell Latin American debt in securitised – or tradeable – paper form. But worldwide the weak demand for direct loans by high-quality borrowers continues, compelling the banks themselves to become major purchasers of securities [22].

The bank's traditional lending area had previously been the short-term loan. Was this affected by the trend to securitisation? Another new feature of the finance world is, unfortunately for the commercial banks, the dramatic emergence of a market in securitised short-term loans. Originating in the United States some twenty years ago and designed specifically to cut out the handling fees of the intermediating banks, commercial paper (CP) has stormed forward. Major American corporations now systematically issue their own paper for terms of up to three months – more than 50 per cent of short-term corporate lending in the States is now securitised in this way. The market has grown in value from $15 billion to $320 billion in the twenty years since its creation [23]. In Canada, the world's second largest national commercial paper market, launched in the early 1950s, issues stood at $11.4 billion in late 1986 [24].

Commercial paper came to the UK as late as March 1986. The value of issues by the end of that year already stood at $1 billion, although issuers must be listed on the Stock Exchange and have net assets of more than £50 million. The Eurocommercial paper market is coming to maturity with nearly 400 programmes at present and, while there are no official figures, it is estimated that outstanding paper is in the $25 billion to $35 billion range.

All this is throwing enormous pressure on the traditional roles and market segment of the commercial banks. As Charles Mitchell of Midland Montagu Commercial Paper told the *Financial Times*, 'Increasingly, a lot of top-ranking corporates see their credits as being as good as the banks'. If this is the case, why should they have to pay for the privilege of using the banks as intermediaries?' [25].

The banks facing the greatest change and the greatest challenge are, then, the commercial and High Street banks. They face the prospect of reshaping their retailing branch structure through the new possibilities of automated and even home banking, reinforced by competition from the building societies. Their role (especially internationally) as direct lenders is being eroded by a world wide popularity of securitised debt. The winners are the major Japanese, American and Swiss finance houses.

In Eurocommercial paper the front-runners are Citicorp Investment Bank, Merrill Lynch Capital Markets, Crédit Suisse-First Boston, Morgan Stanley, Salomon Brothers, Swiss Bank Corporation International, and Shearson Lehman Brothers [26]. And among the top ten lead managers in the Eurobond Market are Nomura Securities, Deutsche Bank, Crédit Suisse-First Boston, Morgan Guaranty, and Salomon Brothers [27]. S. G. Warburg is in both markets the leading UK player, occupying in 1986 seventh position in the Euro-CP dealer league and eighth in the Eurobond Lead Management league.

But commercial paper is only one example of the host of new financial instruments that have emerged in recent years, transforming the nature of international finance. The innovators have been the American investment houses. And it is the range and subtlety of the new instruments that have themselves been major contributors to the world financial transformation. Before we see how this fluid scene has affected the UK, look at the impact of deregulation on London's traditional institutions, and finally assess the competitiveness of the City in the new global setting, we must consider briefly the nature of these innovations.

Transformations I – the new financial instruments

The origins of innovation lay in the pressures on the still compartmentalised international financial system of the late 1960s and early 1970s, as globalisation of the markets took on momentum. The new instruments were essentially investor-driven. The high rates of inflation called for methods of guarding against sudden change. Borrowing or investing at a fixed rate became a gamble. Currencies were more volatile, making exporting more hazardous. Borrowers and investors alike became increasingly aware of the possibilities that lay outside the realm of direct bank loans. What was required was flexibility.

The major innovation of the early 1970s was the Floating Rate Note (FRN) [28]. These bonds came to account for a third of all Eurobond issues by the end of the decade and nearly half by 1984–85. Their great advantage over a syndicated fixed-rate loan was that the rate moved in line with market rates – usually fixed against LIBOR (the London Interbank Offered Rate) based on the rates offered by a number of banks in the Eurodollar markets on any given day at 11 a.m., and adjusted accordingly every six (or sometimes three) months. Initially FRNS were issued entirely in Eurodollars but as part of the worldwide movement toward liberalisation, West Germany, Japan and the Netherlands all permitted for the first time the issue of EuroDM, Euroyen, and Euroguilder FRNs in 1985, with France joining them in July 1986. Fixed-term floaters are for periods of five to seven years, but there are also appeared FRNs with no final maturity data or 'Perpetual Floaters'.

Further refinements included the so-called 'cap' which would allow the interest rate to rise with the index only to a predetermined maximum level, and 'warrants' which give the investor options to purchase additional bonds at a later date in the same or a different currency. To deal with particular tax circumstances (especially in Japan) bonds and notes with 'deferred coupons' have been created (with interest paid as a lump sum only after the initial years). Variations on the theme are 'step-up-bonds', with low interest rates at first and a wider spread later – and their opposite 'step-down-bonds'. Even bonds known as 'upside-down FRNs' have been produced. Instead of the coupon moving up and down with the market rate it moves in the reverse direction, with the coupon reset at a higher rate as general interest rates fall. And perhaps the most bizarre of all (at least in nomenclature) are 'Bull and Bear' issues, created in the US, copied in Japan and then in the Federal Republic in 1986 where they were known as 'Tom and Jerry Bonds'. These are sold in two tranches – they carry the same coupon but, with the redemption amounts linked to the national stock index, the bull tranche amount increases if the stock index rises and decreases if the index falls. Conversely, the bear tranche amount increases if the index falls and decreases if the index rises. The borrower is hedged against market fluctuations because the redemption values of the two cancel one another out. Why create such an instrument? As so often in this era of innovation, it was designed by Deutsche Bank and Daiwa to get round the continuing prohibition in West Germany and Japan on stock index futures and options.

A significant creation were zero coupon bonds – bonds which are redeemed at a par price which includes a calculation of interest and are issued at a sum less the notional interest element. Tax advantages were major reasons for their popularity. These two were not allowed in West Germany and Japan until as late as 1985.

Almost as long established, and similarly designed as a protection or hedge against fluctuations in price, are futures. Commodity futures had long been a central plank in the London and Chicago Commodity Markets, enabling companies to purchase raw materials at an agreed price for future delivery, irrespective of changes in exchange rates or the price of the commodity. And those futures themselves were traded in a secondary market. Likewise, currency futures too had been well known for obvious hedging and speculative reasons. In the mid-1970s Chicago set the pace by introducing interest rate futures and to these share futures have been added. The two competing centres in Chicago, the Chicago Board of Trade and the Mercantile Exchange, are the world's largest. The London International Financial Futures Exchange (LIFFE) was created in 1982. Housed at present opposite the Bank of England in the Royal Exchange, it offers a full range of currency, interest rate equity and gilt futures.

Closely linked to the futures are 'options'. LIFFE has attached options to a number of its currency futures and its stock index futures. If you purchase an option you have the right to buy (call option) or sell (put option) an instrument at a predetermined price within a specified period. If the movement is unfavourable, you can sell, losing only the option premium; if it is favourable, you can decide not to exercise the option. For buying, too, it is a method of taking advantage of favourable changes without risk. Currency options were first traded on one of Chicago's American rival futures markets, the Philadelphia Stock Exchange in 1982. The cumulative volume of contracts on LIFFE has risen substantially and at almost geometric rates. By the end of 1986 it had reached 12 million, while in 1987 daily average volume was twice as high as in 1986! Most powerful areas are LIFFE gilt futures (and in particular the long gilt 15–20 years) and US Treasury bond and note (T-bond, T-note) futures and options. It is in this latter context that the association with the Chicago Board of Trade Futures Market, announced in 1987, is of particular potential. Through a further link with the renowned Sydney Futures Exchange, it is now possible through LIFFE to trade interchangeable (or 'fungible') contracts 24 hours a day [30].

But still more successful in the London options market has been The Stock Exchange. After a slow start in 1978, they took off in 1984 when the British Telecom flotation was endowed with its own immediate option contract. The Exchange Options Development Group expected up to 100 000 options contracts daily by the end of 1987. On the Continent, however, the European leader in the options market is (despite difficulties which we examine in the last chapter) Amsterdam's European Options Exchange (EOE). Founded in April 1978, it has easily outstripped its London rivals in volume with $3\frac{1}{2}$ million contracts in 1983, five million in 1984, seven million in 1985 and some ten million in 1986. Share options represent 84 per cent of trade but the exchange has diversified into currency and gold and silver contracts [31].

Related to futures are financial forwards. Sold over the counter and known as FRAs (Forward Rate Agreements), they are more flexible than futures and have chiefly been used as inter-bank instruments.

But just as spectacularly successful as futures and options have also been *swaps*. Nothing illustrates more clearly how financial innovation has been designed to meet the needs of the international borrower and investor. Originally swaps were combined with new Eurobond issues, the borrowers raising capital in the market where they had advantage and then swapping the proceeds to meet their other currency requirements. Swaps then established themselves as trading instruments in their own right. Essentially they are a technique whereby two parties agree to exchange two streams of interest rates. They may be in the same currency but with one stream at a fixed rate and the other at LIBOR (interest rate swaps – this being the classic type or 'plain vanilla' swap); or they may be at fixed rates but in different currencies (currency swaps); or in different currencies and with different interest rates (cross-currency interest rate swaps or 'circus swaps'). The market has grown rapidly – the European Investment Bank calculated that in 1986 the total of outstanding principal exceeded $400 billion. In all cases the advantage lies in the two parties benefiting mutually from their own most favourable credit, currency and interest circumstances while obtaining through this second party the arrangement they are actually seeking [32].

The remaining area of innovation that should be mentioned are the schemes which from 1981 have been designed to facilitate short-term credit flows – the note issuance facility (NIF, also known as RUF or Revolving Underwriting Facility and SNIF or Short-term Note Issuance Facility). These are medium-term facilities enabling a corporation to issue a stream of short-term notes (Euronotes) which are underwritten by a bank or groups of banks. Though NIFs had a volume of $33 billion in 1985 they are threatened by the rise of a phenomenon we have already depicted as another major form of securitisation, commercial paper. The great advantage of CP to the borrower is that it can cut out the intermediation of the banks – though the underwriting also disappears. In the final analysis these instruments have all been designed for special national – and frequently corporate – circumstances. They are determined by the market conditions.

And so the products come and go. Zero coupon bonds in 1987 had become rare – their tax advantages in the US and Japan had been abolished. In December 1986 the market in perpetual FRNs came effectively to a standstill while the issue of FRNs generally in 1986 was substantially lower than in 1985. Competition from swaps was partly responsible, while generally low interest rates gave a new impetus to fixed rate bonds [33].

What does all this mean for the banks? Above all, highly intensified competition and a changed role, a role that encompasses a securities trading presence in the world's major centres, New York and Tokyo as well as London. As David Lascelles has so succinctly put it:

'The bigger challenge, though, is to *transform themselves from traditional intermediaries between depositors and borrowers, into financial engineers in the capital markets*, positioning themselves between investor and capital-user ...
For many of them it is a matter of their survival in big league

banking, and of keeping up with the needs of their large corporate and government clients which have shifted firmly in favour of the more flexible, and usually cheaper, terms available in the securities markets' [34] (*author's italics*).

The impetus, then, is towards the breakdown of distinctions between commercial banks and investment banks and between banks and securities houses. It was, at bottom, because London and its institutions were in danger of losing out in the global transformation that deregulation grew apace in 1985 culminating on 27 October 1986 in the Big Bang. Preceded by a feverish bout of acquisitions and mergers between Britain's and the world's major banks and securities houses in London, Big Bang swept aside The Stock Exchange's venerable tradition of single capacity and altered the capital participation rules for members. And reinforcing The Stock Exchange's own internal transformation, Parliament in early 1987 radically changed the nature of building societies through the *Building Societies Act*. The day of the financial conglomerate had come.

Transformations II – London's Big Bang and its new institutions

Contrary to its nickname, Big Bang was not quick in coming. Nor was it totally original. And it was not concluded on 27 October 1986.

The first step towards the deregulation of the world's financial centres was taken in New York. The catalyst had been the creation of the off-floor trading exchange NASDAQ. New York's Stock Exchange, already under enormous physical pressure from the expansion in business of the 1960s and early 1970s, was fearful of losing its pre-eminence since it had become a cumbersome and expensive place to deal. Change came on May Day, 1 May 1975. Membership of the Exchange was not made more liberal – it was tightened to prohibit institutions from obtaining membership whether directly or through affiliation with brokers. Trading had to remain on the floor. But fixed commissions were scrapped. The result was dramatic for the players; rates fell by 60 per cent in a few years. Many of the great names like Shearson, Bache, Paine Webber, were taken over or merged. Others disappeared. Business became concentrated in the hands of the big firms [35].

New York's example was to have no rapid effect on London. But pressure was mounting by the later 1970s. It was not only that the London Eurobond market was threatening the attractiveness of the domestic securities market traded on the Exchange. As in the USA in the early 1970s, threats were coming from the new technology. Because of fixed commissions, transaction costs were high. As early as 1972, the accepting houses among the merchant banks evolved a screen-based dealing system that completely by-passed the Stock Exchange. Subscribers on ARIEL – Automated Real Time Investment Exchange Limited – could contact sellers directly, bids and offers were on the screen, commissions were cut out altogether (apart from a transaction fee). The Government refused to let gilts be traded this way. The Stock Exchange reduced commissions in large deals and tried to buy ARIEL out. Eventually it was amalgamated with other automated information systems and lost its dealing facility [36]. But the writing was already on the wall – or rather on the screen. By the early 1980s there were all the signs that another of Britain's historically successful activities was on the wane, hide-bound by anachronistic tradition.

But when it came, the impetus to change was from an unexpected quarter. In June 1976 a Government Order extended the coverage of the 1956 Restrictive Trade Practices Act to services. The Stock Exchange could not claim exemption. A long dispute ensued. In February 1979 the Codes and Rules book of the Exchange was referred to the Restrictive Practices Court. Under scrutiny were to be fixed commissions, single capacity and the membership rules – in short the very stuff of the Exchange's framework which had been in place since early in the century. Any hope that there might be an intervention from the Secretary of State for Trade in the new Conservative Cabinet of Summer 1979, John Nott, was soon dashed. The Conservatives believed in freedom of competition and did not wish to appear to be sheltering the City. Court proceedings were served in October 1979. The Exchange completed its long and complex Statement of Case in March 1981. But there were already signs that competitive pressures were undermining The Stock Exchange's resistance. The abolition of exchange controls had freed the great institutional funds for overseas investment. At the same time, the number of foreign equities quoted in London was rising while, originally as a means of avoiding stamp duty, UK equities were being ever more actively traded in New York through the use of American Depository Receipts (ADRs). Bulk purchases of shares can be made in London (and stamp duty paid), re-registered by a bank in the USA through certificates issued by a depository bank, and subsequently traded in smaller quantities without any further stamp duty. Such moves, together with the prodigious expansion of the Eurobond market, led jobbers in London to feel increasingly isolated. In 1980 the Exchange agreed to allow jobbers access to foreign principals without reference to London brokers. Single capacity had effectively already been breached, albeit in an (initially) minor way.

Another feature of The Stock Exchange that was limiting its competitiveness in the powerful growing securities markets of the 1980s was the relatively modest capital base of members. In May 1982, the Exchange's Council responded by allowing institutional ownership of member firms to rise from the old 10 per cent to 29.9 per cent. This was the breakthrough that was to lead to a radical recast of London's banking and securities structure, and allowed foreign interests significant direct participation in the market. The reasons for working towards an out-of-court agreement were becoming powerful and in the event the new Trade Secretary, Cecil Parkinson, was able to reach such an agreement in July 1983.

The Agreement exempted the Stock Exchange from further court proceedings. In return minimum commissions were to be scrapped within three and a half years, while non-members could become directors of corporate member firms (provided members were still the majority of directors). An independent Appeals Committee was to be set up on issues concerning membership application and Council was to have lay members. There was no insistance on the introduction of dual capacity. But as discussions continued within the Exchange and with the Bank of England it became clear that the dealings systems would have to change. On the Eurobond markets brokers were already acting in both capacities, simply in order to compete with foreign market-makers. The prospects of reduced commissions for brokers who would not have any compensatory right to act as dealers was worrying. May Day, had after all, wrought havoc among members of the New York Exchange. At the same time a 'fair weather only' system that did not guarantee continuity of dealing, even in bear markets, was unacceptable. And while it became clear that change had to come in the system of trading equities, the Agreement also enabled the Bank of England to look again at the structure of the gilt-edged market. This, we saw, had largely been in the hands, traditionally, of two major jobbers in gilts, Ackroyd Smithers and Wedd Durlacher. Before 1971 the smoothness of the gilts market had, to a good extent, been ensured by the Bank's own willingness to buy in or sell to assist jobbers maintain a stable market. Edward Heath's measure of that year, *Competition and Credit Control*, ended quantitative limits on bank advances and relied for control of money supply on interest rate changes. The Bank consequently restricted its role in buying stock. The market was more open but also more vulnerable.

The agreement of 1983 provided, then, the opportunity for a complete new look at market arrangements. In equities The Stock Exchange decided on a modified version, not of the auction market-making approach of the New York Stock Exchange, but of the computing market-making system of the American screen exchange NASDAQ. All firms may become dual capacity brokers and dealers, acting both as agency brokers and as principals buying and selling shares in their own right. They can also apply to become 'committed market-makers', that is dealers who have to make markets irrespective of conditions in the equities for which they are registered. And simultaneous with the new roles for members, their mode of trading was dramatically transformed with the introduction, on the day of the Big Bang, of The Stock Exchange's own screen trading system, the Stock Exchange Automated Quotation System (SEAQ). The stocks registered with the Exchange are classified according to the companies' capitalisation, turnover, number of shareholders and interested market-makers into alpha, beta and gamma groups. For the first two classes, market-makers have to quote firm prices. Trade publication within five minutes is expected of alphas, more time is allowed for betas, while gammas only have indicative prices and delayed trade publication. Alphas include over 50 of the UK's top companies, betas some 500 listed equities, while the gammas include 1200 UK listed equities, but also overseas equities, securities from the Unlisted Securities Market and local authority and government bonds.

SEAQ, which is open from 8 am to 6 pm displays information on three levels of the screen, level 1 the best bids for alpha and beta stocks, level 2 the quotes of all market-makers in a stock, while level 3 is for the market-makers only, enabling them to input bid and offer prices. In addition, there are closed user-group circuits so that market-makers can be in direct contact with major institutional clients. After some early teething troubles in October and November 1986, SEAQ has effectively made a clean sweep of London Stock Exchange dealing. Despite the elaborate refurbishment of the trading floor prior to the Big Bang, its popularity declined almost immediately. The desk system of screens and telephones replaced almost overnight the historical face-to-face dealing on the old Floor. By December 1986, 95 per cent of trading had been diverted to the market-makers' dealing rooms and the Floor has now been closed, ending a centuries-old tradition.

SEAQ is also used for the gilts market, which, like the equities market, was radically altered from October 1986. The two major and four minor jobbers who formerly dealt in gilts have been replaced by twenty-seven Gilt-Edged Market-Makers (GEMMS). The market is, then, vastly more competitive than it was and it is a matter of speculation whether all twenty-seven can possibly survive. Since gilts have to be delivered and paid for in cash the following day, nine companies have been recognised as Stock Exchange Money Brokers (SEMBS), separate from the market-makers, to facilitate the ability of the latter to settle. And alongside the market-makers, further quickening the pace and increasing turnover, is the new category of Inter-Dealer Brokers (IDBS) who deal between the market-makers. All categories are under the supervision of the Bank of England which monitors their ratio of trading to capital and exposure to risk.

A year before the introduction of SEAQ into the domestic UK trading, SEAQ International had been created, a screen-trading system that extends to markets in Tokyo and Hong Kong, France, Germany, Netherlands, Switzerland, Scandinavia, and North America. Its prices can be carried on other national viewdata networks including not only the Exchange's own TOPIC systems and Reuters but also America's NASDAQ and QUOTRON, and Germany's TELEKURS. Though firm price trading is restricted to 9.30–15.30 (to 13.30 for North American stocks), prices can still be quoted outside hours. The significance of *SEAQ International* is to place London Stock Exchange trading firmly in the global 24-hour trading network, with the UK as the middle time-zone between the Far East and the United States.

Who, then, are the players in this bracing new climate? The great shake-up had already commenced, in May 1982 when outside institutions were allowed to take up 29.9 per cent of the capital of jobbers and brokers. The agreement with the Government in July 1983 released a great flood of pent-up demand for access to direct involvement in the London Stock Exchange, setting up alignments and deals that were completed after 1 March 1986, when 100 per cent ownership was permitted.

After the innovatory start in the Eurobond market by S G Warburg back in the 1960s, British banks and securities houses lost out in this, the City's major area of growth. We have seen that the numbers of foreign banks operating in London soared from 114 in 1967, to 400 in 1986 (with a further 47 indirectly represented). Even prior to the agreement between the Government and The Stock Exchange, in 1980 and 1981 there were 353 directly represented foreign banks and securities houses [37]. By 1987 S G Warburg was the only British firm among the top ten Eurobond lead managers, lying in eighth position according to one authoritative calculation in a league dominated by Nomura, Crédit Suisse-First Boston, Deutsche Bank and the three other great Japanese securities houses, Daiwa, Nikko and Yamaichi [38]. British commercial and merchant banks that wanted to have a share of the deregulated capital market cake in London faced stiff competition from the United States and the UK's neighbours in Europe. First in was Security Pacific, which bought a share in the top-ranking broker Hoare Govett as early as 1982. As quick off the mark, however, was Jacob Rothschild who bought through Rothschild Investment Trust a stake in the gilts jobber Wedd Durlacher, and, having sold that stake on to Barclays, bought a further interest in the stockbrokers Kitkat & Aitken, which he again sold, this time to Orion Royal Bank of Canada. The scramble was on. But the competition did not come so much from the giant US securities houses and investment banks such as Salomon Brothers, Morgan Guaranty, or Morgan Stanley. In the event, their very predominance in the much larger London Eurobond market made paying over the odds for access to the UK domestic securities market an unattractive proposition. Like Prudential-Bache and Goldman Sachs, they preferred simply to seek out experienced staff from existing City firms. Merrill Lynch contented themselves with purchasing the small gilt jobbers Giles & Creswell.

It was the US commercial banks who made the running – Citicorp bought two of the most highly regarded of the City's brokers Scrimgeour Kemp-Gee, a top house, and Vickers da Costa, specialists in Far Eastern equities. Chase Manhattan bought two well-known brokers, Laurie Millbank and Simon & Coates. Nevertheless, the principal strategy of the American houses was to build up expertise from within to enable them gradually to move beyond an initial concentration on the stocks of the top 100 UK companies.

But foreign competition for access to the London Stock markets was far from limited to the United States. Most significant was the Union Bank of Switzerland's purchase of Phillips & Drew, a highly esteemed City broker, which in its turn acquired a small gilts dealer and an equity jobber. Other Swiss banks to enter the fray were Crédit Suisse which bought the brokers Buckmaster & Moore and the jobber Harold Rattle. The Austrian Girozentrale & Österreichische Sparkassen also made a broker purchase as did Banque Bruxelles Lambert of Belgium. French banks did not show great enthusiasm, the most interesting acquisition being Paribas's purchase of Quilter Goodison, who had concentrated on European equities.

All in all, twelve European banks are now members of the Exchange, and seven US banks. Surprising at the time was the decision of the giant Japanese banks not to enter the market in this manner but to wait and see. Not even Nomura Securities International took the plunge – but caution turned out to be wise in the unsettling aftermath of the October 1987 Crash.

Meanwhile, the pre Big Bang rush was to result in the emergence of Britain's first true financial conglomerates, for it was the British banks who were most active in the acquisitions battle: altogether fourteen UK banks and a further twenty-two other British financial or trading institutions are now members of the Exchange. Of the original two hundred member firms, there are now some hundred and five that belong in some degree to former outside interests. The remaining hundred are largely provincial partnerships [39]. The first UK banks to move were the merchant banks. Traditionally specialising in corporate banking services and investment advice, they were already being squeezed by the advance of the clearing banks into these areas. National Westminster through the County Bank, Midland through Samuel Montagu, and Barclays and Lloyds through their own merchant arms were already well on the way to evolving into financial conglomerates before the 1983 Agreement. Perhaps the most ambitious move for its size was the decision of S G Warburg & Co. to re-form as Mercury International, taking in not only the top stockbrokers Rowe & Pitman, but the leading gilt jobbers Akroyd & Smithers, and even the old government gilt brokers Mullens & Co. Warburgs had been the only British bank to keep anywhere near pace with the Americans and

Japanese in the London Eurobond market. They now proved that they did not intend to be left behind in the international race for entry to The London Stock Exchange. N M Rothschild bought a share in the jobbers Smith Bros., and a small firm of brokers, Morgan Grenfell, already famed for its expertise in the lucrative corporate mergers and acquisitions business, deployed that expertise on its own account in purchasing a stake in the jobbers Pinchin & Denny and the gilt-edged brokers Pember & Boyle. Kleinwort Benson, (Grievson Grant), Hill Samuel, (Wood McKenzie of Edinburgh), and Hambros all took stakes in brokers, while Baring Bros., and Guinness Mahon added jobbers to their interests.

But the clearing banks, with the notable exception of Lloyds which deals in its own right, formed some formidable combinations. Barclays bought a stake in the top broker De Zoete & Bevan and the leading gilts jobber Wedd Durlacher to form Barclays De Zoete Wedd. National Westminster purchased an interest in another renowned broker, Fielding Newson-Smith and in jobbers Bisgood & Bishop. Midland, through Samuel Montagu, bought a stake in the brokers W Greenwell and also joined the primary gilts market.

By the end of 1984 this first round was over, to be consolidated with further stake holdings when the limit was raised from 29.9 per cent to 100 per cent in March 1986. The explosion of investment banking and its concomitant trading on the Exchange had in a few years transformed the London banking world. Altogether it had cost the clearers some quarter of a billion pounds to enter the UK equities and trading bond scene [40].

Not many believed that the fierce new competition would allow all thirty-five market-makers to survive. Indeed, an early casualty was Midland Bank's Greenwell Montagu Securities, which withdrew from equity market-making in March 1987. And in gilts the switch from a handful of dealers to twenty-seven would seem ominous. But it seems likely that many, if not all, of the contenders will continue in a long war of attrition for ultimately significant shares of valuable markets.

Nevertheless, within the year Lloyd's Bank had pulled out of both gilts and Eurobonds, Chemical Bank from primary eurobonds, Salomon Bros. from EP Commercial Paper and the Canadian Royal Bank from Eurobonds and gilts. Eight houses only were thought to have the lion's share of the gilts market and they included Union Bank of Switzerland's market-makers Phillips & Drew, Greenwell Montagu and Scrimgeour Vickers (Citicorp). At the same time, a gradual shake-out of City staff began, not only from the market-makers that had withdrawn from certain of the markets but others such as Salomon Bros. and L F Rothschild. As many as 750 jobs had been lost a year after Big Bang.

Some UK merchant banks, however, decided not to go down the conglomerate route, but instead to develop their specialism in market niches. Robert Fleming, for example, an outside house preferred to build on their skills in UK electricals and, through their close links with Hong Kong, their skills in Far Eastern securities [41]. Schroders already owned their own firms Helbert Wagg & Co and Anderson Bryce Villiers. Others, like Lazard Brothers, decided to make no acquisitions, probably a wise strategy in the light of the sluggish trading that followed the October Crash. Hill Samuel, which had owned a stockbroking subsidiary Wood Mackenzie, was itself purchased in late 1987 by TSB. TSB (which had been floated in 1986) thus became one of the UK's most diversified financial conglomerates with interests in life assurance, shipping and car rentals.

Transformations were, then, the order of the day both before the Big Bang itself and in its wake. Indeed, the expansion of The Stock Exchange to allow the issuing and trading in securities that would not previously have met the stringent requirements of Exchange listing, had already commenced in 1980. The Unlisted Securities Market opened in November of that year. By the end of 1986 it had been joined by its 500th member, while over 60 had already progressed into full Exchange listing. Total capitalisation for the relatively small companies quoted is already over £4 billion, offering a significant alternative to the main market. But the USM is not without its difficulties. Deregulation has focussed investment interest on alpha and beta stock of the main market, though as we saw, USM securities are featured in the SEAQ trading portfolios as gamma stocks. The major market-makers are National Westminster's County Bisgood, but other major firms such as Capel Cure Myers, Chase Manhattan and Phillips & Drew are also active.

The USM was joined in January 1987 by the Third Market, in a Stock Exchange venture to attract into London the capital market companies that could not fulfil the requirements of the USM, the smallest of whose quoted stocks have capitalisation of nearly £1 million. A second reason was to provide the already existent over-the-counter market with some regulation. For entry to the Third Market a company needs a Stock Exchange sponsor which will assess its standing and record. The sponsor will have to guarantee that there will be at least two market-makers in its shares. Thirty members have announced that they will act as sponsors, while eight have come forward as market-makers. Most of the quoted shares will appear, it is expected, as gamma shares on SEAQ. Some will be placed in the least liquid category, delta, which are not quoted on SEAQ, though information is given on their registered market-makers.

Like the USM in its early days, the Third Market also experienced a rather slow start. Its share index did not recover to its January 1987 level until five months after its inception. Nevertheless the Third Market is still likely to be a significant institution for small businesses, especially as the Small Business Expansion Scheme comes into operation in 1988, emphasising the trend away from the traditional exclusive dependence of such companies on bank loans.

The effect of deregulation was, then, to stimulate business throughout the Stock Exchange. The Bank of England reported in early 1987 that daily turnover since October 1986 in UK and foreign equities had increased by 21 per cent, and although the major British Gas and TSB flotations may have boosted this figure, it is exactly matched by an advance in the USM, a market unaffected by these share issues, of 21 per cent in value and 22 per cent in volume [42].

Immediately prior to Big Bang, the London Stock Exchange, including USM, had a listing of over 7000 stocks and shares with a total value of over £1350 billion. Of these, 4980 were company equity issues, making London the Exchange with the largest number of listed companies in the world. But it is a measure of the international depth of the market that over three-quarters of its value is accounted for by companies of overseas origin, with the US representing over 50 per cent of the total £1122 billion value (on 30 September 1986). Japan follows at 3.7 per cent, then the Netherlands (3.4 per cent) and the Federal Republic (3.2 per cent).

One of the major questions to be answered in the years following deregulation will be London's position relative to the other global centres, New York and Tokyo and relative to the major European exchanges. For while London leads in the number of listing, it is third in terms of capitalisation behind New York and Tokyo, and according to the authoritative periodical *Euromoney* prior to Big Bang in 1985 it had been overtaken in daily and annual turnover by the German exchanges (as a group) [43]. True, the strength of the Deutschmark vis-à-vis dollar and pound is reflected in this ranking, but that cannot obscure the importance for London of Big Bang as a radical stimulus to her future competitiveness and domination of the European securities market.

Perhaps the most important development in this context took place after Big Bang. In 1985, in response to the new regulatory requirements coming into force in the UK in 1987, which we shall discuss below, the London Eurobond traders formed the International Securities Regulatory Organisation (ISRO). Some 56 of its 187 members were already involved in the Stock Exchange and in November 1986 agreement was reached to create a single investment exchange for international equities. The giant Eurobond market would establish itself within the legislative framework of the 1987 Financial Services Act as a 'Recognised Investment Exchange' (RIE) under the title and (regulation) of the Association of International Bond Dealers, (AIBD). But the evolving trade in international equities, boosted by the wave of privatisation such as British Telecom and British Gas in the UK, Saint Gobain and Paribas in France and the huge flotation of Japan's Nippon Telephone and Telegraph in February 1987, will go to a new joint exchange formed from a merger between the London Stock Exchange and ISRO. The new exchange adopted the title 'The International Stock Exchange of the United Kingdom and the Republic of Ireland Limited' (reflecting also the incorporation of the stock exchanges in Britain's other cities such as Manchester and Edinburgh and also of Dublin's exchange of some fifteen years previously). Arguably, the development of the new exchange as a leading international centre, indeed as the world centre, for trading in international shares, is the greatest challenge of the decade, possibly as significant as Big Bang itself.

Transformations III – from building societies to financial houses

We saw that, unlike the banks and The Stock Exchange, building societies had been controlled in their activities by UK law. The 1986 Building Societies Act removed many of the major constraints placed upon them, enabling them to enter an area of concern in this study, the international capital market. Until 1 January 1987 building societies had been compelled to accept an encroachment on their sole area of business, through the entry in 1981 of the commercial banks into the long-term house loan sector. Building societies responded in two principal ways: they became far more aggressive in their search for customers, witnessed by the plethora of advertisements on television during peak viewing hours, and they began to enter the territory of the High Street banks through the introduction of cheque books and the adoption of the very latest generation of Automatic Teller Machines. They had been successful in both drives. In 1986 loans rose by 38 per cent to reach a total of £37 billion and the societies retained 75 per cent of the UK mortgage market [44]. Moreover, their ATM's placed them at the head of the High Street field. Most accept deposits as well as dispensing cash. Many print out balances. The Halifax network even permits the payment of gas and electricity bills and the transfer of funds to other accounts in addition. Five societies have joined up in an inter-connected network known as Matrix, (Anglia, Bradford & Bingley, Bristol and West, Leeds Permanent and Norwich). But more important, the Link network, to which Abbey National and Nationwide belong as well as the National Girobank and Co-op Bank, offers a Funds Transfer Sharing System that extends to the Plus network in the US. In Britain there were 1.2 million Link cards at the end of 1986. Plus has 58 million cards. Already American-Express and Citibank are members of the British Link network [45]. It was a flexibility that the societies badly needed, despite the extra surge in their competitiveness permitted by the abolition of their own interest rate cartel (which had, however, the effect of helping the efficient societies rather than the system as an entirety).

The 1986 Building Societies Act allowed the societies to raise up to per cent on the money and wholesale markets instead of 5 per cent previously. This relieved their dangerously heavy reliance on retail savings as a source of funding, the cause of many mortgage queues in the past. In 1986 the societies became extremely active in the international capital markets. Syndicated bank loans at about £1 billion were still a major feature in their funding but building society bonds raised £750 million, while Certificates of Deposit (CDs) with a maturity of less than a year reached £2.5 billion. Furthermore, after April 1986 the societies became major participants in the Eurosterling bond market (they are restricted to the UK currency) with issues amounting to £2 billion or 25 per cent of the whole market [46].

Not that this may prove sufficient, for another major provision of the Act allows societies with assets exceeding £100 million to enter complete new financial and business areas, ventures that also require capital. The big societies can now offer unsecured personal loans (though total lending in this and the corporate and second mortgage areas may not exceed 10 per cent of the total loans). They may also run estate agencies. By 1987 the societies had already spent in excess of £85 million in acquiring estate agencies. They are also empowered to undertake conveyancing and insurance broking, thus enabling the societies for the first time to offer integrated house purchase services. Stockbroking, managing Personal Equity Plans (PEPs) and pensions are further areas that are permissible and will bring the largest societies such as the Halifax, the Abbey National and the Nationwide (which merged with the Anglia, already the country's seventh largest in September 1987) into direct competition with the great financial conglomerates. And, indeed, in one respect they will go beyond the established business even of these giants by undertaking house building itself [47].

All of this puts the 20 per cent limit on wholesale borrowing under considerable pressure. Fortunately this may be reviewed and raised by the minister to 40 per cent. But eventually the only method will be to become a public limited company (plc) though even then at least 50 per cent of funds will have to be in the form of savers' shares. Control of the societies moves, as we saw earlier, from the Registrar of Friendly Societies to the Building Society Commission, which is responsible for laying down and monitoring capital adequacy, for supervising adherence to the limits on the various kinds of lending and for ensuring that professional standards are maintained in accounting, management and all services offered to the public [48].

And so what originated as modest mutual societies enabling members eventually to own their houses, have become composite firms, combining most of the financial services previously found in many district High Street firms under a single roof. More than that, they are emerging as a force in the international capital market, while some are linked to international fund transfer systems. Indeed, the Halifax no longer restricts its retail activities to the UK. It has opened offices in France as a herald perhaps of a new era in British invisible trade.

After decompartmentalisation – regulation

British building societies remain, despite their new found freedoms, the only UK financial institutions that are directly regulated by British law. But that does not mean an absence of control for the banks and securities houses. The Financial Services Act 1986 sets out an elaborate, many would say hopelessly elaborate, system of self-regulation. Why self-regulation, not direct and specific statutory control as for the building societies? The answer lies in the paradoxical move in the UK and in the world towards liberalisation, towards deregulation. The flows of that life-giving water, money, have quickened and grown in volume during the 1980s on an unprecedented scale. The emergence of financial conglomerates that can trade in capital through screen and local offices globally twenty-four hours a day, firms such as Britain's Mercury International, formerly S G Warburg & Co., with seats on the Tokyo, New York and London Stock Exchanges and offices in San Francisco, means that the flows are unceasing day and night.

The exchanges with the fewest obstacles and the cheapest costs of transaction reap the greatest benefit. London has returned through its effectively off-shore Eurobond market that took off in the 1980s and now the deregulation of Big Bang to becoming not only Europe's major financial centre but possibly the world's major centre. But other centres are anxious not to miss out on the action. The Federal Republic of Germany, which, thanks to its 'universal' banking system, never knew single capacity on its exchanges, had freed movement in outward investment as early as 1957. The coupon tax on foreign holders of DM bonds was removed in the same year. Floating rate notes, zero coupon bonds, swaps and dual currency issues were all permitted from 1985. Foreign banks, provided they were incorporated in Germany, were permitted to lead-manage EuroDM bonds. In France a franc Eurobond market opened in 1985, a commercial paper market was permitted, a highly successful futures market (the Matif) started business in 1986, followed in 1987 by an options market. The restriction on the number of members in the Bourse (the *agents de change*) is to be lifted, and outside companies may take a 30 per cent interest in a broking firm from 1988, 49 per cent from 1989, and 100 per cent from 1990. And already nearly half of the trade in government bonds is transacted outside the Bourse through a Reuters screen network. The Netherlands, already leaders in the options market, began trading in guilder/FRNs, CDs and commercial paper in 1986, while foreign banks, under the supervision of De Nederlands Bank, were allowed to lead-manage Eurobond and domestic issues. The United States scrapped withholding tax, commissions were reduced in the Swiss securities market, Japan permitted from 1984 that foreign institutions could lead-manage Euroyen bond issues, foreign borrowers could issue FRNs, zero coupon bonds and dual currency issues, while withholding tax was abolished. The old protective dykes are everywhere being removed as competition requires freer and freer flows if a financial centre is not to be left high and dry (such as Brussels where the Kredietbank continues to urge further relaxations in withholding tax, the commencement of Euro-Belgian franc bonds and the introduction of the new financial instruments) [49].

Yet while the integration of the world's financial markets can show great benefits to the successful centres and players it remains a source of anxiety to the central banks. For they see not only the erosion of their own powers of control over their domestic financial structures, but the dangers of contagion if just one part of the global system were to be affected by a debt, default or a collapse in confidence. We return to this vital issue in the last chapter, an issue all the more urgent since the stock crash and dollar slide of Autumn 1987. For even within the newly liberalised national systems there are inherent dangers for borrowers and investors - the dangers that intensified competition may tempt financial houses to go beyond prudential limits either through inadequate capital ratios or through undertaking ever riskier transactions to keep business. And beyond that the sweeping away of the old compartments or bulkheads between activities means that confidentiality may easily be breached. The invisible or so-called 'Chinese' walls between the departments of the new conglomerates rely to a frighteningly great extent on the sheer honesty of employees. The names of Collier at Morgan Grenfell and, at an altogether different level of notoriety, Ivan Boesky and his associates (also in Morgan Grenfell as well as other houses) are a salutary reminder that deregulation cannot mean no regulations.

It is as a means to maintaining maximum freedom and, therefore, the attractiveness of London while providing control, that the Financial Services Act laid down a self-regulatory system for the supervision of financial transactions in the UK. Under the Act the Secretary of State for Trade & Industry has powers to define, authorise and regulate the investment business. No-one may engage in this activity without authorisation. But the Secretary of State's powers are delegated to the Securities and Investments Board (SIB) which monitors the entire field. Answerable to the SIB are a series of Self-Regulating Organisations (SROs) with special responsibility for sectors of business. These are The Securities Association (TSA), the Investment Management Regulatory Organisation (IMRO), the Life Assurance and Unit Trust Regulatory Organisation (LAUTRO), Financial Intermediaries, Managers and Brokers Regulatory Association (FIMBRA) and the Association of Futures Brokers and Dealers (AFBD). Matters which the organisations' rulebooks cover include not only information on the membership and direction of an authorised firm, but also the conduct of business with clients, maintenance of adequate capital ratios, construction and monitoring of the Chinese walls in integrated houses, the nature of the SRO's disciplinary powers and the establishment of compensation funds for clients. Each organisation will have a compliance department charged with checking for abuses such as fraud or insider dealing and ensuring that the company's own rulebook (The Compliance Manual) complies with that of the SRC and is adhered to.

Trading itself occurs within the regulatory framework of Recognised Investment Exchanges (RIEs). We saw that the International Stock Exchange of Great Britain and Ireland is the recognised exchange for domestic and international stocks and equity; LIFFE is the RIE for the futures and options market, AIBD, the Association of International Bond Dealers whose province is the vast Eurobond market and has its headquarters in Zurich, has, however, gained a significant concession, reflecting the dilemma facing the British Government: while authorisation for members of the Association to carry on business still comes from The Securities Association, and its trading and resources will also be monitored by TSA, the AIBD is not a full RIE. Instead it is treated as an overseas market like the US stock exchanges. Nevertheless, members still feel that their style is cramped, for the SIB retains responsibility for seeing that the AIBD provides adequate protection for investors in designating it as an exchange. The alienation of the AIBD would, however, be fatal for London's continued pre-eminence in Eurobond trading.

Beyond these regulatory structures, the professions engaged in the investments business are also regulated within the framework of Recognised Professional Bodies (RPBs) which include the Law Societies of England and Wales, and Scotland, the Institutes of Chartered Accountants in England, Wales, Scotland and Northern Ireland and the Institute of Chartered Secretaries and Administrators.

Many firms will thus find themselves falling under the regulations of more than one SRO. It has, therefore, become imperative for them also to establish compliance departments staffed by experts versed in the intricacies of the new rules. And indeed one of the Compliance Officer's central duties is training staff to be thoroughly familiar with the regulations. This is doubly important since not only do the SROs have matching compliance departments that sample trading records, the Department of Trade & Industry Inspectors (who first exposed the chaos in the Guinness takeover of Distillers) have increased powers to question under oath in order to curb insider trading [50].

Beyond these controls, the Stock Exchange itself continues to be responsible for the listing of securities and monitors transactions through its screen trading system (SEAQ).

And adding to the complexity, Lloyds of London is to remain exempted and independent of these regulations, while the wholesale markets in currency, bullion and even financial instruments will come under Bank of England supervision. Firms have to apply to the Bank for exemption from the Financial Services Act, whereupon they come under Bank of England supervision of capital adequacy and a special Code of Conduct.

Even in summary, then, the new framework sounds formidable. Yet no reader can doubt the complexity and trading velocity of the markets that it seeks to monitor and regulate. Whether the number of SROs and their further supervision by the SIB will prove too cumbersome to be effective, can only emerge in a matter of years. Equally pertinent is whether these layers of control, supervision and compliance will deter the very business attracted to the UK by deregulation. Nor do these domestic controls provide more than a local barrier against the abuse of a client's trust. Admittedly, the other major financial centres in the US and Japan are still essentially compartmentalised in the spirit of the American legislation of the 1930s. But the impetus to growth in the off-shore capital markets is strong. The thirst for investment wherever on earth the returns are best will not be slacked – the ageing of the Western and Japanese industrialised populations and their need for pensions provision alone will see to that. Indeed, as we have invariably witnessed in other spheres, once the technology exists it will be used. Global trading on the computer screen is surely a reality that has come to stay. But screens, unlike trading floors, are not restricted to localities. If London's newly regulated system significantly slows down or hampers the flow of world investment trade through the City, that trade could go elsewhere. There are a number of candidates for it in the same time-zone. If the relaxation of the rules for the Eurobond market is anything to go by, however, it is more likely that the regulations will be the first to be modified. And what no regulations can do, of course, is to ensure the permanent stability and buoyancy of the world investment market. What can be achieved, through national banking regulations, is to give Central Banks some measure of control over domestic banking operations. Controlling global currency fluctuations is, however, altogether more difficult in a system dominated by floating exchange rates and 24-hour trading. We return to these daunting issues in the last chapter.

Notes and references

1   *See* the elegant use of the water-money analogy in Dr Andreas Prindl's 'The Andreas Prindl Report: Money in the Far East', *Banking World*, 1986. Dr Prindl is Managing Director of Nomura International Bank in London.

2   *See* Richard Dale, *How Safe is the Banking System?*, The David Hume Institute, Hume Occasional Paper 4, Glencorse, 1986, p. 12.

3   W. A. Thomas gives an extensive historical picture of how The Stock Exchange operated in *The Big Bang*, Philip Allan, Oxford, 1986.

4   Thomas, op. cit. pp. 3–4; Charles Villiers, *London's Position in the Emerging World Securities Market – Accident or Design? A Banker's Perspective.*, The Ernest Sykes Memorial Lecture, 1986, Institute of Bankers, 1986, p. 4.

5   Thomas, op. cit. p. 59.

6   For this and a more detailed analysis of the development of building societies in recent years *see* D. T. Llewellyn, *The Evolution of The British Financial System*, Gilbart Lectures on Banking, 1985, Institute of Bankers, 1985, pp. 22–40ff; and by the same author *The Regulation and Supervision of Financial Institutions*, Gilbart Lectures on Banking, 1986, Institute of Bankers, 1986, pp. 102–3.

7   J. Dundas Hamilton, *Stockbroking Tomorrow*, Macmillan, Basingstoke & London, 1986, pp. 102–3.

8   J. Hills, *Savings and Fiscal Privilege*, Institute of Fiscal Studies, 1984, quoted by Llewellyn, *The Evolution of the British Financial System*, p. 20.

9   Ian M. Kerr, *Big Bang*, Euromoney Publications, London, 1986, p. 14.

10   Derek F. Channon, *The Service Industries*, 1978, p. 64.

11   For the emergence of the Eurocurrency market *see* Hamish McRae and Francis Cairncross, *Capital City, London as a Financial Centre*, Methuen, revised edn, London, 1985, pp. 16–17, 89–91. For detailed accounts of the Eurobond market *see* Ian Kerr, *Big Bang* esp. pp. 14ff and Adrian Hamilton, *The Financial Revolution, The Big Bang and the Explosion of the World's Money Markets*, Viking, 1986, pp. 54ff.

12   *The Banker*, November 1986, p. 69.

13   'Developments in International Banking and Capital Markets in 1985' *Bank of England Quarterly Bulletin*, March 1986, p. 64.

14   Compare Llewellyn, *The Evolution of the British Financial System*, p. 26.

15   N. B. Ritchie and G. Gallety, *The Big Bang: The Financial Revolution in the City of London and What it Means for You*, Northcote House, 1986.

16   Adrian Hamilton, *The Financial Revolution*, pp. 300ff.

17   'Developments in International Banking and Capital Markets in 1985', *Bank of England Quarterly Bulletin*, March 1986, p. 59.

18   *The Banker*, July 1987.

19   *Third World Debt and British Banks*, Fabian Society, London, 1987.

20   *Financial Times*, May 1987.

21   Llewellyn, *The Evolution of the British Financial System*, pp. 25–26.

22 Details of the above in 'International Financial Markets', *Financial Market Trends*, 35, OECD, Paris, November, 1986.

23 Charles B. Young, 'A Foreign Banker's View', in *Bank Strategies for the 1990s*, Cambridge Seminar, The Institute of Bankers, London 1986, p. 47. 'Commercial Paper Markets: An International Survey', *Bank of England Quarterly Bulletin*, 27 (1), February 1987, 46ff.

24 Stephen Fidler, 'Deregulation Aids Fledgling Markets', *International Capital Markets, Financial Times Supplement*, April 21 1987, p. xi. 'Commercial Paper Markets: An International Survey'. *Bank of England Quarterly Bulletin*, 27 (1), February 1987, 46ff.

25 Quoted by Fidler.

26 Andrew Shegog, 'The Year of Living Cautiously' in *Financial Innovations Made to Measure*, Euromoney Supplement, January 1987, p. 13. Alexander Nicoll, 'Eurocommercial Paper, Borrowers' Confidence Grows', *Financial Times*, as ref. 24 above, p. xi.

27 'Euroyen Sector Growth Takes Nomura to Top of League', *Financial Times*, 4 April 1987.

28 For useful accounts on the new financial instruments and their performance *see: Bank of England Quarterly Bulletin*, March 1986, pp. 62ff. and p. 65. P. L. Gilbert, B. Lygum, F. Wurtz, *The International Capital Markets in 1986, EIB Papers*, March 1987, European Investment Bank, Luxembourg, 1987.

29 Clare Pearson, 'Deutsche Bank launches 'bull and bear' offer', *Financial Times*, 4 August 1986, and *EIB Papers* (ref. 28 above), p. 21.

30 Alexander Nicoll, 'LIFFE Volumes Rocket After Big Bang', *Financial Times*, 19 March 1987.

31 *See* 'Euro Options: A Tale of Three Cities', *Euromoney*, October 1986, pp. 42–46.

32 *See* especially *EIB Papers*, March 1987, p. 19.

33 EIB Papers March, 1987: Garry Evans, 'Why New Products Come and Go', *Financial Innovations Made to Measure*, Euromoney Supplement, January 1987 pp. 2–8.

34 David Lascelles, 'A Time to Map New Strategies', *Financial Times World Banking Survey*, 22 May 1986.

35 For an extended account of changes in the US financial scene in 1970–80 *see* Adrian Hamilton, *The Financial Revolution*, pp. 113ff.

36 Gallety and Ritchie: *The Big Bang*, p. 30.

37 *The Banker*, November 1986.

38 *Financial Times*, 3 April 1987.

39 'Change in the Stock Exchange and Regulation of the City', *Bank of England Quarterly Bulletin*, February 1987, p. 55.

40   David Lascelles, 'After the Rush, the Shakeout', *"World Banking"*, *Financial Times*, 8 May 1987.

41   For the fullest account of how 'Big Bang' and its anticipation affected individual banks and houses *see*, Ian Kerr, *Big Bang*, Euromoney, London, 1986, to which we are indebted for many details.

42   As for ref. 39, *Bank of England Quarterly Bulletin*, February 1987, p. 61.

43   'Finanzplatz Deutschland – The How and the Where', *Euromoney Supplement*, June 1986, p. 4.

44   John Edwards, 'Mortgage Market. Competition Grows Fiercer', *Financial Times*, 14 February 1987.

45   'Building Society and other ATM Installations', *Banking World*, November 1986.

46   'The £120 billion Giants', *Euromoney Supplement*, August 1986.

47   George Pitcher, 'Days of Reckoning for the Building Societies', *Observer*, 11 January 1987.

48   *See* Alex Samuels, 'New Law for Building Societies: Building Societies Act 1986', *The Conveyancer and Property Lawyer*, January-February 1987, pp. 36–46.

49   'Brussels: Europe's 5th Financial Centre', *Kredietbank Weekly Bulletin*, 1 August 1986.

50   A helpful though very brief summary of the Financial Services Act is given in the *Bank of England Quarterly Bulletin*, February 1987, p. 60.

4 Financial services – underpinning world trade

Banking for export – export credit insurance

The nature of banking, both domestic and international, is in a state of rapid transformation, as we saw in the last chapter. Traditional bank loans to industry are being replaced by various forms of securitisation, whether Eurobonds, equities or short-term commercial paper. Syndicated loans, which fell from favour in the early and mid-1980s are coming back into fashion. Financial conglomerates formed from groupings between clearing banks, merchant banks and securities traders dominate the financial industry in the post-'Big Bang' era. But despite these changes, a fundamental role of banking in supporting international trade remains. True, banking for export now involves a wider range of services than ever before. But the traditional business of banks assisting exporters financially in a variety of ways remains a linch-pin in the UK's export trade.

The process of exporting after a successful sale is often complex, sometimes fraught with difficulty and requires all the professional expertise of companies' own export departments, of specialist divisions and organisations within the banks, frequently the national Export Credit Guarantee Department (ECGD), and freight forwarders. This is the professional area in which the Institute of Export, through its examinations, seminars and publications is of particular importance in the UK.

The exporter can obtain help from the major clearing banks even before the marketing process begins through the banks' extensive intelligence and information networks which can serve specialist departments in London and international managers located around the UK. Documentation for customs, local import controls and transport, for certifying origin or the fulfilment of health requirements, for the free circulation of goods in the European Community or for obtaining carnets in other countries can be complicated, despite the efforts of SITPRO (*Simplification of International Trade Procedures Board*) to establish systems that are both straightforward and acceptable worldwide. Help in this area is provided by Chambers of Commerce, the Institute of Freight Forwarders and the British Overseas Trade Board. But banks are increasingly anxious to provide their customers with a comprehensive service, and that can include advice on exporting from start to finish, such as NatWest's 'Export Ease' or Midlands Bank's 'International Trade Services' [1].

Obtaining payment is essential, of course. While payment in advance may be possible for small orders, and the open account method (i.e. a simple agreement to pay within a set period) is gaining ground within the EC, thanks to its simplicity, the traditional bill of exchange method is far more common where exporting is outside the Community and/or firm relationships of trust have not been established.

A bill of exchange is written by the exporter and drawn on the buyer. It is formally defined as 'an unconditional order in writing, addressed by one person to another, signed by the person giving it, requiring the person to which it is addressed to pay on demand or at a fixed or determinable future time a sum certain in money, to, or to the order of, a specified person or to the bearer'. These bills can be sent directly to a buyer's bank, but it is more normal for the exporter's home bank to process the bill for collection or indeed handle all the export documents together including the shipping document. An alternative service which enables the exporter to obtain credit in advance of payment from a UK bank is the documentary letter of credit. This letter, sent to the buyer's bank, is binding, once accepted, upon both that bank and the buyer. But defaulting remains the exporter's nightmare, particularly when he is trading with politically or financially unstable markets.

It was to help the exporter in such markets that the Government set up as early as 1919 the ECGD. The ECGD offers exporters specialist insurance to cover the risk that a buyer may not fulfil payment. Some 23 per cent of UK manufacturers' exports are covered by ECGD insurance policies. This department is run on a commercial basis and it may therefore require that a company insures all its exports in order to spread risk. At the same time, like its counterparts in other advanced industrialised countries, the trend in the mid-1980s towards an increase in trade between these countries and a decrease in trade with Latin America and Africa, has led to a decline in business. Moreover, as business declined, increasing claims and bad debts forced premiums up. Together these factors had a further negative effect on business. Table 4.1 shows this decline and indicates the proportions of ECGD business.

The ECGD has, in response to these negative factors and especially bad debts, been revising its programme and has, for example, withdrawn its 'Comprehensive Bank Guaranteed Bills and Notes' and its 'Open Account Schemes' [2]. The clearers are filling this gap with their own schemes. Examples are Barclays' Tradeline and Tradeflow schemes. Moreover, the range of ECGD insurance remains extensive, covering direct default (up to 95 per cent of loss) whether through breach of contract, political disturbance or war, or licence cancellation.

Table 4.1   ECGD 1984–1986

	1984/5 £ million	1985/6 £ million
Total exports insured by ECGD*	17 122	15 672
Buyer credits	2 672	2 478
Short term (up to 6 months)	12 476	11 817
Supplier credits (by deduction)	1 974	1 377
* as percentage of total visible non-oil exports	29.6%	23.3%

Source: Schroders

Cover on major project work can be extended to five years, while other special cover can be obtained for stocks held abroad, or to guarantee payment for services. This increasingly important activity can cover repair and refit work, leasing and technology transfer under licence or royalty agreements. But banks are not excluded from this area. On the contrary they will, as part of their package, act as agents for the exporter to ECGD, or will arrange through insurance brokers (sometimes their own subsidiaries) independent insurance with Lloyd's of London or other London insurance companies.

But the principal banking activity remains export finance itself. This can be either for the supplier or the buyer. In many cases the exporter may be dependent upon the ability of the buyer to raise finance, and if the exporter's own bank can arrange this credit it is clearly a major factor in the decision to purchase. But more often than not the exporter himself will require early finance prior to the buyer's payment. Banks can make advances against bills of exchange for a percentage of the purchase price, but it is more common for the bank to 'negotiate' the bill, that is to purchase the bill. Or, and this we saw was the origin of the merchant banks two centuries ago, bills of exchange can be drawn directly on acceptance houses who sell them at a discount to the discount houses. The bank credits the exporter with the proceeds less a commission, pays it when it matures and debits the exporter. Some major exporting companies sub-contract the business of collecting payment to specialists in debt collection and trade finance known as factoring companies (which are themselves often major bank subsidiaries). An example is Griffin Factors, a part of the Midland Bank Group.

Medium-term and long-term export finance is a traditional business of the merchant banks as well as the clearers. In recent years substantial numbers of major loans on capital projects have been securitised through the Eurobond market, a sector in which London-based foreign merchant and investment banks dominate. Another specialist method of export financing is that of forfaiting. Forfaiting is the sale at a discount (and without recourse in the case of a buyer defaulting) of an exporter's trade debts. It is usually based on bills of exchange or promissory notes that are guaranteed by the buyer's bank and is used where credit is required for up to seven years or even more. The great advantage to the exporter is the receipt of immediate cash without recourse. This work is undertaken by specialist houses, again often subsidiaries of the major financial conglomerates. The ECGD is also a major force in medium-term export finance for it continues to offer bank guarantees, against an insurance policy, on export credit with a term of more than two years. These guarantees can also be used to obtain bank loans to the buyer, or, where the buyer has a number of supply contracts against a major project, a line of credit.

Finally, in this complex field, we must mention services connected with the supply of foreign currency. We review the foreign currency market in greater detail in the next chapter. The essential purpose of these services in the context of exporting is to protect exporters from fluctuations in the exchange rate between the time of contract signature and receipt of payment.

Importers require similar protection when purchase agreements are not in sterling. The traditional method is through the forward exchange contract. But, as we saw in Chapter 3, a major innovation has been the currency options market, which gives the exporter flexibility should the exchange rate move in his favour. Other methods are to borrow in the same currency as payment is to be made (a possibility that is attractive to the expanding company interested in overseas acquisitions), or the Eurocurrency loan. This is a specialism in which both British merchant banks and the clearing banks have been particularly successful.

It is extremely difficult to draw up any rankings among the players in such a broadly defined sector as banking support for exports. One authoritative view is that the British clearing banks with Midland, Barclays and Lloyds at their head dominate both the exporter (supplier) and buyer credit business as well as related services, while the merchant banks are active in niches, concentrating, as we saw, on finance for specific major projects or on particular trading regions, e.g. Morgan Grenfell for Comecon or Baring Brothers for Pemex [3]. An area of particular interest for this study is, however, Buyer Credits, for these are not only a service to exporting industry but simultaneously a financial service sold abroad. In a piece of special research for the study, one of our sponsors, Schroders, looked at Buyer Credits from 1984–86. It is evident from this that the clearing banks account for over half this business and that among them Midland is the clear leader. Among the merchant banks the leader is Morgan Grenfell by a large margin.

Finally, foreign and international banks have made only negligible inroads – Bank of America attained 5.17 per cent by value, Standard

Table 4.2   UK-issued buyer credits 1984–86: clearing banks

Bank	% by number	% by value
Barclays	9.61	7.60
Lloyds	17.30	6.50
Midland	18.26	38.70
National Westminster	7.69	2.35
Bank of Scotland	0.96	0.30
Total (clearing banks)	52.86	54.92

Source: Schroders

Table 4.3   UK issued buyer credits 1984–86: merchant banks

Bank	% by number	% by value
Baring Brothers	0.96	0.44
Hambros	0.96	0.17
Hill Samuel	0.96	0.07
Kleinwort Benson	0.96	2.96
Lazards	2.88	1.91
Morgan Grenfell	11.54	19.20
Rothschilds	0.96	0.25
Samuel Montagu	2.88	4.66
Schroders	7.69	3.60
Total (merchant banks)	29.79	33.26

Source: Schroders

Chartered Merchant Bank 2.35 per cent and Wardleys 1.77 per cent in a total of 11.12 per cent of business. These figures exclude sums for 'sensitive contracts' of the military and naval kind, which would swell the totals considerably, but it seems likely that the same clearing banks would still be in the lead.

From accountancy to 'corporate consultancy'

Britain has four times more qualified accountants than France, the Federal Republic and Japan put together – 120 000 compared to 20 000 in France, 4000 in the Federal Republic and 6000 in Japan [4]. Accountancy firms are the largest single recruiters of university graduates and 10 per cent of undergraduates intend to train in the profession. Quite apart from the significance of accountants within industry (where they constitute almost an equivalent to the professional dominance of lawyers in the Federal Republic), the international accountancy partnerships are dominant in world business. The so-called 'Big Eight' firms are truly international in a profession where, at the moment at least, big is plainly beautiful. In April 1987 Peat Marwick International (as Peat Marwick Mitchell plc, then the UK's second largest partnership by fee income), merged with the Dutch-based international firm Klynveld Main Goerdeler (which was represented in the UK by Thomson McLintock) to form the world's largest accountancy firm, KPMG (Klynveld Peat Marwick Goerdeler) with a fee income in 1986 of some $2.8 billion. With a staff of some 50 000 worldwide, the new firm combines great strength in the USA with a continental European presence that is unrivalled. In all it has 700 offices in over 110 countries, including strong represent-ation in the Far East. KPMG is followed by other global partnerships – Arthur Andersen (fee income 1986 $1.9 billion), Coopers & Lybrand ($1.7 billion), Ernst & Whinney ($1.5 billion), Price Waterhouse ($1.5 billion), Arthur Young ($1.4 billion), Deloitte Haskins & Sells ($1.2 billion) and Touche Ross ($1.2 billion) [5]. The trend towards merger is not over. Price Waterhouse, for example, is seeking a merger with a Dutch partnership, at present part of the Binder Hamlyn group, the world's tenth largest.

The world leadership in the field by the USA, UK and the Nether-lands has historical roots. The early development of the joint stock company in both the Anglo-Saxon countries led to the need for reliable financial reporting that could be made available to the shareholders. In France and Germany, however, where bank lending remained the primary source of corporate finance, such reporting only became impor-tant when national company tax measures were introduced. Thus accountancy practice there derived from state, Roman and Napoleonic code-based law. In the USA and Britain, however, the common law notion of fairness – 'the true and fair view' – remained a central concept in accountancy. And in both countries, as well as the Netherlands, the profession evolved not as an off-shoot of law but as a profession in its own right, straddling art and science [6]. These factors, which made the Anglo-American system more flexible and less culture specific, were complemented by the historical significance of Empire, then the Com-monwealth and the supreme post-war economic importance of the US.

Accountancy is only a shorthand term for the business practised by the great partnerships. In fact, the preparation of accounts and advice on drawing up accounting systems (and adhering to standards and regulations) is only a minor part of their business today. The basis for the remarkable proliferation and expansion of financial services that has exploded the profession in the last two decades was, of course, auditing. Auditing, the independent examination of financial accounts required of limited companies in the UK by law, provided and provides the accountancy partnerships with a vital client network. But reviewing and appraising a company's results, the disposition of its units and liabilities and its financial control systems and procedures gave the auditors a unique and privileged bird's eye view of a company's health and operational processes. From here there was a natural and rapid evolution into what we might broadly term 'corporate consultancy'. Audit remains of course a major part of the accountants' business. For Peat Marwick McLintock after the merger, it is over 70 per cent of their business and it is over 60 per cent for Touche Ross. Moreover, for the major firms auditing grew in 1986 at a rate of over 25 per cent as the big partnerships exploited niche specialisms in particular industrial sectors at the expense of smaller firms. These specialisms included Peat Marwick McLintock in banking and financial services, Ernst & Whinney in brewing, and Coopers & Lybrand in defence and aerospace, for example [7]. The complex and rigorous new regulations that are emerging from the system of self-regulation for the City through the 1986 Financial Services Act impose considerable strain on the financial institutions but may also offer great opportunities for the major accounting firms.

Nonetheless, the major characteristic of the profession in recent years has been its expansion into 'corporate consultancy'. The harsh economic climate of the early 1980s, the rapid incursion of new technology both into office information systems and manufacturing techniques, and the drastic reorganisation of financial institutions, especially in the UK under the impact of 'Big Bang' and the sobering rethink of conglomerate strategies after October 1987, have given the accountants a succession of major business impulses.

At the extreme end of the range is specialist advice given to companies facing cash flow problems or even insolvency. The early 1980s saw, of course, record numbers of bankruptcies. But mergers and acquisitions were, and continue to be, major features of the great realignments that are taking place as companies seek to maximise profits, expand business overseas through direct investments or simply to build business empires. Peat Marwick McLintock and Deloittes have particularly specialised in advice in this area. There is, however, a considerable washback effect from this restructuring on the audit market as the companies being acquired change accountants to those of their new parent companies [8]. A related specialist niche is consultancy on management buy-outs.

Today corporate finance is more complex than ever as the trend towards securitisation continues apace. Here, too, the big partnerships are highly active advising on Stock Exchange flotations, issues of international bonds, entry to the USM as well as the more conventional bank loan method of raising finance. Privatisation is another booming activity; Touche Ross, for example, have specialised in this, advising

Government on privatising British Gas, Rolls Royce and the British Airports Authority among others. Peat Marwick McLintock assisted with Britoil and British Aerospace and have assisted in the policing of such issues in order to control multiple applications.

Financial control is an obvious off-shoot area from auditing and has evolved into the more comprehensive and systematic Treasury management. Treasury management is concerned with four areas, funds management, cash management, foreign exchange exposure management and control of working capital. Each area requires great expertise – expertise for example on the latest financial instruments available for investment, the assessment of risk in global markets, the latest cash transfer systems, the use of currency options and currency accounts and so on. Accountants are in an ideal position to advise a company on all of these as part of a strategic advice service. Specialists in this new art-cum-science are Deloittes Management Consultancy Division.

A more traditional consultancy activity for the accountants is, of course, tax planning. The historically high levels of taxation in the UK led to the early establishment of expertise here and, whereas US accountants and even those in New York have concentrated on the domestic market, the London partnerships took an early lead in international tax advice. It is another area in which firms have sought out specialist niches, Deloittes concentrating, for example, on UK-US tax issues, Arthur Andersen on the co-operation between national tax agencies, Arthur Young on expatriate taxation, Ernst & Whinney and Peat Marwick McLintock on the taxation of financial institutions. Coopers & Lybrand have developed the publication of world-wide taxation surveys in their *International Tax Summaries* [9].

Information technology has been changing the nature of approaches to management. It is a field that is subject almost to daily innovation as software takes the lead from hardware advances. We have seen how computers and new telecommunications systems have altered the City and underpinned its global role. But the sheer range of alternative systems and rival software leads to perplexing problems that affect not only the general operation of financial institutions but their back-offices in the most specific detail. Here too accountants are active in consultancy. Arthur Andersen has set up a worldwide IT activity with offices in London, New York and Tokyo and training centres in Chicago and Geneva. But as computers have opened up new dimensions, particularly in the financial services sector, (from where Arthur Andersen derives 35 per cent of its fees internationally [10]), computers are also open to fraudulent abuse. Deloittes, besides developing expert systems (knowledge-based computerised query systems that map out options for decision-makers) for its own uses, has opened a computer security division.

But technological change has not been restricted to information and financial systems. Manufacturing after the advent of robotics and related automatic factory systems has radically changed – as it had to in both the USA and Europe under the competitive onslaught of the Far East. Even here the accountants are setting up consultancy services. Arthur Andersen has, for example, its own 'Automation, Technical and Operations Laboratory' in Chiswick, London.

Many of these services might loosely be grouped under the term 'Management Consultancy'. Launched in the 1960s, management consultancy originally concentrated on organisational structure and personnel management as well as financial control. The independent firms that emerged at that time and are now among the leaders, PA, P-E and Inbucon, are also active in the IT sector. PA, like Arthur Andersen, has its own manufacturing technology laboratories and computers and telecommunications division. With a revenue in 1986 of £111 million it remains the UK's largest consultancy firm. But increasingly such companies are being challenged by the accountants on their home territory. Arthur Andersen has up to 8000 or half of its professional staff globally working in the general management consultancy field. In both the USA and globally Arthur Andersen had in 1985 the highest fee income of the sector, topping even Towers Perrin & Forster and the renowned McKinsey & Co. in the US by a substantial margin ($477 million compared with $350 million) on a worldwide basis. It was in view of these rapid developments by the accountancy-based consultancies that P-E International and Inbucon merged in January 1988. Another important growth area has been the human resources sector. Peat Marwick McLintock, for example, expanded its human resources team in 18 months from 5 to 35, and is providing services in the areas of organisational strategy, remuneration policy, executive selection and search, personnel management, and development and training [11].

Today the international accountancy profession is, then, far removed from the popular image of a narrow numerical skill, confined to processing numbers on balance sheets. While *The Handy Report* [12] is correct in deploring the low numbers of British managers with degrees or professional qualifications, the negative gloss placed on what appear to be excessive numbers of accountants is perhaps misleading. It is true that through their professional training and numbers they make up to an extent for the absence of a required and rigorous professional management qualification. But, as will have become clear from this survey of the activities of international accountants, they are developing as firms and as individuals enviable expertise in management systems globally. Of course, it may indeed be the very lack of managerial 'formation' as the Report calls it after the *Finniston Report on Engineers*, that provides these partnerships with the market for their rapidly expanding and diversifying activities. Nevertheless, this domestic activity provides the springboard for one of the UK's major and most successful international service industries.

Financial information services – from carrier pigeon to satellites

'As an international bank, our business is entirely dependent upon the free flow of instantaneous communications. In the course of our banking business, we need to have minute-by-minute intelligence from the money markets across the world. In addition, we need to be able to provide fund-transfer services to our customers who move large amounts of funds on a day-to-day basis from one country to another. These same customers need immediate information about their account balances in different parts of the world, the state of the world, and so forth.' – Vice-President of Continental Illinois Bank, 1980 [13].

Information is penetrating all modern industries and above all the financial service industries as its new life-blood, second only in importance to the ultimate sustenance, finance itself. The financial revolution that we traced in the last chapter would have been unthinkable without global telecommunication systems carrying real-time, analysed market data and dealing opportunities. Supporting the dramatic events leading to the 'Big Bang' banking and securities transformation of 1986 were the electronic information systems evolved by independent companies such as Reuters and Telerate and by the banks themselves.

The backbone of modern international banking is provided by SWIFT, the Society for Worldwide Interbank Financial Telecommunications, which was set up in 1977. Today more than 1400 banks belong and 750 000 messages are transmitted daily. It has had an impact not only on the speed of business but on the home procedures of the member banks which have had to accept a standard format for their services. In the coming years SWIFT is to be replaced by a more complex system, SWIFT II, offering over 400 specialist programs. It will be based in the Netherlands [14].

Within their own corporate customer networks, too, banks in the UK, as in the US, are offering ever more sophisticated computerised information services such as Barclays' BarCam which provides treasurers with reports from over 20 countries on a 24-hour basis, and displays balances in real-time or historically for 20 days previously. Barclays, National Westminster and Midland also have foreign exchange reporting systems, with Midland including a currency exposure management service [15].

But the services that are of most importance as a British invisible earning and indeed which dominate the world information industry in a significant number of sectors are those run by Reuters, a British public limited company controlled by the Press Association, the Newspaper Publishers' Association and the press associations of Australia and New Zealand. Its founder was Paul Julius Reuter who started his communications service in 1850 by linking the Berlin to Aachen and Brussels to Paris telegraphs by carrier pigeon. When the Dover–Calais telegraph cable was laid a year later he moved to London and set up his company in the Royal Exchange Buildings. Starting with the telegraphic transmission of stock market quotations from London to Paris he rapidly extended the network through Europe, expanding it to include general news items. He had agents in Shanghai, Bombay and Yokohama as early as 1861. To obtain American news he even laid a cable across Ireland to Crookhaven and sent out cutters from there to intercept the Transatlantic mail boats and receive messages sealed in special Reuters' canisters. The Reuters' column printer of 1883, the teleprinter of 1927 and then in 1973 Monitor, a computerised electronic network for foreign exchange quotations, each in its turn revolutionised the information industry. Today Reuters have business clients in 124 countries and serve the media in over 158.

Before we look at Reuters' financial information services and their competition, we should devote a few words to Reuters' renowned news service. Reuters now employ over 700 journalists and have a further 1300 correspondents worldwide. The network has grown by 50 per cent since 1981. The world is divided into a series of national, regional and area districts, each with an editor. Editorial control of the World Desk passes on a 24-hour basis from Hong Kong to London to New York. There are French speaking services based on Paris and Nairobi, German speaking on Bonn, Arabic on Cairo and Spanish on Buenos Aires. All copy is processed on an advanced integrated computer network. This service is backed by a report and photograph service through the American UPI company that Reuters acquired in 1984 and by Visnews, the world's largest television news agency with 423 subscribing stations in 83 countries. Reuters hold 55 per cent of Visnews shares with the others divided between the BBC and the broadcasting corporations of Canada, Australia and New Zealand [16].

But the bulk of Reuters' rapidly expanding revenue derives from their financial services. In the money markets Reuters' information services dominate. Their 'Monitor' foreign exchange service quotes in real-time on over 108 exchange rates and extends to Eurodeposits in 41 currencies, government securities and certificates of deposit. The new 'Monitor Abacus' provides instant cross-rates and arbitrage calculations. Subscribers in 1986 were some 16 000, making this the greatest single source of the company's revenue [16]. In 1984 this gigantic network was supplemented by a foreign exchange and bullion dealing service that was extended two years later into Japan. Reuters also participated in the explosion of Eurobond trading in London by offering a quotation service from 1975 and later a database providing historical background on each issue. In the USA, Government bond services are dominated by Telerate which, although much smaller globally, (Telerate's world income is only equal to Reuters' US income), holds in the US a unique franchise to distribute quotations from the leading primary dealer Cantor-Fitzgerald. Reuters countered in 1985 with a two-year agreement to distribute US Government bond quotations from MKI Government Brokers Inc. via a satellite network. But perhaps the most significant advance was the launch in 1987 of the Equities 2000 system which will itself enhance world trading in international equities. While it is thought that it will be particularly valuable in those countries like West Germany and Switzerland with no single central stock exchange, it will encounter tough opposition from Quotron (77 000 terminals) and ADP (Automatic Data Processing – 53 terminals) in the USA, from Telekurs in Switzerland and in the UK from The London Stock Exchange's Topic. A survey in December 1986 showed that in the UK, within the banking and credit sector, Reuters were leaders ahead of Telerate, Topic and Datastream but that in investment and insurance Topic was substantially ahead of Reuters and by some margin also in the category auxiliary banking and finance [17]. A great strength of Reuters is, however, the US Instinet system which it acquired wholly in 1987. This system is an equities dealing service which Reuters are extending to Europe and complements their Monitor forex dealing service. In the US Instinet has over 300 broker members and belongs to all major exchanges.

Reuters are also active in the commodities market including tangible forwards, financial futures, and specialist services for crude oil spot prices and futures, shipping (tanker and dry bulk cargo vessel availability), gold and silver coins and precious metals. But this is a fiercely competitive market, particularly in the US where Knight-Ridder has a series of sophisticated services both in tangible commodities and money, while ADP competes with Comtrend and Telerate specialises in the energy sector. Not deterred, Reuters intend to match their Equities 2000 service with Commodities 2000 based on 30 exchanges.

Eighty per cent of Reuters' earnings are derived from overseas. By far their fastest growth area is Europe where revenue grew from £209.4 million in 1985 to £334.1 million in 1986. The Far East and Australasian area is also growing substantially (1985 £112 million, 1986 £146 million), but the competition in the US is reflected in more modest but nevertheless significant and regular growth (1982 £13.7 million, 1984 £48.7 million, 1985 £86.3 million, 1986 £109.3 million) [18].

In another major venture Reuters have purchased Rich Inc., a US company that provides custom-built, semi-automated dealing floors, in addition to what are known as 'smart buildings' for a whole variety of activities ranging from education to hospitals and the police. Rich's latest innovation in the financial sector, using its new manufacturing facility, is TRIARCH, Trading Information Architecture. Rich, which had already grown from 100 employees in 1980 to 500 in 1986, now has, thanks to Reuters, a marketing and sales force based in London of over 50.

In the manufactures export field, too, new technology offers for the future some radical changes in procedure. At present, as we observed, documentation is complex and tedious – and has to be right. Electronic Data Interchange (EDI), or paperless trading, is only in its infancy at present but is being piloted by the DISH Committee based on ports at London, Felixstowe and Rotterdam and using major companies such as ICI, OCL and Rowntree Mackintosh. This techniques for using computers to convey instructions to freight forwarders and thence to carrier and bank have been evolved by General Electric Information Services, GEISCO. The difficulty is that such a system can hardly be on a one-to-one trading partner basis. This means that networks will have to be established and there will even have to be changes in international law to allow transactions to be valid without a paper base. A start has been made at the level of data interchange by the Institute of Export in collaboration with a City software firm, Export Network [19]. In this sector, as in financial information services, the immediate major market will be the European Community, where trade and legal barriers are minimal. Expansion into Britain's largest single visible export market, the USA, can then follow.

British insurance in a global context

By far the largest source of Britain's invisible earnings by any service industry is insurance. In 1986, for example, the total net income of UK insurance institutions was £4260 million (including £1736 million from Lloyd's), compared with £2295 million from banks, £1216 million from consultancies or £572 million from commodity trading [20]. This supremacy has held firm for a decade and more. It is not because the total value of business transacted and receipts from investments exceeds that of the banks. On the contrary, the turnover in income from international lending and other banking services is nine times higher [21]. Nor is it because British insurance companies are the world's largest. Market capitalisation of the Tokyo Fire and Marine Company, for example, is six times higher than a comparable company in the UK such as Royal [22], while Britain's insurance company with the largest capitalisation (in June 1986), Prudential, was ranked only fourth in Europe. At that time Royal was eighth, and General Accident fifteenth, followed immediately by Guardian Royal Exchange, Sun Alliance, Commercial Union and Legal & General. Europe's largest company with nearly three times higher capitalisation than the Prudential is

Table 4.4   Net written premiums 1984

Country	Premiums received in SDRs (millions)
USA	129 365
Japan	53 767
UK	17 548
FRG	12 200
Canada	6 735
France	6 268

Source: OECD Statistics on Insurance, 1987

Allianz [23] (which also owns the Italian Riunione Adriatica di Sicurta, eleventh in European rank, and Cornhill Insurance, eleventh among UK general insurers). Nor can this leading role among UK service industries be explained by muscle deriving from the sheer size of the domestic market. Measured in net written premiums the United States is by far the world's largest market, exceeding Japan twofold, and the UK by over seven times.

The explanation lies in the very low 'import penetration' of the UK insurance and reinsurance markets. In 1986 an equivalent of only some 1.3 per cent of total overseas earnings were paid to foreign-owned parents of UK insurance institutions [24]. Here lies the major difference between the business of Britain's leading composite insurers (that is, insurance undertakings that underwrite a range of insurance activities) and, for example, that of Germany's direct insurance industry. Only 0.17 per cent of German life insurance premium income derives from overseas, and 2 per cent of accident insurance income, rising to 12 per cent if one includes German-owned foreign subsidiaries. But in 1986 Royal derived only 28 per cent of its premium income from the UK, General Accident 33 per cent, Guardian Royal Exchange 37 per cent, Commercial Union 37 per cent and Sun Alliance 50 per cent. The principal overseas markets that account for the bulk of trade, are the USA, Europe (and particularly the Netherlands), Canada and Australia. Table 4.5 indicates how the English-speaking world dominates British insurance export markets.

Not unexpectedly, the United States is the UK's most substantial market but the geographical split in markets varies from insurer to insurer depending largely on their ownership of subsidiaries in particular territories. Royal, for example, has a major US commitment and has recently radically reorganised its American operation following years of countrywide indemnity losses in the early to mid-1980s. It halved its regional divisions to seven, cut its agents from 5000 to 3000 and even moved its HQ from Manhattan to Charlotte, North Carolina

Table 4.5   Geographical split of premium income 1986 (sterling values)

	Commercial Union %	General Accident %	GRE %	Royal %	Sun Alliance %
UK	37	33	37	28	50
USA	34	37	11	47	12
Canada	7	12	9	9	6
Australia	N/A	2	6	3	3
Europe	11	7	16*	3†	13
Other	11	9	21	10	16

* Germany only   † Netherlands only

Source: Greenwell Montagu Research

[25]. Legal & General also has important interests in life insurance in the USA, but is significant in this sector in Australia, too, as is Pearl Assurance. Legal & General has widespread interests, including sub-sidiaries in Holland and France; Guardian Royal Exchange has long held major interests in Germany: it purchased Albingia in 1930 at the time of the great depression and still has an 86 per cent holding. Albingia is itself a worldwide undertaking, specialising overseas in project and factory insurance. But it is also of particular importance to GRE today thanks to its general insurance network in Denmark, France, the

Table 4.6   Premium Income of UK Insurers in Overseas Territories (£ millions)

	General		Long-term	
	1984	1985	1984	1985
English-speaking territories				
Australia	542	452	441	377
Canada	785	895	665	576
Ireland	144	184	356	312
New Zealand	59	60	49	45
South Africa	180	143	139	99
USA	3353	3234	154	142
Non-English speaking territories				
Belgium	158	164	12	12
Denmark	68	77	36	52
France	154	144	63	102
Federal Republic of Germany	245	280	137	145
Netherlands	361	400	277	297
Other (English and non-English speaking)	807	606	135	181

Source: Adapted from ABI, *Overseas Earnings of the UK Insurance Industry*

Netherlands and Belgium, providing GRE with an EC coverage not matched by any other British composite. In all, some 50 per cent of British premium income in fire and accident and in the motor sectors derives from abroad [26]. Table 4.6 gives a precise picture of the relative size of foreign markets.

The historical roots

How did this remarkable record come about? The origins of British insurance are rooted in Britain's history as a trading nation [27]. The most ancient type of insurance protected the vessels and cargoes of merchants and was known to the Greeks and Phoenicians alike. The notion was brought to London as it evolved as a trading port with the Continent of Europe in the fourteenth and fifteenth centuries by Hanseatic merchants and by the Lombards, traders from North Italy. A Chamber of Insurance with which the merchants underwriting marine business (i.e. signing their names at the bottom of the contract) had to register all policies was established as early as 1573. Fire insurance was established to protect not only the merchant's trading interests but his and others' domestic property, too. The instigation for organised fire insurance was the Great Fire of London of 1666. By 1680 the Fire Office had been set up, later to become the Phoenix Company, which pioneered fire insurance for English merchants abroad. By 1786 it had agents in France, Germany and Portugal. Meanwhile, one of the most important events in the history of British insurance had occurred. In the wake of the South Sea Bubble scandal George I awarded Royal Charters to the Royal Exchange and to the London Assurance companies. This gave them a virtual monopoly of marine insurance – but only as corporations. For the Bubble Act of 1720, which enshrined these charters, permitted individual underwriters to continue to underwrite policies. In the late seventeenth century merchants had been meeting to transact their business in London's coffee houses. The most renowned was that of Edward Lloyd. After the Act and during the course of the eighteenth century, underwriting became a significant activity in the coffee-house until by 1771 a representative committee was charged with finding independent premises. Those signing the 1771 committee declaration were referred to in the document as Names. The term has remained ever since for underwriting members. Lloyd's then moved to the Royal Exchange and the true forerunner of this unique institution was created.

Another historical accident had already occurred that was to shape the future of Lloyd's: in 1746 George II had banned reinsurance because of prevalent abuse. This gave a further impulse to the special brand of coinsurance which has since characterised Lloyd's. We return to

Lloyd's, today a major contributor to Britain's invisible earnings, a primary source for London's major broking activities and arguably still the cohesive force for the City's direct insurance activity in a later section. Suffice it to say here that Lloyd's of London's ancient tradition of direct insurance derived from the City's maritime trade. When that trade was given a massive impulse in the nineteenth century by Britain's early industrialisation and later the formation of the world's largest Empire, Britain already possessed a sophisticated system and network of insurance unmatched in the world.

Even in life assurance Britain was historically advanced. Life assurance societies had emerged as early as the beginning of the eighteenth century, and there was even an Act governing their trade by 1774. Scotland was to be particularly significant in this respect for, although her societies were formed a little later, they proved to be among the most enduring of all institutions. Scottish Widows dates back to 1815, Scottish Amicable and Standard Life to the 1820s, and they were followed during the century by Scottish Equitable, Scottish Provident, Scottish Life and Scottish Mutual. Nevertheless, they did not equal in size English giants such as Prudential which held in 1905 half of UK life premiums.

British insurance had accompanied industrialisation at home and abroad with fire, accident and life policies. When the great surge in American industry came during the last decades of the nineteenth century, Britain captured substantial parts of the business. The leading nine British companies then derived half their premium income from the USA. At the same time Lloyd's remained the dominant force in the international maritime business.

Despite two world wars, vast changes in Britain's political, naval and industrial significance, the predominantly overseas character of the leading British insurance institutions has remained. The advent of the motor car and of aviation as major modes of transportation have added huge new sectors to the insurance business. Historically separate companies have amalgamated, the most recent among the composites being the merger of Royal Exchange Assurance and Guardian Assurance in 1968. But that was twenty years ago and the principal features of the insurance pattern have been its remarkable stability and resilience.

New risks – new approaches

Like all trade, insurance and reinsurance run in cycles. Although the very business of the insurer is to spread risk and to protect against loss, the insurance industry itself is exposed to periods of downturn when claims and costs exceed premium income. Yet these cycles are not necessarily tied to general economic cycles, perhaps because insurance is rooted in the very infrastructure of industrial activity, its vehicles and plant and through life and accident insurance in the population itself. Rather the cycles are determined by competition, by price-cutting when too many players come on to the market. The 1960s were lean years for insurers when the Western economies were at the height of their economic miracles. In the early to mid-1980s, when the US economy was booming again, the US insurance market suffered an all-time low with a pre-tax operating loss of $5.5 billion (even after allowing for investment income) and a gross loss of $25 billion – results from which the UK operators were not spared. Yet by mid-1984, premiums were beginning to recover and 1986 saw a swing back into profitability.

Reinsurance companies have been losing for a decade. Neither of the world's two largest reinsurance companies, Munich Re and Swiss Re, has shown profits on its reinsurance activities for years. At Lloyd's one can observe different specialist business cycles at work [28]. Absurdly high US court awards in product and professional liability cases (so high that legislation is being introduced to control them lest insurers withdraw altogether) resulted in Lloyd's general liability account showing losses of £384 million in 1983 and £257 million in 1984. Rashes of shipping losses may occur with or without good reason as when the Amoco Cadiz went aground in March 1978 and three liquified natural gas vessels owned by the US gas production company El Paso were declared unseaworthy through faulty design in 1979. In 1985 there was a sudden series of major aviation disasters including the crash with almost total loss of life of both an Air India and a Japan Air jumbo. It made up the worst year in aviation history. And then in 1987, years of hostility between Iran and Iraq exploded into the tanker war in which both sides set out to damage international oil shipping, with Iran returning blow for blow each Iraqi attack on vessels in Iranian waters. But 90 per cent of the marine war risk business in the Gulf is insured directly or indirectly through reinsurance by Lloyd's. At least Lloyd's Names must be pleased that political circumstances prevented them from ever underwriting the Soviet nuclear power industry.

But none of these risks, gigantic though they may be, necessarily involve operating losses unless competition makes it impossible to set the right premium. The art lies in calculating the risk, based on experience with a class of similar risks whether they be jumbo jets, nuclear power stations, oil rigs – or ferry boats. It is new technology that poses the challenge, when the size and even the nature of the risk may still be unknown. The explosion at Union Carbide's Bhopal plant is one example. As Roger Miller, Secretary-General of the new Association of Insurance and Risk Managers in Industry and Commerce (AIRMIC), has pointed out, damage to the environment from new industrial processes of this kind is only one source of exponentially increasing risk. The consequences of biotechnology could be another; the vulnerability of cybernetic systems to breakdown (with loss of records) and to fraud a third [29]. And those quite apart from growth of damages in court awards, as, for example, the UK courts appear to begin copying US judgments. Indeed as Pat Saxon, Director-General of the Chartered Institute of Insurers, put it to us, insurance is increasingly being understood as international risk management.

Nevertheless, losing on insurance business proper does not mean that the companies themselves have to make overall losses. Indeed, this is far from the case. For just as the Names at Lloyd's may spread their risks by being members of a number of syndicates or groupings that specialise in different sectors, so the big companies spread their risks both across sectors and national markets. In the UK Prudential has bought itself into the estate agency business, where it competes alongside the clearing bank, Lloyds. In October 1987 the French Compagnie du Midi announced that it had bought the UK life insurer, Equity & Law. In West Germany Allianz has bought itself the major Italian insurer, RAS, and Cornhill in the UK after its abortive attempt to take over the far larger Eagle Star. Aachener und Münchener, Germany's fifth largest insurance company, has purchased a controlling share of what had been the German trade union's ailing Bank für Gemeinwirtschaft – and Royal owns 20 per cent of Aachener und Münchener. Allianz has long owned 22 per cent of the Bayrische Hypothekenbank and while Munich Re holds 25 per cent of Allianz, Allianz holds 25 per cent of Munich Re, not to speak of their interests in major German engineering companies such as Europe's largest mechanical engineering group, the Gutehoffnung-shütte AG [30].

So diversification can take old and newer forms. But the major source of profitable revenue for the insurers is through portfolio investment, investment of premium income and investment of revenues. Moreover, with restrictions in the UK on investment abroad lifted and new legislation facilitating private pension building by the self-employed and more affluent employed, British insurance companies (like their continental competitors) have been shifting ever more emphasis on to fund management both for internal company purposes and as a service in its own right for customers. The big Scottish mutual life societies, Prudential, Norwich Union, Pearl, Legal & General, all report growing profitable activity in this area, particularly in the form of unit trusts, especially based on equities investment. In 1986 insurance companies earned £702 million on overseas portfolio investments, Lloyd's £422 million, while pension funds constituted a further £638 million, unit trusts £175 million and investment trusts £188 million (both of which may equally emanate from banks or other financial institutions of course) [31]. Such investments are, however, vulnerable to slides in share prices such as the 1987 crash that ended one of the longest bull markets in history.

Barriers to trade in insurance

We have described in broad terms in Chapter 2 the endeavours of the OECD, by members of GATT and by the European Commission to open up trade in services. The task of liberalising services on the almost global scale that GATT embraces is being examined in the current Uruguay Round of talks [32]. OECD, through its Council, called for an up-dating of its own Code of liberalisation in 1979 and 1982 in view of the growing significance of services in world trade. Its Committee for Capital Movements and Invisible Transactions published a report on its special investigation into insurance in 1983 [33]. This report confirmed that there are still widespread and substantial obstacles to an international trade in insurance. The most prevalent and severe are those obstacles deriving from regulations that govern establishment. In half the OECD countries a foreign insurer cannot operate in a market at all without being established there. Cross-border insurance is thus prohibited in transactions with these countries. Moreover, becoming established may involve being licensed and this may be impossible if the need for the entry of the new insurer and his products into the market cannot be demonstrated. Alternatively, the licence can be restricted to certain classes of insurance.

When a foreign insurer is established through a branch or subsidiary he may still face difficulties such as the levy of special taxes, requirements for deposits of assets or restrictions on the number of foreign nationals who may be employed.

Turning to cross-border trade, insurance services that are essential for international trade, such as insuring goods in transit, are sometimes restricted thanks to the requirement that they should be insured domestically by the importer. And even transactions that constitute central components in the insurance business itself, such as coinsurance and reinsurance, can effectively be reserved for domestic providers. All in all the OECD paints a picture that is complex, with many of the restrictions stemming not simply from local prudential and supervisory rules but from other domestic laws governing taxes, ownership of real estate or employment.

The *causes célèbres* in the battle for liberalisation of insurance have been fought out within the European Community. Articles 59 and 60 of the EC Treaty require freedom of services as an inherent component in the Common Market and directives liberalising cross-border insurance were issued by the Commission in 1976, 1978 and 1979. There was, however, strong disagreement within the Community about what constitutes free trade in insurance. The United Kingdom, for example, held the view that there could be no legal substitute for full competition in an open Community market. At the other end of the spectrum, the Federal Republic of Germany, which has an historical tradition of tight central supervision of insurance saw the matter differently. There, it was argued, the necessary basis for free trade in insurance already existed. Because of the international nature of transport, insurance cover for cross-border business could be contracted by a German transport company or exporter with an overseas insurer. Equally, any individual living in the Federal Republic is free to negotiate insurance of any kind with overseas insurance companies. But what could not occur was for an overseas insurer to enter the German market unless he had established a branch in the Federal Republic or owned a subsidiary and had obtained authorisation from the Federal Insurance Supervisory Board in Berlin (Bundesversicherungsaufsichtsamt). Further it was illegal for a German or a foreign broker to offer a client in Germany insurance from any company established outside the German borders. The purpose of this rule, it was argued passionately, was to protect the client who might be tempted by lower premiums while not realising that the cover was more restricted. Thus demand for complete clarity about what is on offer is known as 'market transparency'.

The dispute came to a head when, in 1983, an insurance agent from Ingolstadt was fined DM.18 000 by the highest appropriate court for selling a German customer an insurance policy issued by Lloyd's. Upon this judgment the European Commission, believing that the spirit of the Treaty had been violated, took the Federal Republic to the European Court of Justice for contravention of the Treaty. The Commission was supported by the United Kingdom and the Netherlands as it was in three other cases against France, Denmark and Ireland, all of which were looked at together by the European Court in coming to its judgments on 4 December 1986 [34]. The cases against the three latter countries were confined to infringements of the Directive on co-insurance. The Court broadly found in favour of the Commission in all 'The Four Cases' as they became known. It reaffirmed the right of companies in one Member State to provide insurance in another without establishment, itself a major breakthrough for companies in the UK and the Netherlands. It also upheld the principle that each Member State must recognise the supervisory procedures through which a foreign company will have passed in order to practise in its own Member State. But, and here lies an ambiguity that will have to be removed in further Community legislation, and probably in a case-by-case testing of the ruling, it did not exclude the need for authorisation by the state 'importing' the insurance service. In certain cases authorisation may still be justified to ensure adequate customer protection, it was argued. While the judgment expressly included both non-life and life assurance, it failed, however, to draw any clear line between the type of insurance that might involve the need for customer protection and that which might not. Thus it did not distinguish between 'mass risks', where large numbers of individuals are insured as in the case of household, car or life assurance, and 'large-scale risks' where commercial companies seek insurance. It remains to be seen where, if at all, the line is to be drawn.

In a further case, however, in which judgment was delivered just one month later in January 1987, there was a substantive ruling on how the EC competition law (which prohibits restrictive agreements and provides for fines of up to 10 per cent of annual turnover) applies to insurance. In this, 'The German Fire Insurance Case', [35] the Court upheld the Commission's decision to declare illegal an across-the-board increase in fire premiums recommended to member companies by the Verband der Sachversicherer, an association of German insurers. The Federal Republic has a long history of insurance cartels, of agreed premiums and regulated adjustments in the light of business fortunes [35]. The Court stated that insurance must be subject to the EC Competition Rules [36] like any other economic activity and that the Association's recommendation was intended to restrict competition. The judgment will affect the role of trade associations in this and other service industries and will mean that any further agreements (insurance is exempted from German competition laws) will have to be notified to the Commission. Moreover, the Federal Insurance Supervisory Board will not be able to insist that an insurer, whether domestic or foreign, should adhere to such an agreement [37]. Together the judgments in this and 'The Four Cases' will result in a substantial change in the European insurance market. It is a change which should benefit the internationally experienced UK insurance companies significantly.

Lloyd's of London and the insurance broking industry

The case brought against Julius Schleicher of Ingolstadt by the Federal German Insurance Supervisory Board was that he sold a client an insurance policy underwritten by Lloyd's of London. Lloyd's and its closely associated broking industry form the last part of our tableau of British insurance in its international context. It is a key part, for Lloyd's forms the cohesive centre of the system, the magnet that has made London both today and historically the heart of international insurance.

The constitution of Lloyd's of London has undergone a series of changes since the move in 1774 to the Royal Exchange, with the most recent called for by the Neill Report in 1987. But throughout centuries of change, one principle has remained sacrosanct and unique to the institution, that the underwriting members or 'Names' are liable for their insurance commitments to the full value of their private fortunes. The great attraction of being a 'Name' is, however, that one's capital can remain invested while so committed and profits from both underwriting and premium investment also accrue. Members belong to one or more (usually at least ten) of the over four hundred syndicates of underwriters that specialise in particular sectors of business. Since the late nineteenth century, when, through the pioneering vision of Cuthbert Heath, Lloyd's branched out from what had essentially been marine insurance business into the growing non-marine business, such as fire, burglary, workmen's compensation, earthquakes [38], Lloyd's has covered the widest variety of risk. Indeed, Lloyd's enjoys the popular reputation for being the place where virtually any risk can be insured, whether it be an actress's legs or a pianist's fingers. But in truth the great sources of premium income remain shipping, property, general liability (not of the exotic kind), motor vehicles, aviation and goods in transit. Table 4.7 (p. 106) shows the performance in the last closed year of business 1984.

The syndicates, which broadly fall into the categories marine, non-marine, aviation and motor, range in size from a few members to several thousand. The total membership, which is steadily rising and now includes many overseas members, is some 31 500. Names are looked after by agents ('pure agents') who act for them in placing them on or taking them off syndicates. The syndicates themselves are run by managing agents (who sometimes also act as pure agents – in which case conflicts of interest can arise).

The managing agents belong to some 114 agency companies that manage the affairs of over 300 syndicates. Business is brought to the agencies and syndicates by Lloyd's insurance brokers, of whom there are over 260. Until the Lloyd's Act of 1982 a number of the major brokers such as Alexander Howden, Sedgwick and Willis Faber owned management agencies. The Act compelled them to divest themselves of these links since it was considered by Parliament to involve a serious conflict of interest to the detriment of the Names and the syndicates generally. Divestment was one of the greatest organisational changes to occur in the history of Lloyd's. It has strengthened the major managing agencies such as Sturge Holdings and Merrett Holdings that have bought up divested agencies [39]. But contrary to some expectations, it has not deterred the brokers from continuing to bring business to Lloyd's. What the 1982 Act failed to achieve after lengthy debate inside and outside Parliament was a 'divorce' between pure agents and the managing agents [40].

While business between the brokers and the agents and underwriters continues to be conducted in the latest, vast version of the famous 'Room' in Lloyd's futuristic headquarters in Lime Street, the governance of the institution has significantly changed since 1982 and will change again. Lloyd's always was and remains, despite severe parliamentary criticism from the Labour opposition, a self-regulatory body. It had been self-regulating in what has to be called a club atmosphere. But the vast growth of business and its growing international complexity have gradually rendered the club tradition inadequate and unacceptable. The gulf between the non-working Names and the

Table 4.7   Lloyd's of London Business Summary 1984

	£m
Accident & Health	
Premiums	162.19
Underwriting profit	33.02
Investment income	17.05
Profit (including PCW syndicates)	36.11
Motor Vehicles, Damage & Liability	
Premiums	323.76
Underwriting profit	7.61
Investment income	25.41
Loss (including PCW syndicates)	(24.09)
Aircraft, Damage & Liability	
Premiums	229.92
Underwriting profit	29.12
Investment income	37.97
Profit (including PCW syndicates)	42.46
Ships, Damage & Liability	
Premiums	903.58
Underwriting profit	186.74
Investment income	122.69
Profit (including PCW syndicates)	233.29
Goods in transit	
Premiums	303.57
Underwriting profit	16.92
Investment income	28.96
Profit (including PCW syndicates)	26.79
Property Damage	
Premiums	666.29
Underwriting profit	119.98
Investment income	65.07
Profit (including PCW syndicates)	132.81
General Liability	
Premiums	364.78
Underwriting (loss)	(256.94)
Investment income	134.95
(Loss) (including PCW syndicates)	(169.74)

Source: Lloyd's of London Global Report and
Accounts as at 31 December 1986.

working Names, and the gulf between Names and managing agents have grown. A series of scandals over the last decade or so have rocked Lloyd's to its very foundations. The first was the Savonita affair, a protracted and complex dispute that evolved when a broker, Malcolm Pearson, became suspicious of a claim for alleged fire damage to Fiat cars carried on a ship called the 'Savonita'. It was particularly complex since Pearson himself was married into the Agnelli family, the founders of Fiat and the Lloyd's Committee refused at first to act and when it did, following questions in the House of Commons, it rejected Pearson's claims. The matter was never satisfactorily settled though it did come to court in Italy. It helped, however, to prompt an enquiry headed by Sir Henry Fisher, which eventually led to the 1982 Act and the first major recasting of the Lloyd's constitution since 1871, when the underwriting society first became a Corporation.

The catalyst in this process was, however, the Sasse affair. Tim Sasse was the active underwriter for a non-marine syndicate, no 762, with 110 Names including Lord Napier and Lord Fortescue, a member of the Swire family of Hong Kong and a brother of a Governor of the Bank of England. Sasse's error was to sign over a general binding authority for underwriting fire and property risks (through the broker Brentall Beard) to an insurance firm in Florida. This 'binder', as such agreements are known, was to become the channel through which a group of crooked operators passed insurance on slum and other high-risk property in the United States and Canada to Lloyd's. Sasse further destroyed his own credibility by manipulating his books and directly taking on bad risks in the computer leasing sector. Though the business thus incurred only ran for a little longer than a year from 1975–76, the final loss was some £15 million. Under threat of imminent court proceedings brought by some of the affected Names, the Corporation agreed to pay £9 million, while the Names themselves had to find over £6 million. The Names' lawyer, Leon Boshoff, put his finger on the root of the trouble when he wrote that, 'the Sasse *débâcle* has finally proved that the modern complexities of Lloyd's operations cannot be controlled by the outdated regulations and controlling mechanisms now in existence. Lloyd's is organised as a club but operates worldwide in a complex industry!' [41].

We have seen that the 1982 Lloyd's Act was important for divesting brokers of their managing agencies. It also created a Council with the power to create binding rules and enforce them upon underwriting agents. It could also require agents to disclose details of their business affairs. The post-1982 Council had sixteen working members of Lloyd's, eight non-working members or 'Names' and three nominated by Council from outside who had to be approved by the Governor of the Bank of England. The executive body was the Committee, consisting of the sixteen working members [42].

Just as Lloyd's seemed set fair on its new course another scandal broke, the biggest of any. In the autumn of 1982, the US broker Alexander & Alexander, which had taken over the Lloyd's broker Alexander Howden, discovered irregularities in the agencies owned by Minet Holdings, the PCW Underwriting Agency and the WMD Underwriting Agency. PCW was named after its leading underwriter Peter

Cameron-Webb and was chaired by Peter Dixon. Set up in 1968 and bought by Minet in 1973, it owned 40 per cent of the much smaller WMD. By summer 1983 it had been established by Minet that some £38.7 million of reinsurance premiums had been diverted by Cameron-Webb and Dixon into off-shore companies and bank accounts they had set up for their own benefit in Switzerland, Liechtenstein, Gibraltar and elsewhere. These sums had, then, been effectively stolen it was judged and much was spent to the direct benefit of Webb and Dixon on yachts, planes, luxury homes, in oil wells, bloodstock and even the financing of a pornographic feature film. This theft was only the beginning of the trouble for the Names involved. By April 1987 the potential losses on the reinsurance were estimated to total some £680 million, mitigated only by the agencies' assets. Between 1500 and 3000 Names were affected. After long and acrimonious negotiations Lloyd's asked the Names to pay £34 million and raised the further monies required to cover possible losses from the brokers involved, other interested parties and its own central fund [43]. The case is not only in the words of Lloyd's Chairman, Mr Peter Miller, 'one of the most shameful episodes in the history of Lloyd's', it also reveals the vulnerability of Lloyd's to the US liability insurance market. For the reinsurance was substantially in the area of US product liability insurance, medical malpractice indemnities and industrial liability. Over the next ten to twenty years, enormous claims could come in for terrible chronic diseases such as asbestosis [44] or the unforeseen effects of new drug administration.

It was while this shadow hung over Lloyd's of London and the Financial Services Act was being passed that Parliament set up the second enquiry at Lloyd's within the decade. Headed by Sir Patrick Neill, Vice-Chancellor of Oxford University, it was to ascertain whether members were as well protected under Lloyd's self-regulation as investors under the SIB. The report concluded that they were not. The Neill proposals which the Government required to be implemented by 1988 through Council bye-laws included doubling the number of outside Council members thus removing the in-built majority of working members. It recommended also that professional underwriters should no longer be permitted to take business for more than one syndicate operating in the same sector ('parallel syndicates'). Underwriting agents have to undergo tests to demonstrate their knowledge of the rules, their honesty and their competence before registration. Within five years no one wishing to become an active underwriter can do so without passing a rigorous examination. Further, an ombudsman to hear grievances from Names was appointed. And the relationship between agent and member was made more transparent. But the Neill report did not recommend that Lloyd's be controlled externally by Government. It will thus continue as a self-regulating body and its ancient traditions will essentially be preserved.

What lies in the future for Lloyd's of London? No doubt it will continue to take catastrophes in its stride as naturally it did with the San Francisco earthquake of 1906, whether it be in insurance and re-insurance of shipping in the Gulf during the 1987 tanker war (90 per cent is ultimately insured at Lloyd's), or of damage done in South-East England in the worst storm for 300 years in the Autumn of that same year. These are sectors where Lloyd's has historical experience and a dominant market position, especially through reinsurance. Aviation is a further sector of great strength even in years of serious air accidents. More ominous is the liability sector which continues to show massive losses, principally as a result of astronomic damages awards made in US courts and the perilously long terms involved in product liability, the so-called 'long-tail' risks. As can be seen from Table 4.7 above, the 1984 loss was £257 million (coming on top of losses of £384 million in 1983 and £425 million in 1982). The problem is not only that these are arguably bad risks. Unlike in the marine and aviation sectors, competi-tion was fiercer when Lloyd's initially entered the market in a big way. There are now fears, however, that, in the light of the magnitude of the awards, insurers may no longer be willing to come forward at all. Certainly, theChairman of Lloyd's, Mr Peter Miller, asked in his state-ment at the close of the 1986 accountancy year 'How far is it prudent to commit underwriting resources in the future to a class of business hedged about with such dangers and uncertainties?'

Another challenge lies in Lloyd's adaptation to high technology. If the same pattern were followed as in The Stock Exchange, electronic transactions could wipe out the 'Room', the symbol of the personal trust invested in the trading partnership between underwriter and broker. A compromise solution has been proposed that the agencies are free to follow. The Room itself is to be connected into a worldwide electronic data interchange (EDI) network stretching to the US, the Far East and Australia and extending to brokers, agents, insurance and reinsurance companies and claims adjustors with law firms [46].

International insurance broking

Nor is Lloyd's without competition, and not simply traditional compe-tition in reinsurance from the great German and Swiss reinsurance companies. In the late 1970s the big US brokers were faced with a saturated domestic market and began actively looking for overseas acquisitions. In an inept act of self-defence Lloyd's Committee passed a rule restricting outside interests to 20 per cent of any Lloyd's broker. This gave impetus to a plan that had already been close to fruition, the creation of a Lloyd's type institution in the USA. The New York Insurance Exchange was established in May 1978. While it is still no major threat to Lloyd's, it can and will grow and shows that unique as

Lloyd's may be, its function could to a fair extent (in the most profitable areas) be carried out elsewhere.

How much competition, more stringent regulatory arrangements and EDI will change the entrepreneurial character of Lloyd's is hard to estimate. No one believes that the effect will be similar to that of Big Bang in banking and investment. But what has changed is the broking world, where parallels with the company realignment of Big Bang can be discerned. In their period of expansion a decade or more ago the big US brokers, Alexander & Alexander, Marsh & McLennan, Frank B Hall were all looking for entries into British broking. The large firms already had historical and amicable trading relationships with their own favourite companies in London. Between 1979 and 1982 these relationships firmed up into partnerships and acquisitions, some friendlier than others. In the end Alexander & Alexander acquired Alexander Howden, Marsh & McLennan acquired C. T. Bowring, and Fred S James, Wigham Poland. Sedgwick, the UK's largest broker, remained independent and indeed in one of the most important moves since the dust settled in the early 1980s acquired in 1985 the world's fifth largest broker by revenue (in 1984) Fred S James. In 1986 it bought the US's eighth largest broker, The Crump Cos., and the smaller Armistead Group, to become the fourth biggest broker in the USA and the third in the world after Marsh McLennan and Alexander & Alexander. The other major UK brokers are Willis Faber (ninth in the world in 1984), Hogg Robinson (eleventh), C E Heath (twelfth), Minet Holdings (thirteenth), Jardine (fourteenth), Stewart Wrightson (fifteenth) [47]. Increasingly, and almost in a reversal of the position a decade ago, the London brokers are committing themselves to the US market. On average the top UK brokers now take 50 per cent of their brokerage in US dollars [48].

But even among purely City firms changes are occurring as divestment of agency interests forces a rethink. C E Heath, for example acquired in 1986 a fellow Lloyd's broker, Fielding Insurance. In June 1986 Willis Faber, already second in the UK to Sedgwick, launched an agreed £254 million bid for Stewart Wrightson, to make the new merged group the world's fifth largest. Naturally, mergers and increasing competition in specialist business are having repercussions on staff. As in 'Big Bang' expert senior staff are of key importance. Only four weeks after C E Heath's merger with Fielding, 28 senior staff left for Citicorp Insurance Brokers, a subsidiary of the UK banking group. Sedgwick in their turn lost four top executives in the oil and gas division to Alexander Howden. In November 1987 five senior executives in the railways and aviation divisions of Willis Faber (previously in Stewart Wrightson) left. One of them had moved from C E Heath to Wrightson only a year before. In this atmosphere salaries started to rise and costs had to be cut. In mid-1986, the Howden Group merged with PWS. Within a short time 60 of the 370 staff were redundant.

There are other signs of tough times ahead. We have mentioned the dangers of the US liability market. The markets in US property insurance and in world marine business are suffering from price-cutting. UK composites are reducing their commission rates to brokers. Lloyd's underwriters are experimenting with reducing their terms of trade for premiums from five months' grace to 90 days, which could profoundly affect the brokers' investment income. The pressure on the smaller brokers will thus continue and we can expect the trend toward merger and acquisition both in the UK and abroad to continue. The 'Big Bang' of insurance broking is not yet over.

Notes and References

1 Midland Bank International's booklet *Services for Exporters* is extremely useful to those entering the export business. This section is indebted to information in it.

2 *See Institute of Export Official Members Handbook*, Cornhill, London 1987, p. 99.

3 We are indebted for this information to Sir John Baring whose bank is a sponsor of this study.

4 *The Making of Managers. A report on management education, training and development in the USA, West Germany, France, Japan and the UK* ('The Handy Report'), MSC, NEDC, BIM, London 1987, p. 12.

5 *Financial Times*, 1 October 1987.

6 Christopher Nobes, 'Financial Reporting in the EEC: why and how it differs', *Management Accounting*, Chartered Institute of Management Accountants, April 1987, pp. 34–35.

7 Janet Bohdanowicz, World Accounting Report; Leon Hopkins, 'New legislation holds promise of audit expansion', in *Financial Times Special Report on Accountancy*, 15 December 1986.

8 *See* Richard Waters 'The battle for audits. New pairings at the takeover dance', *Financial Times Special Report on Accountancy*, 15 December 1987.

9 Clive Wolmar, 'Consultancies. Why London leads', *Financial Times Special Report on Personal Taxation*, 12 June 1986.

10 Sue Landau, 'The Big Bang. The City opens up a new market', *Financial Times Special Report on Management Consultancy*, 13 October 1986.

11 Catherine Hastings, 'Accountancy based consultancies. Diversification sets the trend', *Financial Times Special Report on Management Consultancy*, 13 October 1986.

12 *See* ref. 4.

13 Quoted Juan F. Rada, 'Information Technology and Services', in *The Emerging Service Economy*, edited by Orio Giarini for the Services World Forum, Geneva, Pergamon Press, Oxford, 1987, p. 162.

14   Elaine Williams, 'The SWIFT Network. Banking's unifying force', *Financial Times Special Report on Information Technology in Finance*, 16 October 1986.

15   Elizabeth Sowton 'Systems are streamlined to woo treasurers', as ref. 14.

16   For comprehensive assessments of Reuters' work *see* Flemings Research, 'Reuters Holdings plc', London 1986 and also Kleinwort Grievson Securities Investment Research, 'Reuters Holdings plc', 1987.

17   Survey by Romtec of Maidenhead for The London Stock Exchange.

18   Reuters Holdings plc Annual Report 1986.

19   Roy Assersohn, 'Exporting and Information Technology', *Institute of Export Official Members Handbook 1987*, Cornhill Publications, London, pp. 199–200.

20   *United Kingdom Balance of Payments*, CSO Pink Book, 1987, p. 36.

21   As ref. 20.

22   Nick Bunker, 'Lloyds goes high-tech to ensure key role in market', *Financial Times* 29 May 1987.

23   Information by kind courtesy of Jonathan Walker, Greenwell Montagu Research.

24   Precise calculations of the relative magnitude of foreign-owned insurance companies' business in the UK compared to the indigenous companies are almost impossible. The last available calculations made by the Association of British Insurers in March 1987 go back to 1980 statistics. It showed that 17% of UK general business premiums and 13% of long-term business premiums were under foreign control, ABI, *Overseas Earnings of the UK Insurance Industry*, London, 1987, p. 45.

25   Nick Bunker, 'Royal pushes risk back down the line', *Financial Times*, 25 February 1987.

26   According to the Association of British Insurers, 1985 and 1986 statistics.

27   This section is indebted to Godfrey Hodgson, *Lloyds of London. A Reputation at Risk*. Penguin, Harmondsworth, 1986; Barry Supple, *The Royal Exchange Assurance. A History of British Insurance 1720–1970*, Cambridge University Press, 1970; H. A. L. Cockerell, *The British Insurance Business 1547–1970*, Heinemann, London 1976; G. C. A. Dickson, *Introduction to Insurance, 2nd edn*, Macdonald & Evans/Pitman Publishing, 1984.

28   Nick Bunker, 'Rough draft of the shape insurance is in', *Financial Times*, 4 September 1987.

29   Roger Miller, 'Risk under control', *Association World*, December 1986.

30   *See* Jonathan Carr, 'Munich Re's confidence reflects diversification', *Financial Times*, 19 August 1982 and 'Allianz flexes muscles for its next advance', *Financial Times*, 5 February 1985.

31   CSO Pink Book, 1987 (*see* ref. 20).

32   For a useful discussion of the challenge facing GATT, *see* Gerald M.

Dickinson, 'Barriers to International Trade in Direct Insurance and Re-insurance', in *Trade in Services, Open Markets and Uruguay Round Negotiations. A* conference, London, 1987, pp. 129–52.

33   OECD, *International Trade in Services: Insurance, Identification and Analysis of Obstacles*, Paris, 1983.

34   Court of Justice of the European Communities, Case 220/83 *Commission* v *French Republic*, Case 252/83 *Commission* v *Denmark*, Case 205/84 *Commission* v *Federal Republic of Germany*, Case 206/84 *Commission* v *Ireland*.

35   Case 45/85, *Verband der Sachversicherer* v *Commission*. Judgment was delivered 27 January 1987.

36   For a helpful account *see* Jörg Finsinger, Elizabeth Hammond and Julian Tapp, *Insurance: Competition or Regulation? A Comparative Study of the Insurance Markets in the United Kingdom and the Federal Republic of Germany*, The Institute of Fiscal Studies, London, pp. 51–54.

37   I am indebted in this section to Mr Stanley Crossick of Belmont European Community Law Office, Brussels.

38   *See* Godfrey Hodgson's colourful account, *Lloyd's of London. A Reputation at Risk* (ref. 27 above) pp. 62–5.

39   John Moore 'Era of mega underwriting agency. Divestment at Lloyd's', *Financial Times Special Report on Insurance and Insurance Broking*, 16 April 1986.

40   Hodgson, pp. 318–9.

41   For the whole Sasse affair *see* Hodgson, pp. 246–288.

42   For a brief history of regulation at Lloyd's *see* Jörg Finsinger, Elizabeth Hammond, Julian Tapp, *Insurance: Competition or Regulation?*, (*see* ref. 36 above) pp. 37 ff.

43   Hodgson, pp. 344–372; John Moore, 'PCW victims hit at Lloyd's offer', *The Independent*, 10 April 1987.

44   Nick Bunker, 'The PCW Affair. Still a shadow over Lloyd's', *Financial Times*, 11 April 1987.

45   The *Financial Times* covered the Report in a series of articles in early 1987 by Nick Bunker, 23 and 24 January 1987. The full Report: *Regulatory Arrangements at Lloyd's*, Report of the Committee of Inquiry, HMSO, London, 1987.

46   Nick Bunker, 'Lloyd's goes high-tech to ensure key role in market', *Financial Times*, 29 May 1987.

47   David Thomson, 'The Risk of the Risk Manager', *Financial Times Special Report on Insurance and Insurance Broking*, 16 April 1986.

48   Nick Bunker, 'Brokers. Smaller Players under Pressure', *Financial Times Special Report on Insurance*, 4 April 1987.

5 Markets and exchanges – old and new

In the preceding chapters we have attempted to describe some of the recent developments in finance and financial services which are both worldwide in their scope and at times almost overwhelming in their impact. A variety of economic and political factors have been at work, many of them new and unfamiliar, which seem to strike at the very roots of the conventions, practices and procedures which have long formed the basis of international trade and commerce.

In these turbulent circumstances it is easy to overlook the very much wider range of commercial institutions which have been created over time for the negotiation and discharge of international business transactions. Some of these mechanisms are very old and built into the historic fabric of the City – such as the markets and exchanges for gold, commodities, metal, the Baltic Exchange and Lloyd's Register of Shipping. Others are relatively new operations arising from the trading circumstances of the day, notably the London Foreign Exchange market and the markets in futures and options. There are finally the less structured activities such as overseas markets in real estate and auctions and in sales of works of art.

Each of these areas of operation has its own traditions, its own mechanisms – and its own problems and difficulties. For their record is by no means one of uniform success, and in some cases their future is beset with doubts and uncertainties. For all that, their combined contribution to overseas earnings (including the profits of export houses) is more than £1 billion per year. Moreover, they all in their various ways add to the commercial influence and significance of the City and of the country. And although the short accounts of each in the succeeding paragraphs will do no more than sketch the background, type and scale of the various activities, they should at least provide an overview of a whole range of highly skilled and professional endeavours which in general receive far less interest and credit than they should.

The bullion market

It is a romantic picture. Five participants meeting twice daily to 'fix' the price of gold – stylishly housed at the offices of N M Rothschild as they have been since the market opened – representing firms one of which dates back to 1684, surrounded by portraits of past European monarchs, and signalling consent or disagreement by toying with national flags.

One almost forgets that the commodity in which they deal is politically most explosive and yet in some ways the most prosaic and at times elusive in use of all commodities.

At one extreme gold is almost a form of foreign exchange and, on more than one occasion, has been used to stabilise national economies, to act as a medium of reference for exchange rates, and as a national currency reserve. The commercial uses of gold are by contrast diverse and very practical. It is used, of course, for the manufacture of coins (official and fake), as well as for medals and medallions. About half of commercial gold is used for carat jewellery. Gold has also many decorative and industrial uses, including electronics; and it is of course widely used for dentistry. Finally a substantial tonnage is held as bars for investment.

Annual output of gold is approximately 1500 tons. South Africa sells some half of the world supply, which when related to the US obligation to buy gold offered at $35 per ounce, suggests a volume of world output well in excess of £1 billion per year. Other major suppliers include the Soviet Union, Canada, USA, Brazil and Australia.

The market itself, as a mechanism for private transactions, has been bedevilled by the use of gold as an instrument of monetary policy, with the gold standard, in tighter or looser form, going in and out of fashion in the major industrial countries, such as France, Germany, USA and the UK, as economic circumstances and convenience demand.

Attempts at governmental control of supply, prices and use have more often than not proved disastrous. The culmination of such efforts was perhaps in 1969 when the Bank of England sold no less than $3000 million worth of gold in a fortnight in an attempt to offset an unprecedented level of speculative demand. The attempt failed; the Governor of the Bank of England closed the gold market, and following consultations in Washington with Directors of other central banks, imposed a two-tier system of market trading aimed at separating official intervention in the market from normal commercial dealings. The exchange was closed for two weeks, during which nearly half of London's business was thought to have passed to Zurich from which it has been slow to return.

Over the years things have settled down in the gold market, following the introduction of fairly elaborate processes for channelling orders through a price-fixing procedure. In 1971 'official' influences over the market were still further weakened when the USA effectively devalued the US dollar and at the same time severed its direct link with gold.

Statistics of market transactions are unfortunately even more difficult to detect than other sections of these highly secretive sets of activities.

One of the foremost experts on the subject, William Clarke, estimates that the London market turns over between $1 billion and $2 billion worth of gold weekly, and that London takes 40 per cent of the world gold business and Zurich 30 per cent. To have emerged from at least half a century of political and economic turmoil with this degree of strength in world markets is indeed a tribute to the commercial skills and tenacity of this powerful and well established group of City merchants.

The London Metal Exchange

Of all the City markets, the London Metal Exchange (LME) is perhaps the least glamorous. Its membership is quite small – some twenty ring-dealing members. Entry is expensive and tightly controlled; and whilst it is closely linked with the Soft Commodities Market and with the very speculative trade in 'futures', a relatively high proportion of the market trade involves physical movement and delivery of the products with short-term contracts of no longer than three months.

Above all, however, the market itself seems to be set for commercial decline. The six base metals in which it deals – copper, zinc, lead, aluminium, nickel and silver – are the traditional raw materials for many sectors of manufacturing industry. Over the years they have all in varying degrees been the subject of attack by substitute materials – notably plastics and carbon fibres – in the search for lighter weight and higher and improved technical performance. Few of the markets, however, have surrendered to competition without a fight and, indeed, a few such as copper and aluminium are quite buoyant. The general atmosphere, however, is one of a continuous and gruelling fight with the odds – political, economic and technological – increasingly stacked against the processers and dealers in base metals.

It is for this reason that the collapse and ultimate suspension of the Tin Market in 1985 was such a tragedy both because of the heavy financial losses and for the complex issues which they involved.

Tin has been a toublesome commodity for a great number of years. Its main area of growth was as a coating for tinplate for packaging. However, developments in electrolytic tinning, has reduced the tin coverage of tin plate to microscopic proportions, whilst similarly, both the constitution and use of solder has responded to technological developments in a way sharply adverse to aggregate tin consumption.

The development of tin smelting in production centres has progressively reduced the exports of tin ore in favour of the tin ingot, discouraging overseas expansion in tin smelting in the consuming markets, and producing in the ingot a commodity more readily tradeable in local markets in Bangkok, Malaysia and elsewhere.

Finally, the very active steps of the International Tin Research Institute to expand total demand, particularly within the electrical industries, failed to stem the commercial decline. As a result, the whole market became faced with mounting losses on a scale well beyond the capacity of even the largest broker to cope. On 24 October 1985 the market collapsed. The International Tin Council (ITC), established for some twenty years as a corporate body and designed to manage and control the financial affairs of the industry, declared itself unable to meet a commitment to purchase tin worth £51 million from a leading broker trading on the LME. At the same time, the Buffer Stock Manager of the ITC announced in London that the ITC had no further funds to buy tin and that it was unable to meet its commitments.

The matter proceeded to the courts, where with more than twenty countries involved and represented by perhaps 100 senior and junior counsel there is every indication of a classic struggle developing in some of the more abstruse areas of international law.

Apart from its direct effect on the tin industry, on the tin market and on the LME, there is one major point of issue which throws its shadow over the market mechanisms as a whole. The ITC was established as a corporate entity contracting on its own behalf and not as the agent of its members. It was argued therefore that members of the International Council (led by the UK through the DTI and including 22 sovereign states and the European Commission) could not be held liable under contracts between the ITC and third parties such as traders, brokers and banks. In other words, the International Tin Council, though set up by governments and under their control, by its very constitution as a corporate body, could not and would not be held liable for its debts; and as the ITC itself had manifestly no funds and, indeed, was legally bankrupt, the market members and their bankers were left totally without redress.

A blow of this nature cast doubts not only on the Tin Market but, indeed, on the whole basis of trust of the traditional City markets. The position was not improved by the more recent compulsory winding up of another metal broker (a subsidiary of a big Wall Street merchant house) over the handling of a collateral for aluminium dealings on the LME. The petition covered over £50 million and was submitted by a metal market trader, who was himself a subsidiary of a major Swiss firm.

It is clear that the LME will have some hard thinking to do, particularly over its limited membership, its exclusion of direct membership for overseas firms, its constitution, trading practice and management and particularly its more active participation in futures and options.

Initial steps have already been taken with the setting up of a central clearing house to comply with the provisions of the Financial Services Act, 1986. Conditions of membership and market practice are beginning to show more flexibility, whilst the futures and options market, of which the LME is part, opens up new opportunities both for conventional trading and for speculation.

Despite its many tribulations the LME still remains a major world influence in price fixing, marketing and trading. Aluminium, zinc and lead all show considerable life. It most spectacular commodity is now copper, following the decision in 1978 of Kennacott (the largest American producer) to abandon its own controlled pricing system in favour of London.

The LME constitutes a series of markets which, if only for reasons of prestige, London can ill afford to lose. This particularly applies to the new activities in futures and options described in more detail later in this chapter. It may well be that the City through this new medium will quickly develop the skills and expertise which it has shown in the past, and in this way help to restore the status and prestige of this unhappy sector.

The London Commodities Exchange

The London Metal Exchange may, as we have seen, lack glamour and excitement, although it is sadly capable of attracting to itself quite major and far-reaching commercial disasters.

By way of contrast, the trade in 'soft' commodities through the London Commodities Exchange contains within it many of the elements which give to the City its unique and historic flavour. It may not trade as actively or as widely as its large and aggressive competitor in Chicago (the Chicago Mercantile Exchange), where live hogs, pork bellies and random-length timber are just a few of the huge range of tradeable products. But Chicago caters mainly for the domestic US market and trades only on a lesser scale on the international scene.

New York has the edge in some individual commodities, although London retains its lead in the market for more important commodities such as cocoa, sugar and coffee. We have seen in the case of tin that the local centres of production created a strong market activity in Penang. For similar reasons, Sydney trades actively in wool, particularly in futures, Singapore in rubber, and Colombo and Calcutta in tea with higher trading figures than London.

Soft commodities are, of course, peculiarly at risk both from climatic conditions and in some cases from the narrow bases of both production and distribution. In recent times, frost in Brazil and black pod in Ghana have devastated supplies respectively of coffee and cocoa with prices soaring sky-high from shortage of supply and from the activities of international speculators.

From time to time also the markets are rocked by attempts to corner supply, as happened many years ago in pepper and more recently by the attempts to corner the market in silver by the Hunt Brothers of Texas, who are said to have lost £1 billion in the process.

These are, however, exceptional occurrences in markets which are, by and large, orderly and responsible. Nor are the markets themselves very big. Traders in soft commodities number about 100, of which about a quarter are also members of the Metal Exchange. Entry to the market is expensive, though less so than for metals and there are restrictions on foreign membership. In 1983 according to estimates of the Bank of England commoditiy trade earned £350 million. Profits have remained fairly static in recent years, although with a tendency to decline and of course a number of members have been sharply hit by the Tin Disaster in the LME.

Physical trade in commodities (as opposed to trade in futures) is increasingly transacted through telephone, telex or computer with only a small proportion through organised meetings. Auctions, however, are still held though for a very limited number of commodities such as furs and tea where some 60 per cent of the tea drunk in Britain is said to be bought through auctions.

Futures and Options

Against this background of relatively stable trading, a major new market has now emerged in commodities, that of futures and options. Reference has already been made to the London International Financial Futures Exchange (LIFFE) in Chapter 3 with regards to securities. It is now time to examine briefly the operations of this market in the field of commodities.

The London Futures and Options Exchange (FOX)

We have described (Chapter 3) how both in London and Chicago trade in commodity futures had, by and large, begun as a basic device for safeguarding forward commodity contracts against changes in exchange rates or in the price of the commodity. Owing to the attractions of this form of trading (followed as late as 1985 by both West Germany and Japan) it very soon formed a market of its own, and in due course outgrew its traditional base in soft commodities. LIFFE itself, founded in 1982, still fights on, and with some success, to keep a competitive edge on Chicago, and for this purpose offers a full range of currency, interest rate equities and gilt futures. The market in futures has itself built a parallel market in options where it is in competition with the Chicago Board of Trade Futures Market and the Sydney Futures Exchange.

The London Commodity Exchange was perhaps a little slower to develop than the currency exchange, but early in 1987 the full force of the revolution began to hit this most staid and traditional of City institutions.

In the process of the revolution, the London Commodity Exchange changed its name to the Futures and Options Exchange with the acronym (the subject of some press ridicule) of the 'London Fox'. Its headquarters removed itself from the City to a modern block in London's latest tourist attraction, St. Katherine's Dock. The Exchange assumed corporate status – hopefully avoiding the implications of similar status for the London Metal Exchange. It appointed a full-time Chairman and adopted a high marketing profile. Finally it formed part of the series of self-regulating institutions established in the City with ultimate responsibility through the SIB (Securities and Investment Board) to the Secretary of State.

The structure of the Futures Exchange reflects the range and diversity of the products it handles. As a general rule its business is conducted within the framework of an organised exchange. The constituents are:

1 The London Metal Exchange (LME) for aluminium, copper, lead, nickel, silver, zinc and, hopefully in the not too distant future, also tin.

2 The London Commodity Exchange (LCE) for cocoa, coffee, sugar and rubber.

3 The International Petroleum Exchange (IPE) working with the LCE for crude oil and heating oil.

4 The Agricultural Futures Exchange (AFE) for European wheat, barley, soya bean meal, potatoes and meat.

5 The Baltic International Freight Futures Exchange (BIFEX) established in 1986 at a particularly difficult time for the Baltic freight and timber indices and for the price of commercial oil. Production of forward prices has never been easy in an area at once subject to the political and marketing turmoil of the Middle East and elsewhere.

Some interesting facts and statements have emerged from a survey carried out by the Bank of England in June 1986. The questionnaire, which met with a good response, was circulated to 93 firms including most of the major participants in the commodities futures market and a sample of smaller specialist firms. The facts that emerged included:

1 Shareholders' funds ranged from £57 million to £65 million per firm.

2 The total number of staff employed by all firms in the survey was 5283. Only 13 firms employed more than 100 staff and 26 more than 50. Twenty firms had as few as 20 employees or less. Only 6 firms employed staff overseas.

3 Recruitment is from a variety of sources including school leavers and university graduates as well as experienced traders. There are few organised training programmes and, although limited use is made of

external courses particularly those mounted by The Stock Exchange, on the whole the accepted practice is one of 'learning on the job'.

4 Calculations of turnover and profits are bedevilled by problems of definition and very marked differences in accounting conventions. A sharp drop in average turnover in 1985 was matched by a similar drop in profits (a figure which takes into account contingent losses on tin). Average turnover for some 30 companies appears to have been some £68 million in 1985 – a fall of 24 per cent on the previous year. Total pre-tax profits of 39 firms were £21 million, with an average of £0.5 million per firm.

5 The business of the market was predominantly European-client based. There was a total of nearly 10 000 clients, about three-quarters of whom were located in the UK. Similarly, about 80 per cent of client business stemmed from Europe, followed well behind by North America (7.4 per cent), the Far East (5.2 per cent) and the Middle East (4.5 per cent).

6 In January 1986 80 per cent of total contracts covering soft commodities were placed with the UK exchange. The US exchanges contributed 17 per cent whilst the remaining 3 per cent (cocoa, coffee and white sugar) was transacted in Paris, although there was a surprisingly lively market in potato futures in Amsterdam.

7 Finally, coffee had a substantial lead in terms of commodities traded in the UK although copper, aluminium, raw sugar, gas, oil and cocoa all commanded significant support. In turn particular commodities met varying degrees of competition, especially perhaps from the USA, Paris and Amsterdam.

London's Foreign Exchange Market

Money gives life to business. It is to the industrialist what water is to the farmer. But as currency whose value in relation to other currencies alters daily, hourly and even by the second it can be traded, or rather exchanged, like a commodity. Indeed as a New York banker once put it, 'Foreign exchange is the perfect commodity: it is traded 24 hours a day, is perfectly liquid, deliverable and of consistent product quality'. London's foreign exchange market is the fastest moving of all markets – delays of a few seconds can cost a dealer or his client millions. It is also indisputably the world's largest.

Several factors enabled this, the world's traditional foreign exchange centre, to remain ahead of rivals in the other time-zones, especially Tokyo and New York, and rivals in the European time-zone, Zurich and Frankfurt. Restoration of sterling convertibility in the late 1950s had already helped to restore London's position after the cessation of trading during the war years when Zurich was able to assume a pre-eminence that was to last well into the post-war period. But it was the abolition of exchange controls in 1979, the removal of the prohibition on banks from dealing directly with one another in foreign exchange in London at the beginning of 1980, together with the unprecedented volatility of exchange rates in the 1980s that gave a huge impetus to London as the major market. In the most authoritative survey ever carried out, the Bank of England calculated in 1986 that (after adjustment for doubly-recorded transactions) there was a currency turnover in London of some $90 billion in value per day. This compares with estimates of approximately $48 billion each in New York and Tokyo. And since then the Midland Bank estimates that the daily turnover has risen to some $110 billion. Probably as little as 15 per cent of this turnover reflects the foreign exchange needs of international trade. The remainder is commodity trading, buying and selling currency to protect assets or indeed to swell them, but, increasingly and especially by banks, simply dealing to make profit.

The Bank of England survey showed that some 90 per cent of the trading is between banks with brokers acting as intermediaries for 43 per cent of the turnover. The number of houses participating was remarkably large – the survey included 348 banks alone – but worldwide there are only three to four dozen big players distributed across the trading centres in the Far East, Europe and North America. By far the largest is Citicorp (and has been for a decade or more) which in 1986 earned a profit of some $412 million on foreign exchange transactions. Indeed, the Bank of England established that 78 per cent of the foreign turnover among banks in London was accounted for by foreign banks, with North American banks dominating (41 per cent of turnover compared to 16 per cent for EC banks and 7 per cent for Japanese). The existence of such a successful world market in foreign exchange in London is of course one reason, alongside the Eurocurrency and Eurobond market, for such a remarkable concentration of overseas banks in this single location. And their presence itself generates further turnover. But it should not be assumed that overseas banks dominate, to the exclusion of British banks. On the contrary, both Barclays (which in 1986 achieved a profit in foreign exchange dealings of £123 million) and Midland (£110 million in 1986) rank alongside Citicorp's other nearest rivals, J P Morgan, Chase Manhattan and Chemical Bank.

When it comes to broking, moreover, British firms dominate worldwide and are steadily increasing their global coverage. The leading companies, Mercantile House, Exco, and Mills & Allen are diversifying, despite, or perhaps because of the abolition of fixed commissions in foreign exchange dealing in 1985 (a year before 'Big Bang'!). Together they own three of the four major US bond brokers. At the same time, Exco owns an investment bank in New York (Oppenheimer & Co.) and Mercantile House has become a major financial conglomerate, acting as a primary gilts market-maker through Alexander Laing & Cruickshank and as an inter-dealer broker through Fundamental & Marshall Brokers. Thus we see the same process of acquisition occurring among companies active in this market as we already observed in the banking, securities and insurance broking sectors.

There are four major types of transaction in foreign exchange dealing – spot transactions, forwards, options and futures. Spot transactions (completed no later than the second business day after the deal is struck) account for 73 per cent of London's turnover, underscoring the dominance of trading to take advantage of changes in exchange rates both between the centres in different time-zones and within the market itself. Forwards are sales or purchases of currency at agreed periods in the future, usually one, three or six months after the transaction. The price of the currency is based on its spot value which is then adjusted with a premium or a discount to reflect differentials in interest rates between the first and the second currency. For example, a bank purchases on the client's behalf Swiss francs for delivery in three months and pays for them with US dollars. The interest it will earn on the Swiss francs may only be 5 per cent per annum, while it has to forego a rate of 12 per cent on the dollars it has used. The client will, therefore, be asked to pay a premium to make up for lost revenue. But this is the importer's classic technique for ensuring that he can purchase goods at a fixed price in the future despite any fluctuations in the exchange rate that may occur in the meantime. Likewise, the exporter can ensure that the money he receives at the time of delivery will be the same as when the deal was agreed, irrespective of whether the foreign currency in which the goods were billed has weakened. The same technique can also be employed to protect the value of foreign earnings or assets at the balance sheet date (thus avoiding what is known as 'translation exposure').

These traditional foreign exchange transactions have been supplemented in recent years by currency futures and options. We looked at these in some detail in Chapter 3. Chicago had set the pace in futures in the 1970s and the Philadelphia Stock Exchange introduced currency options in 1982. As we have seen, the London centre for currency futures and options is LIFFE (The London International Financial Futures Exchange). The futures contract is an agreement to buy or sell currency at a future date at an agreed price, the contract being with the Exchange. These contracts can themselves be traded. The currency option allows the purchaser to exercise the right to purchase at an agreed price and on a fixed date but not the obligation. For this the other contracting party charges a premium. Neither currency futures nor options have, however, seemed very attractive to corporations in UK, which continue to prefer the well-established forwards technique. Less than 1 per cent of London's foreign exchange turnover is accounted for by futures and options and LIFFE's strength has remained in the securities area. Swaps, on the other hand, the exchange by two parties of interest rates either in the same currency or two different currencies, have proved a useful technique for adjusting portfolio balances or for taking advantage of overseas funding possibilities without exchange rate risk.

No activity is more hectic than the foreign exchange market. World-wide trading never ceases. As the day draws to a close for players in San Francisco, the market is opening in Tokyo, Hong Kong and Singapore. By their close Bahrain has opened and soon afterwards the European centres begin. By early afternoon in London, New York has started and activities there are bridged by San Francisco which, by extending its day, can trade both with the East Coast of the States and with the Far East. Dealers sit in rooms facing banks of screens, at least three, sometimes as many as six or even eight, which link them to their company's offices round the world and to financial information systems such as Reuters' Monitor which, as we saw in the last chapter, provides real-time information on over 100 currencies. Dealing itself occurs over the telephone. Split-second decisions on the deal of the moment have to be made at the same time as keeping an eye on the flow of diverse and ever-changing information supplied by the screens. While most dealing in London is between sterling and the US dollar (30 per cent) and between the DM and the dollar (28 per cent), it is also necessary to know rates between other currencies. These are provided by Reuters' Monitor Abacus service. And as if this abundance of information were not enough, the volatility of recent exchange rates for example, the sharp changes in the value of the dollar, particularly in the great collapse of October–November 1987, have added to the intensity of the almost climactic atmosphere of the dealing rooms. Small wonder that the dealers are a special breed, people of instantaneous reaction and enormous concentration. Their careers in the room are short, with few continuing into their forties. The rewards are correspondingly high. This and the global trade in securities are the areas for which the banks and the brokers are prepared to pay special premiums to obtain top-flight dealers or simply to retain them. These payments are the so-called 'golden hellos' and 'golden handcuffs' which featured so prominently in the years leading up to 'Big Bang'. For there are two ingredients for success in this dizzy world; an established and efficient dealing team and access to the most up-to-date technology. By the middle of 1987 the Midland Bank had already stripped out what in 1986 had been London's most modern currency dealing room. But in a business where seconds are of the essence, the big players are prepared to invest fabulous sums in both men and machines.

Some contrasting market activities

This section concerns itself with some widely contrasting aspects of the

London markets. Between them they make a considerable contribution to UK overseas earnings, and by their very diversity they reflect the rich variety of trading activity to be found not only within the confines of the 'City', but also several miles outside it in London's fashionable West End.

The activities concerned are:

1 The Baltic Exchange
2 Shipping Intelligence
3 The British Art Trade
4 Real Estate
5 Trading by Export Houses

1 The Baltic Exchange

The overseas earnings of the Baltic Exchange are recorded as follows:

1975: £146 million
1980: £181 million
1984: £270 million
1985: £229 million
1986: £221 million

It should be pointed out that these figures cover the brokerage and other services leading to commissions, agency fees etc. in respect of chartering, sales and purchases of ships and aircraft, and miscellaneous associated activities. They do not, however, include earnings of the Exchange in commodity futures, which for national statistical purposes are included in contributions from commodity trading.

For the British Mercantile and Shipping Exchange (to give it its full correct title) has indeed acquired many fields of activity in its long history. In the eighteenth century, its main business was in commodities – a tradition maintained today by its trade in commodity futures. Some of the commodities concerned are: EC wheat and barley, pig-meal and soya bean oil, and a particularly lively trade in potatoes futures. The Baltic is also associated with the new futures market in shipping freights, a market which was launched in 1985. All these futures are actively traded on the floor of the vast hall of the Exchange. Indeed, with much of the remaining business transacted by telex and by screen, it is commodity trading which accounts for a high proportion of the face-to-face transactions operating in and around the trading floor.

For all that, the Exchange is essentially a ship-broking market, which continues to operate in strength despite the constant decline in tonnage of British merchant shipping. For the market in chartering as well as for the sale and purchase of ships is fully international and London remains at its heart. Chartering agents represent shippers and merchants from all parts of the world, whilst deep-sea shipowners also retain their pressure either directly or through representation. The market is backed by a unique intelligence system and owes much of its reputation to its willingness when called upon to offer services such as ship valuation, and in political terms remains essentially free.

Similarly, the aircraft side of the market, such as the optimal freight and passenger utilisation of British and foreign aircraft is uniquely equipped both in experience and resources to meet sudden demands and emergencies.

The Baltic Exchange claims indeed to be the only truly international freight market in the world. It is thought to account for some two-thirds of the world's shipping 'fixtures' – the greater part made up of tramp shipping, available at any time to go anywhere, and reflecting the unique experience, flexibility and information back-up of this historic and yet up-to-the-minute 'City' institution to which they all look for instructions, for protection, and in times of stress for salvation.

2   Shipping intelligence

The Baltic Exchange, like Lloyd's of London, owed its existence and prosperity to its location in London, which had established itself as early as the beginning of the eighteenth century as one of the world's major maritime trading centres. At the heart of both activities lay the readily available intelligence on ships, their movements and their seaworthiness. By 1734 the information posted for the merchants and shipowners who gathered in Lloyd's coffee-house began to be published as *Lloyd's List*. This was joined in 1760 by the first published inventory of merchant ships, *Lloyd's Register of Shipping*.

Today the *Register* is produced by an organisation of the same name, that is entirely independent of Lloyd's of London. The *Register* is a classified catalogue of all the world's merchant ships over 100 tons gross weight, providing full technical specifications of each vessel, her owner, flag of registration and type. The full *Register* appears once a year but is updated monthly. It offers information that is vital to the shipping industry worldwide and earns some £29 million per year for the UK's invisibles account.

Lloyd's of London, continues, however, to be extremely active in the publication of shipping and commercial intelligence through its wholly owned subsidiary based in Colchester, Lloyd's of London Press. Among its titles is *Lloyd's List*, which appears as a newspaper six days a week and contains the latest news on shipping and shipping movements, off-shore oil activities, freighting, international trade, finance and the Stock Market. It sells around the world with an estimated readership of some 75,000.

Another of the Press's total of 130 publications is the *Loading List*, first published 70 years ago, which is a weekly, comprehensive directory of sea freight services for the UK. It lists ships leaving UK ports for up to 1000 destinations worldwide together with freighting availability and sailing times.

The Press also publishes what might be seen as Lloyd's of London's own equivalent to the now independent *Register*, the *Shipping Index*. This ambitious publication appears daily and lists the current voyages of some 24,000 merchant vessels. Some 200 pages long, it records data on 4,000 ship's movements per day as well as technical information on and full particulars of every ship listed, including changes of ownership, name and flag. Also listed are any casualties and ships that are being decommissioned and broken up. This exhaustive yet constantly changing source of information draws on Lloyd's remarkable network of some 4,500 agents, which was first established in the late 19th century by one of Lloyd's most energetic Secretaries, Henry Hozier. News reaches Lloyd's Press by every means of communication, screen, telex, telephone and telegraph according to the systems available to the agents in various parts of the world. The updating costs alone are some £11,000 per day and, while most subscribers purchase on a weekly basis, this and much of the rest of the intelligence gathered at Lloyd's Press, extending beyond ships and freight to the ports themselves, can be received electronically as well as in the form of hard copy.

This entire activity is a fine example of a traditional City service that continues to flourish by adapting fully to the new conditions of an electronic age.

3   The British art trade

The British trade in art is an excellent illustration of how London, in spite of fierce competition from the most sophisticated and experienced auction houses in New York, Amsterdam and elsewhere, continues to keep its place as the world's leading centre in the sale of works of art and the provision of associated services.

Its two leading firms are, of course, very old indeed. Sotheby's, founded in 1744, has the longest history of any major auction house. James Christie held his first sale in Pall Mall in 1766. And, although Sotheby's, unlike Christie's, have had major changes, particularly in recent years, in ownership and in institutional structure, both firms have succeeded in maintaining a continuous tradition as connoisseurs of the highest order in their trade and in establishing in London the natural focus worldwide for major art disposals.

The trade in art is truly international both in sources of supply and in directions of purchase. The total auction sales at Christie's in 1986 was £581 million, of which rather more than half was overseas and the remainder domestic. By far the largest overseas market for Christie's was the USA with sales of $308 million in 1987–88; followed though a long way behind by Switzerland, Ireland, Italy and a variety of other countries. Sales at Sotheby's in 1986 exceeded £560 million, the result of a tumultuous season, particularly in the Autumn. The sales again were worldwide. Rembrandt's 'Portrait of a Young Girl' sold in London for £7.5 million; whilst a fine Impressionist series realised over £40 million; New York saw records from the sale of a private collection, including Renoir and a sheet of studies by Leonardo da Vinci; Hong Kong brought record prices for Chinese ceramics from the Tao Ko Chao collection; whilst in jewellery a 15th century gold pendant, known as the Middleham Jewel, was sold for very nearly £1.5 million. More recently Van Gogh's works 'Sunflowers' (£24.75 million) and 'Irises' ($53.9 million) have reached astronomical levels, beating all previous records, as a result of the fast-growing enthusiasm of Japanese art-dealers.

The range of products handled by sales rooms is indeed as wide as their sources and their destinations. With the current decline in popularity of 'Old Masters', Impressionists and modern work are beginning to lead the field. There are active markets, too, in furniture, carpets and tapestries, ceramics and glass, in silver and coins, in books, stamps, and vintage cars as well as in jewellery. Most of these categories have their own specialist associations – Society of Fine Art Auctioneers, Society of London Art Dealers, British Antique Dealers Association and the London and Provincial Antique Dealers Association Ltd. Within each association, and in parallel with the leading auction houses, there are well respected specialist firms in furniture, pictures, silver and jewellery which make up between them London's large and growing art dealing community. There are, too, art scholars who act as consultants and advisers and a growing number of foreign dealers. And down the line, perhaps stimulated by such popular TV series as the *Antiques Road Show* there are the suppliers to the vast number of antique shops, antique markets and antique fairs up and down the country and overseas. London is indeed strongly entrenched as the world's leading centre, and there are good reasons for it remaining so:

(a) The United Kingdom still retains much of its unique art heritage on the walls of town and country houses or buried in attics or perhaps cellars. British dealers are well positioned to find out where they are and to keep contact with their owners. There are good reasons (not least taxation and the decline in personal fortunes) why these should continue to be offered in the market and the stream is unlikely to dry up.

(b) The leading firms have established offices and representatives in the most influential centres overseas – New York, Amsterdam, Paris, Monte Carlo, Madrid, Hong Kong, Tokyo, Sydney and Melbourne amongst many others. These are not only centres for auctions and dealing, but also part of a worldwide network of intelligence by which buyers and sellers can be identified, advised and, hopefully, enter the market under their own auspices whenever circumstances warrant.

The London position is, therefore, very strong and by most criteria its strength is growing from year to year. There are, however, a few precautionary signals:

(a) Prices in 1986–87 reached new astronomic levels without any clear pattern emerging either of the directions of purchase, or of the reasons behind these unprecedented levels of bidding. The results of the leading houses very clearly reflect the high sales room returns and could equally sharply be affected by changes in taste, fashion or, more probably, by tightened economic circumstances of the public and private collectors (many of whom are already priced out of the more spectacular contests) or by the withdrawal of some at least of the limited number of individuals overseas who have for so long been forcing the pace.

(b) The sources of the prized pieces in the auction rooms have long been the British estate and country houses. Many have been attracted into the market by the very high level of realisation. Any major weakening of price would reduce the temptation to dispose of the family treasures, and in any case the sources, whilst not likely to dry up, are quite obviously not unlimited.

(3) The top market trade is, as we have seen, dominated by two houses. One of them, Christie's, draws its main strength from the maintenance of the traditions of British society in the narrow range of recruitment of art and specialist staff, in its mode of customer relations and in its sources of market intelligence. Tradition is very strong in this particular market, but much less powerful in the new generation of property owners than in the past.

The other market leader, Sotheby's ceased to be a private limited company in 1983 and became the personal property of a single American entrepreneur, Alfred Taubmann, whose vigorous handling of the company's affairs and of its organisational structure is reflected in results which are startingly good. Once again, however, the legal status of the firm is about to change for largely personal reasons, with a limited flotation planned on the London Stock Exchange, and a proposed two-tier structure of voting and non-voting shares. There is no reason to believe that these changes will adversely affect the company's business in any major way, but this is not a world which welcomes change and uncertainty, and the tradition of security, reliability and continuity, which are startlingly good. Once again, however, the legal status of the long run to any major upset in the firm's top level affairs.

(d) Finally, overhanging the British market is the question of VAT – the proposed liability to the tax (through new legislation of the European Community) of many sections of the trade which are currently free of liability either in whole or in part. It is a complex subject but one which dominates the thinking of many board rooms, of customers and of suppliers in the British art world.

4   Real estate

The direct contribution to overseas earnings of chartered surveyors in 1986 is recorded in the 1987 'Pink Book' as £110 million – a figure almost double that of 1979, the first year where the figures were separately identified for government statistical purposes. The figures, which are subject to the usual reservations of all statistical analysis in this field, represent fees, commissions and retainers paid by overseas clients for the use of professional skills and advice in property valuations, acquisitions, disposals, management and development.

The value of the transactions involved is, of course, very many times greater than this, running into many billions of pounds and dollars and spread over many countries of the world; and the value to the country of professional involvement in a huge financial area such as this, often on a long-term basis. Quite obviously the trade in real estate yields financial and commercial benefits to the country far beyond the remuneration of chartered surveyors or their firms for their particular professional services.

The bulk of the work is for international clients at home and overseas, including contracting to the UK foreign property investors and helping them in developing their worldwide property development. The work is both urban and agricultural, the latter including advice to governments and international funding agencies on development of land and other resources, particularly in the countries of the Third World.

The range of activities includes:

(a) Country houses, farms and estates including farm and estate management.

(b) Residential industrial property – hotels, shops and offices valuations, building services, acquisitions, disposals and management.

(c) Planning, compensation and local taxation and rating.

Of the individual UK firms, the largest operators overseas are Knight Frank & Rutley, Jones Lang & Wootton and Richard Ellis; whilst activities such as those of Sotheby's International Realty in North America and Weatherall Green & Smith in West Germany have carved out for themselves a useful niche in difficult markets. The following are simply illustrative of this important field of operations:

Sotheby's International Realty

This company specialises in marketing in North America, handling especially residential property in the States at the top end of the market, such as, Orange County, New York; Fairfield County, Connecticut and St. Thomas, US Virgin Islands. These are locations where individual properties have realised very substantial prices, often well in excess of

£1 million. Marketing techniques are lavish and accompanied by advertising, public relations and inclusion in Sotheby's own publications.

The International Realty Company often collaborates with Sotheby's in London with joint sales of estates as, for instance, in the sale of Hever Castle in the UK in 1981, when the property was marketed by the Realty Company and the contents sold by the auction house in London.

Knight Frank & Rutley

Of the many worldwide activities of this firm, their operations in Australia, the Far East and Japan are of particular interest, if only because in Australia at least the involvement is very old, whilst the business in Japan has been made the special responsibility of a particularly active department of the London company.

The Baillieu interest in Australia, which now forms the basis of the Australian partnership of Baillieu Knight & Frank, was established in 1885, eleven years before the formation of the London partnership of Knight Frank & Rutley. Its sister firms in Singapore and Hong Kong, together with the developments of the Japanese department from London, now give to the Group experience and resources in wide areas of the Far East quite unmatched elsewhere.

This firm also has companies in New York (as KFR), Brussels and in Botswana, Zimbabwe and Nigeria – a total of 46 offices with 1400 personnel. As a matter of history, they are perhaps particularly proud of having handled the sale of the Crystal Palace built for the Great Exhibition of 1851, and of their very large land sales, which in their early days might, not unusually, total 250 000 acres per annum.

In more recent days, they handled the acquisition of the worldwide headquarters of BP, the largest single property deal in the UK. The New York office arranged the sale by Pan Am of the Intercontinental Hotel Group to Grand Metropolitan for over $5 million; whilst they also advised on the first two major UK property acquisitions by Japanese investors.

One final word on marketing. As a firm dependent for the success of their operations on a skilful and sensitive approach to marketing, it is not surprising to find the high quality of their general publications and literature. The promotional brochure of the Japanese Department, in particular, written half in Japanese, is an all too rare example of the use of language as an effective back-up for some particularly difficult marketing operations.

Europe

As we have seen above, British chartered surveyors have a long history of involvement in overseas property acquisitions and disposals in North

America, Japan, Australia, Hong Kong and in Africa. Property development in Europe was, however, very much a function of post-war reconstruction when many of the British building companies and development trusts secured very large contracts for domestic and industrial building, for retail establishments and infrastructural developments.

Brussels became a particular focus for the activities of British firms, as the city set itself out both to restore and refurbish its pre-war elegance, and to equip itself for the massive demand arising from its particular role in the European Community. New systems of urban communications replaced the old, if rather picturesque, tramway system. Massive buildings were erected or transformed for the Community institutions. Modern motorways flowed to the coast and to the major cities of Western Europe; whilst industrial and domestic development all aimed to keep pace with the demands of firms, factories, shops and individuals who found increasingly in Brussels either their places of work or a focus for their institutional, commercial and individual activities.

British chartered surveyors were very much to the fore both in seeking out opportunities and in deploying their professional skills for both British and foreign clients. Jones, Lang & Wootton, one of the two leading firms in international activities, Richard Evans, and Wetherall Green & Smith, were all to the fore in this phase of post-war development.

West Germany provided a special challenge, but also something of a snare and delusion for many professional firms. Its traditionally conservative property market was largely financed by the German institutions, if only because domestic legislation ruled out significant investment abroad. There was, therefore, plenty of money about – but also plenty of competition both from within Germany and also from abroad, particularly from Holland. The opportunities were clear enough, and a number of British property developers, attracted by high yields and lower costs, sought to take advantage of them. So, too, did the chartered surveyors mostly geared, however, to the fortunes of the British clients.

With the decline in the property values in 1973 (a decline less severe however in Germany than elsewhere), the attraction of the market began to ebb. Most of the British professional firms began to seek their fortunes elsewhere, and removed their presence from Germany; and in the end only two majors remained, Jones, Lang & Wootton with 50 employees spread between Frankfurt, Hamburg and Dusseldorf, and geared largely towards German institutions and domestic clients; whilst Wetheralls, with half the size of staff of Jones, Lang & Wootton, and largely concentrated in Frankfurt, continued developing investment opportunities for foreign, mostly British, clients.

Overseas surveyors worldwide

Out of all these various activities, it is calculated by the Royal Institution of Chartered Surveyors that the contributions of chartered surveyors to the balance of payments in 1986 was £110 million, made up from fees, commissions and other services. Their contribution to British overseas investment is, of course, very much greater than this; and it is on this figure, though largely unquantifiable, that the profession would like to have assessed its total contribution to the British economy.

5 Export houses

Within the annual statistics of invisible exports there appears a substantial figure for earnings from export houses. The figures have increased year by year from £90 million in 1975 to £350 million in 1986. The item covers the brokerage services covered by UK firms in respect of third country trade in goods other than commodities.

Estimates of the profits are based on national surveys carried out by the British Export Houses Association. The latest surveys analysed were in respect of 1977. A separate figure has, however, been given for commodity traders, including earnings from transactions in the commodities futures market. This figure shows a falling tendency and in 1986 was £233 million.

The absence of any up-to-date precise figures is not in itself surprising. The business is complex, embracing many types of activity and, moreover, one in which lines of demarcation between visible and invisible exports are by no means clear. On the other hand, the trade itself is highly significant with deep historical roots and involving large and powerful merchant companies operating in some of the UK's most important overseas markets.

Export houses normally pay cash in the UK to the suppliers and give credit to the buyers. Some export houses trade as principals others as agents. The most generally accepted definition of their roles and activities is listed by the BIEC in their booklet *Services of the City of London* (December 86, pp. 28–29). They are variously to be found as manufacturers' and buyers' agents, as factors, and even as export managers, often on an agency basis. They serve as confirming houses and as export finance houses. Their help is often called in to promote negotiation and execute counterpart trading and in forfaiting. Finally, they act as general merchants deploying, at a considerable profit to the balance of payments, the traditional trading skills and experience on which the UK has built up so much of tis reputation and commercial success in the widest fields of international trade.

Notes and references

General reference works on the City
The City Exchanges, the Services of the City of London, BIEC, revised 1986.

William M. Clarke, *How the City of London works*, Waterlow, London 1987

Coakley and Harris, *The City of Capital*, Basil Blackwell, Oxford 1983

Hamish McRae and Frances Cairncross, *Capital City, London as a Financial Centre*, Methuen London, revised edition, 1985

Sectoral references
1   Gold and silver bullion, Clarke, op. cit., pp. 87–93; McRae and Cairncross op. cit., pp. 190–192.
Gold and freight, *The Banker*, June 1985.

2   The London Metal Exchange, BIEC, op. cit, pp. 17–18.
Metals: *Financial Times Survey*, 7 October 1986.
'Metal Exchange – Trading 20,000 Contracts a Day', *Financial Times*, 9 June 1987.
'Defending the Heavyweight Title', *The Economist*, 26 July 1986.
Stefan Wagstaff, 'The Big Bang Change for LME', *Financial Times*, 30 May 1987.

3   For an account of tin litigation *see* law report by Paul McGrath, *The Independent*, 26 June 1987. Also 'Tin litigation, the UK's wrong priority', A. H. Herman, *Financial Times*, 7 May 1987.

4   McRae and Cairncross, *Capital City*, op. cit., pp. 193–216
'The commodities future market', *Bank of England Quarterly Bulletin*, June 1986.
Mark Cliffe, *The commodity prices and the world's economic recovery*, Capel Cure Myers Croom Helm, 1985
Michael Prest, 'No winners from commodity boom', *The Independent*, 6 August 1987
Robert Staines, 'Coffee planters spill the beans', *The Guardian*, October 1987
There are some interesting publications of the Chicago Mercantile Exchange, including *The Merc at work* and a description of trade and hedging with currency futures and options published 1985.
See also
Nicholas Hogg, *An introduction to options*, Gerrard and National Inter Commodities (SN1) May 1986.
Bifex Freight Futures Review, Issue 1, 1987.

5   Foreign Exchange
For details of the factors contributing to Zurich's importance as a centre for foreign exchange and particularly 'transferable sterling' *see* William M. Clarke, 'Inside the City. A guide to London as a financial centre', George Allen & Unwin, London, 2nd edition, 1983, pp. 183–5

McRae and Cairncross, *Capital City* op. cit., p. 92
'The market in foreign exchange in London', *Bank of England Quarterly Bulletin*, Vol 3, September 1986, pp. 379 ff.

David Lascelles, 'The Banks. Earnings continue to increase', *Financial Times Special report on Foreign Exchange*, 3 June 1987.

Janet Bush, 'Money brokers. Calm follows squeezed margins', *Financial Times Special Report*, 3 June 1987.

Phillip Coggan, 'Corporate Treasurers. Lobbying clout grows', *Financial Times Special Report*, 3 June 1987.

The Bank of England Quarterly Bulletin (as above) and compare Phillip Coggan 'Hedging Instruments. Corporations are changing', *Financial Times Special Report*, 3 June 1987.

6   Fine Art

Geraldine Norman, *The overseas earnings of the UK art market*, BIEC July 1983

Christie's International PLC, *Annual Report and Accounts*

Christie's – History and activities

How to buy and sell at Sotheby's

Professor John Wilton-Ely, *'A future for the past: Art history as our heritage'*, University of Hull, 1983

7   Real Estate

P. Cheesewright, 'The Lure of West Germany', *Financial Times*, February 1987

World service for Japan, Knight Frank & Rutley Japanese Department.

*The international service industries:
sectoral studies*

B: Transport, communications, travel
and tourism

6 By land, sea and air – international transport and telecommunications

Transport's vulnerability

For an international trading nation like Britain which exports a third of its production and imports the bulk of its raw materials, transport is one of the most vital service industries, as vital as finance and, like finance, itself a major exporting industry. Few service industries are quite as closely tied to the fortunes of manufacturing and to the state of world commodity prices. The failure of British manufacturing industry through most of the 1980s to recover output levels of the 1970s, particularly in the heavy engineering areas, exposed British international hauliers, whose reliance on the success of British exporters became manifest. And the severe fuel price rises of 1979–80 coupled with the recession left British Airways deep in the red. In 1980 European airlines (the twenty-one members of the Association of European Airlines) lost nearly $1 billion [1]. But no sector has so clearly shown its vulnerability to changing economic circumstances and has suffered such losses as British shipping, historically the nerve centre of Britain's trading existence. In 1975 there were 1614 UK-owned vessels of more than 500 gross registered tons on the national register. By the end of 1987 there were only 400 UK-registered ships. Indeed, when the Bank of England came to its gloomy conclusion in 1985 that British service industries were following a trend of relative decline commensurate with the decline of British manufacturing, it pointed to the negative balances incurred by shipping as arguably the largest single cause [2].

Yet if the transport sector is especially sensitive to external economic factors, it can also benefit. The huge trade in UK tourism, both inwards and outwards, has been a motor of prodigious growth over the last twenty years, with the charter airlines, the airports, the ferries and their seaports as the principal beneficiaries. And, as in almost all the sectors we are surveying, technology is a key element, contributing to rapid change both in the economics of the industries and in the skills required of those working in them.

Shipping – an enduring crisis

At the turn of this century Britain possessed a merchant fleet that dominated the world; it constituted half the world's registered tonnage. By 1965 it had decreased to 13 per cent of that tonnage [3], following a path not dissimilar to that of Britain's share of world trade. While it grew absolutely to a post-war peak of some 52 million deadweight tons (dwt) just a year after the first oil crisis in 1974, other fleets had grown still more rapidly and Britain's share had fallen to about 9 per cent [4]. By the end of 1986 it had sunk to under 2 per cent. The remaining five hundred or so registered ships of that time were to decrease still further in 1987, and deadweight tonnage was to slump to under 10 million tons, a fifth of the 1975 total. True, other fleets in Europe have suffered also. Norway's merchant marine diminished by 38 per cent in the eleven years 1975–86 (17.9 m dwt to 11.1 m dwt); France by 63 per cent (45.4 m dwt to 16.9 m dwt); the Federal Republic of Germany by 41 per cent (13.5 m dwt to 8.0 m dwt), and Sweden by 68 per cent (12.2 m dwt to 3.9 m dwt) [5]. But a diminution to one-fifth is by any comparison staggering.

What were the causes? The first was the inflation of the oil tanker market. The basic cheap fuel for the world's economic miracle in the late 1950s and the 1960s had of course been oil, with the West and the Far East heavily dependent on supplies from the Persian Gulf. Korea and Japan were offering tankers at highly competitive prices thanks to low labour costs, new building techniques and, as is often bitterly remarked in European shipbuilding circles, to substantial government subsidies. In the UK it seemed a particularly favourable time, in the early 1970s, to make purchases of supertankers, thanks also to a tax concession that allowed one year 100 per cent depreciation of capital costs on ships. In 1974 came the drastic rises in the price of oil, accompanied by the opening of the North Sea oilfields that employed marine pipelines, not vessels, for oil shipment. Further drastic oil price rises in 1979–80 induced the severest industrial recession since the 1930s. Oil trade volume fell 50 per cent between 1973 and 1984, yet because of the timelag between ordering and receiving ships, the world tonnage continued to grow until 1980. The abolition in the UK of the tax concession on depreciation in 1984, a most contentious issue, was a further blow but only an additional, and the Government could argue, a corrective, factor. British oil tanker tonnage had already fallen from 30 million dwt in 1975 to 11 million dwt in 1984. By the end of 1986 it was less than 6.7 million tons.

But the shrinking trade in ocean-borne oil, the long-term relative decline in the British merchant fleet, and latterly the reduction of fiscal support for capital purchases (to 25 per cent in the first year with a reducing balance over 8 years) were not the only factors at work. The world ship market had in any case been flooded by cheap vessels built in the Far East. The fleets of the Eastern Bloc continued to grow and offer their services too. Thus world freight prices did not increase even nominally from 1975 onwards. The unprofitable freight rates were themselves reinforced by the fall in world commodity prices in the 1980s. Iron ore, the second largest bulk cargo after oil, was also less in demand, thanks to decreasing steel production and greater use of scrap [6]. Moreover beyond these largest economic factors, there came drastic technological changes.

Containers have transformed the nature of dry cargo, non-bulk shipping (that is of cargo such as ore, coal or cereals that does not have to be in open-hold vessels and shipped in bulk). Containers can be driven straight on and off ferries (roll-on roll-off) and delivered from door to door on the same trailer or even by the same truck. This development was especially important for Britain, as her whole pattern of trade was in any case changing to a substantially European one, itself reducing the importance of deep-sea shipping, which had previously dominated in the heyday of Empire and Commonwealth trading. Moreover, the modern cellular container ship, which has already reached its fourth design generation in a quarter of a century, can carry as much as seven conventional ships and requires only a small crew as electronic controls take over more and more of the traditional seafaring tasks.

This fateful combination of factors has caused a number of major overseas shipping companies to go out of business, the most spectacular being in Hong Kong, Japan and the United States. Sanco had bought 135 new ships before insolvency. United States Lines ordered twelve new container ships, which had to be sold off at a third of their price of purchase, thus adding to the world's surplus of shipping tonnage. This continues to be as much as 30 per cent despite active scrapping. Competition is extreme and with freight rates set at base survival rates, every possible saving has to be made. So far no British shipping line has involuntarily gone out of business. Some companies, such as British & Commonwealth Shipping, have withdrawn from the industry alto-gether. Others, however, have resorted to what is known as flagging out, one of the most fiercely debated issues of all.

The relative cost of the crew per voyage compared to capital costs and voyage costs (fuel, harbour dues etc.) varies according to the type, size and age of the ship, but it will probably be in the range of 12–15 per cent. European crews have achieved through their unions substantially higher wages and salaries than crews from the Eastern Bloc or particu-larly the Far East – the Philippines or Korea. Furthermore, unions also lay down minimum manning numbers. By reregistering a ship (adopt-ing a flag of convenience) shipowners and operators can reduce crew costs significantly. It has been calculated, for example, that a 60 000 dwt bulk carrier manned by 29 Koreans compared with 28 Germans would reduce crew costs from 12 per cent of total costs per day to a mere 4 per cent [7]. Add to that savings possible in the number of the crew and a significant reduction in the back-up numbers, and the appeal in commercial terms is overwhelming [8]. In January 1986, BP transferred 29 of its tankers to registration in Gibraltar, the Bahamas and Bermuda. In 1987 Shell Tankers transferred a majority of its 40 tankers to the Isle of Man. Ocean Transport & Trading transferred eleven ships to an unnamed offshore register in March 1987. The truth is, of course, that the real decline of British-*owned* ships is not as great as the decline in the numbers still on the UK register. The Isle of Man accounts for more than 75 ships and in all there are some 235 British-owned ships on other registers, of which a fair proportion are registered with British dependent territories – Bermuda, the Cayman Islands, the Bahamas. The total tonnage registered off-shore now exceeds that registered in the UK! [9].

Flagging out has had two major and serious consequences. Firstly, the demand for British seafarers, particularly ratings, had fallen dramatically. Table 6.1 gives the statistics for the British officers and ratings working on ships registered in the UK. While British officers are still in demand on reregistered ships and foreign-owned ships, the requirement for seamen is at its lowest ever. The figures are worrying.

This drastic decline raises the second issue – the strategic implications. The Royal Navy and Britain's army have relied on the merchant marine in a vital support role at times of conflict – for the shipping of supplies, munitions, fuel, troops, and as hospital ships. It is now very doubtful that the fleet assembled at the time of the Falklands crisis could again be brought together. If it were possible, it could only be so with the co-operation of the off-shore registering territories, and foreign national crewmen might be involved [10]. Admittedly, this is not the concern of this book, but the drastic decline in British seafaring manpower is one of the most extreme changes in the whole of the international service sector. In December 1986 the Transport Minister announced three measures to arrest the slide – the creation of a Merchant Navy Reserve, possible assistance with training in excess of immediately required numbers and help with the cost of flying out relief crews. They are, however, no remedy, only a palliative.

Table 6.1   Numbers of seafarers on the General Council of British Shipping Register

	31 Dec 76	31 Dec 84	31 Dec 86
Officers	39 114	16 534	12 688
Ratings	34 812	19 795	17 223

Source: GCBS

Future prospects

The European Commission has shown great concern about the enduring crisis in shipping. The European Community fleet taken as a whole has fallen from over 32 per cent of the world's fleet in 1980 to 21.5 per cent in 1985 [11]. In that year the Commission issued a set of proposed regulations for liberalising maritime trade within the Common Market and for protecting shippers against unfair practices by countries outside the Community [12]. It was largely adopted in December 1986 and includes anti-dumping measures, the promise of co-ordinated action against countries unfairly squeezing Member State companies out of ocean cargo business, and perhaps most significantly of all, the un-impeded transport of cargo by ships of one Member State to and from any other Member State. Thus a British ship could sail from South-ampton, discharge cargo in Marseilles, reload and proceed to Athens, and so on. This applies from 31 December 1989. The same freedom extends to further voyages from an EC port to an outside country from the beginning of 1991. However, agreement could not be reached on allowing cargo to be carried from one port to a second along another Member State's coastline. This is known as 'cabotage' and Britain remains the exception in allowing free access to her own coastline without receiving the right for the same trade along the French, German and Danish coasts. [13]

Ferries

The agreements that have been reached, like the measures announced by the UK, are no panacea, but they could help to consolidate the situation. There are, additionally, areas of some buoyancy. The ferries of north-west Europe now carry as many as 23 million passengers a year, and two-thirds of those are travelling to and from Britain. Certainly the growth of the 1970s (14 m in 1975 to 21 m in 1980) has slowed down [14] but there are still increases recorded on the routes least affected by the Zeebrugge disaster of 1987 and the protracted industrial dispute with P & O Lines in 1988, particularly between south-west England and north-west France and those between Britain's east coast and Scan-dinavia. Both are, however, operated by foreign lines – Brittany Ferries of France and DFDS of Denmark.

Other services have suffered considerable difficulties in recent years. After the merger of Hoverlloyd's and Seaspeed's hovercraft operations there followed a management buy-out and in turn a takeover by British Ferries, a Bermuda-based company. But British Ferries is itself losing money on its Channel Island operations. Moreover, P & O's dramatic return to the ferry business, when it bought European Ferries to which it had sold Normandy Ferries only two years before, has been profoundly overshadowed by the worst British ferry accident since 1953, the capsizing of *The Herald of Free Enterprise*, a Townsend Thoresen vessel, minutes after sailing from Zeebrugge in March 1987. P & O had only taken over Townsend Thoresen a few days before! The bitter dispute with employees over new working conditions in 1988 added to this catalogue of woes.

But a still greater long-term threat is offered by the Channel Tunnel which will certainly cut deep into the trade on short-distance routes, particularly Dover–Calais and the Dover, Folkestone and Ramsgate routes to Boulogne, Dunkirk and Ostend, just at a time when Dover is being extended in a £75 million programme. North Sea and Brittany routes seem less likely to be affected, however.

Container trade

In the important container trade, all is not black. The UK's registered fleet included in 1985 some 7 per cent of the world's cellular container ships, a larger proportion than in any other category of vessel, while Overseas Containers Ltd (OCL) have been a particularly successful line despite the severity of competition. With P & O holding the majority of OCL shares, the company moved back into the Atlantic in 1986, working in partnership with the giant Australian company TNT [15]. The competition is formidable however. Against all odds, for example, the Taiwanese line, Evergreen has grown from tiny beginnings in the mid-1970s to the world's largest container shipping company. It offers round-the-world services in both directions and, it is reckoned, can make profit from routes which for others are unprofitable. Its 55 bright green ships, 150 000 similarly painted containers (which it manufactures in its own factory at the rate of one every 25 minutes) are a familiar sight in Europe's container ports and a striking symbol of the advent of the Far East as a leader in world shipping [16].

World over-capacity, fierce competition from low-cost, efficient Far Eastern lines, and the decline in British deep-sea trading have combined, then, to make the profitable survival of British-owned shipping lines dependent on uncovering specialist niches, such as ferry traffic, or cruising, and on flagging out. The effect on the balance of payments has, as indicated, been dramatic. For whilst the earnings of UK-owned and chartered ships together with payments in the UK by foreign ship-owners came to £3.5 billion in 1986, payments overseas by UK owners and direct to foreign lines was as high as £4.3 billion, a deficit of over £900 million. The bulk of this was accounted for by freight costs for imports into the UK. In 1980 the account had still been in surplus [17].

Britain's ports and associated services

It is inevitable that the transformations in the pattern of Britain's trade since the the 1950s away from the Commonwealth and other deep-sea destinations towards the Continent of Europe should have affected the prosperity and status of British ports. Equally significant has been the growing importance of European industry relative to Britain's. These profound changes have led to a serious reduction in the significance of the UK's traditional Atlantic ports, especially Liverpool and Bristol. Nationally this has been more than offset by increased North Sea and Channel trade with the Continent, and the winners have been ports in the triangle from Hull to Southampton. (In 1965 west coast ports handled 106 million tonnes, east coast 121 million tonnes, by 1984 the split was 99 million tonnes compared with 232 million tonnes) [18]. But this cannot hide the fact that the principal beneficiaries of the post-war era have been the ports of Antwerp, Rotterdam and Hamburg, which are linked by rail, road and inland waterways with Europe's industrial heartland (and in Hamburg's case with East Germany and Czechoslovakia). Indeed, these ports have not only benefited from the expansion of industry on the Continent: the Dutch and Belgian ports in particular have become major centres for the transhipment of goods destined for the UK.

Nevertheless, there are promising signs and considerable optimism. The nineteen ports owned by Associated British Ports, a private company formed from the denationalised British Transport Docks Board in 1983, and including Southampton, Swansea, Cardiff, Hull, Immingham and Grimsby have become highly profitable [19]. Southampton, which was badly affected by a strike in 1984, has been strong in the grain and in the car shipping trade. Jaguars and Range Rovers are exported from here and, while the penetration of the car market by foreign manufacturers is a major element in Britain's deficit in the visible trade balance, the port itself benefits as the importing centre for Fiat, Renault and Spanish-built Ford Fiestas.

Southampton is also one of Britain's more successful freeports, a harbour zone into which goods may be moved without payment of customs duty or import charges (though in Britain unlike elsewhere VAT is still charged!). Here, too, proximity to the Continent has been helpful, yet the leading British freeport is Liverpool with ten resident companies. The freeport system came into existence in 1984, since when it has had a chequered career. Prestwick has had to be closed. Other proposed freeports have not opened. The problem is largely location. Europe's largest freeport, Hamburg, not only serves the north German industrial area: the freeport acts as a transit shipment zone for Eastern Bloc countries (Czechoslovakia has its own docks in Hamburg, for example) and increasingly for Scandinavia. It has 1000 tenant companies and has created 20 000 jobs. Liverpool freeport, by contrast has generated 100 jobs.

Yet it is not location alone that accounts for the success of a port. In container traffic, for example, Southampton has lost first place to that most startlingly successful of all British ports, Felixstowe. Founded by an animal feed merchant, Gordon Parker, who was tired of the poor service he received elsewhere, Felixstowe has grown from a backwater to Britain's largest (and still expanding) container port. The secret was threefold: enthusiasm by a young management team, trouble-free labour relations and the latest, fastest technology. Even before its new Trinity terminal was opened in 1985, Felixstowe was handling over half a million containers and ten million tonnes of cargo per year. The new Loughborough-built cranes at the Trinity terminal are probably the world's fastest, handling a container a minute, while the port also claims to be the first in the world with double-deck, twin-lane ramps for roll-on, roll-off traffic. But the port's specialism is loading and unloading cellular container ships, as is evidenced by the fact that the renowned Evergreen Line uses Felixstowe as its British port, as do also other major lines such as the Japanese K line, Germany's Hapag-Lloyd and Britain's OCL. Significantly, Freightliners, the British Rail container subsidiary, has switched its earlier home at Harwich to Felixstowe.

Owned by P & O, who bought the port as part of the European Ferries operation, Felixstowe undoubtedly owes the rapidity of its expansion largely to its new approach to labour relations. With an effectively closed union shop, (96 per cent membership of the Transport and General Workers Union), the port's labour force has excellent, close relationships with management and a remarkable record of employment continuity. This is backed by a training programme that allows workers to move from one specialist function to another by offering them the chance to acquire new skills. The port works 24 hours a day throughout the year on a three-shift basis, ensuring any ship the fastest possible turn-round time.

Indeed this recipe of the latest technology combined with positive industrial relations has been so successful that a new subsidiary has been established to offer international port consultancy services. It has advised on establishing a container port at Mombasa, establishing a new port, Fujaireh, in the United Arab Emirates, and other projects in India, Thailand, China and elsewhere. It is a useful illustration of the cross-fertilisation between successful industrial expertise and selling the fruits of that knowledge as a export in itself, in this case a service industry that acts as the progenitor of another [20].

But that is nothing new in the long history of British shipping. It was the pre-eminence of the British fleet in the eighteenth and nineteenth centuries together with the first-hand information that this worldwide network brought, which inspired those unique City services, that we have already looked at, The Baltic Exchange, Lloyd's Register of Shipping and Lloyd's Loading List, itself a century old in 1986. The question remains, almost as a counterpart to the emergence of ventures such as the Port of Felixstowe International Ltd, whether the shrinking of the merchant marine will also have a negative effect on the ancillary network of professional services, including not only the Register but even the freight forwarding industry.

Land transport – new prospects for the railways?

As late as the 1950s rail was still the principal method of long-distance and international travel in Britain and on the Continent of Europe. The advent of the motor car as the basic mode of family travel, coupled with the post-war development of motorway networks, pioneered in the 1930s in Germany, and then emulated through most of Europe under the growing pressure of private passenger traffic and also commercial road haulage, transformed the railways increasingly into a specialist city-to-city service for businessmen over medium distances (of 150–300 miles). Today the railways are responsible for little more than a tenth of cross-border holiday travel on the Continent of Europe, for example, and hardly feature in UK-Continental holiday travel at all [21]. Indeed, there is so much concern in the EC for the future of international rail travel that in 1985 the Ministers of Transport drew up a programme of action to improve international services by reducing travel time, and eliminating delays at borders and avoiding unnecessary doubling up between national and local services. Further encouragement is also being given to young people's travel through improved inter-rail tickets [22].

The Channel Tunnel

A revival of international European rail services could, however, be in sight. France has already heavily invested in its high-speed train, the TGV (Train à Grande Vitesse), which travels at speeds of up to 250 mph on specially built tracks from Paris to Lille, Lyons and Berne (from May 1987). The success of this technology (and the final demise of the British tilting train designed to run on existing track) will almost certainly result in its forming the basis for the new train destined to run non-stop through the Channel Tunnel. For the Channel Tunnel is undoubtedly the greatest breakthrough for European, and especially British Rail travel this century. French Rail already plans an extension of the TGV network to the Tunnel [23], and while Britain intends no reconstruction of track the development of new bogie technology by Anglo-French and probably Belgian consortia will bring faster than ever through services from Scotland, as well as London Waterloo, to Paris, Brussels, Frankfurt and beyond.

In freight, where the Continental rail systems, thanks to their larger interconnected networks, have remained far more significant than in the UK, the Tunnel offers the first ever possibility of through freight express trains from the UK to the mainland of Europe. At the same time, Rail Freight International has invested in a new high-speed rail-ferry from Dover to Dunkirk, the advantage over road haulage being that a 10-wagon consignment which can carry the equivalent of 10 truckloads or more can arrive all at the same time [24]. Technology is also offering the possibility, through inventions such as the Finnish Tiphook wagon, of fast railway roll-on roll-off services for trailers [25]. It will be on the longer haul routes that rail, and particularly UK–Continental rail services, could stand to make a revival through such new technology. But whether British Rail will benefit will also continue to depend on the success of British manufacturing exports. At present, as Table 6.2 shows, there is a severe imbalance, with substantially more loaded wagons entering the UK than leaving it, and Britain using Continental wagons for return journeys because of their substantial surplus in numbers [26]. It is a further vivid illustration of the vulnerability of transport to manufacturing conditions, and especially the import penetration of British domestic markets.

The haulage industry also stands to benefit from the Channel Tunnel, allowing faster and more efficient access to Continental roads at a time when the EC intends to achieve a completely free internal market for services.

Eurotunnel, the private Anglo-French partnership floated as a joint venture in 1987 to build and to operate the Channel Tunnel until 2042, estimates that when it opens in 1993 the Tunnel will already carry 44 per cent of cross-Channel passenger traffic and 17 per cent of cross-Channel

Table 6.2   UK–Continent train ferry traffic 1970–1985

		1970	1979	1985
(a)	Thousand loaded units			
	IN	55	48	26
	OUT	29	15	12
	TOTAL	84	63	38
(b)	Thousand unloaded units			
	IN	3	2	2
	OUT	27	35	15
	TOTAL	30	37	17
(c)	Thousand tonnes of goods			
	IN	581	774	793
	OUT	258	300	407
	TOTAL	839	1075	1200

Sources: Annual Digest of Port Statistics (National Ports Council) British Railways Board.
Transport Studies Group, Polytechnic of Central London.

freight traffic. Furthermore, it seems likely that the existence of the Tunnel will itself generate new business and that freight traffic on trains and trucks carried on the shuttles through the Tunnel could more than double in volume by 2003 from the 60 million tonnes transported across the Channel in 1985. The railways in particular are expected to benefit as they come to account for 90 per cent of all passengers travelling without their own vehicles and some 30 per cent of present coach travellers. It is also thought that rail will capture some road freight traffic and a substantial percentage of container and new vehicle delivery traffic.

Road haulage – changes in view

Membership of the European Community has brought Britain an enormous increase of trade with the Continent of Europe, and most of that increased trade (with the exception of fuel and bulk cargoes) is handled by road hauliers, either by means of unaccompanied trailers or powered vehicles, crossing the sea on roll-on roll-off ferries. Yet, although exports carried by road and ferry from the UK to the EC increased from less than 3 million tonnes in 1975 to over 6 million tonnes in 1985, import tonnage rose dramatically from just over 4 million tonnes to nearly 12 million tonnes over the same ten years [27]. In the late 1970s British hauliers benefited from this growth in both directions and had reached, by 1980, a 58 per cent share of the market. But the relative strength of sterling in the early 1980s and the inexorably growing penetration of the British market by imports has reversed this position. By 1985 the share had fallen to 40 per cent. Indeed, despite the new opportunities which will result from the gradual liberalisation of the Community's markets that we shall discuss in a moment, the view of an authoritative Polytechnic of Central London report (prepared for the Chartered Institute of Transport and the Department of Transport) is that direction of trade and exchange rates will remain the principal factors determining the sector's success [28].

Nevertheless, the nature of European haulage will change as the regulations are loosened and it remains essential, if the British haulage industry is to be more than a domestic operation in a Community dominated by European giants, that it enters the new Continental market. At present international haulage movements are governed by quotas of bilateral permits allowing a company an agreed number of journeys per year between pairs of EC countries (with the UK as base for British hauliers and each new country entered requiring a further bilateral permit). There also exist, however, a restricted number of multilateral permits for individual vehicles, issued by the Commission through the Department of Transport, which allow further unlimited journeys to other Member States. The Commission had proposed effectively to go over to the multilateral system by 1992 with an unrestricted number of permits available on the basis not of a quota but of quality of service and safety and financial record. Only 25 per cent of trade would remain covered by bilateral permits.

Although the Council of Ministers had already been successfully taken to the European Court by the Commission in 1985 for not implementing a policy of freedom of services in international transport, it did not fully adopt the Commission's multilateral proposal until June 1988. Quotas on multilateral permits were retained, with increases in numbers until 1991. Cabotage, carriage of goods by a non-resident EC haulier between destinations within a second country, remains prohibited.

But the story will not end here. It is intended that by 1993 free access to the European haulage market will become a reality. Moreover, the year 1992 nearly coincides with the projected opening date of the Channel Tunnel. Whilst this is, of course, a rail link and, as we argued, will strengthen the hand of rail freight operations as well as UK–Continental inter-city passenger services, it is also designed as a vehicle roll-on roll-off system. Potentially the volume of freight carried by road between the UK (especially the Midlands and London) and the Continent must stand to increase absolutely.

New challenges to haulage services

Liberalisation of European services and the prospect of the Channel Tunnel are not the only factors influencing the future of the haulage industry. The UK is arguably the European leader in retailing. Its pre-eminence owes much to retail management's rapid recognition of how information technology could not only keep instant account of stock levels but also the flow of goods from factory and wholesale outlet to the shops. Some major chains developed their own custom-built distribution systems. Others turned to specialist transport companies offering a complete package from transport itself to warehousing and inventory management. Physical distribution management (PDM) has emerged as a branch of management in its own right with a professional institute. Indeed, general haulage has declined relative to these new comprehensive services. This trend has been reinforced by the adoption by more and more manufacturers of a technique pioneered by Toyota in the 1950s – 'Just in Time' manufacturing – which involves holding stock for no more than a few hours' requirements and a constant steady flow of components and materials to the factory. This reduces the need for warehousing and releases capital. But 'Just in Time' can only function where there are systems of ultra-efficient distribution. Nor is it surprising that importers and buyers look increasingly favourably, under these conditions, at delivered pricing rather than ex-works, the traditional British practice [29].

As yet the application of these new approaches to the UK's international haulage industry is in its infancy, with general haulage still dominating. But the American example of integrated express freight services such as those offered by Federal Express or Emery is catching on. Federal Express itself is entering Britain. It is a formidable prospect. In the US, the company which started in 1973, now has 53 per cent of the American express freight market and a turnover of $3 billion [30]. Carriers such as Elan International and TNT, which undertake the whole operation: forwarding, brokerage and customs clearance as well as transport, are also appearing. Moreover the transport will be of the appropriate kind whether road or express air in the company's own road fleet or aircraft. Already the express sector is worth $2 billion in Europe alone.

The future may well belong to such companies offering a comprehensively priced, rapid door-to-door service. As transnational manufacturing grows, particularly within Europe, the need for such services, especially where 'Just in Time' techniques are used, will be compelling. And the growing sophistication of retail systems will further enhance the trend, especially as more internationally owned chains are established.

At the same time, traditional hauliers will find other openings in cross-trading between member countries as the EC multilateral permit scheme gains ground. That will require better foreign market intelligence and an increased role for the professional associations as sources of this information, as the report prepared for the Chartered Institute of Transport argues. The report goes on to stress the need for local Continental offices and for personnel including drivers, operations managers and secretarial staff who can speak the languages of the European Community.

In conclusion, the British international haulage industry faces a time of considerable readjustment. Much will depend on its ability to manage integrated forwarding and transport services, by a variety of modes, across countries with differing languages and using the latest computerised information services. It is a major challenge to management, demanding retraining and recruitment of new talent. But the success of distribution management in the domestic retail market is a sign that the industry can respond and perhaps regain its lost share of UK-European trade.

Air transport – expansion without profit

Air transport is as vulnerable to changing economic circumstances as shipping and road and rail transport. Since the Second World War the whole European air transport industry, including the British, has had to cope with a sequence of new and challenging factors: the emergence of mass traffic, rapidly changing technology, the two oil crises, a steep increase in interest rates in the early 1980s, and just as a period of consolidation was reached in 1986, a severe decline in North Atlantic travel thanks to the Libya bombing and the nuclear disaster at Chernobyl which frightened away a substantial number of American tourists. Moreover, technological change in the airline industry means a commitment to the purchase of new fleets probably before the existing aircraft have reached the end of their economic life and often at a time when the financial resources are not adequate. Falling fuel prices in the mid-1980s further complicated the calculations of when it is prudent to commit capital to more economical aircraft. As a result, European airlines have rarely earned more than 5 per cent net profit in a year, the last time being in 1985, while in the early 1980s they sustained heavy losses [31]. Nevertheless, in the post-war period no airline belonging to the Association of European Airlines has failed. This is partly explained by the sustained growth in passenger numbers and in freight. Yet even with forecasts by the IATA (International Air Transport Association) of a 7 per cent increase in traffic per year in the late 1980s, the Association does not see the finance yet available for the over $200 billion that may be needed by the mid-1990s to replace ageing fleets and purchase extra aircraft [32]. It is against this background that we have to understand the nervousness of many European airlines and governments towards the liberalisation of air services demanded by the European Commission as part of its drive (which we referred to in Chapter 2, pp. 37, 40 and discussed in detail below) for a free internal market in transport services by 1992.

The pattern of the airline industry in the UK and Europe

Of the 48 per cent of world passenger traffic that is international, European airlines have a far greater share than American (in 1984, 35 per cent compared with 22 per cent for the US). While the North Atlantic route is the world's most important, and accounts for 28 per cent of international passenger trade, the European airlines have, in total, access to more of the other major routes, within Europe itself, and those from Europe to the Far East, to Australia and New Zealand and to the Middle East. In terms of international traffic, British Airways is the world's largest airline, the bulk of the great American airlines' trade lying in their domestic operations. The other major European airlines in the world's top ten for international traffic are Air France (in 1985-5th), Lufthansa (6th), KLM (7th), Iberia (9th) and Alitalia (10th in 1985) [33].

But the European industry, and the British in particular, differs from the American in another aspect. Scheduled traffic accounts in Europe and in the UK for less than half of the total volume of trade, indeed in the EC since the accession of Spain and Portugal for only one-third [34]. The European air charter industry is the world's largest and within this pattern the UK predominates. By far the heaviest trade derives from the holiday traffic between the UK, West Germany and other north European countries and Spain. The other major destinations in this largely north–south traffic are Greece, Italy and Portugal. In contrast to the highly regulated nature of scheduled traffic, the charter industry is subject to few controls, except, of course, those concerning safety. In particular it is free from the restrictions on fare-pricing and on relative shares of capacity on routes, negotiation points which form the heart of the bilateral agreements governing scheduled flights.

The growth of charter flights has been prodigious; in the late 1960s it grew twelvefold based on the inclusive tour package of flight, hotel and often meals offered by the major tour operators. When, in the UK, the Civil Aviation Authority took over responsibility for licensing in 1972, it effectively abandoned economic controls and today the UK's charter market is twice as large as the next greatest, West Germany. True, the dominance of the UK is partly determined by Britain's island location. In Britain, air travel is more important for holidays abroad than the private car. On the Continent of Europe the car is still the preferred mode of travel. But we should not underestimate the influence of the tour operators (through the retail travel agent network) on the pattern of holiday-making and their ability from the 1960s to make the package tour the very epitome of mass tourist trade.

Today there are more charter airlines in Europe than there are scheduled carriers. The largest is the UK's Britannia Airways, which carries as many passengers as KLM and flies as many passenger kilometres as British Caledonian. It is owned by Thomson Holidays. The next largest is the British independent operator, Dan-Air, followed by West Germany's Hapag-Lloyd, also a tour operator. In addition, Air Europe (14th largest in Europe) is owned by ILG (International Leisure Group) and Orion (15th largest) by Horizon. The major scheduled airlines also have very substantial interests in the charter sector, however. Europe's fourth largest, Condor, is owned by Lufthansa, the fifth largest, British Airtours by British Airways, the sixth Aviaco by Iberia. As can be imagined, the competition is fierce. Recent years have seen unprecedented price-cutting and attempts by the big tour operators in particular to gain market shares at the expense of profitability. At the same time, the charter airlines are moving to larger, newer aircraft such as the Boeing 757 and even to wide-bodied aircraft such as the Airbus (A300B4), increasing capacity. There can be few clearer illustrations of the impact of tourism on air transport as a concomitant service and of one service industry generating growth in another.

The prospect of European liberalisation

Few subjects are as hotly contested in the European Community as the Commission's proposals for a gradual liberalisation of scheduled air services within Europe by 1992. But for all the debate it must be remembered, as we have now seen, that the scheduled industry accounts for less than half Europe's passenger traffic. It is thus true to say that Europe's, and especially the UK's, air industry is already substantially deregulated. Nevertheless there are still good reasons for the debate: scheduled flights account for most business travel and are therefore of key importance to the efficiency of industry and commerce. Furthermore, we have seen the financial fragility of the airlines and their exposure to rapid economic and technological change. And naturally the third factor to be considered is national interest. Unlike the United States of America, the European Community consists of twelve sovereign states, and their airlines, despite moves towards privatisation, such as that of British Airways in 1987, are still substantially in the ownership of governments.

Comparing fares between, say, domestic US flights and European flights is extremely complex. The nub of complaints by business travellers is that one pays significantly more per mile for flying in Europe than in the US. For example, a single fare in 1986 from London to Stockholm cost £174 (908 miles) but from Los Angeles to Seattle (957 miles) only £67. It is possible to fly more cheaply across the Atlantic with one of the new airlines such as Virgin Atlantic or People Express than to many international European destinations. But, for these comparisons to make sense one has to take into account possible discount tickets which may substantially reduce the relative cost. Furthermore, European airlines can properly claim that their shorter average flights and lower traffic densities make overall operating costs higher than for operators in the US. Nevertheless, the Economist Intelligence Unit has calculated that even if airlines in Europe were to make no further economies, they still have a margin of 15–20 per cent on fares that could reasonably be discounted [35]. Proponents of change argue that lower fares increase traffic; they point for example to the rise in passenger traffic between London and Amsterdam since 1984 following bilateral agreement between the UK and Netherlands to remove restrictions on fares, capacity and the number of airlines able to fly the routes [36].

There was an initial surge of 11.4 per cent growth for 1983–84 traffic, while in 1984–85 this growth was sustained at 10.6 per cent [37]. Moreover, there are now seven carriers to choose from instead of four.

What the European Commission has in mind, is, however, not simply a better deal for travellers by creating circumstances in which fares can be lower and there is a greater choice of carriers and flight, but it is also looking to the matter of principle, the principle of freedom to supply services.

In April 1986 the European Court decided in favour of a French tour operator, Nouvelles Frontières, which had been illegally discounting air tickets to its clients. The Commission then wrote letters to ten carriers warning them that their arrangements for fixing tariffs and pooling services and revenues were contrary to Community competition rules. In 1987, proceedings were continued against three of them, Lufthansa, Alitalia and Olympic Airways. At the same time the Commission put to the Council of Ministers its Air Transport Package. This aimed at four areas. Firstly, fares must be related to the demonstrable costs of individual airlines, while there should be automatic government approval of zones for promotional fares. Secondly, there should be a gradual relaxation of capacity sharing between carriers in bilateral agreements from a rigid 50–50 to 60–40 over three years. Thirdly, there should be greater flexibility for regional air services between minor airports of different member states and between those airports and the major transit airports (or 'hubs'). (Regional carriers are defined as carriers utilising aircraft with 70 seats or less, though some airlines, like Lufthansa would argue for a reduction in the definition to 50). As an additional component in this third area, 'market access', the Commission also wants to see regional carriers allowed to take passengers between second and third countries provided this is an extension of a present network (the so-called 'fifth freedom of the air'). Finally, the Commission seeks to establish clear procedures for the application of EC competition rules in the air transport sector.

It is an evolutionary package, not revolutionary. Its thrust is to make the existing pattern of bilateral agreement more flexible, to loosen regulations not to end them. Nevertheless, as a result of Spain's objecting to Britain using what it claims is non-ceded territory in operating the Gibraltar Airport as what would effectively be a UK airport, agreement could not be reached on the package by the Council of Ministers in June 1987. As the European Single Act came into force in 1 July 1987, the package was lost and had to be resubmitted under the new rules. This meant that unanimity would no longer be required on the Council when it came forward, but either Spain or Britain could still take advantage of the so-called Luxembourg Compromise (whereby it will be recalled from Chapter 2, there is a tacit agreement for other members not to press for a directive if one member's 'vital interests' are said to be affected). In the event, however, agreement was reached: the airport will have both an exit to Gibraltar and a direct exit to Spain. Given the general uncertainty of the scheduled industry, however, the Commission's evolutionary approach, which it intends to take further from 1990, is probably the only feasible one [38]. What is certain is that airlines and Commission alike want to avoid the kind of deregulation that occurred after 1978 in the United States [38].

There is little agreement about the net beneficiaries of the complete deregulation of the American air market that took place in 1978. Certainly, fares were reduced and more carriers competed for the profitable routes. Many new regional carriers emerged. But fare increases were largely achieved as part of a series of price-cutting wars, resulting in a marked instability of tariffs and great disparities between the routes. Indeed some routes of similar lengths cost up to four times as much as others, while average decreases in prices were in fact less after deregulation than before when prices per mile were already falling [39]. New efficient airlines such as People Express have appeared. A number of others, including spectacularly Braniff ('The Big Orange'), have gone bankrupt. Major airlines such as TWA and Pan Am are fighting financial crisis and radically restructuring. In this bitter process a small number of mega-carriers are emerging, surviving by buying up regional lines, establishing route networks based on their headquarters as 'hubs' which feed out and in from the regions and other major airports as 'spokes'. Most successful at this technique has been American Airlines. United have also grown by buying, for example, the ailing Pan Am's Pacific routes. Northwest Orient responded by buying Republic; TWA has slimmed down by the sale of half its computerised reservation system and then bought Ozark. Texas Air, now the US's largest airline, bailed out its subsidiary Continental, purchased a controlling interest in Eastern Airlines, then bought out People Express. As owner also of New York Air, it tripled its size in a year. Thus, unbridled competition in the USA has resulted in the concentration of the industry into an effective oligopoly and it is doubtful whether the consumer will in fact be the long-term beneficiary.

It is feared that if such deregulation were introduced into Europe a number of national airlines would disappear in a similar process of concentration, while special European circumstances would make the financial standing even of the surviving airlines shaky. For in Europe there is direct competition from road and high-speed rail, the high density markets already belong to the charter airlines, costs are higher because of shorter-haul flights and there would be competition from the emergent American mega-carriers [40]. Liberalisation or not, precisely these arguments were used to justify British Airways' purchase of British Caledonian (the rival that was long vaunted in political circles as an example of the open UK air market), with the intention of creating

Europe's first mega-carrier. For even BA and B Cal combined are smaller than any of the US's seven giant airlines and less than a quarter of the size of Texas Air.

Future trends

Whatever happens in the Commission's long-term battle with the airlines, there will inevitably be pressure on the operators to try to achieve economies of scale by mergers. A hub-and-spoke system is already establishing itself in Europe with London and Frankfurt as the principal rivals in the battle to be the dominant European hub for intercontinental flights. Clearly, the size of the major airlines' operations at such a hub and the availability of frequent interconnecting flights to other European centres, the spokes, will determine the rivals' relative success. Again, this is a pointer towards concentration rather than diversification. Even where regional airlines find a niche in new routes from a minor airport, the big carriers may still have an interest in eventually purchasing them. Perhaps the most obvious case is the new London City Stolport, the brainchild of Brymon Airways of Plymouth. Brymon Airways now have to share the new short runway airport, which is only twenty minutes from the City, with Eurocity Express, a subsidiary of British Midland Airways, itself now the major rival to British Airways on the England to Scotland and Northern ireland routes.

Another development which could be of great consequence, blurring the distinction between scheduled and charter flights and thus altering the established pattern, is the growth of single-seat charter offers. We saw that the charter market developed with the package tour. Charter airlines are now beginning to offer seat-only reservations. The dividing-line between the business traveller and the holiday-maker may disappear. At the same time it is a development that could be a threat to the inclusive tour, since many more experienced travellers may prefer to make their own accommodation arrangements.

Any future upheavals should, however, be set against a background of expected continued growth both in business travel, especially as transnational European and international industrial collaboration grows, and in the tourist market. Both are expected by the Economist Intelligence Unit to exceed the growth of GNP (at 3 per cent) with increases of 7.8 per cent for business travel and upwards of 5 per cent for tourism-charter flights into the 1990s. This will provide a welcome cushioning as change occurs through liberalisation, seat-only chartering, and ever fiercer competition from the US mega-carriers. When the EC arrangements for a free market in air transport have finally been implemented in the 1990s, the time will have come for serious

European-US airline negotiations, with both sides seeking to break into the other's hub-and-spoke networks and especially their computerised reservation systems. At present in the US these systems would exclude a European competitor as effectively as any external regulations.

Air freight

We saw earlier in the chapter that express freight is becoming an increasingly prominent feature of distribution networks as new 'Just-in-Time' manufacturing techniques and greater efficiency demand fast reliable delivery of materials and components. Increasingly the express freight companies are turning to air transport as part of a fast integrated service. Already overseas companies are becoming a dominant force. The American firm, Emery Worldwide, is based on a hub at Maastricht with a truck network operating from the airport. Packages can be delivered within a day across Europe. Federal Express has chosen Brussels as its hub, while United Parcel Services, the world's largest parcel freight company, is based at Cologne. From the British side, Red Star now has nightly air services from Southend to Brussels, Basle and Copenhagen. Securicor have flights from Birmingham to Brussels and Nuremburg [41]. DHL has opened a £13.5 million headquarters and sorting office at Heathrow.

As with passenger travel there is much at stake in terms of ground staff employment when it comes to the choice of hub. The British Airports Authority set up a Cargo Task Force to promote Heathrow, Gatwick and Stansted as international gateways both within Europe and for Japanese and American trade. In 1985–86 London, with a throughput of 697 000 metric tonnes, regained second position in Europe behind Frankfurt at 767 000 tonnes but first ahead of Paris at 694 400 [42]. It will be a tough battle. The UK's island position puts it at a disadvantage for instant distribution by road or rail to Continental destinations. Moreover, Frankfurt, which in 1982 already had in the Lufthansa cargo centre the world's largest and highest performance handling facility, completed an expansion in 1986 that doubled storage capacity, while the handling facilities are being improved in parallel to enable this centre alone to handle 800 000 tonnes a year. It is in this context that the Channel Tunnel may become particularly significant for the UK by providing a direct and rapid rail and truck link to the mainland of Europe, especially to northern France and the Benelux countries.

Airports

In concluding this section we look at the airports that are themselves, as can be seen from the example of air freight, major industries. Indeed, it was as such that the British Airports Authority was launched as a private company with a market capitalisation of £1.25 billion in July 1987.

Airports above all have been the beneficiaries of the sustained growth in air passenger and freight over the past forty years. For they are more than landing strips, servicing airlines and their aircraft. The passengers themselves are customers, purchasing duty-free goods, eating in restaurants and drinking at bars. The airports are effectively giant hotel chains but without overnight facilities (these of course being provided by the major hotel chains in close vicinity). Indeed, the profitability of an airport depends to a substantial extent precisely on this passenger consumption side. When BAA was floated in 1987, much of the discussion of its future profitability centred not on the growth of passenger numbers but on the issue of duty-free sales. For it is possible that with the completion of the European internal market, duty-free concessions between members of the EC will be scrapped. This would be a serious blow to British and European airports alike, but until such time, the major debate in the UK centres on how much airport expansion there should be and where.

Heathrow, now with four terminals, already handled in 1986–87 31.7 million passengers, of which 26.1 million were on international flights. It is thus the world's busiest international airport. Gatwick, another BAA airport, reached 16.6 million passengers in the same year. Here the second, North Terminal has raised capacity from 16 million to 25 million. It is already the world's third largest airport in terms of numbers of international passengers. And the UK Government has given the go-ahead to Stansted to be the third major London airport (also part of BAA) with a handling capacity of 7.8 million, rising possibly to 15 million. Luton, owned by the local authority, has a capacity of 3.5 million and is expected to have this increased to 5 million [43]. Then there is the most innovatory of London's airports, the City Airport or STOLPORT (Short Take-Off and Landing Port) which Mowlem and the Docklands Development Corporation have built in conjunction with Brymon Airways from a former wharf in London's disused dockland area. With construction at Canary Wharf developing apace as a much-needed extension of the City's financial service facilities and, with the completion of a light railway connecting the docklands direct to the City, this new airport will be extremely attractive to businessmen for flights to and from destinations such as Paris, Brussels and Amsterdam. Using de Havilland Dash 7 aircraft, the travel time from the Continent to the City has been significantly reduced. If permission were obtained for the use of British Aerospace 146–200 planes, then the network could be extended to Copenhagen, Milan, Frankfurt, Zurich and even Madrid [44]. The capacity of Stolport is intended to be about one million passengers per year. As yet, however, the airport is not connected to the Docklands Light Railway and passengers from the City have to rely on cars or taxis.

Yet projections are such that even this expansion may not be enough. Other airports outside BAA ownership should stand to gain. These include Southend and Southampton (Eastleigh). Nor does this expansion necessarily mean a reinforcement of the so-called North-South divide in Britain. Certainly London and the South-East seem set to be the centre of growth in business and tourist traffic. But the experience of Manchester Airport, since 1987 a public limited company, shows how the regions can benefit from air transport. Manchester is now Europe's fastest growing airport. In 1986 it handled 7.6 million passengers, 24 per cent more than in 1985. Construction of a new terminal and hotel and conference facilities are in hand. Manchester and other provincial airports particularly stand to benefit from regional airline development and new routes. Thirty-two new services came on stream in 1986 with new destinations such as Calgary, Edmonton, Hamburg, Lourdes, Vancouver and Hanover. Interestingly, in view of the analysis earlier in this chapter, Air 2000, a charter subsidiary of the UK's sixth largest route operator Owners Abroad, has chosen Manchester as its base. Moreover, Manchester also is a booming centre for the express freight business, with the volume of cargo (excluding rail) up by 75 per cent from 1985 to 1986.

Airports are, of course, important centres of local employment. In their proximity new industry also tends to grow, attracted by rapid access for business travel and cargo alike. While it remains to be seen whether a privatised BAA will be able to duplicate success stories such as Manchester at Prestwick, Glasgow and Edinburgh, there can be little doubt that as an employer the airport is one of the best possibilities for growth, even in areas of relatively high unemployment. How British airports will fare relative to their more centrally located competitors in France, the Benelux countries and central West Germany is an open question.

We have seen that in Europe, as in the USA, a system of hubs and spokes is evolving, with transit passengers as a major source of income for the airports. Certainly, Heathrow is already well established as one of Europe's major hubs. Some 23 per cent of its passengers use it as a transit centre for flying on to over 200 further destinations. Gatwick with 10 per cent transit passengers and 50 further destinations is less well developed but is arguably part of a London hub. Amsterdam is, however, a significant rival, benefiting from a liberal air transport regime, and centrally placed for the major industrial destinations in north Europe. Indeed, it has been suggested that Amsterdam is making some inroads on London as Europe's biggest hub. A key factor in deciding the future both of airports and airlines will, of course, be the progress made by the European Commission in liberalising air transport services. If mega-carriers emerge as in the USA, then British Airways is probably better placed even than Lufthansa. Heathrow, and perhaps Frankfurt, will then stand to be the major beneficiaries rather than Amsterdam.

Telecommunications

Communications are, and always have been, the nerve centre of trade. Today's high-tech manufacturing is located along motorway networks or beside airports. But rapidly the nerve centre of industry, and especially service industries, is switching in its major dependence away from physical communications to electronic communications. Telecommunications are becoming an enabling mechanism for what has been called the second industrial revolution or what we shall call, later in the book, the cerebral revolution. The cerebral revolution is the transformation of modern economies into wealth-creating systems based less on direct physical factors than on knowledge and information. The Green Paper on telecommunications published by the European Commission in June 1987 puts the point thus:

'The quality – both technical and organisational – of telecommunications will be crucial for future economic growth since it determines the capacity of the economy to generate, and to use efficiently, the *single most important factor of modern "production": knowledge*. The geographic organisation of the infrastructure will strongly influence, just like the nineteenth-century railways, the economic, social and cultural space of tomorrow.

By providing the *conduit* for the enhanced exchange of information and for enhanced information services, the merger of EDP (Electronic Data Processing) and telecommunications will play the role in the field of knowledge and intelligence that was formerly played by energy in the physical enhancement of human strength'. [45]

The key technical development which led to the transformation of what were our familiar telephone and telegraph systems was the convergence of advances in computing for the electronic processing of data with breakthroughs in telecommunications technologies. These were the creation of satellite telephony and the invention of optical fibres.

The enormous initial advantage of satellite transmission was that the system obviated the need for elaborate land connections via copper cable or microwave radio towers and repeater stations. The majority of transatlantic telephone calls are now transmitted via satellites stationed some 23 000 miles above the Earth's surface and received on microwave dishes on the other side of the ocean. In 1964 an international monopoly of satellite transmission and broadcasting was established to avoid unnecessary competition and to create some order in space. Intelsat, a consortium owned by 146 countries and based in Washington, will supply links to any country for a standard annual charge. At present some 75 per cent of all international telephone calls are routed via Intelsat.

But the other major breakthrough, optical fibre technology, provides fierce new competition. Optical fibres transfer signals not in electrical wave form (or as analogue signals) but as light pulses. This requires the signals to be converted into digital form which can be read by computers. Once converted and transmitted over digital networks they are not subject to distortion or interference. Likewise, telephone exchanges, once changed to digital switching, can handle far higher capacities. Moreover, optical fibres can carry prodigious quantities of signal both in terms of speed (565 m bits – or digits – per second) and numbers of signal streams simultaneously. The same fibre could carry several telephone conversations, digitalised videotext and computer data at the same time. In the USA's deregulated telecommunications market AT&T had in 1987 a 95 per cent digitalised switching system and had already laid 20 000 miles of optical fibre. MCI, one of the two other major long-distance telephone companies in the US to have emerged from the deregulation scramble since 1 January 1984, had 23 000 miles of optical fibre. At $86 000 per mile installation costs, this competition could prove ruinous. For what worries the big telephone companies in the US, and increasingly in Europe too, is the emergence of private networks owned particularly by major multinationals, such as General Motors, Boeing, Unilever and Xerox, who will soon be able to rent out excess capacity. At the same time Intelsat sees its future threatened both by private satellite networks but especially from trans-oceanic optical fibre cables. AT&T, British Telecom, and the French DGI (Direction Générale des Télécommunications) are building a transatlantic cable. KDD of Japan is building a trans-Pacific one while the British company Cable & Wireless and another Japanese consortium expect to receive licences to build further cables across the Pacific.

On the economic level there is, then, already considerable excess world capacity, while the enormous installation costs of the new equipment lead to huge initial costs that can only slowly be recouped. While the great advantage of the new digital equipment is that maintenance costs are very low and the hardware has an exceptionally long life, it will be years before the investment can be paid off by the subscribers' usage of the networks. That in itself works against an effective open market, as has been seen in the world's major liberalised telecommunications market, the USA. While local services previously run by giant AT&T have been broken up into seven regional Bell companies (or 'Baby Bells'), long-distance calls are in the hands of only three companies AT&T, MCI and a third, US Sprint (formed after liberalisation as a merger between subsidiaries of GTE and United Technologies) [46].

Set against this background it is hardly surprising that progress towards liberalisation in Europe has been slow. Individual governments have been reluctant to abandon their national telecommunications monopolies, not merely for reasons of sovereignty. Here perhaps more than in any other service industry there are the closest links with manufacturing. Most of the European telephone companies (as indeed the American AT&T) own manufacturing subsidiaries who then have, or had, an effective monopoly over the supply of equipment specially built to suit the particular specifications of the national system. The UK is one of the pioneers in liberalisation both in opening up the equipment market for subscribers and in requiring open tenders for national hardware.

The UK is also the only member of the EC so far to have partly privatised its telecommunications network by selling 49 per cent of British Telecommunications to the public and giving access to the national network to a private company – Mercury Communications Ltd, which from 1988 is also to provide public call boxes additional to those of British Telecom. Certainly, some advances have been achieved more generally in the EC. The European Commission has succeeded in persuading Member States to relax their procurement policies so that up to 10 per cent of purchases must be put out to open tender. Agreement has also been reached that equipment approved in one Member State can be used in another.

Further, a major advantage has been achieved in agreeing to set up a pan-European cellular mobile telephone service by 1991. Thirteen European countries signed an agreement in May 1987 to link these telephones internationally, which at present is impossible. It is a market that could be worth £600 million per year. Two major consortia are already beginning to emerge to develop the necessary digital technology, which could lead the world technically. One could involve the UK's joint venture, Orbitel (Racal and Plessey) with Ericsson of Sweden, and perhaps Siemens and the French CGCT. Another grouping is based on Alcatel of France, British Telecom and the US leader in analogue cellular technology, Motorola. [47]

These developments themselves illustrate the purpose and yet the great irony underlying the policy of liberalisation and telecommunications unification so eloquently advocated by the European commission in its June 1987 Green Paper. Let us take the purpose first.

It is an unassailable fact that telecommunications are the channel for the transmission of the information on which modern industry in both the manufacturing and service sectors increasingly depends. We have already touched upon many vital examples in our analysis of change above – global trading in securities, home banking, EFTPOS, financial, shipping and other information services, airline reservation systems. It does not stop there, however. Electronic mail and facsimile machines are making rapid inroads on conventional postal services, which seem to grow slower even as technology advances. Integrated Services Digital Networks (ISDNs) which will adhere to standardised equipment specification will come to replace the proliferating multiplicity of voice, and increasingly, image systems. Figure 6.1 illustrates the enormous expansion of telecommunications possibilities that have occurred this century and are expected to continue into the next, enhancing both business and domestic life. It is hardly surprising that the volume of international telecommunications traffic is expanding rapidly, indeed far more rapidly than national economies or international trade. At the same time the cost is coming down [48]. As the knowledge content of manufacturing increases, as international service industries rely more and more on information transfer and companies of all kinds assume international patterns of ownership and organisation, we can have no doubt that telecommunications do indeed constitute the latter-day railways of a new industrial epoch. If the European Community is to realise its potential as the largest home market in the capitalist world, it is essential, as the Green Paper argues, that European telecommunications should be liberalised and standardised.

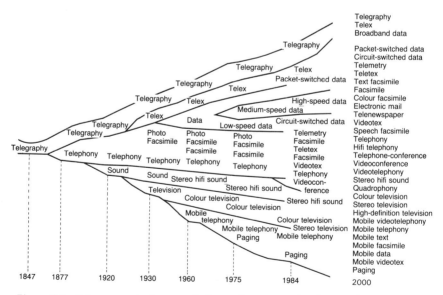

Figure 6.1   Telecommunications: evolution and prospects for the year 2000. (Source: European Commission Green Paper on Telecommunications, June 1987)

But the irony of the situation is this. Europe's present nationally fragmented system has led to the existence of eight major telecommunications manufacturing companies, each with its own relatively small market. The realignment, through European-wide consortia, that is occurring, thanks to the creation of the European digital cellular telephone system, points the way that the industry is almost certain to take as liberalisation of procurement and harmonisation of system take place. For what the Community requires in order to compete with American giants like AT&T, Canada's Northern Telecom or Sweden's highly successful LM Ericsson, are not more competing companies, but fewer with correspondingly larger research budgets. The British companies like Plessey and Racal are already relatively small, particularly as Alcatel of France has merged with American ITT (forming the world's second largest telecommunications manufacturer) and Siemens has bought the European operations of the US company, GTE.

Thus we see sluggish movement towards the opening up of the networks themselves with only France, through new laws in 1986 and 1987, following the route towards competition mapped out by the UK in 1984. Other states such as the Netherlands, Belgium and Spain are granting their national companies greater commercial autonomy, but not breaking the monopoly. Indeed, the report presented in Autumn 1987 to the Federal German Government on the deregulation of the postal and telecommunications system run by the Bundespost, recommended that German Telekom should effectively keep its monopolies for the network itself and for the telephone system. The European future seems to point, then, more in the direction of standardised equipment, as in the example of digital cellular telephones, and more open procurement policies rather than competition among networks. At the same time the opportunity for selling services through the networks does seem more promising. Value-added network services, (or VANS) as they are called, are rapidly expanding. There are 700 running in West Germany on the Bundespost data networks and access to these networks for new VANS is recommended in the government report.

Moreover, there is the prospect of far keener intercontinental competition at network level as optical fibre cables come on stream across the Atlantic and Pacific, supplementing the satellite system. The UK is well represented in these ventures. As and when the European monopolies finally become eroded, the UK, through its experience of a relatively liberal system should be well placed to compete both in the network sector itself and in the services supplied over those networks.

As in other areas we have examined, the trade figures in this sector are imprecise. Furthermore, the statistics published in the CSO Pink Book are an aggregation of results of the telecommunications industry with the postal services. These overall figures show a resistant deficit over the last decade (£98 million in 1986). The telecommunications industry is of the view that its activities, which are expanding, are in surplus since imports of such services are low. The export categories are principally in consultancy (selling the systems abroad), in fees from implementing systems, maintenance (service contracts) and return from investment. Cable & Wireless, for example, can earn £80 million per year from Hong Kong where it owns 80 per cent of the domestic network and 100 per cent of international telephone traffic, by far its most profitable territory and activity.

At present, the greatest opportunities for British companies lie in installing and advising on new systems in the developing and newly developed countries. British Telecom has set up a special overseas division to develop exports of the new technologies. The most promising areas are the Middle and Far East, and Africa. The US is largely self-sufficient.

In Europe a successful future will, then, closely depend on greater European progress towards liberalised systems to allow British companies to offer new services. But such progress, in the view of the European Commission, will be essential if industry is to receive an adequate infrastructure of information technology to compete with Japan and the USA. Both the UK, through its Alvey Schemes I and II, and the EC, through ESPRIT I and soon ESPRIT II, have put substantial funds at the disposal of industry, universities and research laboratories in order to further European-wide development of information technology. But the appropriate implementation and realisation of much of the research on the software side will depend on the availability of open and harmonised European-wide systems to accommodate the facilities created.

Notes and references

1 Marcel Pisters, 'The economic situation of air transport', *ITA Magazine*, Jan–Feb 1987, p. 9.

2 'Services in UK economy', *Bank of England Quarterly Bulletin 25*, 3 September 1985.

3 Rt Hon John Moore, MP, Address to The General Council of Shipping, 10 December 1986.

4 These and the following statistics, where not otherwise indicated: General Council of British Shipping, *Statistical Brief*, October 1986.

5 Rt Hon John Moore, MP, *see above*, ref. 3.

6 For a useful survey of the varying features of the different categories of cargo see B. Volk, *Seaborne Trade Forecasts 1984–85 – A Synoptical Review*, Institute of Shipping Economics and Logistics, Bremen, 1985.

7 *See* B. Volk, *Shipping Investment in Recession*, Institute of Shipping Economics and Logistics, Bremen, 1984, p. 31.

8 *See*, for example evidence given to the House of Lords Select Committee on the European Communities, *European Maritime Policy*, HMSO, March 1986, p. 182.

9 Kevin Brown, 'Shipping and ports. The squeeze tightens', *Financial Times Survey*, 14 April 1987.

10 *See* the paper by Sir Edward du Cann, *Time to hoist the Red Ensign. The decline in Britain's merchant fleet and how to restore it*, Bow Publications, London, 1986.

11 *Financial Times*, 18 December 1986.

12 'Progress towards a common transport policy. Maritime transport', *Bulletin of the European Communities*, Supplement 5/85, European Commission, Luxembourg, 1985.

13 The House of Lords Select Committee on the EC in its 'European Maritime Policy' (ref. 8 above) had supported the idea of cabotage.

14 *See* Tony Peisley's most informative article, 'Sea ferry travel and short cruises. Travel between the UK and continental Europe' in *Travel and Tourism Analyst*, Economist Intelligence Unit, January 1987.

15 Andrew Fisher, 'Pressure on freight rates', *Financial Times Shipping Report*, 27 May 1986.

16 Andrew Fisher, as above, and 'Profile Evergreen: world leader', *Financial Times*, 27 May 1986.

17 CSO Pink Book.

18 Eric Pollock, 'A shift in Trading Emphasis', *Transport*, August 1986.

19 Kevin Brown, 'British Ports. Struggling to compete against European rivals', and 'Profile: Associated British Ports' in *Financial Times Shipping and Ports Report*, 14 April 1987.

20 This information is derived from Lloyd's Loading Lists Special Supplement to celebrate a century of existence of the port, May 1986, entitled 'Port of Felixstowe'.

21 Stephen Wheatcroft and Geoffrey Lipman, 'Air transport in a competitive European market – problems, prospects and strategies' *Economist Intelligence Unit Travel and Tourism Report 3*, September 1986, pp. 164–6.

22 *Tourism Policy and International Tourism in OECD Member Countries*, OECD, Paris, 1986 pp. 82–3.

23 Details of Eurotunnel and its financial prospects derived from its prospectus published 18 November 1987. On French Rail plans, *see*, for example Andrew Cornelius, 'On show ... the super train with a platform the length of Europe', *Financial Guardian*, 28 May 1987 and the *Financial Times*, *Special Channel Tunnel Supplement*, 13 October 1987.

24 *Export Times*, June 1987.

25   Kevin Brown, 'Wagon design may produce ro-ro trains', *Financial Times*, 6 June 1987.

26   For statistics on intra-European rail freight traffic, *see* James Cooper, Mike Browne, David Gretton, *Freight Transport in the European Community: Making the most of UK opportunities*, Transport Studies Group, Polytechnic of Central London, March 1987, p. 93.

27   For this information and much of the analysis in this section we are indebted to the Polytechnic of Central London London Transport Studies Group Report, above ref. 26.

28   As for refs. 26 and 27, *Recommendations Report*, p. 4.

29   For discussion of these changes, *see* the Polytechnic of Central London Report, Michael Brown, 'Achieving efficient distribution,' and Peter Martin and John Harlow, 'Express freight and the exporter: towards a new partnership', *Institute of Export Members Handbook 1987*, pp. 147–151 and 139–142.

30   Kevin Brown, 'Profile: Federal express. Strong presence from hard work', *Financial Times Survey of Courier and Express Freight Services*, 15 March 1987.

31   *See* Marcel Pisters, 'The Economic Situation of Air Transport', *ITA Magazine* 41, Jan–Feb 1987, pp. 7–11.

32   Michael Donne, 'Air Transport. Running into losses despite expansion', *Financial Times Survey of Aerospace*, 9 June 1987.

33   For this section I am indebted to Stephen Wheatcroft and Geoffrey Lipman, ref. 21 above, especially Chapter 2.

34   *See* the important article by Heini Nuutinen, 'Charter airlines in Europe. Traffic, tour operators and the impact of liberalisation', *Travel and Tourism Analyst*, Economist Intelligence Unit, November 1986, pp. 19–36.

35   'Europe's Air Cartel. Break it up, but not the American way', *The Economist*, 1 November 1986, pp. 19–23.

36   Tim Dickson, 'Battling to break the price barrier', *Financial Times*, 21 March 1987.

37   Ronald Katz, 'Liberalisation of air transport in Europe. Regulatory developments and commercial projections', *Travel and Tourist Analyst*, EIU, London, March 1987, p. 15.

38   I am grateful to Mr Frederick Sørensen of DG VII at the European Commission for a very valuable discussion of these issues.

39   Jacques Pavaux, 'Airline deregulation in the United States: was it a mistake or a friendly hoax?' *ITA Magazine*, May 1986, pp. 15–21.

40   *See* Pavaux, ref. 39.

41   Philip Hastings, 'European services, delivery schedules increasing', *Financial Times Survey of London's Airports*, 16 March 1986.

42 Michael Donne, 'Cargo. Fierce rivalry from Continent'. *Financial Times Survey of London's Airports,* 24 March 1986.

43 Michael Donne, 'Study expansion set to continue', *Financial Times Survey of London's Airports,* 24 March 1986.

44 'Unquiet take-off at London's Stolport', *Management Today,* April 1987, pp. 104–115.

45 *Green Paper on the Development of the Common Market for Telecommunications and Equipment,* European Commission, Brussels, COM (87) Final, 30 June 1987, p. 44.

46 For further useful information on the technical and economic aspects of the modern telecommunications industry *see* 'New lines for old: a survey of telecommunications', *The Economist,* 17 October 1987.

47 David Thomas, 'Mobile communications. Moving nearer a unified market', *Financial Times Special Report on High Technology,* 9 July 1983.

48 J F Rada. 'Information technology and services', in *The Emerging Service Economy,* edited by Orio Giarini for the Services World Forum, Geneva, Pergamon Press, Oxford, 1987, p. 145.

7 Tourism, hotels and leisure-related industries

Introduction

'Tourism may become the greatest single economic factor in world trade by the beginning of the 21st century'.

This prediction of growth (contained in the BIEC Annual Report 1984/85) is a startling reminder that tourism throughout the world has already developed by several orders of magnitude beyond the traditional image of the industry.

So far as the UK is concerned, however, there existed for many years something of a credibility gap between the observed economic and social significance of the industry and its public image. This image was acquired through long periods of decline and fading glories in the fashionable Victorian and Edwardian resorts and spas, to be replaced by a string of run-down seaside towns with their seedy hotels and boarding houses; with brash picture postcards and souvenirs; and with wet and windy beaches. Visitors to London, particularly from overseas, were there for quick killings, whilst the brief pilgrimages to Edinburgh, York, Stratford, Oxford and Cambridge, Winchester, Salisbury, Chester, Canterbury and Bath were all accepted by the natives as a profitable seasonal influx of business which demanded little real effort from themselves either by way of investment or in supply of trained personnel to cater for the special needs of the visitors.

It was perhaps inevitable, therefore, that the UK was something of a slow starter in the world league of modern tourist centres. We had, of course, little help from the most powerful salesman of all for the industry – sunshine. Moreover, British coasts and countryside, with the possible exception of the Lakes and the Scottish Highlands, seem to attract little interest from overseas tourists. By contrast, our major strengths – the country's historic, architectural, social and cultural heritage – were in general poorly marketed and starved of financial support for development and promotion.

As a result, the UK tourist industry found itself in competition not only with the traditional centres of Switzerland, Austria, Italy and France, but also with the many newer ones, particularly Spain,

Portugal, Greece, the Mediterranean Islands, the Caribbean and, to a lesser extent, North Africa, the Eastern Mediterranean and the Far East. Some part of the growth in world tourist trade did indeed find its way to the UK only to find a travel industry ill prepared for expansion; prices of hotels and food rocketing sky high, and a local population only too often more aware of the nuisance factor of increased tourism than of its commercial and economic advantages to the country.

And so for many years the world's inveterate travellers – the Dutch, the Germans, the Japanese, the Scandinavians – found little incentive to break their existing modes of holiday-making. If they felt the need of more adventure, the prospect of visiting the UK appeared less exciting than other alternative places pressed upon them with increasing intensity by foreign governments and their tourist agencies. Exceptions were the USA, attracted by the historic link with the UK and by the use of the English language, and also a growing student body from north-west Europe seeking low-cost holidays with a minimum of expense on travel.

At the same time popular taste in the UK, with more frequent short breaks from work, found longer holidays at home less and less attractive either in quality or in price. Hence the increasing mass of tourists leaving the UK every holiday season by land, sea and air, and hence, too, the urgency of generating a compensating flow into this country of tourists from overseas. For there were indeed very good economic reasons both for maximising the attractions of holidays in the UK for British families (a most important form of import saving) and for ensuring that as much as possible of the foreign trade in tourism was diverted to these shores.

The reasons were both economic and social. It was becoming increasingly clear that tourism as a labour-intensive industry offered considerable scope for employment at all levels of skill and experience. At the same time there began to emerge in the late 1960–70s a healthy surplus on the balance of payments which showed every sign of continuing into the indefinite future. There was, therefore, every reason for Government stimulus to the industry. A considerable step forward was the passing of the Development of Tourism Act of 1969. Under the Act the English Tourist Board (ETB) was created to develop and market England's tourism; and to encourage the provision and improvement of travel facilities in England. Similar bodies were created for Scotland and Wales. At the same time a further statutory body, the British Tourist Authority (BTA), was charged to promote the attractions of the UK for tourists from overseas. The boards also had statutory duties to advise the Government on tourism and to administer grants and loan schemes. The boards also liaised with regional and area travel centres and with local authorities. In the course of time, common services between the BTA and the ETB were developed, in their general developmental and promotional activities, in research, and in specialist areas such as education and training.

The stimulus provided both by the Act itself and the new institutional developments which it generated proved remarkably effective both for domestic and overseas tourism, and went some way towards overcoming the weaknesses which had held back the industry for so long. Moreover, the steady devaluation of the pound from 1967 and then in 1974–75 was a great magnet. We had surpluses on the travel account for much of the 1970s with deterioration setting in during the 1980s. This in turn led to a new anxiety for the future of the industry.

The urgency of the situation was sharply and unexpectedly underlined by the 40 per cent decrease in 1985 in visitors from the USA – a decline partly due to alarm at international terrorism, partly due to the worsening of the economic situation in the USA and to adverse exchange rates.

Whatever the reasons, the result was to give a new impetus to promoting on a wider basis a fuller understanding of the real significance of the tourist industry. It also led to renewed efforts within Government, educational establishments, and firms to ensure that the British tourist industry in all its many facets was equipped in finance, and perhaps even more so in trained manpower, to take the strain of the industry's move into so prominent a place in the national economy.

Definition of the tourist industry

If, as a non-resident of the UK, you come from overseas to enter hospital, you are a tourist. So, too, if you come to visit relatives, on business or for a business conference or exhibition, as a student on a course lasting less than twelve months, or simply to take a holiday. An 'international tourist' for official and statistical purposes is defined as a resident of one country who visits another country and stays there for a period of less than twelve months but more than one day. The definition excludes travellers visiting another country to take up pre-arranged employment there and certain other categories, such as, military and diplomatic personnel and airline crews on duty. The entire expenditure in the UK of international tourists is put to the credit of our balance of payments.

On the other hand, if you travel abroad as a UK resident, everything you do and pay for, including accommodation, eating and drinking out, shopping and entertainment are all totted up and marked against the country's overseas accounts. Fares to the UK whether by land, sea or civil airlines and paid to UK carriers are put to our credit. On the other hand, payments by UK tourists using foreign carriers are debited against the UK. The whole equation is then entered into our national accounts – the income from overseas tourists as invisible earnings, and the money spent abroad by UK tourists as imports. There emerges a net trade figure which, as often as not, is near the point of balance and which in 1984 and 1985 showed a surplus. In other words, the earnings of the UK tourist industry have generally more than paid for all the vast number of UK holiday-makers going abroad each year. This is in marked contrast to Germany, for instance, whose adverse balance on travel has reached a staggering figure of some DM30 billion in a single year.

Statistics of the industry

The tourist industry is extremely diffuse and, as will be seen below, embraces many different activities. Moreover, parts of the industry, particularly in the UK, share a mixed economic purpose, and, indeed, a number of developments, particularly in recreation and leisure, which, whilst helpful to tourism, are primarily targeted at general social and community welfare. This makes it particularly difficult to isolate figures distinctive to tourism and allowance has always to be made for points of overlap.

The prime sources of statistics are the OECD reports on international tourism supplemented by its comprehensive tables, many of them disaggregated on a country-by-country basis; and entries under 'travel' in the UK Balance of Payments, 'Pink Book'. To complement these generalised national figures, the industry as a whole has also had many bodies at work on tourism statistics. These include the OECD, the European Travel Commission, the tourist authorities of England, Scotland, Wales and Northern Ireland, the training boards and professional institutes and local authorities. In addition, there have also been a number of special surveys with a large statistical content sponsored by the CBI and the British Invisible Exports Council. Similar work has also taken place within the universities, polytechnics and institutes of higher education.

Out of all these figures it is not easy to derive a simple consistent statistical picture of the industry as they all reflect, to a greater or lesser degree, difficulties and differences in definition, demarcation and harmonisation. The following, however, are some of the main points which appear to emerge on both the national and international scene:

1   Total number of visitors

Table 7.1   Overseas travel statistics

Year	Visitors to the UK (thousands)	UK Residents visiting overseas (thousands)
1968	4 828	7 269
1973	8 167	11 740
1978	12 646	13 443
1983	12 464	20 994
1984	13 644	22 072
1985	14 449	21 610
1986 (P)	13 844	25 181

(P) = Provisional figures

Source: International Passenger Survey (IPS) 1986, *Public Business Monitor MA6*, October 1987

2   Countries of origin

The main country of origin of our overseas tourists has traditionally been North America, accounting for more than a quarter of the total number of visitors. The American figures, however, showed a sharp decline early in 1986 prompted by fears of terrorism, atomic radiation following the nuclear disaster in the USSR, and the weakening dollar exchange rate.

Table 7.2   Origin of visitors to UK (1986)

Country of origin	Number of visits (thousands)
USA	2288
European Community	6888
Other west European countries	1413
Other countries	2699

Source: IPS 1986.

3   Earnings

Overseas earnings in the UK from international tourism gross more than £6 billion per year, out of a total turnover of the industry of some £20 billion. Net earnings ('exports' less 'imports') vary from year to year. In both 1984 and 1985 the travel industry showed surpluses on balance of payments of £500–£600 million, but for the various reasons already cited 1986 showed a substantial deficit.

In 1985 business travel accounted for £245 million, whilst the remainder was contributed by tourists who were here for 'leisure' purposes.

4 Expenditure

Table 7.3 Travel: Contribution to balance of payments

Year	Income (£m)	Expenditure (£m)	Balance (£m)
1976	282	− 271	+ 11
1978	2507	− 1549	+ 998
1983	4003	− 4090	− 87
1984	4614	− 4663	− 49
1985	5442	− 4871	+ 571
1986	5435	− 6070	− 635

Source: CSO 'Pink Book' 1987, Table 1.3.

The main items of expenditure by overseas visitors in 1985 were estimated as follows:

			£bn
(i)	Accommodation and hotel expenses		1.5
(ii)	Eating and Drinking out		0.8
(iii)	Travel including internal transport, but excluding fares to UK paid to non-British carriers		
	Internal transport	0.625	
	Fares to British Carriers	1.227	1.852
(iv)	Shopping		1.950
(v)	Entertainment including leisure-related activities		.250
(vi)	Other services		.326

(Source: BTA – Shopping and Consumer Surveys)

5 Duration of visits

In 1985 overseas tourists to the UK totalled 14.5 million with an average stay of 11.7 nights. More than 9 million of these visitors spent the whole or part of their stay in London. For comparative purposes, the total number of visits and trips within the UK (both domestic and overseas) is estimated at 140 million with an average duration of 4.7 nights. The regional impact of foreign tourist spending was as given in Table 7.4.

Table 7.4   Overseas tourism – expenditure by region 1986

Region	Expenditure (£m)
England:	4872
London	3132
Northumbria	65
Cumbria	25
North-West	165
Yorks and Humberside	124
East Midlands	80
Heart of England	185
East Anglia	157
West Country	218
Southern	126
South-East	355
Thames and Chilterns	224
Scotland	352
Wales	100
Northern Ireland	17
TOTAL*	5388

*Includes oil rigs, day excursions, unspecified areas, Isle of Man, Channel Islands.
Source: International Passenger Survey 1986 (ETB 1986)

6   Investment

Over the six months to June 1986 projects to a total of £247 million were completed, nearly double the previous six months. They include 49 quite major undertakings. At the same time, projects to the value of £600 million were under construction with a further £100 million committed to projects of mixed use, of which tourism was an important element. Of the total investment, a third was earmarked for hotels – including some large new provincial hotels in Brighton, Manchester and York – and some major units in and around Gatwick Airport and in London Docklands. There is also a major capital programme for the expansion and refurbishment of hotels, particularly in Central and Greater London.

Outside the hotel sector, the major investment programmes were for historical and cultural facilities and for leisure/sports activities. Other spending was earmarked for self-catering, for marinas, and for theme parks, whilst no less than £100 million has been spent or earmarked for conference and exhibition facilities. The largest single investment in this category is for the Queen Elizabeth II Conference Centre in Westminster costing £60–70 million and funded by the Department of the Environment. The big Central Station Conference and Exhibition Centre in Manchester costing £14 million is just one of the tourist developments in that city. It has been privately financed with the backing of an insurance company.

The financial institutions on the whole, however, have taken little interest in investment in the tourist industry, regarding it as a low-profit, high-risk investment. The hotel and catering sector has in the main been privately financed, whilst local authorities have been very much the leaders in the provision of development finance for tourist and leisure-related projects. Overseas investment in the industry both inwards to the UK and outwards comes largely from the big hotel chains. But other organisations may be involved. For example, the very large investment in the Sherwood Forest Development Complex, including 600 self-catering chalets and large leisure annexe, and costing in all £31 million, came from the Sportshuis Centrum in Holland.

7 Employment

Employment in the tourist industry is extraordinarily difficult to calculate and its further potential equally hard to estimate. Jobs are in fact very widely spread both geographically and by type of activity. The industry employs a large number of part-time workers many of whom are women. There are also an exceptional number of self-employed and working proprietors, a depressing proportion of whom are forced out of business almost as quickly as they enter it. For this and many other reasons, there is an exceptionally high figure of wastage in some sectors, perhaps as high as 33 per cent per annum of the total labour force. The best estimates suggest total employment to be in the region of two million made up as follows:

Hotel and Catering	900 000
Travel and Transport Services	500 000
Leisure-related Services	450 000
Self-employed and working Proprietors (not including above)	200 000
Total Employment	2 050 000

Source: DOE Quarterly Estimates and IMS Estimates June 1985

These figures may reasonably be regarded as a fair working base. Beyond the base, the scope for growth is very substantial and it has been estimated that approximately 50–75 000 quite new jobs are created each year. If allowance is made for the high turnover of labour, then the total recruitment for the industry in a single year totalling some hundreds of thousands constitutes a very significant figure indeed in relation to the employment situation of the country.

Moreover, a study of the investment projects referred to above shows that much of the employment both in the hotel sector and in the wider aspects of the industry will be provided, at least in the future, just where, from an employment point of view, it is most needed.

Barrow, Birmingham, Manchester (four major hotel projects), Portsmouth, Salford, Stockton, Leeds, Falmouth, Hull, Camborne, Plymouth, Sherwood Forest, Exeter, Wakefield, Wigan, Bradford, Gateshead and Liverpool are all centres of significant and, in some cases, very large projects. They include hotels, leisure and sports centres, heritage developments and the improvement of the countryside. By no means all of them are exclusively directed at overseas visitors, but between them they reflect an exciting atmosphere of growth, imagination and confidence.

Activities of the industry

As will be apparent from what has been written above, tourism is not so much a single industry in the conventional sense of the word, as a group of consumer services and activities directed to a common purpose – the satisfaction of human needs when out of the home, when enjoying holidays or when engaged in business, educational or social pursuits.

A directory of nearly fifty occupations is contained in two publications of the English Tourist Board together with an analysis of training requirements and career prospects for each. They list four main categories of labour deployment – hotel and catering, leisure, transportation and tourism organisation. To these may be added a fifth category of employment – trade fairs, conferences and exhibitions – whilst there is a large but non-calculable number of people who find employment in relevant aspects of retail distribution including duty-free shops, merchandise and displays aimed at the tourist trade, and overseas investment in shops and franchises.

1   Hotel and catering management

Jobs comprise managerial posts such as hotel, conference and banqueting managers; house skills such as receptionists and office clerks, housekeepers, porters and room attendants; and many other 'craft-based' posts, such as chefs and cooks, waiters and waitresses, and kitchen and bar staffs. Outside the hotels there are publicans and bar tenders, guest-house managers, holiday centre staffs, and managers and staff for caravan and chalet sites and institutional catering.

2   Leisure facilities and entertainment

The diverse jobs in this category reflect the nature of the facilities and often call for specialised knowledge and skills. The range includes managers of theatres, museums and galleries, and historic properties; zoos and wild-life parks, sports centres, parks and gardens; and boat hire. In addition to the managerial and technical staffs, most of these activities call for attendants and security staff as well as maintenance staff and craftsmen, some of them very highly skilled.

3   Travel and transportation

This category includes aircraft, ships, ferries and hovercraft, all of them needing captains and cabin staff, and in addition a wide variety of crews and maintenance staff. There are also trains, coaches and buses, car hire and taxi drivers.

4   Tourism organisation and marketing

This category includes tour operators and agents; management of the large tourist groups; the local staffs of Tourist Authorities Information Centres. In the main centres of international tourism there is a requirement (all too rarely met) for well-developed language skills as well as, of course, a knowledge of local geography, history and facilities.

5   Conferences, trade fairs and exhibitions

This is an important set of activities, whose significance extends beyond its not inconsiderable contribution to earnings, employment and investment. Success in this field does much to enhance the international reputation both of the British tourist industry itself and of the UK economy. A more detailed study of the field is given towards the end of this chapter on pages 189–91.

Education and training

These broad categories of employment and the nature of skills and occupations which they absorb have determined the pattern of education and training in the industry. It is an industry where until relatively recently it was largely a matter of learning on the job. There have, of course, long been exceptions – well-established schools in Switzerland, France, Italy and America which have both taught the crafts of the trade to the highest international standards and, particularly in the case of the American schools, helped to guide the transition of the industry from small, family-based units to very large establishments deploying modern management skills and subject to the rigid planning and financial disciplines taught by the American business schools.

For the greater part, however, units in the UK tended to be small and family-owned, if not managed. The large luxury hotels at the top end of the business employed, almost as a matter of prestige, Continental managers and *chefs de cuisine*. The smaller and less pretentious hotels and catering establishments, whilst they have had their share of overseas visitors (many of them on package holidays) have been largely concerned with catering for British tastes and expectations.

It was against this background that a few pioneers in the industry began in the early 1970s the slow job of constructing a training framework for the UK industry and, beyond that, an educational structure adequate not only for a growing and more sophisticated domestic demand but also able to stimulate the development of international tourism whose exploitation, as we have seen, had become a matter of economic concern.

It was, in fact, not simply in numbers that the industry found new challenges. It had to cope with changes in types of ownership, including the absorption of single units into huge, often heterogeneous, groups, many of them owned and directed from abroad. It is interesting to note that not only have British firms successfully coped with the entry of foreign groups into the British market, but also that British firms have themselves expanded rapidly overseas, including latterly the purchase of substantial establishments and chains in the USA. Examples are the purchase of Holiday Inn by Bass, of Hilton by Ladbrokes and Travel Lodge by THF.

There were changes, too, in scale, with moves to larger units; in food and administrative technology; and in customer expectations. All this and more required to be taught and learned in an industry which had very little education tradition and extremely low academic credibility. Moreover, as we have seen above, much of the newer development in the UK was taking place in areas of the country hitherto almost completely unfamiliar with international and, indeed, domestic tourism.

It is against this background that we shall look at the problem of education and training in the industry, and seek to describe what has been achieved and what still remains to be done. For it is the tourist industry, arguably more than any other in the UK which has been led in its process of transformation and rapid growth, by changes in education and training.

The structure of education and training in the tourist industry

The general pattern of education in the industry is largely determined by a number of distinctive features, some of which have been touched on above:

1 The huge labour wastage and annual cycle of replacement of the labour force each year. To a significant extent, therefore, recruitment is as much concerned with replenishment, largely of short-term and seasonal labour, as it is with providing for the growth and development of the industry.

2 The number of seasonal and part-time workers, some men, but mostly women, and between them accounting for more than half of the total recruitment.

3 The number of new and old employees who come from backgrounds outside the industry. The course at Sheffield Polytechnic, designed for former steelworkers from Corby, is a case in point and indicates the determination of the industry to help ease unemployment in particular areas.

4 The number of entrepreneurs and self-employed with a high rate of business failures and representing a particularly volatile element in the training sector.

5 The number and variety of additional and new jobs in the industry, generated not only by the growth of the hotel industry itself, but also by the demands of bar meals and snacks in public houses; by the growth of contract catering, partly as a result of the privatisation in hospitals, schools and other institutions; by the demanding requirements of conferences and exhibitions, not only for catering and personal services but also for office reception, language and communication facilities; and by the expanding range of tourist requirements, often in conjunction with local authorities and including sports leisure, farm tourism, and the more subtle exploitation of various aspects of the national heritage.

Together, these factors present a huge challenge on many fronts to those responsible for education and training in the industry. It must be said, however, that for a large proportion of the actual and potential employees the sheer weight of numbers and the nature of the work make it totally impracticable for more than the simplest form of on-the-job training under the control of local managements, and helped by a variety of training guides, publications and short courses organised by firms, by the training boards and the tourist authorities.

Beyond this, however, there is a substantial body of people requiring more structured modes of education and training. They include nearly 100 000 school leavers and former students of technical and vocational colleges, and a very large number of adult employees, both actual and potential who are looking to the industry as one of the few areas of employment growth in the country. Their wish is to update existing knowledge and to acquire new skills that will carry them forward to progressive careers within the industry at varying levels of craft, skills, technology, professional and managerial expertise. It is to these very large groups that the main thrust of effort is being directed by the professional associations, training boards, Manpower Services Commission, educational establishments, and by firms.

Education provision in the UK

More than fifty boards, associations and institutes are listed as bodies whose activities, in whole or in part, are concerned with education and training for tourism and leisure. Many of these bodies have in turn their own regional and area structures. In Whitehall, several Ministries – the Departments of Education and Science, of Employment, of Trade and Industry, of Agriculture and of Environment – have aspects of tourism within their portfolios. So do almost without exception, local government authorities. Statutory bodies such as the tourist boards and authorities, the Manpower Services Commission and several industrial training boards all have immediate and widespread responsibilities in the field, as have the Business and Technician Education Council (BTEC), the Scottish Vocational Education Council (SCOTVEC), the Council for National Academic Awards (CNAA) and the City and Guilds Institute of London. More than four hundred local authority colleges, institutes of higher education, polytechnics and universities mount between them nearly 1000 courses in transport, hotel and catering, travel and tourism, sport and leisure and horticulture. In most cases the courses lead to awards at different levels from diploma to higher degrees and are monitored by a wide range of professional and examining bodies. These courses are in turn supplemented by introductory courses in the fifth and sixth forms of schools and by private institutions operating outside the formal education system.

Increasingly, teaching institutions make use of an expanding range of 'distance learning' techniques under the general guidance of the Hotel and Catering Industry Training Board, and will very soon be looking for still wider dissemination of materials from the recently-established Open College.

Last but not least, are the training activities of private firms, from the large country house training centres of international companies, to the often feverish attempts of the proprietor of the very small hotel, restaurant, public house, or even bingo hall, to familiarise himself and hopefully one or two members of his staff with at least the rudimentary skills of financial control and general management, of technology developments and of professional skills.

This volume, diversity and quality of training activities is perhaps unique in British industry. It has indeed been said, and with some truth, that the educators have not only supported the efforts of the operators in the industry but established a dynamic partnership with them for the development and growth of almost every aspect of the industry.

It is clear that it is beyond the scope of this study to do more than describe briefly a few of the main organisations and establishments in the field. For the most part their concern is with domestic as well as with international tourism, for this is an area where visible and invisible exports are very closely interlinked. Their success in international tourism in particular is very much a function of how far the efforts of educators and trainers are reflected on the ground in the capacity of the industry to attract, welcome and satisfy the needs of their overseas guests.

Professional institutes, associations and training boards

Hotel and Catering Industry Training Board

This is one of only five statutory Training Boards remaining from the twenty-four set up by the Industrial Training Act of 1964. The 1964 Act itself has been amended on several occasions, resulting not only in the very sharp reduction in the total number of statutory boards in existence (although often to be replaced by non-statutory national training organisations), but also, so far as the Hotel and Catering Industry Training Board is concerned, in a reduction in the number of firms remaining in the scope of the Board and subject to its statutory levy.

The response of the Board to this decline in its levy income has been to sharpen its competitive edge, to continue to offer its services to all companies in the industry, both exempt and non-exempt and to conduct a commercially viable operation on a wide front, covering the mounting and operation of courses, programmes for management development and training skills, publications, research and consultancy. The total number of delegates attending courses offered by the Board went up from 8000 in 1984–85 to 11 000 in 1985–86, generating income of nearly £1 500 000; two-thirds of it from sales to firms on a commercial basis. The balance came principally from small business start-up programmes funded by the MSC and other agencies.

Three major developments are of particular significance to the Board's current activities and to its scope for future development.

1 Agreement with the Brewers' Society facilitating the participation of this important section of the industry in the activities of the Board.

2 Overseas consultancy, now made possible to the Boards through a recent amendment of the Industrial Training Act.

3 The development of open and distance learning which is covered in a separate section below. The prospects to the Board opened up by this particular development are very exciting indeed. This technique fits very neatly into the Board's already deep involvement in YTS schemes, adds significantly to the geographical spread of its teaching and offers a real

prospect of tackling in depth the huge numbers requiring education and training in almost every aspect of the tourist industry.

The Hotel, Catering and Institutional Management Association

There are a large number of professional institutes and associations whose interests impinge to a greater or lesser extent on the tourist industry. They include the Institutes of Export, Transport and Linguists, and more immediately the Brewers' Society, the Association of British Travel Agents, and the Institute of Travel and Tourism (ITT).

The Hotel, Catering and Institutional Management Association (HCIMA) is the professional body for managers and potential managers in food and accommodation services management. The Association has set itself three priorities:

1 To win greater recognition for managers throughout the industry.
2 To set and monitor standards.
3 To help managers and potential managers develop and maintain their knowledge and ability.

The ITT offer what they claim to be the only professional management qualification in the world in their particular field. They run their own examinations, which in turn lead to six grades of qualification from Fellows to Student members. At each level they seek to maintain an appropriate balance of academic knowledge, institutional experience and practical skills. Optional studies permit of specialisation in individual sections of the industry. They also allow for partial exemption for pre-entry knowledge, experience and qualifications.

The Association is rightly proud of its success in fighting for recognition of both itself and its members in a field which for long was notoriously resistant to the very concept of professionalism. Its success is reflected in the steady rise in membership which now totals 23 000 in all grades, of which 2000 are overseas.

Its councils and committees have amongst their members an exceptionally wide spread of people of high position and influence in the industry reflecting between them commercial companies, academic institutions, local authorities and the armed forces.

Over-the-counter selling

There are three institutes and associations particularly concerned with over-the-counter selling. They are: The Institute of Travel and Tourism (ITT), Association of British Travel Agents (ABTA) and the City and Guilds Institute of London.

There are approximately 12 000 counter and reservation staff and some 2000 management and professional staff working in travel agencies.

There are in addition a very large number of travel operators (dominated by some ten large companies) many of whom provide services to visitors from abroad. The training resources include the joint operations of the ABTA National Training Board (a non-statutory body but very active in many aspects of the field) and the specialist sections of the City and Guilds Institute of London, a chartered institute which is almost exactly one hundred years old. In addition, BTEC and SCOTVEC offer appropriate modules in the Higher National Diploma curricula.

ABTA National Training Board and the City and Guilds Institute have between them launched their Certificate of Travel Agency Competence (COTAC) and higher level Certificate of Travel Agency Management (COTAM), incorporating such fields of study as financial administration, office organisation and law. These qualifications in turn, together with the British Airways TRAVIS Diploma, are approved for various grades of membership for the Institute of Travel and Tourism – a body aimed at developing the professionalism of its members within the industry.

These Institutes, Associations and Examining Bodies are concerned with developing and recruiting educational infrastructure in the industry, which at the same time is flexible enough to cope with the very large numbers making their way, often from a fairly low start and at very different levels, through the variety of craft, commercial and management skills which give careers in the industry their special attraction.

Distance learning

Amidst all this variety almost everyone employed in the industry will have one thing in common – working conditions which are not only strenuous but, as often as not, subject to hours of work which are irregular and often anti-social.

This constitutes something of an educational nightmare, particularly in those sections of the industry composed of very small units and often located in the remoter areas of the country. To cope with these conditions, the development of distance learning, to which reference has already been made, can be something of a lifeline. A *Distance Learning Directory* – a directory of tourism-related courses – has been compiled by the Education and Training Unit of ETB/BTA from information contained in the *Open-Tech Directory*, which in turn works in the closest collaboration with examining bodies such as BTEC, SCOTVEC and, at a higher level, CNAA and the universities.

The *Directory* presents an exciting picture. Costs of the individual courses vary from £30 to £400 depending on duration and on back-up support in terms of audio or video cassettes, workbooks and tuition; whether face-to-face, by television, in company, or, exceptionally, during class provision in colleges and universities. Some lead the whole or part of the way to academic or professional qualifications; some, such as the flexible management development programme of Strathclyde University Business School, probe fairly deeply into the various aspects of general management as do the courses at Henley Management College through its distance learning company.

Other courses are more sharply oriented towards some particular aspect of the industry. The Foundation Course on Rural Tourism at Dyfedd Open-Tech is designed for farmers who are considering providing facilities and accommodation for tourists. The Hotel and Catering Open-Tech course is conceived as a self-instructional management development programme for actual or potential managements and operational units. It allows for assignments to be marked by a training board assessor and for the issue of certificates. Other projects include the BII Pub Business Programme offered by the Institute of Innkeeping, the Open-Tech Transport Project for Road Transport Operators and their staff, and a series of self-standing training packages in the retail travel trade provided by ABTA (in conjunction with the City and Guilds Institute) and academically aimed at COTAC levels 1 and 2 and at COTAM.

Finally, an ambitious scheme for co-ordinating at a national centre open-learning material for amenity, horticultural and land-based leisure has been launched at Capel Manor Open-Learning Unit at Waltham Cross. It is aimed at those employed in local authority leisure departments, garden centres, private gardens, countryside parks and 'anyone helping others to enjoy the environment'.

This intensive deployment of open-learning techniques is indeed an encouraging portent for the future. It is an encouragement which is being helped along by training boards and organisations and the major examining bodies, in addition to the Open-Tech, and hopefully in the future, the Open College whose proposed activities offer almost unlimited scope for promotion and innovation.

Establishments and courses in the UK

In the previous sections we have referred to the main institutions, training organisations, examining boards and government agencies, with the responsibility to plan and pilot education and training in the tourist industry.

It is time to take a brief look at the teaching establishments themselves which are, of course, the vehicle through which these plans are instituted and brought direct to the public whom the whole system is designed to serve.

The formal teaching is at many levels, caters for very large numbers of students and covers a multitude of courses and subjects. There are about 350 local authority colleges in England, 45 in Scotland, 40 in Wales, 25 in

Northern Ireland and one each in Jersey and Guernsey. They include colleges of further and higher education, colleges of commerce and technology, and colleges of agriculture, farming and fisheries. In addition, almost all the polytechnics have courses either directly aimed at the tourist and catering industries or impinging less directly upon them.

A small but growing number of universities offer degrees or postgraduate awards in the field. Private colleges offer courses in catering, food technology and hygiene which are often themselves complementary to sixth form courses in schools in domestic economics and allied subjects.

Finally, a number of larger firms, particularly the larger hotel groups, travel organisations and retail distributors, run their own schools and centres combining the basic principles of theory and practice of the industry with an intensive up-date of their own particular crafts, technologies and commercial skills. The subjects covered by this complex of courses can be grouped broadly as follows:

1 Hotel and catering
2 Travel and tourism
3 Transport
4 Sport and leisure
5 Horticulture

Sadly, few of them are designed specifically for the tourist from overseas. Equally, however, all of them are aimed at improving the efficiency and attractiveness of the industry, and therefore maximising the income arising from international tourists, as well as contributing to import saving from domestic customers persuaded to take their holidays at home rather than abroad.

Individual establishments

It is clear that in a teaching area involving some 500 establishments and more than 1000 courses, it is impossible to comment on more than a very small proportion and, indeed, to do full justice either to them or to the many others whose activities are well worth consideration. The following comments therefore are intended simply to give a fair impression of the direction, levels and variety of teaching in this highly diversified area.

1 Universities

It was no easy job to gain acceptance for higher professional education within an industry as full of brilliant pragmatists and entrepreneurs as the hotel and catering industry. Traditionally, it has been craft-based, with skills either handed down from generation to generation, acquired through formal and informal apprenticeship within industry, or simply on the job, often learnt from bitter experience.

It was, however, through the efforts of such people as Professor R Medlik that higher level university courses were conceived, initiated and an educational programme developed. Based on what had previously been the Battersea Polytechnic but which received its charter as Surrey University in 1966, Professor Medlik engaged in a long battle both to gain acceptance amongst companies in the industry for a management rather than a craft approach to higher education, and within the university for academic acceptance together with an allocation of resources to promote his planned programme of work.

Since Medlik's retirement, the department has continued to expand greatly in numbers and in range and level of teaching, and perhaps of more than symbolic importance and intended to mark the management-based approach to the subject, the department, itself within the Faculty of Human Studies, has been renamed the Department of Management Studies for the Tourism and Hotel Industries.

There are, moreover, other universities in the UK, such as Strathclyde and Ulster, who have taken up the challenge. It is perhaps because of the increase of this particular level of activity that warning voices continue to be heard, that the higher education within the industry may be moving in the wrong direction – too much theory at too high a level and too little attention to craft and tradition. It is, of course, a battle which permeates many aspects of management and industrial education and it is something which is uppermost in the mind of academic staffs particularly in polytechnics and in colleges.

2   Polytechnics

There are very few polytechnics which have failed to find a place for some aspects of the tourist industry, either within their specialist programmes or as options within the general framework of courses in business studies. Prominent amongst these institutions, are polytechnics at Huddersfield, Leeds, Manchester, Portsmouth, Newcastle (in association with New College Durham), Sheffield and Brighton. The combination of theoretical and applied learning is a natural for polytechnics, and much of the work in this area is quite excellent.

3   Institutes, colleges etc.

The number of courses offered in this sector is very large indeed, with many of the individual courses quite admirable both in concept and quality. Between them they reflect a progression from local craft-based colleges to institutes for further education and research within a modern thrusting industry making its way both in national and international markets.

At the top end of the sector are such colleges as the Dorset Institute of Higher Education, which claims the first Honours Degree in Tourism in the UK; and which, under the guidance of Patrick Laverick, acts as a high level consultant to government and to the European Community; and Blackpool and Fylde College, one of the largest and oldest teaching centres in the UK for the tourist and travel industry, which through its complex of courses combines a competence in the higher management of the industry with a thoroughly practical approach to the professional and craft aspects of hotel and catering operations.

The industry is particularly fortunate to have this diverse range of educational facilities at the local and regional levels, offering support both for the industry as it is today and for the challenge of future development and expansion.

Conferences, trade fairs and exhibitions

Business visitors coming to the UK to attend conferences, trade fairs and exhibitions represent a small but highly significant segment of the overseas visitors market.

Conference statistics

Income from business travel to the UK in 1985 totalled £1520 million, nearly a quarter of the combined earnings for business and leisure. To make up this total it has been estimated by the BTA that 157 000 people came to visit trade fairs, conferences and exhibitions (one per cent of the total overseas visitors), and that they spent between them in the UK some £74 million. The average trade fair/conference visitor, moreover, spent more per visit (£469 in 1985 exclusive of fares) than either the average visitor to the country or the average business visitor.

About half of the trade fair/conference visitors come from countries in the EC. West Germany is by far the largest source of visitors to British trade fairs and exhibitions, but the USA (with a total expenditure of £13 million) spent more per head on this type of visit than any other single country, contributing rather more than one-fifth of the total revenue.

Significance of trade fairs and exhibitions

The revenue generated by this set of activities is, therefore, by no means negligible, but the significance of the activity goes well beyond this.

1 It is an important source of investment and development by government, local authorities and by private enterprises. Some of the projects are very large, such as the great National Exhibition Centre at Birmingham and the Queen Elizabeth II Centre in Westminster which cost £60–70 million. Other major developments include the G-Mex complex on the site of the old Central Station in Manchester, the Rosetor Conference and Exhibition Centre in Torbay and the Alhambra Theatre in Bradford. The new multi-million conference centre at Olympia has many outstanding features both in design and equipment, not least its booths for simultaneous translation into eight languages. Elsewhere in London there are extensions at Wembley, the rebuilding and refurbishing of Alexandra Palace, the purpose-built Barbican Conference Centre in the City and the many adaptations and extensions of hotels, halls and academic establishments.

2 London will continue as a major focus for conference activity. In 1985, for instance, some 150 000 visitors stayed in London during their visit to trade fairs and exhibitions. On the other hand, more than 120 000 of these visitors found their way to other centres in the UK, and with new developments and increased facilities this number may be expected to grow. Apart from projects in Manchester, Torbay and Bradford, which have been mentioned above, there is a large international conference centre in Harrogate. The early days of this centre were fairly rough, but certainly the centre does not lack in size, resources or ambition. Elsewhere in Yorkshire there are important conference centres in Leeds, Doncaster, Scarborough and Bridlington; whilst other provincial centres include Cambridge, Eastbourne, Southampton, Brighton and, of course, Birmingham. The capital involved is substantial and the ventures are by no means low risk, but for all that the prospects remain bright.

3 With the capital programmes go jobs – in construction, in equipment, in hotels, restaurants and public houses and in the conference centres themselves. The latter call for a variety of skills including secretaries, translators and interpreters; technicians for rapidly developing conference technologies; a wide range of managers and house staffs; and specialists in advertising, public relations and in the press and media. A growing number of jobs are outside London and can in themselves make an important contribution to the revitalising of inner cities and of the more 'difficult' urban and rural areas.

4 Finally, there is the very prestige and worldwide repute which accrues from successful operations in this competitive, highly skilled and international market. Moreover, conferences, trade fairs and exhibitions themselves offer a service to the service industries – a focal point

for the gathering together of knowledge and skills over highly diversified areas of professional and business thinking, and for the dissemination of the combined wisdom and experience of the participants to almost every country of the world.

The future of the tourist industry

The previous pages have painted a bright, perhaps over-roseate, view of the UK tourist industry. Its achievements over the past twenty years have indeed been significant.

It is true that its net contribution to the balance of payments stands no sort of comparison with major earners such as insurance, banking and financial services. On the other hand, it has attracted to Britain sufficient overseas visitors, whether for business or for pleasure, to pay for the increasing number of UK residents pursuing similar activities abroad.

In the broadest sense of the term, however, it is both a substantial earner of foreign exchange and, to the extent that holiday-makers are encouraged to stay at home rather than go abroad, it is a considerable import saver.

Quite apart from its overseas earnings, the domestic industry has added significantly to the income of many UK-based companies, most particularly in hotel and catering, in domestic travel and in certain sectors of retail distribution.

It is also a considerable employer of labour with a capacity for creating some 50 000 new jobs a year. It is true that London still remains a focus for a considerable number of overseas visitors, as do many parts of the Home Counties and South of England. But thanks to the efforts of the British Tourist Authority and the national and local tourist boards, there are signs of a wider spread of investment which often means more jobs and money just where they are most needed. The level of investment in the industry continues to be good, even to the extent that British companies now feel confident enough to buy out American interests in hotels and other leisure-based industries at home and abroad.

Finally, there has been a real attempt to tackle the problems of training and retraining at every level in the industry. Professional associations, training boards, academic establishments and private firms are all very clearly seen to be working together, to an extent which is quite unusual. Though it would be unrealistic to suggest complete agreement in the industry on the direction and pattern of individual training initiatives, both the volume and achievements in education and training are clear to be seen.

Opportunities and constraints for the future

The steady progress of the industry has had its hiccups in the past twenty years, reflected most recently in the series of deficits on overseas trade in 1980–83, and the 40 per cent fall in visitors from the USA in 1986 as a result of terrorism in the UK, and the falling exchange rates and economic recession in the USA.

All or any of those factors could be at work again in the future. There are, however, some special problem areas which merit the attention of all engaged in the industry.

1   Barriers to international travel

These are still surprisingly numerous and bothersome. Tourism now appears on the agenda of the Uruguay Round of GATT and many sticky problems are likely to arise. The conceptual framework prepared by the OECD forms a useful platform for discussion as a whole. So, too, do the national series on trade in services submitted to GATT by thirteen different countries.

Visas and conditions of entry are particularly tiresome in Eastern Europe and, until 1988, the USA. Tourist documentation varies from country to country and will greatly benefit from the type of harmonisation which is now proposed for the European Community. Restrictions on the export of certain local currencies bear particularly heavily upon the nationals of the countries concerned, but they also affect foreign visitors who find, as in Yugoslavia, very strict limitations on the amount of currency they can bring in and the amount the can take out.

Tourism promotion offices are, in some countries, the subject of government monopoly, whilst elsewhere there are tight local, regional and governmental controls on promotional activities by foreign countries. Limits on duty-free purchases vary considerably, between countries. The sharp restrictions, for instance, on duty-free purchasing imposed by France in 1983 (though short-lived) had an important and significant impact on the French tourist trade. Finally, travel by land, sea and air are the subject of many agreements which sharply restrict the customers' freedom of choice and in many areas (particularly in Europe) significantly add to the cost of personal and business travel.

2   International organisations

The World Tourism Organisation (WTO) based in Madrid has 109 full government members and more than 150 organisations from the private sector. Its aims are to propose measures to simplify entry and exit formalities, and to develop a set of standard procedures and recommended practices which would form the basis of a draft convention for its members.

There are other organisations, too, with special interests in travel and tourism. They include the International Monetary Fund (IMF), International Civil Aviation Organisation (ICAO) and the Brussels-based Customs Co-operation Council (CCC). There are many other national and international bodies who wish to have their say in Uruguay on the future of tourism which seems likely to prove not the least controversial subject tabled for discussion.

3 Competition

Tourism is worldwide. It is by and large a growth industry with particular potential in foreign earnings and employment. As a result there are few countries of the world which do not wish to have their share of the action. Competition is keen and sophisticated – and grows from day to day. It is this atmosphere in which the UK tourist industry has to live and thrive, and in the main it has made a pretty good job of it. For the future, they have everything to gain from supporting the efforts described in the previous section to ensure that world trading and tourism is free and fair. In some respects, however, tourists may meet even more difficulties, at least in the immediate future.

In the present world conditions of terrorism, drug smuggling and illegal immigration, it is difficult to conceive of any relaxation of customs and immigration control procedures at points of entry in the UK, at least where it is also the point of entry for the EC. Our efforts should, therefore, be directed to ensure that all barriers to travel are aimed simply at the protection of national and European security. Beyond that the British response to competition should be the vigorous pursuit of these wholly commercial activities, and in particular the UK should:

1 Identify its points of national weakness in the market – and its strength. This means a lesser emphasis on sunshine and beaches and more on history, heritage and the countryside.

2 Maintain an increasingly sensitive approach to the very real environmental problems arising out of the growth of the industry. These include pollution of air, sea and land, the appearance and upkeep of main tourist centres and the avoidance of overload of resources both in the tourist centres themselves and in the means of access to them.

3 Accept that London is, and will remain, a tourist best-seller and put a lot of effort into its promotion; but at the same time encourage the tourist boards and authorities to intensify their efforts to secure a more even spread of visitors which they have done, with a certain amount of success, in their imaginative approach even to the 'difficult' tourist areas.

4 Look for growth points and go hard for them. In the UK this means activity holidays, farm tourism, business travel and perhaps above all a major emphasis on exhibitions and conferences. But remember that the latter is regarded as one of the major 'plums' of the market. Almost every country in the world has it targeted and competition is fierce and sophisticated. Organisation of these events needs to be smooth and competent. Back-up resources must be first-class including secretarial, audio-visual equipment, translation and interpretation. Food and accommodation must be both good and value for money. Above all, it must be remembered that the English language, if properly exploited, gives the edge to the UK location over most of the alternatives.

Finally, the tourist industry can only be as good as its managers and staff. The future of the industry does, indeed, depend on the standard of education and training. A good start has been made. What is needed now is a continuing commitment to its extension and development by all concerned – central and local governments, industrial companies, banks and retail houses, academic establishments and all who see in the industry a satisfying and progressive future.

Notes and references

1 Facts and Figures – Employment, Jobs and Investment

Jobs in Tourism and Leisure, ETB and Institute of Manpower Studies, 1986.

Employment in Tourism, James Morrell, (BTA), May 1985.

The Facts about Tourism and the Leisure Industries, ETB, 1985.

Britain's Tourist Industry, British Invisible Exports Council Annual Report, 1984–85.

Tourist Investment Report January-June 1986, ETB.

'Labour Markets for Hotel Industries of Member Countries', Note by OECD Secretariat, February 1986.

Department of Employment, quarterly estimates of employment and Institute of Manpower Studies estimates, June 1985.

European Travel Commission (Annual Reports) and World Tourism Organisation.

Overseas Trade Fairs/Exhibitions – Visitors to the UK 1985.
International Passenger Survey, Department of Employment and BTA/ETB Statistical Research, March, 1987.

2 Professional Institutes – Annual Reports, Courses etc.

Hotel and Catering Advisory Board.

HCIMA Reference Book, 1986–87.

Association of British Travel Agents (ABTA).

Institute of Travel and Tourism (ITT).

Distance Learning Directory, ETB-BTA from information supplied by the Open Tech.

Handbook of Careers in Tourism and Leisure, ETB, 1985.

Directory of Courses in Tourism and Leisure, ETB, 1985.

Facts about the Tourist and Leisure Industry, ETB, 1986.

3 General Reading

Annual Reports, BTA and ETB.

Strategy for Tourism Development, ETB, 1987.

R. S. Medlik, *Paying Guests*, CBI, 1985.

Robert Banks MP, *New Jobs from Pleasure*.

Tourism Policy and International Tourism in OECD Countries, OECD, 1976.

R. S. Medlik and D. W. Airey, *Profile of the Hotel and Catering Industry*, Heinemann, London, 2nd edition, 1978.

'Hotel and Tourism Development', paper delivered to Joint Planning Session, International and American Hotel Association, by J. A. Bodlender, United Nations 1983.

Peter Buckley, 'Tourism – An Economic Transaction Analysis.' *Tourism Management*, September 1987.

'UK Conferences and Exhibitions' *Financial Times Survey*, 13 January 1987.

P. J. Buckley and S. F. Witt 'Tourism in Difficult Areas (Bradford, Bristol, Glasgow and Hamm)', *Tourism Management*, September 1985.

Amin Rajan, *Hotels and Catering – Services: The Second Industrial Revolution*, IMS Butterworth, 1987, pp. 76–98.

Bruce Tanner and Harry Goodman, 'The Hard Work of Running a Leisure Business', *The Director*, August 1985.

D. F. Channon, 'The Rise of Property and Leisure – The Leisure Providers', *The Service Industries, Strategy, Structure and Financial Performance*, Macmillan, London and Basingstoke, 1978.

P. J. Buckley and S. F. Witt, *The International Tourism Market in Eastern Europe*, January 1987.

8 Construction, Engineering and Design

Introduction

The civil engineering industry has many facets, the principal ones being design, construction and project management. These are the subject of this chapter. The role of the materials and components suppliers and the financiers, and many other skills which play their part in the complex business of building and maintaining built structures, large and small, should not, however, be overlooked.

Britain's openness to the outside world, thanks to its massive trade and investment in the Empire, resulted in the British construction and civil engineering industry adopting an internationalist approach as early as the mid-nineteenth century. The Indian railways, roads, harbours and imperial buildings are examples of British design; Macadam designed roads worldwide, Brassey developed railways in Europe, and projects like the Aswan Dam in Egypt and the Cantilever Bridge in Quebec, Canada, are further examples. In Latin America there are many others.

The early civil engineers James Brindley, John Rennie, Thomas Telford, and the Stephensons, were self-taught craftsmen, stonemasons or toolmakers who constructed large scale public works. This was made possible by the development of modern mechanics, hydraulics and materials, for instance Portland cement, cast iron and steel. The first engineering societies were formed in France between 1716 and 1750, whilst the Society of Civil Engineers in London was formed by John Smeaton in 1771 to promote the building of public works, with members who were not only engineers but also entrepreneurs and lawyers. The teaching of civil engineering only got under way at universities in the UK in the 1820s.

The UK consulting engineering professions pioneered the exporting of independent consultancy services (mainly in today's Commonwealth countries) as long as 130 years ago and provided a model for other countries, soon followed by those from Europe and North America. At first they were both designers and doers, managing their projects and campaigning for them, profiting from their own equity stake in the great days of empire building. Since then the UK professions have built up an envied track record of high achievement through independent advice, integrity and professional ethics combined with a service deploying high-calibre people trained to the highest levels of proficiency in the latest techniques.

None of these essentials must be thrown away, but the UK industry now faces serious challenges. New ways of providing these services must be found to prevent professionals from other countries taking over the UK's potential markets. The threat is posed by new perceptions, needs and resources encountered overseas.

As a study by the Committee on Invisible Exports stated nearly a decade ago 'The British professions should retain, and if possible enhance their capacity to provide unrivalled services, if necessary in increasingly specialised fields.' [1].

New strategies are needed for retaining, or even increasing, the UK market share for consultancy and construction services as the world moves rapidly from an energy economy phase, into the information economy, where products miniaturise but information multiplies explosively (as we have had reason to observe in so many other sectors).

Engineering consultants

Functions, and contribution to developing countries

The functions of the civil engineer are performed in three stages which come before, during and after construction; these are:

site investigations, feasibility studies, research and design;
co-ordinating contractors and other consultants;
maintenance.

Many specialised consultancies have developed in the industrialised countries, and have contributed much to the development process in other countries, often through Technical Assistance Programmes. Such work not only generates invisible earnings, but can also be the source of business opportunities for other suppliers. Not all consultants and aid agencies are fully aware of this opportunity. However, UK consultants have to consider their professional independence, which requires that their work should be divorced from purely commercial considerations. Certainly, there is a powerful feeling in developing countries that assistance should be directed towards the country's eventual self-sufficiency and this includes self-sufficiency in technical expertise.

Thus, on construction projects a large element of the transfer of technology is in essence an exchange of experience. Local associates and joint-venture partners learn from working on projects, and are progressively more able to carry forward future projects unaided. On many projects a condition of the appointment is that counterpart staff should learn new techniques by working alongside more experienced expatriate staff.

The essentials of success in working abroad are firstly, humility in the face of other people's problems; secondly, a sense of what is relevant; and thirdly, and perhaps most important, a respect for the constraints of implementation. Working overseas exerts greater strains than working at home, and this stress affects people and their way of life, the finances of the firm and the administrative and logistic support services. Communication takes on a greater importance, and so does mutual trust and understanding between people taking decisions, often in isolation.

Two of the chief constraints to growth of UK overseas business are the financing of work-search activities, and funding working capital. More working capital is needed because of larger and more protracted projects overseas, inflation, exchange variations, on-demand bonds, and higher turnover for each unit of technical input.

Greatly extended payment periods exacerbate the endemic under-capitalisation which is the norm for a large part of UK consultancy where the main assets are the brains which walk out of the office each evening. Slow and unpredictable payments make forward cover difficult and expensive, and in many of the exotic currencies earned, the forward market is thin or non-existent.

Education and training

The professional engineer must have a university degree or a recognised qualification at an equivalent level. The university course is three years long (or four years if of the sandwich type) and is followed by a course of practical training supervised by a qualified engineer. Mid-career training is now arranged between universities and employers.

Although project management has not always been recognised in the UK as a management discipline, and indeed has arguably been misunderstood, significant support has now developed at some academic centres, for example, at the University of Reading, the Management College at Henley and Brunel University. In addition the Major Projects Association has been created to act as a focus for all the elements of project management.

A principal problem has been the availability of adequate opportunities for experience at home. Many potential opportunities remained closed because public sector authorities preferred to maintain their own projects departments which were thus not open to young outside consultants. Pressure on these authorities has brought some change to their policy in the development of young engineers.

The British Consultants Bureau

The BCB was set up by the Board of Trade in 1965 to promote the interests of British consultancy engineers abroad. It is a multi-disciplinary organisation of about 300 UK consulting firms with over 30 000 staff. About 45 per cent of the member firms are engineers, 25 per cent are architects, and the rest are quantity surveyors, management consultants and a wide range of other professionals including mining and agricultural consultants, and those from the nationalised industries.

The BCB is the only representative body of consultants in the UK concerned with capital investment overseas. Its members have a hard-won reputation for independent judgement, honesty and technical excellence. It contains in its membership the majority of British consulting firms who are working worldwide and is the focal point for government liaison for consultants working overseas. It is independent of contractors and suppliers.

The objective of the BCB is to collect information on overseas engineering prospects, and to provide a focus for overseas countries needing consultants on capital projects so that suppliers and customers can be introduced to each other. The BCB organises missions to markets, acts as a link between government and consultants, briefs embassies and high commissions on the work and expertise of consultants, and maintains close links with the construction industry. It is a constituent member of the Confédération Européenne des Bureaux des Ingénieurs (CEBI), which maintains links with FIDIC (The International Federation of Consulting Engineers) and CEDIC (The European Confederation of Consulting Engineers).

Each year, the Hon President of the BCB, HRH The Duke of Gloucester, announces to its AGM the previous year's export earnings (which later appear in the CSO Pink Book). The five years run of figures from 1982–1986 is:

Table 8.1 Export earnings (in £m)

	1982	1983	1984	1985	1986
Consulting engineers	568	561	577	562	508
Process engineers	301	296	319	282	250
Architects/others	104	120	124	111	103[*]
Chartered surveyors	73	74	92	99	110
Management consultants	44	46	48	53	54
Totals	1090	1097	1160	1107	1025

Source: CSO Pink Book 1987
[*] The figure of £103 m for 1986, following the practice of previous years, largely arises from architects' fees but it also includes the Nationalised Industries Overseas Group and a notional amount for miscellaneous professional earnings.

Construction contractors

Nearly all civil engineering commissions include an element of construction work, and the design will take account of the siting of the structure, its function, economics and visible impact. The main need for construction arises in the following sectors:

transport – roads, bridges, canals, railways, tunnels, airports
maritime and hydraulic works – harbours, docks, jetties, dams, flood defences
public health – drainage, waste disposal, water supply, anti-pollution schemes.

Contracting, unlike manufacturing, has never been able straightforwardly to quote a price for a product produced in a factory in quantity, following the development of a prototype. Although the risks associated with this process are present in contracting, there are many others as well. Major contracts involve high costs and long time scales. The project has to be designed, and then created on site, where the conditions may turn out to be quite different from the assumptions on which the bid was based. Weather and ground conditions can materially affect the cost of construction, and contractors are increasingly exposed to these risks. They therefore wish to have the responsibility for both design and construction in order to retain greater control over the total risks. The struggle to win business internationally has not only intensified, but so has the nature of the competition.

The traditional role of the contractor is to take the financial risk of carrying out the construction work. This has often been unappreciated or undervalued by those who point to the emergence of indigenous firms overseas, and assert that it is not necessary for the UK to maintain a project contracting export capability, provided the consultants continue to be successful. But in modern service industries, it is the role of organised management which is crucial, and can only grow through keeping together teams of experienced individuals.

Very substantial resources are needed in order to mobilise construction teams in remote locations under primitive local conditions. Contractors can often be at the mercy of local officials whose experience of the site may be limited but who are, nevertheless, charged with taking critical decisions.

Marketing and bidding costs are increasing, and capital commitments have to be arranged in the form of bonds at all stages of a contract from the bid onwards. Not only do these incur servicing costs, but also have serious implications for the contractor's balance sheet as contingent liabilities. The practice whereby clients require the posting of unconditional guarantees, or on-demand bonds, has long been a matter of concern, because they can be called in without any justification given.

Once called, the funds are lost, unless the contractor has the ability to negotiate a satisfactory settlement, or to obtain a favourable arbitration award.

Much of the business of contractors overseas involves the provision of buyer credit, and they have to assemble attractive proposals to match those from competitors outside the UK who benefit from lower interest rates, and more favourable government policies on the deployment of aid funds or co-financing with international aid agencies.

The Export Group for the Constructional Industries

Founded in 1940, the EGCI is a non-profit-making trade association, financed entirely by its members. Its membership is open to all UK lead project contractors and major subcontractors active on the international market. EGCI provides the collective expression of the UK international project industry to the UK government, and represents the industry in its relationships with foreign governments, international funding agencies and commercial funding institutions, FIDIC (Fédération Internationale des Ingénieurs-Conseils) and FIEC (Fédération Internationale Européenne de la Construction) and EIC (European International Contractors).

EGCI holds regular meetings with civil servants and government ministers from the Foreign and Commonwealth Office, the Overseas Development Administration, the Ministry of Defence, and the Exports Credits Guarantee Department. It maintains active connections with the Bank of England, banks, acceptance houses and the private insurance market.

EGCI maintains a liaison committee with the British Consultants Bureau with the aim of bringing about a closer relationship between consultants and contractors in pursuing both common policy objectives and particular projects. Close relations are also maintained with the Association of Consulting Engineers, the Federation of Civil Engineering Contractors, the Building Employers Confederation and other sector exporting groups.

Package deals, turnkey contracts and management contracting

Consultancy

There is a growing world market for package deals offering both design and construction services. Ways to include finance in the package and to make turnkey propositions without waiting to be asked are having to be devised. Consultant teams can act as project managers and honest brokers, mediating between conflicting interests, and provide technical, training and management skills on a long-term basis.

Consultants recognise the need for a partnership between themselves and organisations experienced in running large-scale utilities needed by the developing world. However, many developing countries wish to develop their own consultancy professions and this is reducing the market for UK professionals in traditionally strong areas. At the same time the turnkey multinationals from the USA and Canada, with strong European input, together with equivalent operations out of South Korea and Japan are also an ever increasing threat to the consultant's traditional markets.

These trends highlight the fact that competition has come increasingly, not so much from higher standards of technical performance, rather than from the financial packaging of the services and the vertical integration of consultancy services with finance, construction and operational skills.

The factors which have to be taken account of, but not necessarily imitated, when putting together a new response, are: (i) that aid funds are often tied to the use of donor countries' services; (ii) the increasing use of consultancy services by competitors as loss leaders to gain a foothold for large engineering contracts or some other economic market; (iii) the practice of tying military aid to the use of the donor countries' services; (iv) the deployment of industrial, commercial and banking financial muscle to subsidise the price of consultancy, even offering it apparently free; (v) government grants, subsidies and insurance services may be used to subsidise the price of consultancy.

Thus, whereas the traditional British strengths of a high quality service linked to financial independence and integrity will no doubt continue to provide a distinctive marketing message and competitive edge, they are no longer sufficient in themselves. In the future consultancy will have to keep ahead of changing markets by offering new services or combinations of services without loss of independence for the consultancy and financial services, and taking due regard of the inherent conflicts or interest in assembling new packages.

More consultants are beginning to see the advantages of the managerial partnership of management contracting over their traditional advisory role, as evidenced at the 21st Anniversary Conference of the British Consultants' Bureau in 1986. It was also suggested there that consultants were not doing all they could to assist in the divestiture of state organisations, or to make use of combined World Bank and private resources. Consultants need to develop country-specific solutions, with fewer exhaustive reports, and seek a greater involvement at the strategic level of management.

The added value of UK net exports will also have to be increased through the improvement of consultancy services marketed overseas in a way which also improves the export chances for UK building and civil engineering contractors, materials suppliers and the financial services sectors supporting these activities.

Contracting

In the past much of the international contracting work undertaken by British firms followed an historically established pattern. It was carried out for colonial governments, clients in the older Commonwealth countries, or British and European private companies. The management of such investments tended to be entirely in the hands of technologically competent expatriates, and standards of performances expected were not much different from those in the UK.

The ending of colonial regimes and the granting of independence to many countries resulted in great changes. One of the chief problems was and, regrettably, still is the lack of people in the newly independent countries who are competent to run the organisation needed to manage the large investments. The World Bank and other agencies are concerned about this and devote resources to assist in the development of competent institutions. Some investments have, nevertheless, failed to deliver their planned output or other benefits, and some have simply fallen into disrepair. In the OPEC states there have been problems through their inability to deploy people with the level of technological education needed to run complex plants, though recruitment of expatriates has made up for this deficiency to a large extent, particularly, for example in the Middle East where the management of hospitals has been contracted out to private firms.

Recognition of this new problem is shaping the thinking of all international financial institutions, and providing a new philosophical foundation on which their developmental strategies are being planned. Contractors feel that the pressures of population growth, the changes induced by new found independence, the rate at which simple agricultural methods have been destroying the environment, and the rising expectations fuelled by international communications, make it impossible for rural self-help approaches to succeed any more.

What appears to be needed is an improved institutional structure which is competent, responsible and self-sustaining to accompany the physical investment. It has been agreed in the UK that this position could be reached more quickly by the privatisation of many state holdings. This could provide the basis for a new partnership in management between the developing countries and those with a surplus of such skills. However, the fears of a new form of imperialism or economic domination from private multinational corporations is still widespread, and a reluctance to receive back again expatriates as managers, rather than as advisors. This situation requires creative thinking by both contractors and consultants from the UK.

The project business has moved to a high added value operation using high technology and advanced know-how. Sensitive political, social and financial circumstances in the developing countries have added most substantially, then, to the complexities of the activity. The challenge to the UK construction industry is how to adapt to these circumstances while at the same time competing with companies in the newly industrialised countries that have the different business approaches outlined in the section above.

Turnkey operations

The complexity of the roles of those involved in projects has, then, increased. On the traditional construction project there were just three parties: the client, consultant and contractor. In modern turnkey projects specialisation involves many different firms and relationships are changing so as to meet developing competition.

Many of the larger contractors prefer to deal directly with the client by means of turnkey or design and build contracts. In such situations the contractor employs the consultant, or the design work is done in house. Many clients prefer such an approach, since they expect to get a more economical outcome where design and construction expertise is combined. However, the World Bank, and many other official clients continue with the traditional arrangements, which enables them to call for a number of tenders to be submitted from contractors for the construction phase.

In the traditional form of contract, the consultant is employed by the client on a scale or lump sum fee basis to:

carry out feasibility studies;
produce designs;
prepare specifications for the construction, organise the tendering process with contractors and advise on the selection of a contractor;
supervise the construction of the works.

In the UK the consultant has traditionally been an independent professional, usually belonging to an association which upholds a code of ethical behaviour. Members of the Association of Consulting Engineers, for instance, could not incorporate their partnerships, which have to be controlled by a majority of chartered engineers. The British Consultants Bureau permits incorporation, but requires certain assurances on the financial independence of its members.

A high proportion of construction projects overseas used to be carried out under the Contract Conditions of the Fédération Internationale des Ingénieurs-Conseils (FIDIC), which are largely based on the British

Institution of Civil Engineers' Model Form of Contract, since British engineers have always played an important role in FIDIC. A principal feature of these conditions is that the engineer had an independent role when, for example, certifying variations to contracts, which is a common occurrence. One of the reasons that this form of contract is used less now is that clients are more reluctant to cede authority for increasing their expenditure. Contractors have had experience of cases where the standard FIDIC conditions have been varied by the client without the necessary revelation to the contractor having been made, which in turn increases his risk.

Consultants are feeling the pressure of the increasing demand for a single package including finance with engineering and project management, but do not have the balance sheet strengths needed to take on responsibility for the construction phase. They are therefore seeking ways of forging stronger links with the international financial community. Consultants are finding ways of closer co-operation with contractors so as to become more flexible over working methods and contractual arrangements.

Management contracting

The complexity of modern contracts and the demand for shorter construction periods has led to the growth of management contracting. Under this arrangement a contractor manages the project on behalf of the client on a fee basis in the place of the consultant. The responsibilities of the management contractor can vary from managing the work of both the designer and construction firm, or solely the building work. Such contractors will be strong on management and procurement skills, and will be experienced in complex and rapid methods of construction. For these skills to be developed, a strong UK contracting industry is needed where training can be carried out and practical experience gained.

Management contracting has been growing in the industrialised world for new construction, and to a lesser extent for the management of plant operations. Management contractors are able to build up a team used to working with each other within an established company culture. There are signs that the World Bank is open to using this approach, but working it out in practice requires ingenuity if the sensitivities of the recipient countries are not to be aroused. Local employees have to be brought increasingly into the control of the partnership in order to create their own corporate culture which can continue once the contractor has departed.

To make management contracting a success the contractor must have full responsibility for performance, even though the client retains control of the contract. In the case of difficulties the home organisation of the contractor must be responsive in support and deploy people of high quality. The training of local staff remains a priority.

Management contracting of operations may lack the excitement of new construction, but has good long-term prospects for reappointment and a lower risk profile.

Consultancy in water supply, technology and management

British standards in water technology have long been accepted as among the best in the world, and as such have proved a very good basis for overseas consultancy, particularly in the poorer and less developed countries. The field includes feasibility studies, management, operation/control, manpower planning and training in areas in which expertise has been developed over very many years both nationally and within the regional water authorities of the UK.

The range of subjects includes water supply and distribution; sewerage and sewage disposal; water quality and pollution control including waste; river management and quality; land drainage; sea defences (erosion); fisheries and recreation management.

In areas so fundamental to the infrastructure of developing countries, it is not surprising that the advanced knowledge and technology involved has met with increasing demand. It so happens, too, that in recent years the incidence of floods and drought have affected vast areas of the world on a scale and intensity very rarely experienced, at least in recent times.

A fair amount of the water consultancy overseas (as well as in the UK) has therefore of necessity been of an emergency and remedial nature. But there have also been a good number of developmental projects in which British skills and experience have played a major part, often involving one or more of the UK Regional Water Authorities.

The Anambra State Water Corporation of Nigeria, for instance, has launched with the UK Southern Water Authority programmes for the renovation and extension of the water supply system – programmes which include consultancy on operational procedures – administration, finance and engineering. An even more comprehensive consultancy programme was undertaken by the Severn-Trent Water Authority in conjunction with the Water and Sanitation Authority of Lahore in Pakistan. A major survey is under way on training needs in conjunction with the Madras Metropolitan Water Supply and Sewerage Board, including the establishment of a centre which will undertake the training of employees of other water authorities in India. A variety of projects in Qatar, United Arab Emirates, Jamaica, Saudi Arabia, Egypt, the Sudan, Sierra Leone, the Philippines and Nepal cover technical assistance and staff training in the operation and development of water supply and dealing with problems of sewerage and sewerage systems.

The commercial value of these projects is, of course, very hard to assess as consultancy is often an element in very large enquiries and contracts received by consulting engineers for the environmental development of the country concerned. It is worth mentioning, perhaps, that the provision of administrative and consulting services provided by the Thames Water Authority for the preparation of a general study and drawings for water sanitation in the Buenos Aires area of the Argentine, and completed in 1986, was valued by the British Council at £160 000. It suggests the fees earned by the water consultants and by the local authorities and involving more than fifty countries make a significant contribution to UK overseas earnings.

The water industry in the UK is in the process of major reorganisation and the overseas consultancy contracts seem likely to face further changes of administration, co-ordination and control. It would be a pity, however, if the primary and lucrative foundation on which its current business has been built were to be eroded or weakened in the process of reorganisation and possible privatisation of the industry.

Export prospects and returns

Outlook

The major factors affecting the exports of construction and engineering are the general level of international economic trading activities, the level of aid to the under-developed countries, the underlying strength of the domestic market and the reduction of non-tariff barriers. As we saw in Chapter 2 if non-tariff barriers are to be reduced both in the construction and the consultancy service areas, there will have to be a concerted effort, particularly by EC member states and other members of the Group of Ten during the Uruguay Round of GATT. UNCTAD is a further vital forum that will need to be convinced of the advantages of trade liberalisation, especially in the service sectors.

A danger in the UK lies in the severe reduction of activity in the construction industry since high-points in the late 1960s. Home output plunged in the wake of the first oil shock (*see* Figure 8.1) and then continued to slide until 1980. It is encouraging that export earnings offset this loss to an extent for those companies with an overseas capability (*see* Figure 8.2). Moreover, as both tables show, membership by consultants of the BCB has risen in the period 1973–86, reflecting a growing awareness of how vital exporting expertise had become. Nonetheless, as Sir Andrew Derbyshire stated at the 1986 BCB Conference, it is questionable how much further the domestic construction

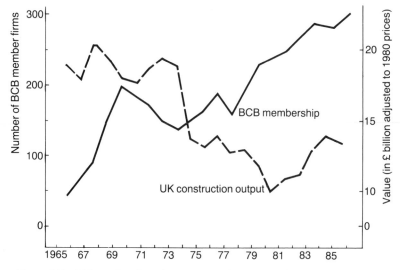

Figure 8.1   UK construction: home output (constant prices). (Source: DoE)

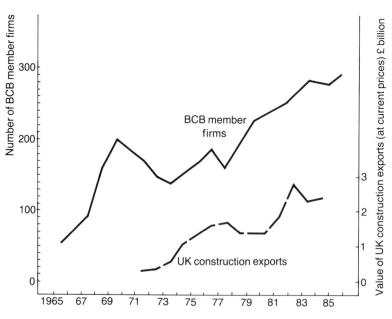

Figure 8.2   UK construction exports. (Source: BCB and DTI)

industry can shrink before the credibility of UK consultants abroad is undermined [2].

Turning to a worldwide perspective the outlook is still for continued heavy spending on armaments and defence projects. Although an undoubted stimulant to the economies of the chief hardware suppliers, and of some importance to UK consultants in their home markets, it is not of wide significance overseas for UK firms. If international tensions were to decrease, leading to reductions in defence spending and resources were diverted as aid to the developing countries, this could give an enormous boost to consultancy and construction markets.

A report of the Commission of the European Community published in 1984 [3] pointed to new services and openings in the markets of the developing countries, to add to the traditional building project services. They included agricultural and rural development schemes, management of water resources, development of alternative sources of energy, improvement of living conditions (such as cheap housing, water treatment and recycling of waste), small scale industrial and craft projects, rehabilitation of public and industrial firms, assistance with management and running of businesses and their maintenance and training programmes, and the management of large-scale projects.

Exporters have more recently had to adjust to the loss of spending power in the former oil rich states, especially in the Middle East, once their major market. Severe political and economic turbulence in many countries such as Iran, Iraq, Libya, Nigeria, Sri Lanka and in various Latin American states has severely limited opportunities in those areas.

Strong moves are being made by the UK's competitors from both old

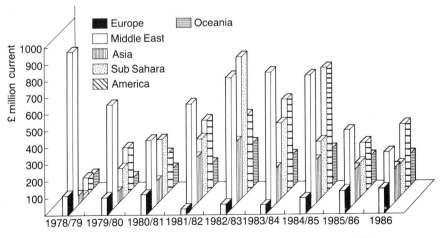

Figure 8.3 Contracts obtained by British Construction contractors: £million current. (Source: DoE)

and new areas. The American competition is benefiting from the lower dollar, the South Koreans from lower wages (something the Indians and Brazilians stress in their sales literature), and the Japanese are buying into European firms to tap aid from the European Development Fund going to the African, Caribbean and Pacific states under the Lomé convention. Figure 8.3 illustrates the changing fortunes of the UK construction industry since 1978. Particularly noticeable is the fall in Middle East and Sub-Saharan work since 1982/3.

Export values

Up to 80 per cent of the value of a contract is in the equipment and materials supplied, and much of this can come from the country of residence of the contractor. The proportion varies from about 35 per cent for roads, to 80 per cent on power stations. A study by the National Economic Development Office in 1982 showed that where the lead contractor was British, the proportion of British supplies was much higher than when the lead contractor was foreign. Other studies have shown that many of the supplies come from small businesses which lack the resources to be exporters on their own account. British contractors thus act as the marketing edge for a large number of other firms.

Calculations by the Export Group for the Constructional Industries suggest that for every £1 bn of project contracts won by British contractors overseas, 6600 jobs are produced in the UK and abroad for British employees with those contractors. British suppliers benefit to the extent of a further 20 000–25 000 jobs. At present levels, this means that for each job about £4500–£5500 is spent from the aid budget, a lower figure than the cost of annual unemployment benefit per person. If indirect employment achieved through the multiplier effect were to be included, then the cost per job might be as low as £2500.

Figures for the earnings of the consultants are published by the Central Statistical Office, and the values of the construction contracts on which the contractors are working are published by ENR (*Engineering News Record*), but the foreign earnings of those contractors are not recorded separately anywhere and are therefore not known.

Consultancy markets

Although UK professionals have been involved with large projects overseas for well over a century, in common with the patterns of consultancy exports of many other countries, the big increase in work abroad only came with the enlarged deployment of world aid funds starting in the 1960s, and at an even greater rate with the rapid development of the oil-rich countries in the 1970s. It was also partly the product of modern communications and air travel. Before that the task of reconstructing the basic fabric of economies shattered by the Second World War, and then creating the post-war industrial miracle kept consultants fully stretched at home. The abrupt end to this second phase, partly induced in 1973 by the sharp oil price increases of the OPEC countries, forced many firms to increase the proportion of their work overseas, and many more UK firms to seek work outside the UK for the first time. There they met brisk competition from consultants of the other major western countries working overseas for the same reason.

The main markets for UK consultants for the past fifteen years or so have been countries in the Middle East, Africa, South America and South East Asia. Many of the star performing markets have suffered severe reverses (e.g. Nigeria and Iran), whilst whole continents have been afflicted with economic malaise (e.g. Africa and Latin America).

New markets, such as Indonesia and China, are few and far between and generally have tougher characteristics needing higher levels of investment by consultants to win projects than can be afforded by all but a handful of large firms.

A study for the Scottish Development Agency found that countries which offer least difficulty for architects are Brunei, Malaysia, Hong Kong, Nigeria and those in the Middle East, and indeed a large number of UK firms already work there despite the great competitive pressures. More difficulty is experienced in Europe, although penetration exists in the Netherlands, Spain, Portugal and Greece. Other nationalities have gained a far greater share of markets in the older Commonwealth countries such as Canada, Australia and New Zealand.

The USA has huge potential but can satisfy its requirements from its own firms. Opportunities for specialists exist, and many UK building contractors have obtained work there. The most difficult areas for British consultants are the greater part of Europe and Scandinavia, Brazil, Japan and South Korea.

The *Engineering News Record* [4] of America estimated that in 1986 the UK engineering consultancy sector held 13 per cent of the world market, second only to the USA, nearly double that of France, Germany or the Netherlands; and more than double that of Japan and Canada. By contrast, the UK construction firms held only 7 per cent of world markets, lagging behind the USA, Japan and South Korea.

The proportion of work held by the British engineers in four broad areas of the underdeveloped world, i.e. Latin America, the Middle East, Africa and Asia, is second behind the USA in the two largest markets in the world, that is the Middle East (ratio 30 per cent : 17.6 per cent) and Asia (ratio 24 per cent : 20 per cent), (two markets which also grew more than the others). The UK came third behind France and the US in Africa, the third largest market (ratio 18.3 per cent : 14.6 per cent : 11.5 per cent).

In Latin America, which is in effect a US preserve, but only a third of the size of the first three, the UK did not rate.

The North and South Committee on Needs and Resources (NASONAR) of FIDIC has shown that there are quality resources underemployed in the developed world, whilst there is a dire need in the countries of the South, where they cannot be afforded. The conflict between market forces and politically acceptable forms of transfer of wealth and technology have to be overcome so as to deploy more widely technical and managerial skill on appropriate development projects.

Construction contracts

Engineering News Record publishes statistics gathered annually from a voluntary questionnaire returned by contractors around the world who are on the journal's list. Despite the self-selected nature of the sample, the figures are the only comprehensive set available from which to assess the size and geographical spread of projects.

Figure 8.4 shows the changing values of new project contracts each year since 1978, expressed in current US dollars, the market shares obtained by the leading contracting countries, and the location of the projects in broad regions. It should be noted, however, that the output of plant manufacturers is not included, and the work of subsidiaries is allocated to the country where the parent is based. In the case of the UK, many American-owned firms operate here that have a significant share of the world market, and were this added to the UK's share, it would make the UK a close third to Japan: much of the economic benefit of this business does accrue to the UK. When analysing the world market for

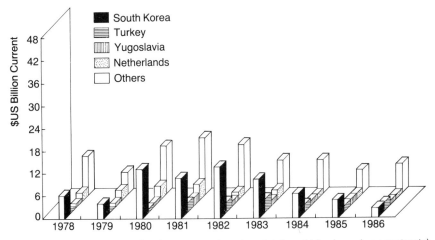

Figure 8.4   Building, civil and process engineering: total world business (new contracts) market shares 1978–86. (Source: ENR/EGCI)

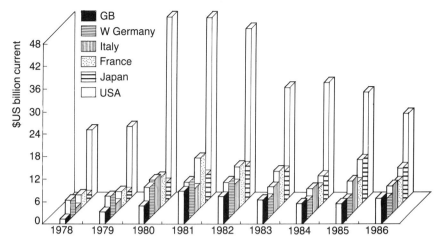

Figure 8.4(cont.) Building, civil and process engineering: total world business (new contracts) market shares 1978–86. (Source: ENR/EGCI)

projects, it is helpful to draw a distinction between countries which are:

developed (ie the members of OECD);
newly industrialised (NICs);
developing, with oil exports (mainly OPEC members);
developing, without oil exports (LDCs).

In recent years many of the major projects have been carried out in the OPEC countries, financed from oil revenues, and in the non-oil-developing countries, financed largely by the international funding agencies such as the World Bank, and development aid from OECD member governments.

The balance of contracting work between countries will change as new firms emerge in the developing world, and indeed some international agencies give preference to local contractors, but most of these countries have not yet acquired the range and depth of skills necessary to create and sustain the high standard of services needed locally. Local contractors are increasingly linking up with international partners, and some governments require foreign firms to form local companies with significant or even controlling shareholdings to be held by nationals. Major contractors still view such requirements with caution thanks to the lack of success in many such partnerships in the past.

Many contractors from the LDCs and NICs operate successfully in the international market, having based their comparative advantage on cheap labour. Initially, their growth was generated by contracts from their own governments who were either blind to the risks involved, or willing to underwrite them when accepting bids at very low prices compared with those from international firms. The role of Western consultants was also instrumental in assisting emerging contracting firms to obtain the necessary know-how both in design and project management. However, there have been some notable financial disasters involving NIC firms which has made all concerned more cautious.

In the past, projects have consisted of the construction of transportation routes and facilities, the introduction of irrigation and drainage systems, the provision of water supplies and sanitation facilities, and protection against certain natural disasters. More recently energy generation projects have grown. This pattern will continue in the developing world, whereas in developed countries projects may be more concerned with modernising the infrastructure; where also the balance between government and private sector work may alter, privatisation continues.

In the developed world and the richer developing countries which largely finance their own projects either government agencies or the marketplace will decide on the source of funding and relative priorities. In the poorer countries the problem is different, since they are dependent upon grants, and outside finance which has to be serviced by fragile economies. This leads to considerable intervention in the decision making process by the donors and lenders, and their advisers. The latter do not always appreciate the importance of investment in the infrastructure to the development process, which is becoming ever more urgent due to greater global interactions, and the rapid growth of enormous conurbations needing water, sanitation, health care facilities, urban transportation and power supplies.

UK co-ordination

The UK Department of Trade and Industry states that it is government policy that 'there must be a combination of industrial and banking activity with co-ordinated government policies relating to exports' and in the context of exports that a 'partnership is needed between the government and the private sector'.

To achieve synergy, consultants need to stand closer to sources of money and financial advice, in order to serve clients better and assist where possible with any associated exports.

The ability to connect together banking, currency and other financial services, with accountancy, management consultancy, economics, planning and the building and allied professions would greatly enhance the packaging of UK services, as might a widening of the range even further in selected circumstances to include construction contractors and materials and component suppliers. This would open up new possibilities which could be exploited in order to protect market shares. At first, close communications would be organised for the exchange of information on markets, prospects and bids, but later the connection could develop into associations or joint venture groupings.

The adding together of disparate services into new, and possibly multinational, hybrid associations should ensure that clients are offered the latest relevant expertise and secure better access to finance, insurance and to information systems. Furthermore, only large groupings will have the financial muscle needed to compete worldwide with firms from Japan, South Korea, the Continent of Europe and Brazil which are backed by large industrial, commercial and banking concerns.

In the financial world the ability of finance and securities houses to offer a wider package of services has partially accounted for the tendency towards mergers between service companies, and between goods and services companies. The hybrid nature of these newer transnational conglomerates enables them not only to diversify risks, but also to maximise the use of their own information systems, thus gaining unmatched advantages in world markets. There could be a lesson here for the construction and engineering sector.

Competition

Competition for capital projects is intense, and only those firms which can demonstrate high levels of technical and managerial ability are likely to obtain them, and then only by offering a keen price and an attractive financial package.

The technical know-how and managerial content of projects constitutes much of their added value, enabling the UK to remain competitive in the face of the emergence of new local firms overseas. Contractors usually face high financial risks due to the unforeseen contingencies which always arise on projects. Projects are awarded to firms after an assessment has been made of their technical, managerial and financial abilities, and of their bids, with the award usually going to the lowest tenderer.

In the 1970s the chief competition to UK consultants was felt from experienced professionals out of developed economies with similar backgrounds, such as the USA, Canada, the EC, Scandinavia, Japan and Australia. This was also the period of ascendancy for the large turnkey firms with in-house consultancy, principally operating from North America but with large offices in Europe and the Middle East. They included such names as Bechtel, Parsons, Fluor, Foster Wheeler, Kellog, Lummus, Procon and Lavalin. Large Japanese trading houses were also well represented. More recently professionals from developing economies such as India, Brazil and Pakistan have been strong competitors in third world countries. Turnkey operations from South Korea and Taiwan have also been a feature.

Foreign consultants usually have to ally themselves with local firms, even if no additional expertise is deployed thereby, and in some countries, particularly in the Middle East, a sponsor is needed, who is seldom a professional.

An association with a local firm can be important for an understanding of local professional practice, the building industry, and conformity to local codes and procedures; and for interpretation of local language, culture and politics. Local national indigenisation decrees require this in many developing countries.

Barriers to trade and the liberalisation of trade in services

Any moves which liberalise the trading structure so as to increase the world market for services are seen to be of benefit to the developed and developing countries alike, because costs can be cut, quality increased, the transfer of skills and technologies can be speeded up and an increase in specialisation achieved on a wider base.

In addition to the many barriers found in developing countries there is continued protectionism in the European Community, the USA, Canada and Japan. Qualifications are not recognised and there are strict immigration and labour laws and local ownership rules. Government procurement is based on national preference and local content policies, and there are hidden subsidies.

These problems are being addressed by the Liberalisation of Trade in Services (LOTIS) Committee of the British Invisible Exports Council (BIEC). Formed in 1982 to assess the international climate for services trade negotiations, it provides a co-ordinated UK private sector response to international proposals, which it expresses to the UK Government, the Commission of the European Community, and to the international trade bodies such as GATT, OECD, and UNCTAD. From the start LOTIS has included a representative from the consultancy sector nominated by the BCB. In turn LOTIS plays its part as a member of the European Community Services Group which speaks out for the Community's service providers on the CEC's priorities for removing international obstacles to free trade in services. Both these organisations maintain contact with other similar groupings around the world.

The major focus for negotiations on trade in services since 1986 has been the Group of Negotiations on Services (GNS) at GATT in Geneva. Studies commissioned by the OECD in Paris, have specifically covered the interests of both consultancy exports and the international activities of construction services. These studies looked at the main obstacles to trade faced by these sectors, particularly in developing countries which formed their major markets. They found that national regulations required government procurement from local companies, imposed minimum requirements for local content, restricted imports of equipment and construction goods, made difficulties over obtaining visas and work permits, and other necessary authorisations. Overseas foreign exchange procedures and inequitable taxation impositions were also widespread. The main distortions in the developed countries arise from government subsidies, especially for export credits, and through tied aid.

Role of UK Government

The Government has to maintain a strategic view of the industry, considering both its home and overseas markets, the economic environment which is influenced by levels of interest rates, and take into account that British contractors are more exposed to risks than many of their most powerful competitors which have closer relationships with their domestic banks and a cosier dependence on their governments. British success in competing for investment projects is extremely sensitive to government policy.

The challenge to government is carefully to integrate and orchestrate its policies and facilities for export promotion. Exporters want this to include pressing for a true European common internal market, maintaining good diplomatic relations with overseas countries likely to provide the best markets, improving the autonomy and efficiency of the Export Credits Guarantee Department so it can offer better facilities and ensure there is no gap in cover between its policies and those of the private insurance market, reacting quickly with appropriate assistance to exporters when needed to match the offers of competitors by overseas governments. Other needs include improving the double tax treatment for income earned overseas by permitting the pooling of foreign and UK sources of profit for relief, co-ordinating the assistance and services from all the government agencies concerned, and ensuring that the public sector exporters co-operate with and do not compete against private sector firms.

It is clear, above all, that effective operation in this group of activity will demand the greater possible co-operation between the government and the professional, banking and industrial sectors.

Export Credits Guarantee Department

ECGD, which we looked at in Chapter 4, is a separate government department for which the Secretary of State for Trade and Industry is responsible, and is of special importance in these sectors. It is assisted by an Advisory Council, focusing on its commercial operations, the Treasury, from which consent for its transactions is needed, the Export

Credits Guarantee Committee, an inter-departmental committee including a representative of the Bank of England, and the Projects Exports
Policy (PEP) division of the DTI, which is concerned with projects
deserving special support from the Government.

ECGD's insurance policies for non-payment, exchange risks, and
credit and bond support are vital for the construction and engineering
sector's export activities, and are unrivalled elsewhere in the world,
apart from the French scheme. A representative of contracting, but not
consulting, interests has served on the Advisory Council for many
years.

Project finance [5]

Projects are financed in many ways either using the client's own funds,
borrowed funds, grants or a combination of sources. In the developing
countries loans and grants predominate, with bilateral aid from
developed countries being a major factor. In developing country
markets construction activity is heavily dependent on external aid either
under bilateral programmes, or from the World Bank, European
Development Fund, and other regional aid organisations such as the
Inter-American Bank, the Asian Development Bank and the African
Development Bank.

Much of this aid is channelled into very basic projects, and this helps
to stimulate other developments. Examples include irrigation and soil
improvements; roads, bridges, railways, ports and airports; dams and
pumping stations; houses, schools, hospitals, medical centres; energy
exploration, mining and telecommunications. Commercial developments might also occur including hotels, offices, and shops, but if
private finance is involved competition is intense.

The development of financial packages for the entire project, covering
all the design work, with all frills such as foreign currency swaps,
co-financing, currency and interest rate swaps and cost escalation cover,
is already a necessity.

The way in which a project is financed can assume great importance to
contractors as it materially affects their ability to secure the work in the
first place. Projects paid for in cash from commercially raised funds are
mostly located in industrialised countries or the most advanced
developing countries. Even where the client is a private firm, there may
be a substantial public authority involvement, for example, where there
are grants or subsidies to persuade clients to invest in a particular
country or region. Private clients are often developers.

Projects which are partially funded with credit facilities arise in the
richer developing countries, such as the oil-producing states or sometimes in developed countries. The contractor may himself be involved in

arranging part or all of the credit, and success in doing so may be a material factor in obtaining a contract. UK finance houses in the City of London have long experience in such financing, but availability of funds and the terms of credit depend upon conditions prevailing in the money markets. A further important factor is the availability of credit insurance in the private market or from the Export Credits Guarantee Department.

Contractors from some countries such as Japan and Germany can have a natural advantage when offering credit because of the close relationships between the banks and powerful industrial organisations, and the contractors. Their low rates of interest have been a further advantage in recent years.

The variety of elements which can be incorporated into financial packages is almost infinite, involving the use of official development aid from an international funding agency, or from one or more national aid agencies. Such projects would be located in developing countries, to which aid makes up about 36 per cent of all financial resource flows. Practically all water projects, for example, have been financed by Arab funds or from aid programmes. This situation is likely to persist for a long time in the future.

The international funding agencies

The World Bank consists mainly of two agencies:

The International Bank for Reconstruction and Development. The IBRD raises funds mainly in the capital markets, secured in effect by the guarantees of the 149 member countries which provide its capital. Loans are made to governments who wish to use the funds for eligible projects.

The International Development Association. The IDA is funded by direct contributions from member governments, and the funds are lent to the governments of the poorest nations on generous concessional terms for interest rates and repayment periods.

In 1985 the total value of loans approved by the IBRD and IDA was US \$14.4 billion. About 25 per cent went to agriculture and rural development, a further 25 per cent to power generation and energy projects, 14 per cent to transport, and 5 per cent to industry, education and water supply/sewerage.

The International Finance Corporation is also part of the World Bank, and it lends only for private sector development projects. Other international aid agencies include:

The Inter-American Development Bank
The African Development Bank
The Asian Development Bank
The Arab Funds

The European Development Fund, which is an agency of the European Community, concentrates 60 per cent of its lending on the African, Caribbean and Pacific group of countries, which together with the European Community are signatories to the Lomé Convention.

The EDF plans its lending programme in five-yearly cycles; the budget for the period starting in 1986 amounts to ECU 8.6 billion. Of this 52 per cent is lent on works contracts, 30 per cent on supplies, and 18 per cent on technical co-operation and services. The UK usually obtains about 4.5 per cent of the works contracts, 20 per cent of the supply contracts, and 15 per cent of the services contracts.

Each country has its official aid agency. The Overseas Development Administration of the Foreign and Commonwealth Office performs this function for the UK. Geopolitical and developmental considerations are uppermost in the criteria applied by the ODA in its lending programme.

World Bank procurement and funding

When the World Bank provides a loan to a developing country, the responsibility for the management and execution of projects remains with the recipient country, but the World Bank retains a good deal of influence over the procurement process. An international competitive bidding process is insisted upon for most contracts, and the procedures laid down in the World Bank Procurement Guidelines are mandatory for the parts of projects they fund. Bidders cannot be required to offer financing, and bids are evaluated on a cash basis so as to exclude any financing terms which may be voluntarily offered.

Contracts have to be awarded to the lowest bidder, and a requirement to incorporate up to 15 per cent by value from local suppliers and contractors may be sought. No limits are set on bidding for contracts, and pre-qualification standards are low or omitted, so UK contractors have not evinced much enthusiasm for World Bank funded business.

The World Bank normally finances only a portion of the cost of a project, and the borrowing country may use an entirely different procurement procedure for the part financed in other ways, provided that the project's timetable, quality, or financial viability is not adversely affected. The term 'parallel financing' is used for situations where the World Bank funds part of a contract awarded under its aegis, and the remaining finance is provided from other sources such as export credits or tied aid. Where funds from the World Bank and another body are jointly used to purchase a common list of goods and services, this is termed joint financing, and the World Bank's Procurement Guidelines have to be followed. This deters those who wish to secure a commercial advantage from offering bilateral tied aid, although they may indicate 'their ability to provide financing for the balance of the funding not provided by the World Bank', but this cannot be taken into account when evaluating their bid.

The World Bank has pioneered a scheme of co-financing whereby funds from their loans and a donor country's bilateral aid are combined to finance projects. About a dozen countries have such agreements with the World Bank, and the UK is about to follow suit with the system, although similar ad-hoc arrangements had been made by the Overseas Development Administration in the past. The new scheme has improved the position for contractors as they are now consulted on forthcoming projects, and a senior director of a contracting firm was a member of the delegation to the World Bank to discuss the proposals.

The World Bank has funded more than 2300 projects with a total cost of over US $300 billion in the last ten years. Of these about one-third involved co-financing with one or more lenders. Official development agencies helped co-finance over US $17 billion on 700 projects, with about US $11 billion of export credits for almost 150 projects. Co-financing is a practice common to all funding and aid agencies.

Aid budgets

In 1984 the total aid from OECD countries increased in real terms by 6 per cent, yet the UK's contribution fell by 3 per cent, largely due to a drop in bilateral assistance. The total of UK aid now amounts only to 0.33 per cent of GNP, compared with the OECD target figure of 0.7 per cent, and this proportion will fall over the next few years because aid budgets are to be pegged in real terms.

UK aid is divided almost equally between multilateral and bilateral aid, whereas many major countries give up to five times as much bilaterally as multilaterally. This is a big change from 1970 when the UK's ratio was eight to one. It is only the bilateral aid which can be tied to the purchase of British goods and services, and so this source of advantage for exporters has been severely curtailed.

Until recently UK aid was solely in the form of a cash grant, which was appropriate until developing countries were offered loans at low interest rates which were effectively subsidised with aid funds. The UK has followed this practice in China and Indonesia to enable contractors to make more competitive bids.

Commercial funding

Commercial capital for projects has to be raised mainly in the principal world financial centres, but despite the keen competition to lend funds, it can be difficult to match terms offered by foreign contractors able to raise long-term loans in their own country for periods such as 20 years. Contractors become exposed to the exchange rate risk from the bidding stage onwards, and hedging against this risk can be expensive. Recently even the ECGD Tender to Contract Cover has become so expensive as to be almost prohibitive.

Contractors from countries with stable currencies and low interest rates, such as Japan and West Germany, start with a big apparent advantage, although the risk of the local currency depreciating against the currency of the loan is real but is often overlooked. This risk can be mitigated by softening the terms with development aid, enabling interest rates to be lower, and repayment to be over a longer time and starting with a grace period. This maximises the chance of the investment generating earnings which can keep up with the repayment of the borrowed funds.

British contractors have felt handicapped by the slow reaction of the Government in providing aid for mixed credit packages, and the lack of keenness in the terms. This has forced them to bring in foreign contractors to projects solely to gain access to the advantageous financing available to such overseas partners.

Limiting international competition in financing

One aim of the Development Aid Committee (DAC) of the OECD is to limit competition in aid, and this is enthusiastically supported by the British Government.

The DAC oversees a mechanism for setting minimum interest rates on loans, with a matrix of rates, 'consensus rates', depending on the classification of the borrowing country as between 'relatively rich', 'intermediate' and 'relatively poor'. Repayment periods are also laid down. These consensus rates of interest are reviewed every six months, and altered under an automatic formula agreed on in 1983.

The provision of mixed credits incorporating grants is also controlled, such as the British Aid and Trade Provision, which amounts to about 5 per cent of total UK aid. In any one package the aid concessionality component must exceed 35 per cent in an attempt to prevent the funds being used on a wide scale in this manner, and the USA would like to see the minimum increased to 50 per cent.

One problem for the UK is that the concessionality proportion on soft loans is calculated in relation to the differences between the consensus figure and domestic interest rate. This results in low interest rate countries, such as Japan and Germany, being credited with high concessionality at very little cost, compared with the UK's position, although recently the introduction of differential discount rates will progressively reduce the comparative advantage from low domestic interest rates.

In summary the activities reviewed in this chapter find themselves at what may be a turning point in their futures. The increasing complexity of overseas projects at a political, financial and even social level – and especially in developing countries is accompanied by growing competition from the newly industrialised countries. These problems are exacerbated by the decline in British overseas aid as a percentage of GNP, and particularly of the bilateral type. A continued low level of UK construction is a further factor. The future will require more UK-overseas joint ventures, but above all closer collaboration between consultants and the construction industry and between both these and finance houses. There can be few clearer examples of the intimate and vital link between production industry and the international service sector [6].

Notes and references

This chapter was first drafted by Peter McGregor, Director, Export Group for the Construction Industries. The authors are also indebted to Sir Andrew Derbyshire, Mr Julian Arkell and the staff of RMJM Consultants and to British Water International at Newbury for their research into the international operations of the water industries.

1 *Overseas Earnings of the British Professions*, Committee on Invisible Exports, London, November 1972.

2 'The Future for Consultancy: BCB Objectives and Achievements'. Paper given by Sir Andrew Derbyshire to the BCB 21st Anniversary Conference, London, July 1986.

3 'Private Sector Perceptions of Community Interests in the Liberalisation of Trade in Services'. Report by SEMA for the Commission of the European Communities (DGI), Brussels, July 1984 (not published for sale).

4 'The Top 200 International Design Firms in 1986'. *Engineering News Record (ENR)*, Highstown, NJ, USA, August 1987.

5 Of value in this section was *Barclays Bank/Euromoney – Guide to Export Finance*, Euromoney Publications, London, 1986.

6 Other sources of information for this chapter included:

Encyclopaedia Britannica, 15th Edition, Chicago and London, 1974.

The Marketing of Scottish Architects – Worldwide. Scottish Development Agency, Glasgow, 1986.

Francis Baden-Powell – article for *International Practice of Architecture*. (Drafted May 1987).

J. Arkell and I. S. Harrison, *A Sectoral Study on the Relevance of the OECD Conceptual Framework to International Trade in Consultancy Services*. London May 1987. (Not published – the study was commissioned by the OECD and submitted to them.)

Leaflets published by British Water International:
The Synopsis of the Water Industry in Britain
Planning, Operation and Development
Organisation and Management

9 Trade in knowledge, experience and specialist skills

It has often been said of the UK that its capacity to invent and innovate far exceeds its capacity to exploit. It is perhaps another facet of the same national characteristic that whatever its position in the world league of economic powers, there are still a very large number of countries which look to British knowledge, experience and specialist skills as one of the mainsprings of their own economic, technological and educational development.

The practical expression of this trade in knowledge and expertise, whilst by no means trivial, is of course a small fraction of the benefits accruing to the recipient nation, or indeed, though less directly, to the UK itself. Some of the more obvious commercial by-products in terms of construction, engineering and consulting contracts have been touched on in the previous chapter. This chapter looks at this total trade in a wider perspective, and identifies some of the many and often surprising directions in which British specialist knowledge and skills are offered on world markets and the various national and international agencies, institutions and firms through which the trade is negotiated and financed.

The areas covered in this chapter comprise:

1 *Education* – overseas students; consultancies and contracts abroad; other fee-earning activity overseas.
2 *Health-Care* – courses and seminars, pre- and post-qualifying; propagation and dissemination of specialist knowledge; overseas contracts for hospitals, medical schools etc.
3 *Legal services abroad*.
4 *Tourism* – overseas consultancy.
5 *Intellectual property* – (i) Patents, trademarks and copyrights. (ii) Creative arts – royalties from films and TV, books and music.
6 *Computing software*.

Education

In previous works the authors have explored in some detail the concept of education as an exportable product. It is not a concept which found ready acceptance in some purist academic circles; nor so far as overseas students are concerned has its obvious cultural and commercial value proved an immediate attraction to the spending departments of the UK Government.

For all that, overseas education has been, and continues to be, a scene of very considerable activity. There have, it is true, been setbacks in recent years arising from some harsh and frustrating policy decisions. However, the record is impressive; and whilst various attempts at quantified cost/benefit analysis have proved less than convincing, there seems little doubt of the overall value to the country of British overseas education and training.

The activities can be broadly grouped as follows:

1 Overseas students
2 Educational consultancies overseas
3 Other revenue from overseas educational activities

Overseas students

The total number of students in the UK in 1985 has been estimated by the Overseas Students Trust, using a variety of statistical sources, as 332 819. Of this 284 950 were in private sector schools and colleges (spread over 320 institutes) and the remaining 47 869 were in publicly funded institutions, including universities, polytechnics and colleges. The following tables show the distribution in both public and private sectors by type and level of institution.

It will be seen that within the private sector colleges, by far the largest number (266 000) are studying English with an average duration of 10 weeks per course. Using this estimate for English studies the Trust calculated a total equivalent full-time student number for the private sector of 86 500 overseas students.

Table 9.1   Overseas students in private sector colleges, 1985

Institutions specialising in:	Number of institutions in the UK	Total number of overseas students	Full-time equivalent student number
English language	200	264 600	66 150
General, non-advanced education	64	6 500	6 500
Professional and vocational training	45	10 250	10 250
Higher Education	11	3 600	3 600
Total	320	284 950	86 500

Source: OST, The Next Steps, p. 75

*Table 9.2   Expenditure on fees by overseas students in publicly financed institutions –
1984/85*

	Level of fees	Number of students paying overseas fees	Total expenditure on fees
Universities	£		£
Medicine, etc.	7650	2 471	18 903 150
Engineering and science	4150	13 128	54 481 200
Arts, etc.	3150	14 086	44 370 900
Public sector			
Advanced	3180	11 471	36 477 780
Non-advanced	1750	6 713	11 747 750
Total income from students paying overseas rate of fees			165 980 780
Income from students paying home rate of fees			5 489 538
Total (Publicly financed institutes)		47 869	171 470 318

Source: OST (*as above*)

Aggregating Tables 9.1 and 9.2 above, the grand total of full-time
equivalent students for the academic year 1984–85 was as follows:

Private sector colleges	86 500
Publicly financed institutions:	
Universities	29 685
Public sector advanced	11 471
Public sector non-advanced	6 713
Grand total full-time equivalent students	144 369

Contribution to balance of payments

1 The 'Pink Book' (1987) estimates annual foreign exchange earnings
from overseas students as follows:

	1985	*1986*
	£ m	*£ m*
Fees	269	302
Other expenditure	290	329
	559	631

Source: CSO 'Pink Book' 1987, Table 3.6

The figures include fees and expenditures, both in the publicly funded institutions as well as in private schools for students who are in the UK for twelve months or more. Earnings from short-stay students are entered under Travel and Tourism and not separately differentiated.

2 The Overseas Students' Trust have attempted a more comprehensive calculation of overseas students' revenue from all sources – fees and expenditure on essential and non-essential goods and services both in publicly-financed and private institutions. Their calculations for 1984–85 work out as follows:

	Private sector £ m	Publicly-funded sector £ m
Fees	288	171
Essential expenditure	202	155
Non-essential expenditure	69	45
	559	371

Total on fees and expenditure: £930 million

Gross total estimated revenue from overseas students is £930 million. So far as balance of payments is concerned £80 million has to be deducted from the total for the contributions from British sources, mostly scholarships and awards, leaving net earnings of £850 million.

The precise figures are of little significance in themselves, nor would the Trust seek to minimise the degree of approximation inherent in their calculations. There is a paucity of hard data, particularly for the private sector, whilst the demarcation between essential and non-essential expenditure, if not arbitrary, certainly reflects a major element of judgement. There are also of necessity major omissions in both categories of expenditure. For all that, the orders of magnitude are certainly correct and they give support to the claims of the Trust that overseas education, if not already there, is on its way to becoming a billion pound industry.

Student numbers – trends 1979–86

The following tables show the trends in student numbers by sector and level of study from 1978–86 and also by countries of origin from 1979–84.

The figures are confined to publicly financed institutes and exclude the private sector. They therefore reflect most directly the effect of changes in government policies in fees and grants and were in part recorded at the time of maximum impact. There are signs in more recent years of some stabilisation of the figures and indeed, as far as post-graduates are concerned, of some partial recovery.

The statistics, together with some later research carried out for the Trust in 1986–87, suggest some of the new trends in the UK overseas

Table 9.3   Overseas students in publicly financed institutions, by sector and level of study 1978–86 in 000s

| | Academic year beginning in | | | | | |
	1978	1980	1982	1984	1985	1986
Universities						
Postgraduate	18.3	16.4	15.9	17.7	20.1	21.5
Undergraduate	20.3	19.4	17.3	16.9	18.9	20.5
Total	38.5	35.8	33.3	34.6	39.0	42.0
Public sector higher education	22.1	19.7	15.3	13.6	14.0	14.7
Total higher education	60.7	55.5	48.5	48.2	52.9	56.7
Non-advanced further education	27.1	19.5	8.1	7.3	9.8	8.3 *
All students from abroad	87.8	75.0	56.6	55.5	62.7	65.0 *

* Provisional
Source: DES, November 1987

Table 9.4   Numbers of students from top twenty sending countries in publicly financed institutions – 1979 and 1984

		1979 Number of students	Percentage of total enrolment			1984 Number of students	Percentage of total enrolment
1	Malaysia	14 739	16.7	1	Hong Kong	6 935	12.4
2	Iran	8 356	9.5	2	Malaysia	5 600	10.0
3	Hong Kong	6 954	7.9	3	USA	3 438	6.1
4	Nigeria	5 263	5.9	4	Nigeria	3 221	5.7
5	USA	3 585	4.1	5	Greece	2 289	4.1
6	Greece	3 029	3.4	6	Iran	2 023	3.6
7	Iraq	2 487	2.8	7	Iraq	1 568	2.8
8	Zimbabwe	2 254	2.6	8	Germany, FR	1 496	2.7
9	Singapore	1 841	2.1	9	Singapore	1 329	2.4
10	Jordan	1 739	2.0	10	Libya	1 250	2.2
11	Sri Lanka	1 673	1.9	11	Kenya	1 056	1.9
12	Cyprus	1 655	1.9	12	India	1 012	1.8
13	Turkey	1 274	1.5	13	Cyprus	980	1.7
14	India	1 200	1.4	14	France	971	1.7
15	Kenya	1 199	1.4	15	Brunei	946	1.7
16	Germany, FR	1 185	1.3	16	Norway	906	1.6
17	Sudan	958	1.1	17	Canada	805	1.4
18	Pakistan	941	1.1	18	Irish Republic	780	1.4
19	Canada	934	1.1	19	Pakistan	705	1.3
20	Libya	928	1.1	20	Saudi Arabia	627	1.1
Total		62 203	70.7	Total		37 937	67.7

Source: OST, *The Next Steps*, p. 18

student population:

1 In the five years (1979–84) the total number of publicly financed overseas students fell by about one-third. The bulk of the fall was in the first three years. After this there was a period of stability followed by a slight rise in the years following 1984.

2 A very high proportion of the fall was at the lower end of the educational spectrum – the colleges and institutes offering non-degree courses.

3 By contrast the universities showed a slight rise with a distinct bias in favour of post-graduate students. In 1986–87 there were in fact more overseas students at universities than ever before at both undergraduate and post-graduate level.

4 Polytechnic numbers after a rapid fall showed a tendency to stabilise after 1981.

5 Social and business studies held their numbers well at universities at both post-graduate and undergraduate levels. Engineering and technology were surprisingly weak in all sectors of higher education. Numbers of science and mathematics students showed increasing strength, particularly at universities. There was a general decline throughout in non-advanced further education.

The total decline in numbers was of course in great measure due to the imposition of 'full-cost' charges on all overseas students (other than for the EC and one or two other selected categories). It was intended as a simple cost-saving measure (estimated at £186 million per year) in pursuance of a government policy which, whilst welcoming overseas students for education and political, commercial and developmental reasons, maintained that in general overseas students' education should not be subsidised by the British taxpayer. It allowed, however, for carefully targeted scholarship support to selected individuals and categories of students in accordance with national priorities.

The basic calculations have been brought into sharp question by the British Council, by educational and social economists and in particular the Overseas Students Trust, an educational charity since 1961. The Trust promotes education of overseas students in the United Kingdom in conditions which are both congenial and understanding. Backed by rigorous analytical studies and statistics it has maintained that the marginal costs of overseas students were overstated. By contrast the parameters of income derived from students were too narrowly drawn and in total widely underestimated.

Whatever the validity of the arguments, there is no doubt of the results of the policy. Numbers, as we have seen, fell steeply – at times to cause embarrassment to individual institutions, especially the engineering and technical faculties of polytechnics and technological universities. So far as the polytechnics were concerned, the decline in numbers was also aggravated by the sentiment of many local authorities against spending ratepayers' money in the teaching of overseas students, an activity which in their judgement brought little benefit to the local community.

There were also some side effects on the general pattern of the student body most of which might have been forecast. The shift to advanced higher education, particularly at post-graduate level, raised the average age of students very considerably. The preferential fee basis for students from the EC increased the proportion of that particular cohort of students. Similarly the combination of higher fees, adverse exchange rates and the selective targeting on the higher levels of advanced education sharply reduced the numbers from the poorer and developing countries of the world and from the Commonwealth.

Finally, local difficulties in Nigeria and Iran cut back two of the most prolific sources of overseas students. However, Hong Kong and Malaysia (though at a lower level) maintained their place on the ladder of subscribing countries side-by-side with the USA, Greece, Germany, France, Canada and the Irish Republic.

In addition, the development of national education systems, as in India, and the active marketing of alternative opportunities, particularly in Australia and the Far East, sharpened the adverse reaction to British policies which were thought to be unwelcoming and perhaps even churlish. There seems little doubt that this loss to the country of educational business, which is impossible to quantify, will be extremely difficult to replace.

Educational contracts and consultancies

Awards, programmes and monitoring of overseas students, all demand continuing consultation and co-operation between universities, polytechnics and colleges, government departments at home and abroad, and funding bodies, charitable foundations and firms both in the UK and overseas.

Much of the responsibility for the smooth running of the educational programmes rests with the Technical Co-operation and Training Department of the British Council working in collaboration with the ODA as well as with DES, FCO, DTI and other concerned departments. There is, however, one aspect of the Council's activities of which the advantages are not only more obvious but also financially quantifiable – the work of the Educational Contracts Department.

The authors have been privileged to study a full chronological list of educational training projects administered by the Department from 1975–86. The list includes more than 100 contracts for teaching, consultancy and educational development spread over more than thirty countries. Many of these countries are developing countries of the Third

World, in the Middle East, in Africa and in Asia, and also increasingly in China. There are projects, too, in Venezuela, Greece, Turkey and Portugal. A team is at work on the national transport plan for the Argentine, whilst industrial contracts include the supply of textbooks to Sierra Leone and Indonesia.

Many contracts are funded by the World Bank, Asian Development Bank and similar bodies. Their value ranges from quite modest sums for small but significant local projects, to very large projects for developing the educational infrastructure of the countries concerned. The projects include an integrated textbook scheme in Indonesia in collaboration with the Publishers Association (value £462 000); a second contract funded by the European Commission and worth £414 000 to assist the Faculty of Science at the Yarmouk University of Jordan – a project led by the North-East World Institute which also involves the University of Salford and the University of Wales at Bangor. Huddersfield Polytechnic have accepted a training contract under World Bank auspices for more than 100 trainee lecturers in engineering. The training will employ a Polytechnic lecturer on loan to Indonesia. The whole contract is valued at £2.9 million. The Bell Education Trust arranged a study tour for 30 language trainees also from Indonesia, again under the auspices of the World Bank. A very large programme (value £2.4 million) is under way in Turkey in collaboration with the RCA of the USA to up-grade eight post-secondary education schools and technical training centres.

In Singapore, following pioneer work many years ago by the Polytechnic of Central London, a centre for computer studies is now being developed by ICL (Singapore) in conjunction with the British Council; whilst also in Singapore, Loughborough University are helping to develop a college of physical education under a contract worth £790 000.

Finally, and perhaps most exciting of all, is the contract of the World Bank (value £2.36 million) to improve the Chinese television and polytechnic systems. An advisory panel has been established, whilst the British Council, in collaboration with several UK educational institutions, provides administrative and professional support to the project and short-term specialists for a period of four years.

Other educational revenue

The above list is, of course, selective and can in no way pretend to be complete in its coverage of public-funded contractual activities. There are, in addition, a great many fee-earning activities quite outside the area of public funding. These include as demonstrated in Tables 9.1 and 9.2 the large and growing activity in the teaching of English as a foreign language, some of it drawing on public funds, but a great deal more in private language schools, particularly in the south-east of England.

A number of academic entrepreneurs have also for years been

cultivating individual contacts resulting quite often in self-financing contracts for consultancy and academic development, many of several years' duration.

There is also the large range of overseas examinations conducted by the Royal Society of Arts, the City and Guilds Institute and the London Chamber of Commerce Examination Boards. Their fee-earning capacity is very large indeed as is their contribution towards the educational development of many countries throughout the world.

The British Council have themselves encouraged and advised on many of these efforts whilst recognising the limits of public funding to support many worthwhile enterprises.

Health-Care

Twenty years' ago there were around 20 000 overseas student nurses under training in this country. The figure now is appreciably lower – perhaps one-third of its post-war peak. This is largely due to the greater availability of teaching and training resources in the developing countries, as a result of continuous expansion of hospitals, clinics and medical research, much of it through ambitious projects which, as with education, are financed by the World Bank, Asian Development Bank and other funding agencies.

There are, unfortunately, other circumstances peculiar to the UK which already affected the intake of overseas medical students at universities, colleges and medical schools. The most obvious is the increase in undergraduate fees for medical students at universities to £8450 per annum in 1986–7, an increase of 69 per cent on 1980–1. Then there is the cost and availability of student housing particularly in London and the South-East. Finally, there is the dwindling public reputation of the British National Heath Service which, whilst in professional terms at least is by no means always justified, nevertheless makes it increasingly difficult to resist the aggressive marketing tactics of other countries which appear to value more highly the presence of overseas medical students.

The increase in post-graduate medical fees has been in line with fees for undergraduates and they bear particularly harshly on students from the developing countries and the poorer members of the Commonwealth who, despite the targeting of government grants in their favour, remain at a disadvantage compared with European Community students (who by and large pay nothing for tuition) and the wealthier nations of the OECD who can best afford to pay.

Fortunately, the worldwide reputation of the UK medical profession has ensured a strong and continuing market for post-graduate students and for the overseas participants in seminars and short courses in one of the many medical and professional specialisms on which the country's reputation has been built. Many of these are sponsored by the British Council, whilst others are organised and largely financed by individual drug and pharmaceutical companies and foundations, such as the Wellcome Foundation, the Boots Company, CIBA/Geigy, Shell and ICI. Many of the courses are high-level and concerned with the propagation and discussion of recent advances in medical knowledge and research. Others are aimed more generally at up-dating the progress and knowledge of hospital staff both at home and abroad. Most of the courses are planned in collaboration with the British Medical Association and also with the British Health Education Council (BHEC) who play a crucial role in monitoring developments worldwide, in disseminating information on current contracts and tenders, and in promoting and exporting medical equipment and services. For there are few areas of specialist skills with such clear links between research, consultancy and overseas sales.

Exports of services and medical equipment

Exports in this area are in the main in the form of visible goods. Frequently, however, when large contracts or bids are concerned, successful bidding is preceded by a period of consultancy, and by laboratory and analytical testing. Often, too, particularly for underdeveloped countries, the contract includes commitment to consultancy sometimes for a period of one year, and also acceptance of students for training in UK hospitals, universities and medical schools.

The success of British efforts in this field is sharply reflected in the statistics, published by Customs and Excise for exports of medical equipment over the past five years, extracts from which are given in Table 9.5. In 1962 exports of medical equipment from the UK totalled £348 144 million. The comparable figure in 1986 was £598 974 million. Every year in this five-year period showed an increase over the previous year.

In each year the three largest customers were USA, Federal Republic of Germany and France, whilst the bulk of the fifty top-ranking export countries, including as they do the most medically aware countries of the world, displayed in their purchasing policies their respect for the level of British technology and their confidence in British medical equipment. It is interesting that China and the Soviet Union have been rising in the list of importing nations, whilst Japan, India, and Australia all maintain a prominent position in our export market.

The size and scope of the tenders are very wide indeed. The current list, published by BHEC, includes a project for management of a new hospital and the building of a pharmaceutical unit in Saudi Arabia; a new hospital development in Hong Kong; the supply of medical

Table 9.5 UK exports – pharmaceuticals and medical equipment

Country	Value – £m	% of total
USA	98.840	17.63
FR of Germany	62.943	11.23
France	38.047	6.79
Saudi Arabia	22.224	3.97
Irish Republic	21.922	3.91
Italy	21.427	3.82
Japan	20.783	3.71
Netherlands	19.239	3.43
Australia	17.241	3.08
Denmark	17.029	3.04
Sweden	15.326	2.73
Belgium/Luxembourg	13.000	2.32
Iran	10.348	1.85
South Africa	9.640	1.72
Spain	9.448	1.69
Canada	9.146	1.63
Switzerland	8.815	1.57
Nigeria	7.934	1.42
Iraq	7.135	1.27
Egypt	5.831	1.04
Norway	5.812	1.04
Hong Kong	5.291	0.94
Soviet Union	3.440	0.61
China	3.147	0.56
Turkey	2.556	0.46
Libya	2.509	0.45
Mexico	1.979	0.35
Others	71.327	12.73
Total	560.494	100.00

Source: Statistics from the DHSS

equipment in Burma and Singapore, dental instruments in Chile, radio-isotope equipment in Bangladesh and X-ray equipment in France.

All these contracts and tenders are, of course, subject to the keenest competition in terms of both finance and technology. The British success rate does, however, appear to be consistent and growing.

Legal services

The lawyers of the City of London, with their wide-ranging experience and expertise, have long provided an underpinning to the overseas operation of governments, institutions, companies and individual clients. Some of their firms are very old. A recent merger for instance joined together two firms founded respectively in 1801 and 1900. Many of them are also very large. This same firm, Clifford Chance, as now merged, employs more than 1000 staff in 14 different countries, about half of their employees being professional lawyers.

The services of these firms, though far-ranging, are at heart commercial. For this is their tradition and the source of their expertise. For the same reason, they are most at home when advising and operating in overseas commercial markets, for there are few countries of the world without a past (and often quite recent) involvement of one of the firm's branches, offices or representatives. Moreover they have been able to take in their stride the new political and economic influences which are increasingly at work worldwide in legal affairs. Many have been described elsewhere in this book – liberalisation of international trade and protectionism, with the developing work of GATT on the one hand and protectionist measures in USA, Japan, Germany and elsewhere; the many legal implications of the Financial Services Act in the UK; and the huge proliferation of laws, directives, and orders emanating from the European Commission.

This same flexibility and professional expertise also goes some way to explain why British lawyers, in spite of mounting competition from many developed countries of the world, continue on the whole to maintain, and even expand, the international standing of both firms and individuals, and to increase the UK overseas earnings from their international activities.

Overseas earnings of the UK legal profession

As in other areas of our sectoral studies, we have found formidable difficulties in quantifying the overseas earnings of the legal profession. The sums are surprisingly large, and the chief statistical source (the Pink Book of the Central Statistical Office) shows a steady progression in foreign earnings of solicitors from £15 million in 1974 to £88 million in 1985. The figures are based on VAT returns from 1974 to 1977 supported in subsequent years by surveys conducted by the Bank of England on behalf of the Central Statistical Office.

A more detailed questionnaire and enquiry, however, carried out in conjunction with the Law Society and the British Invisible Exports Council, suggests that the earnings both in 1985 and in earlier years, may have been seriously underestimated, and the Pink Book for 1987 shows a figure for 1986 of £190 million. The figures have been aggregated from many sources including fees from non-residents, income from overseas operations and earnings from seconded staff. Even the new figures may underestimate the real total earnings of overseas activities, particularly as the figures are confined to firms and exclude profits and earnings from non-resident individuals. Whatever the precise figure, an estimate of some £200 million per year may be considered a fair valuation of the profession's contribution to the UK balance of payments.

Range of legal services

The overseas work of the City firms reflects, as we have said above, the character of their domestic work. Its heart is in commerce – banking and financial work, securities issues, mergers and acquisitions, general corporate and commercial work, litigation, arbitration (industry, public and international) shipping, aviation, real estate etc. By and large it is the legal counterpart (and more) of the City's major international merchant bankers.

The English language is widely used for international contracts and for arbitration. English courts are felt to be relatively accessible; English judges free from political influence; English lawyers well informed and competent.

Overseas branches often started in a largely domestic context, particularly in Belgium, France and Holland, advising British companies on corporate strategies, taxation, and gradually in bridging the gap between the different national legal systems. There followed a more broadly based position in international business in North and South America, Tokyo, Hong Kong, Japan, Singapore and the Middle East. Finally the European community, with its complex institutional structure, its laws, and its directives, often bearing upon trade and industry, added enormously to the work of this growing number of legal specialists in the field.

The legal profession and the European Community

The first responsibility of a lawyer is to guide his client through the successive hierarchies of the Community systems – the Council of the European Community, the European Parliament, the Court of Justice, Court of Arbitration, the European Patent Office and a wide range of regional and specialist committees. In addition there are many committees of the Council of Europe, and other wide-ranging bodies such as the European Council of Human Rights and the International Court of Justice at the Hague, which is the principal judicial organisation of the United Nations.

The major commercial issue in Community work tends to revolve around international trade such as the dumping regulations (which repeatedly involve Japan), customs queries, and questions arising from GATT; and anti-trust work, where the British firms are called upon to represent clients directly before the Commission and in the Court in Luxembourg. The Commission is particularly active in the anti-monopoly area, and handles up to 200 cases per year. Involving, as many of them do, the small print in the Treaty of Rome, the work is time-consuming and often frustrating both for the lawyer and his client. Advice on Directives is particularly keenly sought, as many, in draft form at least, appear extreme in their provisions and too often unwork-able in practice. The seeking of legal advice is in many cases pre-emptive, and at least one British firm in Brussels issues a regular newsletter in this area.

The Community have in part succeeded in clarifying the status of lawyers from member states, with members of the EEC free (subject to one or two local restrictions) to represent their clients in Court provided that the individual concerned retains his domestic title (e.g. 'barrister') and conforms to local regulations and also of those of the home state. Both France and Germany, however, impose restrictions on the estab-lishment of a Branch in a member's state. Indeed, Germany prohibits the establishment of foreign lawyers independently – a ruling which has been under question at the Court of Luxembourg.

Growth of legal firms overseas

The speed and scope of overseas development in legal affairs is reflected in the number of firms established overseas, their size, and their geographical spread. We have already referred to one (perhaps the largest) Clifford Chance, which has a total of 1000 employees, with offices (including associated offices) in 14 countries including London, Paris, New York, Tokyo, Singapore, Saudi Arabia, the United Arab Emirates, and Bahrain. They have special arrangements with the People's Republic of China, providing for mutual secondments of lawyers within offices in Hong Kong and Beijing.

Hong Kong, which employs the British legal system, has been the scene of very special activity of British lawyers. The Law Society of Hong Kong made enquiries on behalf of this research of 21 London firms who had opened up offices in Hong Kong. They received 20 replies (itself a near record by market research standards!) and their figures establish beyond all reasonable doubt, the size and speed of the development of local legal firms. Johnson Stokes and Masters, for instance, have several offices in Hong Kong, as well as at Kowloon and a branch office in Tokyo. They have some 60 partners (including a significant number of Notaries Public), and nearly 100 associated solici-tors, a list notable not only for its size but also for its increasing number of Chinese admitted both as full and assistant solicitors.

Baker & McKenzie with its worldwide string of some fifty offices spreading from New York, Washington, Sydney and Melbourne,

Mexico City, Rome, Zurich, Tokyo and Taipei, opened in Hong Kong in 1975 with 3 qualified solicitors. They now have 15 resident and 7 non-resident partners, 28 solicitors admitted in Hong Kong and 16 other lawyers not locally admitted and a support staff of more than 200.

Linklaters and Paines (L & P) opened an office in Hong Kong in 1975 with one partner and (shortly after) one assistant. Following a trial period of joint venture, L & P London now have in their Hong Kong offices four resident partners, eleven other fee-earners (nine Hong Kong solicitors, one waiting admission and an Australian solicitor) and two articled clerks from London on six months' rotation.

There seems, indeed, to be consistent growth throughout all these respondent firms – some quite modest and others like McKenna starting with one partner and one assistant in 1980, and employing in May 1987, 17 solicitors of whom 6 are partners, whilst Slaughter & May increased their qualified professionals from 3 in 1974 to 22 in 1987.

This short account of legal activity in Hong Kong, which no doubt can be matched, though in varying degrees, elsewhere, indicates quite clearly the particular contribution of the legal profession to development overseas and the large and growing opportunities for fee-earning activities for the United Kingdom. Its current financial contribution of perhaps £200 million of foreign earnings is in itself very substantial, but possibly only a fraction of the value of their activities to the British and overseas economies.

Tourism – overseas consultancy

The growth and rapid changes in this group of industries have been described in Chapter 7. The growth has indeed been so rapid and widespread as to make a very major impact on the economic and social development of the countries as a whole and on their individual cities, towns and villages.

It follows that in many areas there has arisen a need for specialist help and advice and in turn those few people qualified through education and experience to act as consultants to the industry find their services in very great demand both at home and overseas.

As well as being the leading academics in the field – Medlik, Archer, Gladwell, Laverick, Lickorish to name just a few – they are also leading figures in the provision of consultancy advice to British and overseas companies as well as individual firms.

Side by side with the academic establishments, a firm of chartered accountants, Stoy Hayward, offer, through their wholly-owned company Howarth & Howarth UK Ltd, a major consultancy practice specialising in the provision of advisory services to the tourism, hotels and leisure-related industries. The company has set out to advise on worldwide hotel planning and operations, conference centres, leisure and multi-facility operations and restaurants. In addition they mount a large number of seminars and training sessions on various aspects of hotel planning, management and control.

There is one other firm which merits mention in a specialist field of consultancy in the industry. Abela Manufacturing Services Ltd is Lebanese-owned, registered in Belgium and London-based with operating branches throughout Europe and the Middle East.

Its business is to advise on providing total back-up requirements for services based overseas, for oil terminals and pumping stations and for similar types of development projects throughout the world. They identify, select, train and monitor the personal needs for both start-up and subsequent operations. They advise on equipment and arrange accommodation and facilities for recreation. It is a fascinating niche in the consultancy market and one which, in the case of Abela, has developed into a very sizeable business.

It is not possible, in the case of this and other consultancy operations, to evaluate their precise commercial value at home and particularly overseas. It can be safely said, however, that there are few major centres in the world for tourism or for personal services to staff overseas which have not benefited at some stage in their development from the professional advice of British academics, business consultants and specialist service companies.

Trade in intellectual property

'Intellectual property', says the preamble to a White Paper ('Intellectual Property and Innovation') presented to the UK Parliament in 1986, 'is important to many areas of government policy concerning industry, commerce, science, technology and education'. The overall objectives of intellectual property laws, it continues are, 'to protect and reward, and thus to provide an incentive to innovation and creativity, whilst ensuring that the resulting rights and obligations strike a fair balance between the originator, his competitors and the user'.

So much is clear and, indeed, objectives such as this are behind a great deal of thinking of governments, industry and the creative arts. It found its most recent expression in the 'Copyright, Design and Patent' Bill of October 1987, to be enacted in 1988.

Amongst the specific provisions of the Bill are,' to restate the law of copyright, to make fresh provision on the rights of performers, to confer design rights of original design ... to amend the laws of patents, to make fresh provision penalising the fraudulent receipt of programmes, to make the fraudulent application of use of trade marks an offence, to enable financial assistance to be given to certain international bodies'.

The field is wide, significant and complex, reflected not least in the mammoth size of the bill, with its 277 clauses and 75 pages of schedules. Quite clearly, however, detailed discussion of the provisions of the Bill, is beyond the scope of this book and, in fact, only partially relevant to its purpose. The following remarks will, therefore, be confined to the following aspects of intellectual property:

1 General significance, scope and size of the field and its overseas earnings.

2 Probable changes in the law affecting the export potential of intellectual property.

3 Some policy implications for international trade affecting competition policy and monopolies, the Uruguay Round of the GATT, and the probable negotiating stances of the technically advanced countries, the NICs and the developing countries of UNCTAD.

The scope of the field and overseas earnings

The main indicators of the size and scope of overseas earnings are the figures for royalties etc., contained in the CSO Pink Book. The estimates cover amounts payable or receipts by UK residents (other than oil companies, banks and insurance companies) for the right to use patents, processes, trade marks, copyrights etc., the manufacturing rights and the use of technical 'know-how', and amounts payable or receivable in respect of mineral royalties. The figures also include royalties on printed matter, sound recordings and performing rights. Earnings from films and television are recorded separately, whilst royalties included in the contract price of UK exports and imports are covered under visible trade.

The royalty figures paid out and received from related companies (defined as overseas parent companies, branches, subsidiaries and associates) and earnings from and payments to non-related companies are listed separately.

Out of these statistics the following broad picture emerges for 1985. (The 1986 figures recorded in the 1987 Pink Book are unfortunately not disaggregated).

Highlights of the figures are as follows:

1 Intellectual property makes a positive contribution to the UK balance of payments which totalled in 1985 £416 million. After steep annual rises from 1976 the revenue from films and TV has since levelled out. In the years 1983–86 there was in fact a sharp rise and again in 1985, perhaps due to some exceptional receipts. But the figures for 1986 appear to have reverted to the level of previous years.

Receipts for royalties show a steady increase, mostly to non-related concerns. Payments to related concerns have shown a steady rise to a

Table 9.6 Royalties, film, TV – 1985

		Credits £m	Debits £m
1	*Royalties*		
	Related concerns	332	368
	Other concerns	459	151
		791	519
	Net related concerns	− 36	
	Net other concerns	308	
	Total net credit	272	
2	*Films, TV*		
	Credits	335	
	Debits	191	
	Net credits	141	
3	*Total net credits*		
	Royalties	272	
	Films, TV	141	
	Total net credits for royalties etc., films, TV	416	

Source: CSO Pink Book 1986

peak of £530 million for 1986. Payments to non-related concerns show some rises but at a much lower level.

2 The UK has succeeded in increasing its surplus on licences and patent income. The USA (by far the largest) and the UK are in fact the only industrialised countries to achieve such a surplus. Japan has the greatest deficit in this trade, and West Germany, though still funding only half of its expenditure out of revenue earnings, has substantially increased its receipts over the past ten years.

3 The steady increase of royalties from 'non-related concerns' illustrates a distinctive feature of British trade policy, in so far as they show the lesser significance of direct overseas investment as a source of licence and patent income, compared with the USA and, most significantly, West Germany. British inventors tend to spread their licence business very broadly, maximising their income from fees and royalties, but often irrespective of direct interest in overseas manufacture and commercial development. This is thought to be a major point of weakness in the longer-term policies of the UK companies.

Spread of overseas licences

The DTI annual survey of overseas licence transactions gives the best, albeit rather incomplete indications, of the spread of technical licences from the UK. The chemical and allied industries, easily the largest sources of revenues, account for some third of the total income. Motor vehicles contribute one-fifth, as do mechanical and electrical engineering. Substantial contributions also come from food, drink and tobacco, rubber and paper, printing and publishing.

North America is the leading destination for UK licences (some 30 per cent) followed by Western Europe (some 25 per cent) and 18 per cent to other developed countries. It is estimated that the total trade associated with the UK overseas royalty transactions was of the order of some £6–7 billion.

It should be noted that these figures refer to 1983. They are compiled from a total of 1200 firms contributing to the DTI survey, and omit any form of technical collaboration which does not involve royalty payments – an omission which is perhaps less significant to the UK than elsewhere in view of the high proportion of sales to non-related concerns and which, for the most part, are therefore subject to royalties and licence payments.

The 1987 Bill

At the time of writing, the Bill was only in the very early stages of its passage through the parliamentary process.

Some of its main provisions are as follows:

1 Original designs are to be protected against copying for ten years, although licences will be available, as of right, after five years. Copying necessary for the provision of spare parts is, however, permitted.

2 Performers and recorders of film companies will be permitted to take civil action in county courts against bootleggers, with sanctions brought into line with arrangements for copyright.

3 Patent actions will also pass to county courts instead of falling within the existing jurisdiction of the High Court. The intention is to make such action cheaper, quicker and less complicated.

4 Exclusive rights for pharmaceutical products are to be expanded from 16 to 20 years, a clause welcomed by the industry as giving more time for market exploitation from research and development which, in most cases, has been costly and protracted.

5 Authors, artists and film directors now have the right to be identified on their works and given legal right of compensation for unauthorised reproduction and modification. Film directors welcome the first specific mention of film directors in British copyright, but the

Directors' Guild, aware of the complexities in enforcement, are already lobbying for clarification and amendment.

6 Similarly, artists are pleased at the reversion to the first 'Hogarth' Copyright Act of 1735, but are already planning to follow the example of their distinguished predecessor to clarify and tighten the 'moral right' which is written into the Bill as a new concept in British law. It is contemplated that artists will now maintain control of their work, both with regard to directions of sale and standards of reproduction, even after assignment of copyright. This particular provision is in line with the Berne Convention and the Copyright Convention signed by EC countries.

7 Despite intense pressure over many years, the Bill does not introduce a levy on blank tapes to compensate copyright holders. At the time of writing the battle over this contentious issue is still warming up.

8 On the other hand, unlimited fines or up to two years' imprisonment may be imposed for making or distributing materials infringing copyrights, with heavy penalties also for trading in pirated goods. A new offence makes counterfeiting liable to unlimited fines or up to ten years' imprisonment.

9 After a lengthy process of consultation, it has been decided not to change the legal status of the Patent Office. It remains directly under central government and it is not to be privatised, presumably on the assumption that much of its work will be passed to the European Patent Office in Munich. Vigorous efforts are, however, contemplated to enable the facilities of the Patent Office to be more intensively commercially exploited through access to its reservoir of technical and scientific information.

International property rights and the international trading system

The 1987 Bill, as discussed above, will undoubtedly strengthen the patent and copyright position of British manufacturers, inventors and creative artists. It removes a number of weaknesses in existing legislation. It introduced new protection, particularly for design, and embodies within the legislative framework, the principle of 'moral rights'. It admits new offences and increases the penalties for existing ones, particularly for breaches of copyright for illicit publication and distribution and copyright patented material and for counterfeiting. The Bill is reasonably comprehensive and, on the whole, well balanced.

And yet the very introduction of the Bill, with all its concern and safeguards for individuals and firms in the UK and for the British national interests, illustrates in itself, the anomalous situation of intellectual property rights within the international trading system. For the Bill does not attempt a philosophical defence of its basic concept, that intellectual property rights are best developed and best defended on the basis of legislation of individual nations; that every national and every individual has the right to a fair economic return on the results of his or her creative work; and that, in particular, the rewards of technological progress should properly belong to the individual or corporate entities who gave them birth, and that there should be an accrual of commercial advantage and financial returns to the originating nation as a whole.

It is true that international bodies exist to monitor developments in national legislation and that there are in addition a series of conventions to help their harmonisation. A specialist agency of the United Nations, the World Intellectual Property Organisation (WIPO) aims at the modernisation of laws on intellectual property and on the centralisation of measures for their harmonisation. The Paris Convention (under WIPO) covers wide areas of the field and in particular requires that one contracting state gives the same protection to individuals of other contracting states as it grants to their own nationals. The Berne Convention, also administered by WIPO, covers literary and artistic works, whilst the Universal Copyright Convention (UCC) operates, though less comprehensively, in the same field as the Berne Convention. Administered by UNESCO, this latter agreement draws its strength from including (quite exceptionally) in its membership the USA who have, by and large, refused to join numerous other conventions and agreements, including Berne, on the grounds that the agreement in question violates their domestic laws, that the US law is stronger, or that it is not in American interests.

International patent agreements in particular arouse little enthusiasm amongst the strong technological nations because of the limited membership of many of them, inadequacy of enforcement, unwarranted demands on patentees and licensees, differences in procedure requirements, or because, in many cases, they are easily violated and difficult to defend.

Intellectual property and monopoly

Weaknesses, then, there certainly are in the international trading system, and many of them despite pressures particularly from the USA, are proving highly intractable. In addition, efforts are being made within the European Community (with fair prospects of success) for a common code amongst its members on intellectual property rights.

There remains, however, one major conceptual obstacle to any real speed in liberalising international practices in this field. Patents and copyrights are of their very nature expressions of whole or quasi-monopoly and as a result form a series of barriers to free flow of international trade.

The GATT, to whom this whole question is due to revert in the near future, is by its very nature dedicated to removal of barriers to trade, whether by way of tariffs, quotas, agreements or by implication, concessionary rights to patents, or technical 'know-how'.

Meanwhile, the large number of countries which form the bulk of membership of UNCTAD have neither the technological nor financial resources to keep pace with this trend by their own efforts. They consider that they themselves enjoy a right to 'knowledge goods' wherever they may arise and at a price to suit their own ability to pay. Without such concessions they feel that scientific and technological progress will consolidate rather than narrow the North-South divide and increase the gap between the industrialised countries of the world and the poorer nations who are being left behind.

This is one of the more difficult issues facing the negotiations on trade liberalisation in the services, which have already been discussed in Chapter 3. It will undoubtedly feature prominently in the continuing discussions in UNCTAD and also in the Uruguay Round of GATT negotiations.

Exports of British films and television

The international film and television trade is dominated by the USA. True, the UK, France, India, Japan, the Soviet Union, and surprisingly perhaps Hong Kong, are all major producers of films sold internationally. Nevertheless, in films especially, the USA is pre-eminent. In Europe, it has been calculated, American films account for 80 to 90 per cent of cinema attendance in some countries and an average of 47 per cent in the UK, France, Italy and West Germany combined. In television the networks tend to devote rather more time to domestically produced material but, nonetheless, some three-quarters of imported programming on European television originates from the USA. On the other hand, the USA is an extremely difficult market to enter on any scale. No more than 2 per cent of total programming derives from overseas [1].

Nevertheless, the British film industry has shown a consistently powerful overseas performance during the 1980s with receipts increasing year by year from £97 million in 1981 to a peak of £260 million in 1985, dropping to £209 million in 1986. The drop reflects, as we indicated earlier, adverse dollar–pound exchange rate fluctuations as the dollar weakened. Net receipts in 1986 showed a UK surplus of £103 million. While the USA remains the largest single market (at 52 per cent in 1986), the EC has steadily grown in importance throughout the decade, accounting for 30 per cent of sales in 1986. Among the most prominent successes of recent years were *My Beautiful Laundrette* by Film Four International, *Room with a View* (Merchant Ivory Production) and *The Mission* (Goldcrest Films) [2].

Though the receipts from television programmes sold overseas were some £100 million in 1986, import penetration, largely from the USA, is much greater, leaving a surplus of £12 million. Nevertheless, the UK is the world's second largest exporter of television programmes. The USA, followed by Australia, are the UK's most successful markets. The UK shares with the USA one enormous comparative advantage, the possession of the English language. While English is not the world's most frequently spoken mother tongue (that honour goes to Chinese), it is both the first language of a substantial number of the wealthiest industrialised markets and the world's international language. There are some 409 million native speakers of English compared with 352 million speakers of Hindi and Urdu and 265 million Spanish speakers. Small wonder, then, that in many cases West German film producers have resorted to filming in English and dubbing back into German for the domestic market.

This very wide potential market for television programmes is reflected in the number of countries to which British TV companies sell their products. In 1986–87, for example, the BBC sold £40 million worth of programmes, representing 8500 viewing hours to some 100 countries. Central Television, which won the 1987 Queen's Award for Export Achievement, sold a wide range of programmes to 80 countries, with a total output of 1600 hours. The countries ranged from Australia and the USA to Iceland and Kuwait. Granada sold a record 3983 hours to 88 countries, Yorkshire 650 hours to 75 countries, Scottish 75 programmes to 23 countries. In all, in 1986 the reputation of British television was such that sales were made to more than 200 countries worldwide. That is not to say, however, that all markets are especially lucrative. Prices worldwide are fixed according to the USA 'Global Prices for TV-Films', to which all western countries adhere. The prices are calculated on the basis of size of population and the number of TV sets. This means that a film that makes a return of $40 000 per hour on Canadian Television only brings in $100 per hour in Bermuda. Haiti pays $150 per hour, Thailand ten times as much [3].

What sort of British TV programmes are most successful internationally? They tend to fall into a number of clearly defined categories. By far the most important, the bread-and-butter of the British TV (and film) export trade, are those programmes and films related most closely to what the outside world regards as typically British. The BBC's best-selling programme is *Elizabeth R* made in 1971, followed by the *Six Wives of Henry VIII*. Czechoslovakia recently became the forty-seventh country to buy the BBC's complete Shakespeare series. Other BBC successes that demonstrate this clear British image include *Vanity Fair* and *Blackadder the Third*. The international popularity of programmes set in British historical backgrounds, often with a strong romantic quality, is well illustrated by the films that led to the Queen's Export Award to HTV in 1986: *Robin of Sherwood, Return to Treasure Island, Jamaica Inn, The*

Master of Ballantrae. Granada have been successful overseas with *Sherlock Holmes*, *The Jewel in the Crown* and that rather different view of British life *Coronation Street*! BBC's Miss Marple films have sold even to the Republic of China, while *Bergerac* has been dubbed in French, German and Spanish.

Another category of major importance are programmes based on the performance of pop music, also a British cultural speciality. Central Television's *Tina Turner – A Private Dance Tour* of 1985 sold to 55 countries. *The Pointer Sisters* by the same company was seen in over 30 countries, *Duran Duran* in 47. One of the BBC's greatest successes in the USA is *Top of the Pops*.

Another part of the staple diet of TV exports are the wildlife and natural history programmes made by the BBC and a number of the independent companies. *The Kingdom of the Ice Bear* and *Living Planet* are just two highly successful examples from the BBC.

A further looser grouping are again programmes that are un-mistakably British but do not derive from romantic geographical or historical settings. On the contrary, possibly the most successful of all is that scurrilous satire of British (and international) public life, Central Television's *Spitting Image* which has twice won an Emmy Award and has been sold in its entirety even to Spain. Then there are programmes as dissimilar yet culturally British as BBC's *Dr Who* (shown in 200 cities in the USA), Thames' *Benny Hill Show*, TVS's female detective series *CATS Eyes*, Anglia's thrillers *Cover Her Face* and *Tales of the Unexpected*.

A final category are those programmes made with a deliberate appeal to the American market. Central Television's *Vietnam* and *Kennedy* (which was pre-sold to the USA and eventually seen in 27 countries) are examples. LWT's *Dempsey and Makepeace* is another variation on this theme. It is a crime series featuring a dynamic American policeman operating for the Metropolitan CID and partnered by an attractive yet cool blonde English girl from the upper classes.

In fact partnership in TV programme-making is today hardly confined to the fictitious characters of the films themselves. As production costs rise, while in the case of the BBC at least, licence fees are pegged at fixed real prices, co-production with overseas companies becomes an increasingly good business proposition. Not only are costs spread: wider markets seem guaranteed. Central Television's *The Bretts* was made for the American TV Company WGBH Boston for the PBS network. Granada's *Lost Empires* was underwritten for broadcast on WGBH Boston by the Mobil Corporation. Thames' film of the America's Cup *The Challenge* was co-produced with Australia's Nine network and subsequently sold to 13 countries.

The BBC, largely through its dynamic commercial arm, BBC Enterprises, was involved in 90 co-productions in 1986, of which 80 per cent were with American companies and many of the remainder with

Australia. The attraction to the overseas partners are the exclusive sales rights they enjoy in their own domestic markets. BBC co-production revenue rose in 1986–87 by 25 per cent to £9 million.

What of the future? The challenge lies in fuller exploitation of video, cable and satellite. BBC Enterprises is placing great emphasis on sales of inexpensive videos. They are also deeply involved in the sale of educational materials. A group of the independent TV companies have together invested in Super Channel, which broadcasts by satellite to West and North Europe. An English-language channel which broadcasts programmes from both the independent companies and the BBC, Super Channel's largest markets are the German-speaking countries, Austria, Switzerland and West Germany, where it reached in 1987 some 3.9 million households, and Benelux countries with 4 million households. In third place are the Nordic countries with 1 million households. In the UK, by contrast, it reaches only 111 000 households. The principal source of revenue for Super Channel is advertising. This has shown dramatic growth. In 1985 receipts were £5.5 million, in 1986 £9.6 million, in 1987 receipts reached £13 million. The sources of the advertising are, moreover, pan-European, thus representing a major new UK invisible export. Super Channel competes with another UK-based satellite channel, Sky, which is owned by the newspaper magnate Rupert Murdoch [4]. This channel has adopted a rather different broadcasting strategy, with a heavy emphasis on pop music and original industrially sponsored programmes.

The outlook for European satellite television seems to depend on two major factors. The first is the potential for advertisements that can transcend national cultural and linguistic boundaries. The range of goods that can use the same campaign across several countries is arguably restricted. The second is the outcome of the race to launch two new satellite transmission systems, Luxembourg's Astra satellite (which is backed by British Telecom as a consortium member) or British Satellite Broadcasting (BSB). It is more than possible that the format of the broadcasting will be different in each case, entailing two reception dishes if a household wishes to receive both. Altogether it is an area in which British television is the leader.

Books and royalties as exports

The UK book industry is very large both in domestic and international terms. In 1985 the turnover of UK publishers reached the £1 billion mark for the first time, while royalties reached £37.5 million [5]. While statistics for world comparisons are not satisfactory since different countries have different bases for calculating numbers of titles, UNESCO figures suggest that the UK produces annually the fourth largest number of titles behind USSR, USA and surprisingly perhaps, the Federal Republic of Germany. The next most prolific publishing nations are Japan, France and Korea. Of the top seven, Germany produces the most titles on philosophy and religion but is second behind the USSR in social science. The UK, however, occupies second place behind the USSR in pure and applied sciences. In literature the USSR and West Germany are well ahead of the UK which also trails behind Japan and France. The USA is, however, even further down the league in this category. The importance of the UK in the science area is reflected in her exports as we shall see.

Recent years have seen enormous upheavals in the ownership patterns of publishing houses. In 1985, for example, Octopus bought Heinemann for £100 million, Longmans purchased the family publisher Pitman for £18 million and another private publisher MacDonald & Evans, while Penguin went on a spree, buying Hamish Hamilton, Michael Joseph, Elm Tree, Rainbird, Sphere and TBL Book Services. This trend has continued since. For example, in 1987 the Reed Group bought Octopus, thereby making it the UK's largest publisher.

The next table shows the top eight UK publishers by turnover in 1985.

Table 9.7   UK publishers by turnover 1985

		£ m
1	Octopus	138
2	Longmans	124
3	Collins	121
4	Penguin	113
5	Macmillan	87.4
6	OUP	87.04
7	ABP	76
8	Hodder	44.5

Source: Book Trade Year Book, 1986

If, however, we judge size by the number of titles, a very different picture emerges with the leaders the academic publishers Oxford University Press, and Cambridge University Press followed by Macmillan.

Exports are of enormous importance to the UK book industry. Reliable statistics are again exceedingly difficult. *Whitaker's Directory* lists some 12 000 UK publishers, of whom 2000 publish the majority of the 50 000 titles per year. Only 206 of these supply sales statistics to the Government's *Business Monitor* and 51 to the Publishers' Association's *Statistics Collection Scheme* respectively. Nevertheless, they do represent the major firms and certainly provide an order of magnitude for overseas trade. The *Business Monitor* calculates that in 1985 the UK exported some £592 million worth of books, which represented an increase of 33.7 per cent in real terms since 1981. In volume terms this was some 290 million books, a remarkable record. Royalties, calculated by the *BM* totalled in 1985 £41.9 million, a surge of one-third since 1984. For imports we have to turn to a different source, the overseas trade statistics, and these are not entirely reliable since they exclude books sent by post to a value of less than £100 and are quoted at wholesale purchase price. The figure for 1984 is £263 million, which should, to take account of postal imports, be increased to approximately £320 million. It would appear, therefore, that there is a substantial surplus of exports over imports.

The next table shows the great importance of what we might call knowledge-based books in exports compared with fiction and imaginative works. The categories are, of course, not hard and fast but give an indication which will also hold true for royalty payments.

Table 9.8   Exports of UK books by category 1985

	£ m
School books	53.9
University and professional	90.2
Mass market paperbacks	52.8
Specialised*	14.1
General†	66.3

* Includes reference books, religious books, maps, guides.
† Includes general fiction, non-fiction, adult and children's.
Source: Book Trade Year Book, 1986

The significance of the UK educational and training sector in the trade emerges still more clearly when we consider that somewhat over half of all school books produced are exported, half of all university and professional books and some 54 per cent of children's books. Of the other categories one-third are exported (36 per cent in the case of general books).

The UK's largest market is Western Europe, though its fastest growing market (by 87 per cent since 1981) is the USA. Contrary to what might have been expected, the next table of export markets also shows that non-English speaking markets are today more important than English-speaking ones, notwithstanding very substantial sales to these. This bears out the importance of English as the international language.

For the Western European markets school and university/professional publications are the most significant categories (61 per cent 1985), while for the USA university and professional books accounted for nearly half. A different pattern pertains in Australia and New Zealand where the most dominant category is mass market paperbacks. In Africa there has been a dramatic fall in purchases by Nigeria since 1981, falling from £67

Table 9.9   UK's export markets for books 1985

	£ m
Western Europe	161.5
USA	141.2
Australia	94.0
New Zealand	15.5
Africa	64.9
Rest of world	198.7

Source: Book Trade Year Book

million to £15.5 million in 1985. South Africa is still a major market and, until the fall in value of the rand, had been growing rapidly. Again, the dominant categories were school books and university and professional books.

While it is true that, strictly speaking, sales of books overseas are visible exports rather than invisible we have looked at them in some detail for these reasons. Firstly, they tell us of the provenance of the related longer-term invisible receipts in the form of royalties and are therefore the only way of establishing the trade pattern in this sector. Secondly, they illustrate the power and importance of English as the international language, not only of trade but of science, learning and even, to an extent, entertainment. And thirdly, they emphasise a basic theme of this book, the significance of education for the prosperity of the UK as an exporting country, since the bulk of book exports to our major markets in the advanced industrialised world derive from authors engaged in that sector.

Music

There are few areas where visible and invisible exports are so mutually interdependent as in the music trade. There are few fields, too, where technological developments in recent years have so transformed the nature of the tradeable products both in physical goods (mostly discs, cassettes and records) and in invisible – the recordings, tapes and reproductions which for artists, composers and publishers, constitute the main source of royalties earned by them in overseas markets.

It is technology, too, which has made it increasingly bothersome (and sometimes impossible) to calculate royalties due both on sales and on performances and, as we have seen earlier in this chapter, it is one of the objectives of the new UK Bill on Intellectual Property to maintain the moral and legal rights of musicians, artists and composers over the copyright, reproduction and marketing of their creation.

The UK and world sales

The main source of statistics is the annual year book of the British Phonographic Society (BPS).

The total turnover of all domestic recorded music markets was valued in 1986 at $12 billion. The market was led by the USA with 36.5 per cent of total sales of national recorded music. Japan took second place with 11 per cent whilst the UK tied in third place with West Germany, each with 7 per cent of total world sales.

It is, however, worth noting that the UK led the world in terms of nationality of artists. Over 50 per cent of all record sales in 1986 were by artists originating in the UK. It is interesting that the country most resistant to British music is Japan where Japanese and Korean records dominate and western music is often adapted.

The Beatles were important in opening up world markets for British music and since then UK artists have had an increasing influence. In Europe, 40 per cent of the 1986 best selling singles were by Britons and only the French took more of their own market than the British. The Australian top hundred regularly contains between 35 per cent and 40 per cent of British records with its own music often accounting for only 10–15 per cent.

Contribution to balance of payments

1 Artists' royalties

It is estimated that British artists received in 1985, a total of £228 million in royalties from outside the UK, compared with £32 million earnings by foreign artists in the UK in the same year. Details are as follows:

	Earnings by UK Artists 1985	Earnings by Foreign Nationals in the UK 1985
	£ m	£ m
In USA	115	17
In EEC (exc.UK)	58	4
In rest of world	55	10
	228	31

Source: BPI Year Book

It is estimated, therefore, that the contribution to the balance of payments from artists' royalties was £197 million. It should, however, be noted that the figures refer to artists' royalties only – publishers, composers and producers earnings are not included.

2   Performing rights

The Performing Rights Society collects royalties on behalf of British composers, authors and publishers and received in 1986 £26.45 million from performances and broadcasts overseas. In the same year £12.72 million went overseas for the same purpose. The net balance of £13.75 million can therefore be devoted to the contribution of the industry to the balance of payments.

The performing royalties come from nearly 40 different countries throughout the world. The distribution of income and expenditure for 1986 was as follows:

	Received £ m	Spend £ m
USA	10.56	9.05
France	3.06	1.13
West Germany	2.00	0.66
Netherlands	1.38	0.14
Italy	1.21	0.24
All other countries	8.24	1.48
Total	26.45	12.72

Source: The Performing Rights Year Book 1987–88

3   Visible exports

The visible exports of music products from the UK in 1986 is calculated at £76 million, with a favourable balance over imports of some £20 million.

Trends in the industry

The music industry never stands still and there has been some significant development in the past few years. In particular, compact discs (CDs) have shown a growth of around 200 per cent per year in the first four years since their launch in 1983. At the end of 1986 they sold 4 million units (£56.5 million) in the UK, the equivalent of 6 per cent of the album market. The growth of CDs overseas is equally strong. Popular music remains the main category of both record and tape sales followed by 'middle of the road' music, and then classical music with an average of some 10 per cent. Classical music has, however, been one of the chief reasons for the growth in demand of compact discs and now accounts for 29 per cent of sales in volume, and 52 per cent in value in the section of the market.

Conclusion

It would be seen that this is a lively, fast-moving market, both at home and overseas. The competition remains extremely strong, but it does appear that the British music industry is well placed, particularly in terms of its artistic creativity, to anticipate further continuous growth in the future.

Computing software

Computing software is one of the fastest growing of all sectors that we have examined, yet its contribution to invisible earnings seems to be expanding still more rapidly. We say 'seem', since this is possibly the most difficult sector of all to track statistically in an area that we have already seen is statistically problematic. Exports are not measured by the customs authorities since there are no tariffs to be levied, only a 6 per cent tax on the carrier medium e.g. the tape or disc. Expertise can be exported over the telephone or through on-line transmission from computer to computer. A company may easily purchase an overseas package for a few hundred pounds and then re-export it in bulk for millions; or vice-versa a product may be sold cheaply abroad and only exploited there. And lastly, there is the possibility that overseas earnings by UK subsidiaries are not sent back to the UK but used on the spot for further research and development. It is perhaps for all these reasons that the Government's *Business Monitor* estimates total sales to foreign clients for 1986 to be £106 million [6]. The Computing Services Association, however, which bases its statistics on returns from member companies considers £327 million to be more accurate [7]. This is a remarkable figure, showing massive growth from the estimated £180 million for 1986. Again, it is difficult to make a direct comparison with growth in overall turnover for the UK software industry. The CSA's figures show here a rise from £1484 million in 1986 to £1788 million in 1987 but the membership was not constant. Nevertheless, it does emerge that UK exports are growing more rapidly than the activity as a whole.

This is particularly encouraging since it is known (despite the absence of any figures at all for imports of software) that the UK still imports more than it exports. It is again the USA which dominates world trade both as an importer and an exporter and probably accounts for half of all trade. Certainly the USA is the UK's largest export market for software, followed by Europe and then the Commonwealth [8].

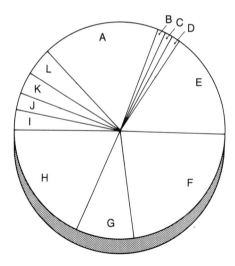

Key:

	Business sector	%	Revenue £m
A	Processing services	16.1	
B	Database services	1.0	
C	VANS	2.1	395
D	Facilities management	2.9	
E	Consultancy	15.6	278
F	Bespoke software	22.0	394
G	Software products	9.3	167
H	Combined hardward and software	18.5	331
I	Training	1.9	34
J	Contract staff and recruitment	5.1	91
K	Third party maintenance	2.3	42
L	Other	3.1	56
	Total	**100**	**1788**

Figure 9.1   Structure of UK computing services industry 1986. (Source: Computing Services Association)

The make-up of the industry can be seen from Figure 9.1. From this it will be seen that software itself dominates the business while, surprisingly perhaps, consultancy accounts for only 15.6 per cent. Indeed, if we consider exports alone, that share falls to only 5 per cent.

In this sector as in others that we have explored, especially perhaps in this chapter on trade in knowledge, the advantage of the English language is again paramount. Firstly, this makes the UK an attractive European and Commonwealth distribution base for a trade dominated by the USA. Thus, a major feature of the software export trade in the UK is that much of it comprises re-exporting. Secondly, there is the worldwide adoption of English as the standard language for the terminology of information technology and data processing.

These advantages are, as we saw, reflected in the substantial growth in the value of exports both absolutely and as a proportion of total revenue (from 12 per cent in 1986 to 18 per cent in 1987). Moreover, the number of exporting companies that are members of the CSA rose in the same period from 55 per cent to 63 per cent, against a substantial increase in the size of membership from 252 companies in 1984–85 to 280 companies in 1986–87. It is significant that the great majority of these companies (75 per cent) are British, while of the seventy that are in overseas ownership 65 belong to US companies. One might think in this connection of the remarkable proliferation of software companies that have sprung up in and around Cambridge during recent years, largely under the direction of former Cambridge graduates.

Indeed, so vigorous, young and competitive is the industry that in software no single company holds more than a 5 per cent share of the market, a striking contrast to the computer hardware sector where the major companies dominate. IBM, for example, has 50 per cent of the UK hardware market alone. This trend towards a growing variety of companies with their own specialisms and software niches is, however, set to continue. With it employment, too, is rapidly expanding. The workforce among the CSA membership has nearly doubled in five years and has been growing at a compound rate of growth of 11 per cent (*see* Figure 9.2). This has been accompanied by a still more dramatic rise in the sale of hardware by the CSA membership, moving from £129 million in 1985–86 to £204 million in 1986–87.

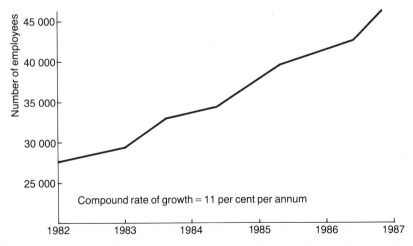

Figure 9.2 Staff employed by CSA members. (Source: Computing Services Association)

The UK's major hardware manufacturer, ICL, has recognised that for entry into the fiercely competitive European market in time to take advantage of the completed Internal Market in 1992, computing services are as important as hardware. This company has therefore adopted a strategy of exploiting two major niches in France, the retail sector and the financial services sector. ICL is strong in the retailing activity in the UK as a supplier of both hardware and software, matching the forward-looking approach of that industry. It has also benefited, like a number of other UK companies, from the great opportunities for software development and sales provided by Big Bang. Should financial services follow a similar route of transformation in France, ICL hopes to benefit. In West Germany on the other hand, where it has purchased a German software company, ICL is concentrating on computer-integrated manufacturing systems and, at the research level, is collaborating with Siemens in Munich. Here it is working on artificial intelligence projects.

In the UK the Government-sponsored Alvey Research Fund has given a very substantial boost to information technology research. This was paralleled in the European Community by the first phase of the more massive ESPRIT programme, the European research project for information technology. The second phase of both programmes, it is expected, will shift the emphasis from hardware developments to software and systems engineering. For it is becoming apparent that this is the area in which battle will be joined with the USA and Japan for the major share of the world market in the 1990s and the early decades of the next century.

Notes and references

Overseas students

We have been greatly helped in our work on overseas students by several divisions of the British Council and also by Mr Martin Kenyon and his colleagues of the Overseas Students Trust, to whose publications and statistics we have made several references in the text.

General references:

Statistics of students from abroad in the UK 1984–85, The British Council.

DES Statistical Bulletin – Students from Abroad – Department of Education and Science, London.

The British Council Report 1985–86.

The next steps: Overseas student policy into the 1990s, Overseas Students Trust, 1987.

Peter Williams (ed) The overseas students' question: Studies for a policy, for OST, Heineman, 1987.

P. R. C. Williams, *They came to train*, ODA, London, 1985.

Gareth Williams, Maureen Woodhall, Una O'Brien, *Overseas students and their place of study*, OST, London, 1985.

Educational contracts:

D. Liston and N. Reeves, *Business studies, language and overseas trade*, Pitman Publishing, London 1986, Chapter 7.

Using Britain and *Bridging the skills gap*, British Council, Educational Project Dept.

Chronological List of Education and Training Projects 1975–86, British Council Educational Contracts Dept.

Health care

The British Health Care Export Council (BHEC) through its weekly bulletin, is the general point of communication for British health care activities overseas. Its information to members includes tenders, conferences, exhibitions, seminars and trade missions.

Other reference points:

(i) Annual directory on health care – equipment, services, and supplies (BHEC).

(ii) Medical Services and British Medical Bulletin (Courses Dept) – the results of British research initiatives (British Council).

(iii) HM Customs & Excise – statistics on medical equipment exports.

(iv) *Pharmaceutical Industry and the Nation's Health*, statistical bulletin, Association of the British Pharmaceutical Industry (ABPSI).

Legal services

There have been particularly useful discussions with the International Directorate of the Law Society (Babette Brown); with Messrs Lovell, White & King; and with Clifford Chance and Belmont in Brussels. The Hong Kong Law Society (by courtesy of Robin Peard of Johnson, Stokes and Masters) have provided valuable information on the development of the British legal profession in Hong Kong.

Other more general references are:

CSO 'Pink Book', 1987, table 3.6 (with revisions on previous years).

David Mullock, *The overseas earnings of the legal profession*, BIEC, Sept. 1986.

Notes for guidance – Legal Practice Directorate (International) – Law Society April 1987.

EEC Council Directive, 'to facilitate the effective exercise by lawyers of freedom to provide services' – (EEC 77/249 27 March 1977).

The establishment of business in Great Britain by a foreign corporation, Lovell White and King, July 1987.

'Inter alia – Costly protection from what?', *Solicitors' Journal*, 12 January 1987.

Survey of Growth of British Legal Business in Hong Kong, Hong Kong Law Society, 1985.

Chartered Institute of Arbitrators Annual Report 1986.

Tourism, hotel, leisure and related industries

The main educational references are given in Chapter 7. So far as consultancy is concerned much of the material is contained in the publications by the industry, universities, colleges and polytechnics. Post-graduate work in particular often has a consultancy content as, for instance, the options at Strathclyde Business School in tourism for developing countries.

At the cross-national level the report by Patrick Laverick of the Dorset Institute of Higher Education on education and training for careers in Tourism in the European Community (June 1984) was an important consultative document for government policies.

The statement of experience published by Howarth & Howarth (UK) in 1986 forms the background of the worldwide consultancy activities of this particular firm.

We are indebted to the company's managing director, Jonathan Bodlender, for his information and advice.

Intellectual property

Patents, know-how and licences:

The White Paper basic to recent legislation was 'Intellectual property and innovation' – issued by DTI (Cmd. 9712) in April 1986.

The White Paper has a useful bibliography (pp. 77–78).

The resulting Bill is the 'Copyright, designs and patent' Bill of 28 October 1987.

A particularly relevant critique is that of Robert P. Benko, 'Intellectual property rights and the international trading system' in *Trade in Services, Open Markets and the Uruguay Round Negotiations*, A Conference, London, 1987.

A variety of comments on various aspects of the Bill were published in *The Independent*, 31 October 1987.

A useful piece of the general theme appears in the *Kluwer Handbook of International Trade* (3.4 author John M. Skilbeck) Kluwer Publishing, London, 1986, Vol 1.

British films, TV, software etc.

Particular references, numbers as indicated in the text.

1   For this and other quantified information above *see* Steven S. Wilkinson and Stephen S. Siwek, 'Telecommunications and Entertainment: Trade in Films and Television Programming' in *Trade in Services, Open Markets and the Uruguay Round Negotiations*, A Conference, London, 1987, pp. 83–98.

2 'British films and TV earn £114 m overseas in 1986', *British Business*, 2 October 1987, p. 32.

3 'TV-Export: Ende der Einbahnstrasse', *Der Spiegel*, 22/1986, p. 170.

4 This section is indebted to interviews with the BBC and IBA (conducted for us by Liz Anstis) and with Super Channel, where we are particularly indebted to

Mr Richard Hooper. Annual reports from the television companies provided further information.

5 This section's statistical information relies on that supplied in *The Book Trade Year Book*, 1985.

6 *Business Monitor Quarterly Statistics SDQ9. Computing Services*. Quarter Two 1987, HMSO, London, Table 2.

7 *Computing Services Association Annual Report*, 1987, London, p. 9.

8 We are grateful to Mr Douglas Eyeions and Mr Tony Lewis of the Computing Services Association for this and other information in this section.

9 David Thomas, 'Software becomes a priority as ICL tailors its products', *Financial Times*, 28 October 1987.

PART III

The education and training dimension

10 The cerebral revolution – challenge to education worldwide

'The revolution that has followed the industrial revolution is not a service revolution but a cerebral one in which value is added not by skilled hands but by skilled minds'

This extract from a remarkably perceptive short leader in *The Economist* (22 August 1987) sets the theme for this chapter on the challenge to education. Indeed the article as a whole, although not exclusively slanted towards invisible exports and overseas tradeable services, forms an exciting and imaginative backdrop to our book. For it identifies the real significance of the world move to 'service-based' economies, and the richness and variety of opportunities provided to all who are willing and equipped to take them.

Education and training are the keys to a nation's ability to cope with far-reaching challenges of this kind, just as in a previous generation industrial training and commercial education helped (though by no means always adequately) to take the strain of the move from agriculture to manufacturing as the nation's major employer.

The challenge to education is therefore to adapt the system once again to wholly new circumstances, both as they are today and as they almost certainly will be in the future; and to engineer such changes as may be required in disciplines, in curricula, in teaching methods and in attitude. Its aim must be to feed into the labour force a new resource of skills – managerial, technological, and operational – which will not only be superior, both in quality and in relevance, to anything previously achieved, but able also to match the standards of international competition. For the other industrialised countries, though often from different starting points, are themselves faced with problems very similar to those in the UK.

We have, therefore, in this chapter taken a quick look at the new influences of work in current educational development, arising in particular from the progress of technology and the changing patterns worldwide of industrial commercial activity. In this way we have been greatly helped, particularly in the social and human aspects, by the publications of the ILO in Geneva and by their having made available to us a digest of publications from many countries of the world. We have looked in more detail at the expression of these influences on schooling and vocational training in France, Germany and Japan before considering the situation in the UK with special reference to recent initiatives and to the major Education Reform Act of 1988.

Thereafter in Chapter 11 we have taken a closer look at vocational, professional and management training and education, in the UK as a whole and also in the major sectors of international finance and in overseas tradeable services.

Education and training – new influences

Three main factors which increasingly influence the thinking of academic and professional establishments throughout the world are:

1 The speed, direction and scale of technological change in manufacturing, in commerce, in the professions and in administration.

2 The revolution in international trade, both in the nature and origin of tradeable products and in the processes by which this trading operates.

3 The impact of all these changes on the human and social infrastructure of the individual countries; and the requirement for the teaching of new knowledge and skills at every age and at all levels within schools, higher education and within firms.

An examination of the first two of these factors forms the core of the sectoral chapters of this book. We now turn more specifically to the new influences at work on the educational systems both of the United Kingdom and, by way of comparison, of France, Japan and the Federal Republic of Germany.

Technological change – social and labour implications

Computers and the progress in automation which they have primed in almost every field of human activity, are already reflected in the variety of technological courses on offer in almost every country of the industrialised world, as well as in publications and in academic research. They cover computer hardware and software, with applications ranging from the most routine of operations in offices, shops and in factories, in hospitals and in the home, to the probing of the limits of knowledge in astrophysics, in ballistics, and in engineering.

There is, however, a very different aspect of this technological change which tends to dominate intellectual thinking – the very scale of the social and labour problems which it generates, associated as they are with demands for new skills, new areas of deployment and fresh patterns in almost every sector of the social system.

The International Labour Office, based in Geneva, has perhaps the chief concern for the effects on a world scale of a progressive shift of demand towards a smaller elite of highly trained and highly skilled labour. The direct consequence of this trend is the recruitment of lesser-skilled, lower-paid, and often, part-time workers, who are destined to form a high proportion of the total workforce of the future. The literature on the labour implications of these shifts in demand is large and growing. The ILO has set itself to monitor the impact of the new technologies for both the industrial and services sectors, and has published a summary of its findings in a recent publication *Technological Change – The Tripartite Response 1982–85*. A search and print-out carried out for the authors by the ILO revealed 500 titles and short extracts of literature in the field of service industries published since 1980.

In the face of technological developments of this nature and on this scale, the ILO is quite right to be concerned with the massive changes taking place in the composition and size of the country's labour force.

Equally dramatic, perhaps, though in a different way is the report of the UK Manpower Services Commission that more than two-fifths of the 257 000 jobs created in the UK in 1986–7 were filled by women working part-time, whilst only 8.6 per cent (22 000) were filled by men: 46 000 were taken by women working full-time (*MSC Annual Report 1986–7*, p. 10, diagram 2.1). These figures were taken against a background of rising service-sector employment of 341 000, and a fall in numbers employed in manufacturing by 130 000. It is clear that in the UK, as elsewhere in the world, not only are there major shifts in the type of employees, particularly between men and women, but also in the sector and nature of their employment, with ever-increasing employment in the services, and with a sharply diminishing intake within manufacturing industry.

Elsewhere a valuable statistical analysis of labour in the service industries was prepared by Amin Rajan and published in 1987 by the Institute of Manpower Studies at Sussex University for the Occupational Study Group. Its particular value is as a manpower-based study and its wide coverage makes a valuable contribution to the debate on the business and jobs outlook for the UK growth industries. It was itself a follow-up of a survey of wider scope covering employment of all the industries of the economy. The special value of Rajan's latest work is its exclusive concentration on the service industries – seven sectors in all covering between 6.5 million workers, one-half of the employees in the service sector and over a quarter of the national manpower.

Even more comprehensive is the work of Dorothy Riddle in the USA on the role of the service sector in world development, not least because of the close contact maintained by the author with national and international institutions such as the World Bank, OECD, GATT, UNCTAD, and LOTIS in the UK. The bibliography contained in Professor Riddle's book is itself a work of most meticulous scholarship and illustrates very clearly the range and coverage of recent academic activity in this field.

Mention should be made of the work by Orio Giarini (Services World Forum 1987) which again features some valuable bibliographical material in this area.

The publications of the ILO and the other sources quoted above constitute a most valuable compilation of the progress of computerisation and robotisation throughout the world; its probable effect on the pattern of labour and skills, and the steps being taken by governments, trades unions and firms to secure agreements on redeployment of the labour force both in manufacturing and services, on training and retraining and on redundancies and unemployment.

Attempts at quantification reveal, however, the usual wide discrepancies amongst research analysts in the field. Figures from the British Robot Association (BRA) quoted by the ILO show, for instance, that on a world basis Japan leads the world with 64 000 installed machines, compared with 20 500 in Western Europe and 13 000 in the United States. The Chairman of BRA maintains that there has been, 'too much media hype' over robotisation and that they should be seen for what they are, 'tools for use in industry'.

On the other hand, reports from Eastern Europe (CMEA New Prospects 1984) state that member states in Eastern Europe planned to produce 200 000 robots by 1990, and from Soviet Government sources it is calculated that the current robot population in the USSR is already in the region of 65 000.

Nor is there any greater degree of agreement of the effects on the total labour force of computerisation or high technology in the production and service industries. The Institute of Manpower Studies at Sussex University takes a cautious note on the speed at which redundancies of some 250 000 in the production sector can be made up the near future, while the OECD and Stanford University in the USA both tend to emphasise the scope for spectacular change in employment leading not to fewer but different jobs.

What can, however, be said with some certainty is that areas of particular interest to this book, notably banking and insurance, as well as other service industries, are likely to be amongst the most sharply affected by these technological factors, as indeed they already are.

Information technology and automated processes of administration permeate the whole scene not only in terms of hardware and software, but also in opening up to the groups of workers concerned new opportunities for simplifying procedures and for the exploitation of procedural and commercial possibilities. It follows that skills as new and valuable as these are rarely as abundant as required, and those who have the good fortune to have, or have acquired, the requisite aptitudes, expertise and skills, find they can sell them at a premium in very many markets at home and overseas.

The most dramatic illustration has been the money markets of the world particularly in the UK, where a unique combination of circumstances induced pressures with which neither the personnel nor the equipment have been fully able to cope.

The effect on personnel has been all too clear, particularly in The Stock Exchange and the money markets of the City. Plans for 'Big Bang' were in general thorough and sensible, hinging in the main on advanced computerisation of financial transactions and clearances. Training and recruitment were hopefully adequate both in the Exchange itself and in the many individual partnerships and firms, many of whom as a result of deregulations and mergers found themselves facing new challenges and, as often as not, types of business with which they were sometimes unfamiliar. In the event the volume of business initially proved quite overwhelming and beyond the handling capacity of the computers and of their back-up services. The situation was aggravated by the activities of the many foreign banks who, operating either from London or from their home bases in New York, Frankfurt, Tokyo and elsewhere, poured their business into London to take advantage of the new market conditions. The equipment situation proved on the whole susceptible, at least in the short term, to alleviation by pauses and short cessations of activity, although the backlog of work, particularly clearances, was especially severe and frustrating.

The personnel problem, however, proved far more intractable as firms rushed into an unseemly scramble to lay their hands on any available talent either in the UK or elsewhere. Huge premiums were offered by way of vast salary 'golden hellos' safeguarded wherever possible by 'golden handcuffs'; and changes in top management structures with very rapid promotion to the few matched by the side-stepping and often redundancy of those less well equipped to meet the challenge. Traditional loyalties were undermined and some of the oldest and most reputable firms changed almost overnight their style of business and mode of operations.

It was to be expected that in these highly volatile conditions, company scandals would arise both in the processes of merger and in transfer of top personnel. The scale and nature of these scandals (with the media overkill) added another dimension to the general turbulence, which did not abate when the stock market crash of Autumn 1987 took the heart out of the labour market, but brought with it further uncertainty concerning the future.

The total effect of this disturbance has been to call in question the scale and relevance of the general and professional training in the UK and, in particular, our capacity to introduce into our young people in schools, colleges and universities and, indeed, to many of their seniors, the ability to cope with constant changes and uncertainty. This is the true challenge to our national systems of education and training, as it is also to our main competitors abroad.

Vocational training in France, Germany and Japan

France

The French education system is by reputation elitist, heavily structured and centrally directed. It is perhaps best known for the care and skill with which the best brains of the country are progressively segregated, groomed and refined to take their place at the highest levels of industry, commerce, the armed forces, in administration and in government.

It therefore comes as something of a surprise to read in a recent work of Hilary Steedman (National Institute Economic Review 1987) of the thought and care devoted to vocational training well down the line, not only in the interests of the individuals themselves, but as a way of priming the total reservoir of skills available to meet such situations as described above.

The system has, of course, its weaknesses, particularly a lesser exposure to the world of work at the early formative stages such as there is in the USA, Germany, and increasingly, in the UK. So far as industry is concerned, this is to some extent off-set, at least in advanced education, by the special statutory role of the French Chambers of Commerce and by the high quality of the vocational training of the cities, regions and departments throughout the country.

In basic education, however, the French philosophy, derived as it is from traditional attitudes, aims at ensuring that boys and girls leave full-time education with a broad range of subjects behind them, with emphasis on literature, mathematics and languages, particularly English and to a lesser extent German.

Within the system there are four national administrative levels of vocational examination available to young people below the level of Higher Education. These levels are the CAP (*certificat d'aptitude professionnel*), the BEP (*brevet d'enseignement professionnel*), the BTn (*baccalauréat de technicien*) and the BTS (*brevet de technicien supérieur*). The Steedman study concerns itself specifically with clerical training where the same four levels apply. It should be said, however, that the term 'clerical' has little of the perjorative undertones that sometimes apply in England. Indeed, the system is flexible enough to permit (subject to attaining satisfactory standards) a passage from the lowest grade to the most senior. At the top this implies familiarity with quite sophisticated aspects of information technology, modern administrative procedures, and a good working knowledge of typing, word processing and modern office systems as well as some training in management and decision-making. It is clear that a system such as this provides a continuous reservoir of skilled young 'clerical' workers equipped and ready to meet the changing complexities of the commercial world which lies ahead.

There are, of course, similarities to and differences from the British educational system. In particular, the subjects and higher French standards are roughly comparable in the UK with levels of progression of BTEC. But there are some substantial differences:

1 The vocational options, both clerical and others, form part of a much wider range of studies common to the schooling system as a whole as opposed to the narrow base of the normal British curricula.

2 The options themselves are an integral part of the total school curriculum. They last three years and lead to standards of performance that are understood and expected by parents, employers and students themselves. In Britain it is normal to have a single subject vocational qualification often gained through part-time study.

3 The numbers in training in France are very large compared with Britain. For every person qualifying in England to a level corresponding to the French intermediate or higher clerical qualification, there are roughly ten who passed these qualifying examinations in France in the early 1980s.

4 In industrial terms, the French system is not work-related on this basic school level, nor is there within the schools the close relationship with industry and commerce that has begun to develop in the UK. It is possible, therefore, as indeed has happened in the past, that well-qualified young people may exceed the demand, with the consequent danger of unemployment and waste of resources.

The various schemes in the UK of YTS (after schooling) and TVEI (during schooling) have this element well in mind. If, therefore, the schemes in the UK succeed in raising standards somewhat more closely related to those in France, of which there are all too few signs and, moreover, if the concept of the combination of these standards both in general and vocational education is more widely accepted than it is now by British employers, then there is the prospect over the years that the British system with its proposed national curriculum, its emphasis on vocational training and its strong work relationship may develop unique virtues of its own different from, but not necessarily inferior to, the French system of vocational education.

Federal Republic of Germany

We have emphasised above the relatively minor influence within the French vocational educational system of work-related experience. The

German system by contrast has preparation for work as its main motivating force and a number of unique features of the system derive from this concept. It is on this aspect that we have chosen to concentrate as being of particular relevance to the theme of this book.

We have carried out our own research in West Germany and drawn on the series of articles in the *Journal of the National Institute of Social and Economic Research* (particularly Prais & Wagner, May 1985).

The German school system has two main features:

1 Comprehensive schools (*Gesamtschulen*) have generally remained a small-scale experiment. Similarly the private option remains relatively unimportant. As a result the vast majority of children, after attending their primary schools, enter the mainstream of compulsory secondary education within the State system.

2 Germany has not adopted a common school system for children of all abilities through to the end of compulsory education. Instead they have adopted an ability-related, three-stream, selective system through which children are directed after parent/teacher consultation and not by test into one of three types of school – *Hauptschulen, Realschulen, Gymnasien*. It is the individual objectives, teaching, and achievements of these three types of schools that between them feed into the German economy an impressive stream of young men and women related by preference, ability and training to the world of work which they will enter either immediately or after further higher or professional education.

Hauptschulen

Catering as they do for the lower ability grades, they are intended to provide a general basis for work in practical and technical fields. They cater for just over half of all school pupils and nine-tenths of their intake achieve certification. Ten subjects are taught including mathematics and a foreign language, and certification demands a pass in all but one of the ten subjects.

The standard is high in relation to the basic ability range. It has been estimated that only 27 per cent of English students of the same ability range would reach certification level, whilst in mathematics the German average attainment in the lower half of the ability range equals the average of all English pupils.

Realschulen

The *Realschule* is a preparation for young professional and technical careers, providing an education to 16 plus and qualifying for entry into technical colleges. These are the *Fachoberschulen* for further training prior to employment, and the *Fachhochschulen* are roughly equivalent to a polytechnic. Again certification requires the students to reach a satisfactory level in about ten subjects at which four or five are examined, including mathematics, German and a foreign language, at a level roughly equivalent to 'O' level. In 1984 some 438 000 were certificated at this level, a very solid core of young people consciously educated and trained as a band of technicians, managers and professionals for the German workforce of the future.

Gymnasien

One of the reforms inspired by Wilhelm von Humboldt as long ago as the first decades of the nineteenth century, is the traditional academic-based school with certificate exams for the *Abitur* or *Hochschulreife* taken at the age of nineteen or sometimes twenty and qualifying the successful students for attendance at a university or polytechnic. As in the other schools they offer a very wide range of subjects and many specialist options. A linguist, for instance, may take up to three foreign languages to the age of nineteen alongside other subjects, including mathematics and science. Not surprisingly, however, the breadth of the study at this level of schooling leads to lower levels of knowledge in Germany than that tested in English 'A' level, although the latter is taken one or two years' earlier. The bulk of German university undergraduates comes from the *Gymnasien*. Students there have behind them a general school education extending over ten subjects until they are at least seventeen or eighteen years of age.

Vocational schooling

Preparation for later vocational training proper already begins at school in both the *Hauptschulen* and *Realschulen*. In the *Hauptschulen* in Berlin, for instance, a special preparatory course (*Arbeitslehre* or work tuition) begins at 13 and reaches as many as eight classes per week for those aged 15 and 16. Visits are paid to companies, whilst in addition there are classes on office practice, on various aspects of technical and manpower operation, manufacturing techniques and on budgeting and statistics. Some of these elements, particularly company visits, have invaded even the traditional *Gymnasium*.

Following these introductory classes within each category of school there are the comprehensive provisions for compulsory vocational schooling at *Berufsschulen* (vocational schools) incorporated within the German 'dual system'.

Some pupils attend specialist vocational schools full-time for training in certain trades for careers as nurses and in some technical occupations, other schools provide routes into polytechnics or universities for those without the *Hochschulreife* (or university entry qualification). By far the most important activity is that carried out under the dual system of traineeships coupled with attendance at *Berufsschulen*. This involves the trainee in a two and a half to three-year training programme organised jointly at the workplace and the vocational school.

The framework for training in some 430 trades is laid down by the Federal Government. This states the skills to be obtained and outlines curricula and examination requirements. The companies employing the trainees then carry out their schemes with regard to these regulations in collaboration with the Federal states who have responsibility for the instruction given in the vocational schools. Finally the chambers of commerce and the various trade associations supervise the training and devise the final examinations.

Despite the recession of the early eighties and the substantial number of unemployed in the Federal Republic, this type of vocational training has grown year by year for a decade. In 1976 1.3 million youngsters had trainee employment. In 1986 it was over 1.8 million.

Total numbers in vocational schools rose from 2 million in 1976 to 2.5 million in 1985. When we consider that the number of young people of the appropriate age for such training is in sharp decline, with a drop in the general school population from 10 million in 1976 to 7.5 million in 1984, the achievement is startling.

What is the special significance of this healthy training infrastructure for West Germany's internationally tradeable service industries? An exact statistical assessment is not possible. It is exceedingly difficult in many cases even to distinguish between service industries and manufacturing. Restricting the service industries to those whose primary concern is direct transactions with customers and with activities such as financial and administrative services, transport, the distributive trades, health care, hotels and catering, entertainment and domestic services, we find that in 1986 of 93 occupations, 930 000 young people were in training in primary and manufacturing industry and crafts, against 827 000 in the service industries. We cannot know how many of the latter contribute or will contribute to German invisible exports. It would be impossible to calculate how many hoteliers, how many bank employees, or how many secretaries are directly or chiefly involved in the international or tourist side of their business. Nevertheless, we can observe that all these service industries can potentially cater for foreign customers, that over 45 per cent of all German trainees are in these industries, and that the branches of particularly great interest to this study are very powerfully represented. By 1985 there were some 71 000 trainees in banking and insurance, and nearly 25 000 were training as managers and accountants. (Statistics based on *Statistisches Jahrbuch 1987*, Bonn, pp 362–363).

One of the paradoxes of German education is that for all the strength of vocational training more prestige is traditionally attached to academic education. The *Gymnasium* has remained the most cherished school goal as has the university in contrast to the polytechnic. Over the last decade, notwithstanding great fluctuations in the total numbers of children of secondary school age, the total of pupils attending *Gymnasien* has constantly exceeded those in the *Realschule* by some 700 000 or 40 per cent. The social prestige derived from possessing an academic background also helps to account for the huge growth of the universities since the 1960s, for which there is no parallel in Britain. *Bildung*, the development of the whole personality, thought to be achieved through education based on theory and cerebration, remains generally more admired than *Ausbildung*, practical and therefore more humble training.

Clear signs are now emerging, however, that this historical situation is changing. As a result a significant proportion of those now taking up trainee posts in their late teens are pupils with the *Abitur* who would normally have gone straight to university or polytechnic studies.

Between 1980–81 and 1986 the percentage of applicants for traineeships with university or polytechnic entry qualifications rose from 7 per cent to 15 per cent, their absolute number increasing threefold to some 90 000. And the fields which they are entering are substantially industries which are engaged in international business. Of the ten most popular trades chosen by these young people, banks came first, industrial sales and purchasing second, sales and purchasing for the distributive trades third, taxation and accountancy fourth, industrial and commercial administration fifth and insurance seventh. This ranking order was for 1983.

When we look at those professions with the highest proportions of trainees with these top school qualifications we find they are exclusively in the service industries, with a heavy concentration on those that are engaged in international business. All those entering sales and marketing in air transport in 1983 were *Abiturienten*, 74 per cent of those entering advertising, 70 per cent the book trade, 60 per cent data processing, 52 per cent shipping sales and marketing, 50 per cent travel agencies, 49 per cent sales in the hotel and catering industry, 47 per cent in publishing and 41 per cent banking. (Statistics from *Berufsbildungsbericht*, Bonn, 1985)

But there remains a major question. How is this great commitment to youth training financed?

Both Federal Government and the states are very heavily involved – the vocational schools that are not part of the dual system (that is, the full-time schools) cost nearly 4 billion Deutschmark, whilst the part-time *Berufsschulen* which are the linch-pin of the 'dual system' cost 2.6 billion Deutschmark. However, these contributions by *Land* and *Bund* are dwarfed by the contribution made by industry and commerce through the actual employment of the trainees and apprentices together with their in-house training. This totals some 66 per cent of overall expenditure. Government, Federal and State, can be said to supply the framework and infrastructure but the substance comes from the productive and service sectors. In a word, German industry and commerce has learnt to value training as a worthwhile investment. On average seven out of every hundred employees in German industry and commerce are trainees.

Japan

Modern Japanese education, like so much else in modern Japan, owes its post-war growth and development to influences drawn from the western world rather than from its own indigenous cultures. And again, as in many other aspects of its national life, because of its late entry into the field, Japan tends to have drawn the best from post-war schooling and educational developments in USA, Germany, UK and elsewhere.

From these various sources the Japanese have devised a system which, despite its diverse origins, is in the main not only distinctly Japanese but also well adapted to the Japanese role in worldwide industrial and commercial development. So far as industry and commerce are concerned, there are features of Japanese traditions which appear to be directly reflected in the national systems of general and vocational schooling. Japan is a country where by custom and practice career progress is largely within a single firm, and promotion to successive levels of seniority, particularly at the very top, tends to be gained through length of service and organisation. It follows that in-company experience, resting on a sound and broad-based system of general introductory schooling, is (or has been) the foundation of the country's approach to the maintenance and expansion of the labour force. It follows, too, that it is not a system which readily leans to elitism in education, but is more concerned with the production of a large number of people, the vast majority of whom are educated to a very high average standard within broadly based general and vocational curricula. Moreover, elitism, if associated as it often is with impatience and intolerance of tradition, can itself be a disruptive element in the traditional framework of career progression. It is true that the rapid introduction of new technologies associated with the influence, and often physical presence, of multinational companies has imposed variations on the system to permit more rapid movement in the careers of high flyers with special skills. For all that, the system on the whole still remains geared to producing the maximum number of students with the highest possible average performance as a national reservoir of labour for industry and commerce, and indeed to all other forms of economic and social activity.

Schooling and vocational preparation in Japan

Over 95 per cent of boys and girls now stay at full-time schooling until the age of 18, in contrast to the 32 per cent of 16- to 18-year-olds in full-time schooling in England. There have been many studies, some going back over 20 years, comparing Japanese achievements within those years with that of other countries.

The Japanese educational system can in fact produce results in almost all these areas which can stand comparison with their foreign competitors. Their concentration, however, is on the intermediate levels in technology, commerce and administration, and here they can fairly claim to lead the world both in the very high average standards they set and in the numbers successfully attaining them.

Their strength derives from a number of distinctive (though not necessarily exclusive features):

1 A very high level of mathematical and scientific attainment, particularly in the early school ages. Comparisons have been carried out by the International Association for the Evaluation of Education Achievement (IEA). The figures seem to establish beyond reasonable doubt that Japanese pupils in mathematics are particularly far ahead of their British counterparts, reaching at the age of $13\frac{1}{2}$ a level which might be expected of British pupils at the age of 16 and these are figures which were confirmed in the most recent survey in 1987. Comparison of achievement in science showed similar trends, although not perhaps so spectacularly.

2 The close integration in Japan of lower secondary school education (a three-year course for ages 13–15) and upper secondary school education (also for three years for ages 16–18). Ninety-five per cent of Japanese pupils successfully passed their examinations for transfer to the upper secondary school – corresponding roughly to the British 16-plus examinations (GCE 'O' level, GCE 'A-O' level or GCSE), the latter exam being aimed at some 40 per cent of the intermediate range of students.

3 Until the age of 15 Japanese schooling is compulsory and free. At upper secondary school there is a parental contribution both in the 'prefectural' publicly financed schools and in the 'private' or 'national' schools, corresponding in part to the old British direct grant schools, and possibly to the more academically talented of the British public schools.

4 The official policy up to the end of the lower secondary school is that schooling shall be the same and equal for all, following the American pattern. The whole classes are taught together without streaming, and, with classes of some 40 people, teaching is on the whole textbook-based, a narrow curriculum with few optional subjects, a longer school year

and with fewer school holidays. It is a system geared to 'value for money' including allocating to pupils ancillary tasks such as cleaning classrooms and helping with midday meals etc. It would, however, seem to be a system in which the less able would be left behind by the more able, whist the latter in turn were held back by the drag of large all-ability classes and a fairly unimaginative approach to classroom teaching. It is perhaps more geared to producing a respectable average level of achievement, rather than one which is aimed at securing their full potential out of the best.

5 The dilemma, by no means peculiar to Japan, has been approached by them in three ways:

  (i) By recognising that Japanese parents wish, and the Japanese economy requires, that their children share with them a respect for education at the highest possible level. This implies that children will be prepared to work to close the gap between them and their brightest school fellows.

 (ii) On this basis it is assumed that parents will be prepared to seek out and to pay for extra coaching in areas of their children's weakness. In turn, the educational administrators are expected to be both pragmatic and understanding in their approach to the provision of this additional teaching.

(iii) By recognising that at quite early stages academic 'hierarchies' will develop, even within 'prefectural' schools and in certain areas. Parents will seek out the top-most schools in the hierarchy, whilst at the same time provision needs to be made for remedial teaching, coaching outside school hours and for supplementary selective specialisms according to students' needs, and catering all the way up to the high flyers. Some of these will be at schools which will themselves have close links with universities and institutes of higher education.

It is through this dual system, costly in time for students and teachers, and in money for parents, that the Japanese have succeeded in pursuing a path which would not be possible in any other country. A notionally egalitarian and 'comprehensive' system of early in-school education with a high degree of selectivity for the later stages, it provides incentives for optimal performances for both staff and pupils and, with parent co-operation, helps to guide and direct children up to the age of 18 to the appropriate type of school (technical, commercial and 'national' or private) to a realistic level of educational ambition and achievement; and to the particular specialisms (some of them quite specific) provided by the very large range of technical colleges, special training schools, commercial schools and other training institutions of which there is a prolific supply throughout the country. Above all the system ensures that whatever final form of specialisation emerges as appropriate, it is built on a sound base at upper and secondary school level. There is, moreover, sufficient direction to ensure that in all the vocational secondary schools, about half the school day is devoted to general subjects such as languages, history, geography, mathematics and science. A foreign language, English, is taken for two years at secondary school, and for all three years at the commercial schools. In this way the pupils at technical schools emerge with a sound knowledge of general subjects and of languages, whilst conversely the commercial school students have a level of attainment in mathematics and science beyond the range of their British counterparts. The Japanese child, therefore, whether moving to higher education in universities and polytechnics, or moving into employment in industry and commerce, has an educational background of supreme flexibility and relevance to whatever career he or she may eventually choose. It is the result of long hours spent in the classrooms and in subsequent coaching. It demands of parents a willingness and capacity to pay, and above all else it assumes a national attitude to education and to sheer hard work which it is difficult to match elsewhere.

Schooling in the UK

Compared with France, Germany and Japan, the UK educational scene presents a far from happy sight. There are, of course, problems in other countries – riots in the streets in Paris in protest against proposed entry restrictions to higher education; grumbles in Germany at the late entry in the world of work of graduates who normally complete their cycle of academic and professional education around the ages of 27–28, with a possible consequent entry into the higher ranks of business of too many academics and not enough practitioners; and conflict in Japan over reconciling the ruthless fast-track career requirements of the new generation of technologists and business graduates with an environment geared to slower and more orderly advancement, normally within the context of a single firm.

The problems in the UK are perhaps more fundamental, and ironically stem, in part at least, from the long-established academic institutions of England and Scotland and, to a lesser extent, of Wales and Northern Ireland. For it is this traditional pattern, particularly in England, which was most affected by the Education Act of 1976 which, after a period of hesitation and profound political argument, finally required local education authorities to introduce a system of comprehensive all-ability schools for all publicly funded secondary schools within their areas. At the same time, the 'direct grant' schools were phased out, leaving to the individual schools (including many of the major grammar schools of the country) the option of full integration into the State system, or becoming independent with little or no entitlement to public funds. In the event 119 of the 170 direct grant schools chose independence, though often with great reluctance; and in consequence massively reinforced the independent sector of national education and opened up a major divide between public and private education. This divide, with its political and social, as well as academic, implications is one of the major issues in the debate of the Education Reform Act of 1988. The figures for school leavers in 1986 were as follows – they apply to England only:

	Numbers of students (thousands)
Maintained schools:	
Comprehensive schools	629.06
Grammar schools	20.59
Other secondary schools	41.34
Total	690.99
Independent schools:	45.22
Total school leavers	736.21

It will be seen that independent schools represent some 6 per cent of the total school leavers, whilst the combined totals from independent and grammar schools is approximately 10 per cent.

Level of achievement

Against these statistics should be set figures for levels of achievement. The criteria are results in examinations for the General Certificate of Education at ordinary level (GCE 'O' level) and at advanced level (GCE 'A' level). These are the grades of major significance for entry into higher education. (But *see* note 2 below).

	Percentage leavers with 5 or more 'O' levels grade A–C or grade 1 CSE
Comprehensive	22.7
Other secondary	11.5
Grammar	78.0
Independent	75.8

	Percentage of leavers with one or more 'A' level
Comprehensive	13.3
Grammar	55.0
Independent	65.2

As a percentage of this age group in 1984–85, 16 per cent of boys had one or more 'A' level, and 15.3 per cent of girls. In the same years 16.8 per cent of boys had five or more 'O' levels, and girls 16.3 per cent. (*Source*: Statistics of Education – Schools (DES 1985))

Notes on the Statistics

1 The criteria used above, GCE 'O' and 'A' levels, are of most relevance in relation to entry into further, higher and professional education. The Certificate of Secondary Education (CSE) is open to boys and girls in any school after completion of five years' secondary education, and is meant for pupils of about 16 years of age who are around the average in terms of ability for their age group.

2 All existing 'O' level GCE examinations and the CSE have been superseded by the GCSE (General Certificate of Secondary Education), for which the first examinations were scheduled for 1988. Although the grading of individual pupils was almost certainly be affected by the new curricula and modes of examination, it was not expected that there would be any major change in the relativities of achievement as between types of school.

3 A new grade of 'AS' level examination (advanced supplementary level) is aimed at expanding the range of the total curricula and reducing the degree of specialisation of candidates preparing for higher education. The future of this examination will also need to come under review in the light of the new curricula changes contained in the Education Act of 1988.

4 The overall significance of the statistics quoted above highlights both the relatively small numbers of total school leavers entering higher education, and amongst them the disproportionately large number who come from independent schools and some of the maintained grammar schools.

International Comparisons

International comparisons, some of which were quoted earlier in this chapter, show how the UK compares with some of its international competitors. A summary of relevant statistics is contained in the *Grund-und Strukturdaten* published by the Ministry of Education in West Germany. It gives the percentages of young people committed to post-school education within various age groups. The figures are for 1984:

	Age group 19–26 %
FRG	20.8
Denmark	21.4
Italy	17.4

	Age group 18–25
	%
France	20.4
Netherlands	17.3
Ireland	13.00
UK	9.00

The figures in the UK are by any standard very low and compare poorly with their continental competitors. It should be said, however, that part of this discrepancy might result from the relatively high proportion of British students who cease their post-school education well below the age of 25.

The Education Reform Act 1988

The figures show up very starkly the fundamental problem of British education, which the new Bill is seeking to tackle. It is clear that, whilst the traditional 'public' schools and the former 'direct grant' schools are maintaining a level of achievement equal to any in the world, the UK has so far failed to build into its public sector a level of achievement to ensure for the country a broader reserve of young men and young women in numbers and educational achievement comparable with the major industrialised countries of Europe, of USA and, least of all, Japan.

A number of independent schools have, it is true, problems of their own. Fees continue to rise, reflecting increased costs and averaging now some £4000–6000 per year for boarders and £2000–3000 for day pupils. The financial commitment for boys, and increasingly for girls, bears particularly heavily on parents in these sectors of the economy which were formerly the main catchment area for the large London and provincial grammar schools, many of which as we have seen are now in the independent sector. Even greater in its implications is the pressure on headmasters and headmistresses to show 'value for money'; increasingly to be reflected in the rate of success of applicants for universities and polytechnics, and their level of achievement in public examinations and, subsequently, in career prospects. This in turn aggravates one of the major problems of British education – increased specialisation in those areas of teaching of particular interest to the universities and to potential employers. There is, therefore, little room in the curricula of most independent schools for a serious approach to newer subjects such as information technology, science, the arts and a wider approach to language learning.

It is, however, in the public sector, particularly in the comprehensives (some 80 per cent of the total secondary schools) that the major problems arise. Many of these schools are very large and often result from the amalgamation of two or more schools in the same area. Many are located in inner cities and in the more deprived areas of London and the major industrial conurbations with a student mix which reflects the complex ethnic composition of their catchment areas. The schools are under local authority direction and in some areas have been caught up in the extremes of local political controversy. Many of the schools (though with some outstanding exceptions) have been short of funds for building maintenance, for textbooks and teaching materials, and for extra-curricula activities. Morale amongst teachers has been low, beset as they are with seemingly endless disputes, by and large over pay and conditions of service, and an acute feeling of a fall in status of their profession and a lack of public understanding and sympathy for their problems and difficulties.

Parents are often worried and almost frightened for the future of their children, whilst the children all too often reflect clearly in their examination results and in their general character development the uncertainty and often almost turmoil of their schools. Within this general context it is too much to expect of a single Education Act that all the problems in the schools will be solved or that the British education system as a whole will regain its former standing in the world (or indeed its dignity). But the Act does address many of the right problems, and if it can be freed from its political overtones and the requirements are adequately funded, then the prospects for the future are far from bleak.

Its main provisions include the introduction of a core curriculum for public, and possibly private, sector schools – not, it is true, aimed (as in certain countries) at ten certificatable subjects, but certainly with a wider range than now and with more emphasis on English, mathematics, science, technology and a foreign language. The Act also allows the more frequent monitoring of progress of children from the age of 7, whilst the newly introduced GCSE will rely more on continuous assessment and on skills than on written examinations and the presentation of knowledge. It seeks to reduce the power of local authorities, and allows for schools to opt out of local authority control without losing entitlement to public funds. It seeks to increase the influence of parents in the schools' general direction and administration, including a major say in the vital decisions as to whether or not to seek to opt out of the public system.

The possibilities are, however, that like its predecessor Acts of 1902, 1918, 1944 and 1976, it will prove a watershed in educational progress in the UK. The Act has many weaknesses and it is already something of a political football. But in the end it may well permit the British education system to pass from the centre of the political scene and revert to a truly professional activity. It would produce an orderly path in academic development and, hopefully, make a major contribution, as it has in the past, to the social, industrial and commercial well-being of the nation.

Notes and references

1 Information from the International Labour Office

Our comments on the ILO follow personal visits to their Headquarters in Geneva, where we were greatly helped by Mrs Medva Sarfat. We are also grateful to Mr Von Muralt for the time which he made available to use and Mr Anton Faymann of the Hotel and Tourist Division.

We have made considerable use of specially prepared extracts from the ILO Digest of Relevant International Articles and Books. We have also referred to the ILO Social and Labour Bulletins and also to other publications of the ILO, including their book on *Technological Change – The Tripartite Response 1982–1985* (Geneva 1985).

2 Sources of international information

Many of the international statistical comparisons are extracted from the Internationaler Vergleich section of *Grund-und Struktur Daten* for 1987–88, published for Der Bundesminister für Bildung und Wissenschaft (Bonn, December 1987).

There are also a number of useful figures published in 'Competence and Competition' a report by Amin Rajan on training and education in the Federal Republic of Germany, the United States and Japan, prepared by NEDO and published by MSC 1986.

A very valuable source of information is the series of articles relating to schooling, vocational training, productivity and economic performance in France, Germany, Japan and the UK. The articles by S. J. Prais in conjunction with Karin Wagner were published by the NISER in the years 1981, 1983, 1985 and 1987.

Much of the information on German education in industry was collected by Professor Reeves following extensive consultations during his six months secondment as visiting Alexander von Humboldt fellow at the University of Hamburg. Particular points of reference, mainly statistical, are indicated in the text.

3 Education in the UK

The Manpower Services Commission (MSC) has covered many aspects of the subject in its publications. Of particular relevance to the theme of this book is the account of the Industrial Training Bill (Bill 37), December 1985, which extended the overseas activities of the training boards.

Other relevant publications of the MSC are:

Adult Training – National Priority Skills Scheme 1987–88
Industrial Training Organisations, 5 January 1985
The Effective Non-Statutory Activities of the Training Organisation, NASTO July 1986

4 General reading includes:

David Liston, *Education and Training for Overseas Trade*, BOTB, 1975.

'The Dramatic Rise in Female Part-time Workers in the UK' Labour Research Report, *ILO Social and Labour Bulletin*, March 1987.

Amin Rajan and Richard Pearson, *UK Occupation and Employment Trends in 1990*, for ISM, Butterworth, 1986.

Michael Durham, 'The Pull of the Magnet Schools' *Daily Telegraph*, 21 September 1987.

Open Learning Directory, MSC April 1988.
How not to lose the Trade Wars by Cultural Gaffs. An interesting comparison by John Pfeiffer on the Japanese bargaining rituals and their significance to the progress of the USA and Japanese trade, *The Smithsonian*, January 1988.

11 Post-school education in the UK: vocational, professional and management

From the classroom to the world of work

It is clear from what we have written in Chapter 10 that schools in the UK have been going through an unhappy time. The weaknesses of the British scene are obvious and much publicised. The strengths are perhaps more difficult to identify and quantify but, nevertheless, are real enough and give hope for the future.

Many of the 'public' schools in England and the former 'direct grant' grammar schools are very old (a few can trace a continuous history of more than 600 years). They are proving not only resilient in maintaining the best of their own traditions, but also flexible enough to absorb, and often pioneer, major changes in curricula, in educational technology, in examination routines and in developing industrial co-operation. Moreover, as we have seen, their level of achievement in public examinations is well up to world standards.

The Scottish schools system has maintained much of its traditional structure independently of England. The schools are much nearer to the Continental system in the breadth and length of their examination curricula. Unfortunately, the teaching staffs in Scotland have been upset even more than in England by disputes over pay and conditions. But, for all that, many of their fine city schools continue to be amongst the best in the world.

So, too, are the Welsh grammar schools, inheriting a fierce national pride both in educational standards and in sport, but struggling not unsuccessfully against the depressing economic environment of their catchment areas, lack of funds and the general educational malaise.

On a more general level, the principle of comprehensive all-ability schools has won slow but increasing acceptance. The principle is itself far older than it is generally thought to be both in the UK and abroad, and some of the outstanding problems, in so far as they derive from educational as opposed to social considerations, are clearly capable of solution in the light of the growing experience of the schools themselves and of similar institutions overseas.

In the public sector, too, the sixth-form colleges are proving a useful bridge between school and higher education. In many cases they already have an impressive record of success in 'A' level examinations and in subsequent entry into the universities and polytechnics; whilst a number, which were based on private schools with a good sixth-form, remain amongst the most popular sources of recruitment for the university sector.

Outside the schools, but increasingly impinging upon them, there are many new initiatives sponsored by government and by government agencies which are seeking to bridge the gap between academic and vocational aspects of education. Their aim is to introduce more practical technology-based teaching in both schools and colleges in co-operation with industry and, in this way, to provide a more natural transition from the classroom to the world of work and to open up career possibilities in science, technology and engineering. The new proposed national technological schools, a good deal of whose financing will come from private sources, are a further move in this direction.

The Manpower Services Commission, in association with the Department of Employment, Department of Trade and Industry (Department of Enterprise) and the Department of Education and Science, have launched a great number of initiatives including the Youth Training Scheme (YTS). The Technical and Vocational Education Initiative (TVEI), provides the basis for practical vocational training both at pre- and post-16 levels. It introduces a new, practical ethos and atmosphere into the schools.

Side by side with these initiatives have been attempts to bring under control Britain's confused and confusing system of vocational qualifications. The National Council for Vocational Qualifications (NCVQ) was established in October 1986 following the government review of vocational qualifications (April 1986) and a White Paper, 'Working together: Education and training' (comd 9823 July 86). The remit of the NCVQ has been summarised as follows:

'1 To establish a framework of vocational qualifications which is comprehensible and comprehensive and to facilitate ... programmes and the continuance of learning.

2 To influence vocational qualifications themselves by relating their standards more clearly to the standards of competence required in employment.'

At the same time, the Vocational Accreditation Council has made progress in its efforts to regulate the activities and awards of teaching establishments outside the state system.

Finally, the establishment some years ago by DES of the Business and Technician Education Council (BTEC) has brought together two areas of sub-degree certificates and diplomas which formerly operated as separate entities. Similarly, the Council for National Academic Awards, currently the largest degree-awarding body in the country, has played a crucial role in evaluating the curricula standards and awards of the non-chartered bodies in higher education, some of whom in turn have reached such maturity in their specialised areas as to have earned accreditation status in both under-graduate and post-graduate areas of work.

The prospects for success of these various efforts are perhaps less good than they might be, if only because of the highly complex interaction in the UK of political, educational and social attitudes. Indeed, the very size and complexity of the problem, with its huge financial implications, appears to be a deterrent to progress, particularly in a country where the contribution of education to industry, business and commerce, and to the economy as a whole, has been consistently undervalued.

There is, however, one area of business where the UK already has something of a lead over many of its international competitors and where the prospects look good for this lead continuing in the future. The field is that of professional education and training. It is, moreover, an area of particular relevance to the general theme of this book – the development, both in new entrants to the profession and in existing members, of the skills and attitudes required for successful participation in international trade and services. The commercial involvement of these professions has already been discussed in the sectoral chapters. We now look more closely at the work of the professional institutes, associations and educational establishments in their efforts to face up to the challenge of education in their respective spheres. This in turn leads at the end of the chapter to a more general discussion of the vexed question of management education and efficiency.

Professional education

The professions concerned are as follows:

1 The Stock Exchange, 'The City' and Financial Services
2 Accounting
3 Law
4 Banking and financial services
5 Insurance
6 Transport

The Stock Exchange and the City

The public image of the British stockbroker is clear enough – upper-class, wealthy, well-connected and addicted to the better London clubs. He is above all pragmatic and confident in his own commercial judgement and in his ability to trade successfully through the historic, informal, yet deeply entrenched practices and conventions of the stockbroking business.

What is (or was) less clear is his recognition of specific requirements for entry into the profession other than personal recommendation and the required level of financial resource; or any need for professional or commercial qualifications other than a modest course, mounted either in-house or through a very limited number of universities and polytechnics, for final registration into The Stock Exchange.

This picture is, of course, over-drawn and less than fair to many who have fought so hard to maintain the momentum of their business in face of continual change in recent years. However, it remains true that, whilst the registration of individuals working in the Exchange began in 1934, there were no examinations at all until the 1960s. Recruitment has been in the main from the public schools, often part of a family tradition. On the other hand, the system has been flexible enough to permit 16-year-old school leavers to work their way up to 'blue buttons' (reporting prices on the floor), to traders, and in due course to become partners in their firms. It was a cosy, protected atmosphere, paternalistic and hierarchical – and on the whole it worked well, as it did in rather a different way in the older merchant banks and other finance houses.

Change, however, has now caught up with the 'City' with a vengeance, and blown away many of the traditions and practices which were both its strength and its weakness.

1 Most of the London partnerships (the old brokers and jobbers) are now parts of international or UK conglomerates, as described in Chapter 3. Many belong to major banks, with established graduate recruitment policies.

2 The sophistication of securities is now far greater than even five years ago, with hosts of new financial instruments created and then in many cases set aside as conditions change. Indeed the creation of new products has become an important part of merchant banking – financial futures and options (described in Chapter 3) are but one example of a burgeoning new field.

3 The new technology has resulted in global, 24-hour trading from information displayed on screen. The Floor, the face-to-face dealing area on the Exchange and the traditional hub of all activity, is gone except for option trading.

4 The new examinations, instituted 1986–87 as The Stock Exchange became a self-regulating organisation (SRO), themselves make new and different intellectual demands on entrants.

Thus, the range of entrants today is much wider than it was in previous years. A worldwide economic sensitivity is important for investment analysis and advice, whilst specialisation is growing in all aspects of investment and securities management, with a consequent call for graduates in economics, business studies, accounting, banking and mathematics.

Side by side with specialisation, the need has, however, developed for more broadly based skills, particularly in marketing and international trade. The demands grow for sharper responses than hitherto in telephone and screen trading, for instant decisions, and for absorbing information rapidly from the screen – a combination of commercial flair and academic achievement – most improbably to be found in the traditional method of recruitment (where lack of success in any public examination was no disqualification), and poles apart from the attitude noted above in our preamble to this section.

The Stock Exchange examinations

From 27 October 1986 all those who trade or advise clients will need to pass the first tier of Stock Exchange examinations in order to enjoy registered status. At the end of 1987 examinations were in place for those who advise clients on transactions in securities and operate for their firm as 'Registered Representatives'. Those who are directly involved in dealing will need to pass the Registered Traders examination, which, however, does not authorise activity as an adviser or in soliciting orders. Options Traders are treated separately and have their own examinations, as do Registered Inter-Dealer Brokers and Money-Brokers (for details of the new structure of The Stock Exchange *see* Chapter 3). The examinations all focus on knowledge of the regulations now governing the market as supervised by the Securities and Investments Board (SIB) and in technical knowledge of the subject. For the Registered Representative this includes dealing practices in The Stock Exchange and other major exchanges (such as New York and NASDAQ), types of securities, settlement procedures in The Stock Exchange, principles of listing, investment and accounting analysis and investment taxation. The examinations last between $1\frac{1}{2}$ and 3 hours, can be taken at any time during the working day in a purpose-built video-based examination centre in the Exchange and require answering multi-choice questions. Because the examination is computerised, results are available by the next day.

To become a member of The Stock Exchange after reaching Registered status, all have to take the Securities Industry Examination, passing a compulsory paper on regulation and compliance together with two specialist papers on, for example, investment analysis, private client investment advice and management, institutional investment advice, financial futures and options and fund management. Though these papers of three hours are not all identical in format, they follow a common pattern. A section testing technical knowledge and technology, a practical case-study section for which materials are provided (or a SEAQ simulation may be played) and a section requiring the exercise of judgement and analysis in the form of an essay.

The implications of this for the candidates are twofold. Firstly, evidence of greater academic ability is required than previously. This is proving particularly tough on the young traders whose skills traditionally lay rather in dealing itself. The pass rate in their examination is only one-third, which itself has severe training implications. At present there are evening classes offered at City University Business School, City Polytechnic and some private tuition colleges, lasting three months for Registered status and six months for Membership. Henley Distance Learning has evolved a series of video and audio-type learning packs for both levels of examinations. However, no provision has generally been made for students to obtain day or block release, let alone for the organisation of in-house tuition. This contrasts sharply with the USA which has had registration examinations of even broader range for many years and where the major companies, like Merill Lynch, produce their own materials and have their own training systems. Such is the speed with which the securities world is moving, that training and retraining will have to become part of the normal career pattern. Firms will have to see it as part of their investment programme if they are to continue to compete effectively in the global market against other Europeans, such as the Germans, and against the Americans and the Japanese for all of whom apprenticeship or successful completion of formal qualifications is an essential professional requirement.

Accounting

The spectacular developments in the accounting profession were covered in Chapter 4.

The Royal Charter of the Institute of Chartered Accountants in England and Wales, which dates back more than a hundred years, contains as a principal objective to 'recruit, educate and train'. Other accounting bodies have similar objectives amongst them the Institute of Chartered Accountants for Scotland and Ireland, the Chartered Association of Certified Accountants, the Chartered Institute of Management Accountants and the Chartered Institute of Public Finance and Accounting.

With so many key bodies in the field, the need for harmonisation, both at home and overseas, is clear enough. The Central Council for the Accounting Bodies (CCAB) maintains a general overview of the educational standards and practices of the profession, whilst in particular the Board of Accreditation of Educational Courses, operating on behalf of these four London-based bodies of CCAB, are asked to confirm that courses are:

1 properly constructed with sufficient accounting thrust;
2 provide adequate coverage of the professional subject;
3 are properly assessed;
4 are taught by an appropriate number of qualified accountants.

Within this framework individual bodies can then determine which courses they choose to approve. The entry requirements vary considerably between bodies.

The Chartered Accountants for Scotland for instance have a graduate entry of 92 per cent, whilst the Chartered Institute for England and Wales count nearly 90 per cent graduates out of their annual student entry of more than 6000. A minimum entry level of the major accounting bodies is 5 GCE 'O' levels and 2 'A' levels, with a general requirement for proficiency in English and mathematics.

Amongst the graduate entry of the Chartered Institute for England and Wales for 1985, 44 per cent had a first degree in business studies and 23 per cent in science and mathematics. Significantly less than 5 per cent had first degrees in engineering. Forty-five per cent of the 1985 entry had first or top seconds – a very high level indeed for a profession which has not been traditionally regarded as a natural outlet for the academic high-flyer!

More than fifty universities and polytechnics offer degrees in accounting/accountancy, either (exceptionally) in isolation, or within a combined honours degree, or in combination with such subjects as business economics, finance, data processing, law or European studies. Postgraduate studies include international financial management at Reading and Glasgow, finance and accounting at Cranfield (for MBA) and finance and technology at Imperial College for MSc and for DSc. There are at least six degrees in accounting (minimum 3 years) at polytechnics, colleges and institutes; a degree in European finance and accounting at Leeds Polytechnic; a large number of technical and vocational courses; and HNC/HND courses either as full-time courses on their own or in many cases as an option in HND business studies.

Recruitment policies

With all this wealth of educational opportunity, much of it newly created, what signs are there of a major impact on the profession, of new thinking and of new responses to the difficulties and opportunities seen to beset accountancy perhaps more than any other profession?

Opportunities there most certainly are, reflected as much in the growth of the annual entry as in the eagerness of employers faced with persistent demands for new blood, to find out what is on offer, to beat their competition in the chase after the brightest and best in the field.

The major accountancy companies are the most buoyant recruiters in the UK, particularly of graduates, of any individual sectors. The largest, Peat Marwick McLintock, for instance, recruit nearly 1000 graduates per year, whilst other firms, such as Coopers-Lybrand, Price Waterhouse, Touche Ross and Arthur Young each recruit several hundred graduates each year. They look for no specific subject in the degree; although reflected in the total recruitment figures for the profession, there is a general preference for broader-based subjects – such as the inter-disciplinary business studies – rather than for degree courses more closely linked to accountancy itself. For the same reason, the more general approach of many Oxbridge courses is found attractive, although recruitment is in fact across a wide spread of universities and polytechnics.

Skills and personal qualities

This recruitment policy is determined very largely by the evolution in the work pattern of practising accountants, and by the consequential change in requirements both of people and of skills. The introduction of new technology and accountancy software has coincided with an ever intensifying expansion in both industry and commerce in financial control and management efficiency. Together these factors as we saw in Chapter 4, have shifted accountancy companies across into management consultancy as a major part of their work. As a result many day-to-day accountants, almost from the start of their careers, are not so much what we might call accountancy technicians, as investigators and auditors. Numeracy clearly remains important, not least for the traditional accountant. But so, too, are the skills of analysis and above all of presentation and communication.

Recruiters, therefore, look for young people with self-motivation, not traditionally the strongest feature of the accounting profession, and an open, self-confident social manner. Their written and oral command of English also has to be excellent. As a result candidates stand not only on their academic achievement, although the class results of graduate entrants shows it still to be important, but also on their activities in school, college and university. Accounting companies are looking, especially amongst their potential high flyers, for leadership qualities and evidence of ability to work in teams and against time.

Accountants and overseas trade

British accountants have long been familiar with the technical problems in accounting, in consolidation and in presentation arising from the overseas operations of the larger UK companies. In recent years, however, their overseas ramifications have grown apace – through multinational companies, the growth and complexity of trade within the Community, and most recently the impact of the UK 1986 Financial Services Act particularly on the location, operation and merging of British and foreign finance houses.

The resulting spread of accounting offices and staff is indeed dramatic. Touche Ross, one of the largest firms in the UK, employs 2800 staff in the UK and 236 000 abroad with representatives in over 90 countries. Peat Marwick had in 1985, 360 offices in 102 countries. Now following its merger with the Dutch firm KMS, this combination becomes the world's largest accounting company, with a network on the Continent of Europe comprising some 14 000 employees.

Training

This physical presence abroad has of course considerable implications for the competitive strength of the British accounting professions, and through them for the British and foreign companies which they serve. It also has implications for training both general and professional.

With regard to general training, we have already seen how the recruitment policy of the firms is strongly influenced by the range of scope of responsibility that a young accountant may have to undertake, both at home and particularly overseas. In one direction, however, there is less than unanimity amongst the firms – the importance of a foreign language to the aspiring accountant, perhaps reflecting the traditional concentration of many companies in the USA and Commonwealth countries. For all that, if young British managers are sent to offices with no language other than English, foreign languages can become crucial. The same applies, of course, at more senior level, particularly as project leaders in international negotiations, company take-overs etc. The prevalence of French in English schools makes a good basis for learning. Spanish is also considered useful, but there is a serious dearth of people with Portuguese (for Brazil) and with Japanese, and a limited but important need for the Far Eastern languages such as Thai and Malay. On the whole, however, no foreign language policy is discernable in British firms – a situation all too common in almost every aspect of British overseas trade.

Training within the profession

So far as the Institute of Chartered Accountants is concerned, the trainee will be expected to pass the examinations necessary for Chartered status in three years and generally speaking the time for study has to be found outside working hours, though a few companies arrange two to three months' block release for tuition in private schools. Training is an arduous task for many and a good number do not complete their qualifications and leave the profession.

The Institute of Chartered Accountants of Scotland has a two-year scheme and itself provides a system of a 3- to 4-week block release when candidates come together to study at the Institute's own Education Centre in Glasgow or Edinburgh.

Entrants can, of course, go into a number of departments, but a common feature of training is a maximum exposure to different types of work through direct involvement in a diverse series of business audits or consultancies. The audit, which can get to the root of a company's financial structure and strategy, is perhaps the most popular introductory activity. It was, after all, the source of the new dominant diversification of accounting companies into management consultancy. For those with a foreign language or interested in rapid international experience, a secondment of six months or more to an overseas office, which could be anywhere from Canada to Hong Kong, is common. But whether the trainee is at home or abroad, involved in general audit work or selected for specialist training, such as receiverships or taxation consultancy, the same need for team-work, quick decision-making, and marketing is evident.

Law

Recruitment and training

In common with many professions, recruitment for solicitors in England has since 1979 been by graduate entry only. This is followed by one year at the College of Law for those with law degrees, or two years for graduates of other disciplines. Finally the recruit is accepted for two years as an articled clerk to a firm of practising solicitors, in return for which for many years a premium was payable to the host firm, but for which the articled clerk is now paid at a rate comparable with those of a trainee in one of the larger industrial companies.

The completion of this cycle of six or seven years entitles the recruit to admission as a full professional member of the Law Society and to a practising certificate. The maintenance of the latter is now, however, subject to the successful completion of a three-year part-time course in post-qualifying legal education.

There are in addition two grades of legal executive, with qualifications administered by their own institute, open to recruits with sub-degree qualifications, and entitling the executive to work with legal firms or in the legal departments of companies, though with less than full professional status.

The training of solicitors in Scotland is under the control of the Law

Society of Scotland and incorporates the main features of Scottish Law, whilst qualifications of barristers are obtainable only at one of the Inns of Court in England, the Faculty of Advocates for Scotland, and the Honourable Society of the Inns of Court of Northern Ireland.

The law degrees at universities and polytechnics form the natural source of recruits for the profession. There are some fifty such degrees offered in the United Kingdom, many of them with specialised options and a number featuring a training in a foreign legal system together with a foreign language. These include King's College, London, Birmingham, Kent, East Anglia and Surrey Universities. The potential demands on the professional lawyers are, as we have seen, very diverse and in a state of constant change. They, therefore, require of entrants the capacity of quick response, articulacy and a broad knowledge of affairs and skills in communication. Professional competence in law can come later and is perhaps best learnt either at Law College or in articles; the handling of international affairs is best handled by the firm itself, wherever possible through an appropriate posting within the firm at home or overseas. The need for languages is perhaps appreciated now more than it ever was, and there are discernable efforts to make good the weaknesses in languages of the average school or college leaver.

The Law Society is conscious of all that needs to be done, and the Overseas Directorate in particular is trying hard to incorporate the international dimension as outlined in Chapter 9 within the general scheme of education and training within the profession. There is still a long way to go, but the stake is very high and the omens are far from discouraging.

Banking and financial services

It is appropriate that the Institute of Bankers, now more than 100 years old, should at last have received in 1987 its Royal Charter. For it is a recognition not only of the years devoted to establishing, promoting and monitoring professional standards of practice and education and of securing their worldwide recognition, but also of the fact that at no time during the past century has the profession itself faced more threats, or been offered more opportunities, than it has today.

The membership of the Institute in 1986 was 115 000. Of these 90 000 were in the UK and 25 000 abroad with overseas local centres in Cyprus, Hong Kong (with nearly 10 000 members), Kampala, Lusaka, Malta and Mauritius. Some 250 polytechnics and colleges offer courses in banking, leading to membership of the Institute (with, in addition, a newly-created certification), and entitling candidates to sit for the Banking Diploma which is the basic qualification of the career banker. Holders of the Banking Diploma are entitled to become Associates of the Institute

(AIB) and also to enter for the Financial Studies Diploma, the highest of the Institute's academic awards. This particular course was launched in 1985 and, after a slow start and high failure rate, now seems set to attract an annual entry of more than 800 candidates.

The most recent innovation, and indicative of the new outward thrust of the profession, is the International Banking Diploma, introduced in 1987, and carrying with it the hopes of all who look to the Institute to reflect in their curricula and their awards a firm grasp in an international context of banking law, accountancy and monetary economics.

Finally, the hierarchy of the Institute is completed by its elected Fellows, of which there are some 3000, in addition to its Honorary Officers and strong Central Council, and a Headquarters staff split between London and Canterbury.

The membership of the Institute shows a steady, if modest, annual improvement. Its courses and curricula seek to be responsive to new influences and directions within the banking world. It has a strong and representative institutional structure, including widespread local centres at home and overseas.

The future of the banking profession

And yet some serious question marks hang over not only the Institute itself, but also the entire profession which it serves. Has the world of banking changed so completely in the past century and particularly in the past decade as to have leapt beyond the limits of the very word 'banking' as traditionally conceived in the UK? Is the banking profession itself in the process of being pre-empted by a profession of quite a different character devoted to the provision and handling of global financial services which are at the moment variously rendered by the British clearing banks, the merchant banks, The Stock Exchange and a miscellany of finance houses? Is the description 'Institute of Bankers' and are the very terms of its new charter adequate to describe the professional knowledge and expertise which must increasingly become the Institute's field of deployment? Above all, are the young men and, increasingly, young women who are trained and groomed through the Institute's curricula and examinations for full professional entry into banking, prepared for what is in fact becoming a highly diversified group of professional and commercial activities, operating in many cases through a single corporate entity but demanding a wide range of skills and professional expertise which the banking qualification alone, even at the highest level, can no longer be left to provide?

In considering these questions, two major points need to be made:

1 Firstly, in fairness to the Chartered Institute of Bankers and to the

directors, trainers and recruiters of the individual banking firms, it should be said that these are precisely the questions which many of them have been asking of themselves. In October 1986 the Council of the Institute approved the concept of a full-scale review of the Institute's role and activities, and in December 1986 Philip Wilkinson, Group Chief Executive of the National Westminster Bank was appointed to the chair of the review body. The review body's terms of reference covered the purpose, image and membership of the Institute, its qualifying and non-qualifying activities, its role overseas and the governance and funding of the Institute. At the time of writing the findings of the review body had not been published.

2 Recruitment policies of the banks are, of course, under constant scrutiny in the light of these various factors. It should be said, however, that whatever adjustments are made, and in some cases they are already very great, there is little if any feeling that the basic professional training of the Institute should itself be radically altered, much less rejected or abandoned. There are many points of criticism in detail, particularly in the somewhat traditional approach to retail banking, the scope and content of the international coverage (except in the new International Diploma), and on aspects of the new banking technologies. But despite the increasing involvement of the banks in business outside the traditional range of banking, there appears to be a general wish to preserve the basic standing and integrity of the profession itself. And it is most generally considered that the education offered by the Institute is by and large on the right lines.

There is, however, felt to be an urgent need for a new dimension at least for recruits aiming at the top – something over and above the professional competence of the new entrant to banking and more akin to the commercial and management skills so zealously sought after in many fields of business activities.

This need is reflected, and to a very small extent satisfied, by the increasing prominence of banking as a discipline in higher education. There are, for instance, first degrees in Banking and Finance at the City University, at Loughborough, within the University of Wales (at Bangor and Cardiff), at Heriot Watt and at the City of London Polytechnic, whilst Leeds Polytechnic have pioneered a first degree course in Banking and European Studies. There are post-graduate courses in Ulster and Heriot Watt, and research facilities at the City University, City of London Polytechnic, Glasgow College of Technology and Leeds Polytechnic. There has also been a most encouraging increase in part-time courses in Banking at every level of higher education and a great variety (often stimulated by the Institute and, in many cases, held at the banks' own training centres) in post-experience short courses, seminars and conferences. There is little doubt that as a result banking education is showing progressive improvements both in breadth and in depth.

Beyond this, however, there remains the still greater problem of the general thrust of educational development within a profession which is changing fundamentally in character and is so continuously on the move. The response of company recruiters and training officers shows two main trends:

1 A new profile of requirements for the would-be high flyers in the profession.

2 An increasing participation in top-level programmes such as the MBA, and an attempt to reshape at least some of the courses either in whole or in part to meet the requirements of commercial as opposed to manufacturing enterprises.

The new profile

Recruiters are no longer primarily concerned with the subjects that graduates in particular have taken at first-degree level. Holders of banking degrees, it is pointed out, are not necessarily going to be good bankers. Mathematics at good school level (though by no means an essential prerequisite) shows in our trainee sample to be of some statistical significance in graduate selection. The same is true of economics. Recruitment appears to be overwhelmingly from the whole field of arts and social studies, including languages, with only a relatively small proportion from science and engineering. It is perhaps, however, worth noting that in Scotland there is a very substantial recruitment even for management trainees from school leavers, whilst, as a result of union constraints, graduates cannot effectively be employed at all in Ireland, with the result that the University of Ulster exports its banking graduates to more receptive markets.

Recruitment in general is, however, concerned at least as much with basic character requirements as with academic achievement. The search as we have found in other sectors is for flexibility, ready and effective response to change and well-developed analytical, numerical and communication skills. A proven capability for learning languages is thought to be helpful, particularly for those with an eye on international operations; but skills in any particular languages are thought to be best provided as required by post-experience training either through an appropriate overseas posting, or by using specialist language centres.

Similarly, a working knowledge of computers and of more advanced banking technology is best acquired, it is thought, in the course of professional and in-house training, although it is a paradox (an aspect which is touched on later) that in a profession so affected by revolutionary developments in technology, little credit in recruitment is given to candidates with technological expertise.

Post-qualifying education

This pursuit of managerial skills has led to widespread interest by the banks in MBA type courses, both in the UK and overseas. In the British business schools, in particular, nominations from both merchant and clearing banks have from the start formed an important element in the student mix. Banks have also supported post-experience degree and diploma courses in management departments of universities, polytechnics and colleges. But with this experience has come some disillusionment resulting in particular from the strong manufacturing orientation of America and British management teachers and of much of the case material which forms the basis of their teaching.

There are doubts, too, as to whether 'open' courses with their wide range of participants and what is still basically a broad academic approach to management teaching, can satisfy the most urgent needs of the banking profession. This they see as the need to familiarise their new graduates with the changes resulting from 'Big Bang', in particular the involvement of the banks in security dealings and the internationalisation of The Stock Exchange. More young bankers will have to become familiar with capital markets, securities trading and the new financial instruments. They will need to understand the impact of the 'time zones' – both the benefits of London's geographic position set conveniently for trading purposes between New York and Tokyo, and the need for speed both in thinking and communications to get full benefit from the advantages which location has placed at their disposal. The young bankers will need to live with the influx, possibly only temporary, of skilful, highly paid traders in bonds and financial instruments to whom worldwide thinking and split-second decisions have long been a way of life, and also with their mobility either voluntary or increasingly enforced. Finally, and on a far longer time scale, there are the international banks and banking professionals who have poured into London in large numbers and who are the products of professional training and experience in many cases very different from their own.

In all these circumstances it is not surprising to find a move away from the orthodox general MBA courses to full or part-time courses, custombuilt for banks and associated services, and often mounted in close consultation with the Chartered Institute of Bankers. A part-time evening MBA course of the City University has been designed for young professionals working in the City of London and is aimed to cause as little interference as possible with the daily work. The Centre for International Banking and Finance offers support, particularly in research, for this and other similar associated courses at the University.

The work of Dr Jim Byrne (formerly at the Centre for Banking and International Finance at Manchester) broke even more completely with the traditional pattern of the MBA with a series of tailor-made eight- or three-week courses in development/merchant banking and commercial banking with special reference to the Third World. The courses are aimed at banks both in the UK and in the developing world and have attracted very large numbers.

Finally, the possibilities of video-led distance learning, at Henley and elsewhere, are being actively explored particularly by the Banking Information Service and will no doubt feature prominently in banking education in the future. We return to banking in relation to the wider aspects of management education in the concluding sections of this chapter.

Banking education – some worries for the future

There are, perhaps three main worries for the future.

1 Banking is a profession which has for more than a century been largely based on a school-leaving entry, followed by in-depth professional education at the banks' own training centres, at polytechnics and colleges teaching to the Institute's examinations and on-the-job training through carefully supervised postings at home and overseas. The numbers involved are very large, attitudes entrenched and the processes of change often long and painful.

The career path of graduate trainees, no new feature of the banking system, has never been easy and still continues to be difficult. The fast-track high-flyers (propelled by the MBA or other post-graduate awards) will obviously need toughness and tenacity as well as flexibility if they are to achieve the rapid advancement which both they and their employers had in mind when setting them on this particular course. Wastage is already high, although probably no higher than in many other business contexts. For all that, it remains a worry and could turn into disillusionment particularly amongst top management. Finally, the influx of 'whiz-kids' with high salaries and often unrealistic expectations is obviously a major unsettling influence. Some of the most influential of the top banks feel, however, that this particular influence, though often necessary and healthy in itself, will quite soon shed many of its overtones and excesses. The sharp cut-back of a number of the leading employers in America and in the UK since October 1987 has already had a sobering effect and a settling down process is generally expected.

2 In the long term the more worrying factor are the general staff implications of the recent changes, particularly the increasing spread of acquisitions and mergers and the new developments in banking practice and technology. We have already discussed some of the more obvious effects in both domestic and international banking. There remain to be considered the implications for the staff – managers and skilled and semi-skilled clerical staff – of the steady growth of the size of individual

units and the near total automation of banking transactions and the reduction or elimination of very many of the manual operations.

So far as labour supply is concerned, it would appear that, despite its narrow educational base compared particularly with German and Japanese competition, British schools and universities are producing young men and women of the quality and in the numbers required for top management purposes. Moreover, they are coming forward at an age young enough to permit extensive, post-graduate and post-experience training, in contrast to their German and Japanese counterparts whose protracted schooling period includes a considerable element of vocational training but, particularly if followed by a first university degree, delays the release of graduates on to the market until the age of 28 or 29.

The success of the British system is illustrated by the recruitment by some foreign bankers in London. Nomura Securities of Japan, for instance, expanded their total staff in London from 200 to 500 in $2\frac{1}{2}$ years and some 70 graduates were sent to Tokyo for a three-month training period in banking practice and in languages.

The real worry, however, is not so much the quality/quantity training or indoctrination of the new top management stream in the profession which possibly receives a disproportionate amount of attention and costs a lot of money, as the growing imbalance in the labour force as a whole, particularly in the huge army of unskilled and semi-skilled staff.

It is clear that the development of large concentrated, highly-automated, multipurpose units leaves very little room for all but the selected few to seek career progression in retail banking which has hitherto absorbed a very large proportion of banking staffs. There, of course, remain at the branches openings at junior manager or supervisory level with, however, little opportunity to exercise higher management skills.

So far as clerical jobs are concerned, those that remain at branch level will at best be semi-skilled, many of them part-time and providing little opportunity for advanced clerical work either for men or women. As a result the gap between those who are going fast and those who are left behind is becoming dangerously wide.

Here the narrow base of the British education system shows to its greatest disadvantage. In Germany, for instance, as has been described above, the combination of company-based apprenticeship and carefully graded in-house training feeds into the firm a continuous stream of young people educated and trained for jobs at every level all along the line.

It is true that bank employees in Germany who have pursued their academic studies to doctorate level (and there are plenty of them about) are strongly placed for promotion to the highest positions or to positions just below. The products of German schools and colleges with their relatively broad schooling and their vocational training are equipped also to make a bid for a wide range of more general and intermediate positions and, in exceptional cases, to go to the very top. The gap between them and their graduate colleagues is no longer as wide as in this country, and, except for a limited number of specialist positions, advancement in Germany is by no means simply a function of the higher level of pre-entry education.

In sad contrast are the thousands of British bank clerks, both men and women, who have entered the bank straight from school and find themselves constrained by the narrow base of their school education and by their limited post-entry training and experience. They see little hope of participating in a major way in the new and exciting prospects opening up for the profession; on the contrary for all too many the prospect is one of ever increasing routine, of machine processing, or early retirement and, possibly, even redundancy.

Insurance

Unlike accounting and banking, insurance has never fully established itself as a self-standing academic discipline. There is not a single degree in insurance at UK universities, although management degrees at both City and Nottingham University incorporate insurance options. An innovatory course in risk management at the Glasgow College of Technology took eight years from planning to final approval by the Council for National Academic Awards.

There are, of course, many specialists working in the industry with high academic qualifications of their own. They include actuaries, accountants, economists, lawyers, surveyors, arbitrators and men and women with full academic training in marketing (both domestic and international); in estate management; in computers, engineering and technology; whilst particularly for risk assessment and valuation, there is scope for engineers and technologists. Common to most entrants in the industry is competence in mathematics, a facility particularly sought after by recruiters; whilst for sales and marketing staff, there is special emphasis on interpersonal relationships and skills in presentation and communication.

In the absence of any single umbrella degree, or indeed of any academic institution equipped to take the lead in teaching and research, much of the responsibility for general patterns of education and training in insurance and for the safeguarding and development of professional qualifications must rest with their own Chartered Institute. The individual specialist institutions and associations, such as those for actuaries, accountants and engineers remain, of course, responsible for the particular level of expertise fed by their members into the industry. The overall harmonisation and co-ordination remains, however, with the Chartered Institute of Insurance, the Association of British Insurers (ABI), the British Insurance Brokers' Association, with Lloyd's and with the Association of Insurance and Risk Managers in Industry and Commerce (AIRMIC).

The Institute dates back to 1897 and received its Charter in 1917. It has nearly 60 000 members of which more than half are qualified as Fellows or Associates. The Institute's basic educational award, the Associateship diploma (ACII) is attained by passing nine subjects (subject to certain exemptions). Courses are taught at approved colleges and polytechnics and normally involve three years' part-time study. Many students attend evening classes, although there are a few firms in the industry who give day release to approved employees. Study and examination centres are widely spread over the country and overseas, as part of a comprehensive tuition service approved by the CII, assisted by a hundred qualified tutors, and operating on a non-profitmaking basis, as a Division of the Education and Training Trust of the CII.

Progress to the Fellowship of the Institute (FCII) involves further study and additional examinations in five subjects at advanced level, though again there are exemptions for high academic achievement and for certain levels of experience.

Additional to its basic awards, the Institute offers a Life Assurance Salesman's Certificate (for which postal tuition is provided by the CII Training Service) and a Certificate of Proficiency in insurance. This most recent and important addition fills a gap which was noted by the authors in another publication. It is aimed at staff of any age working on insurance matters in industry and commerce, who wish to obtain a broad knowledge of insurance at a basic level, but who do not wish, or are not qualified, to pursue a full professional insurance qualification. In the business world, where risks and the consequent need for insurance now obtrude almost universally to a growing and alarming extent, this extension of insurance teaching is greatly to be welcomed.

The profession draws additional strength from the resources of the College of Insurance at Sevenoaks. Operating as a Division of the Education and Training Trust of the CII, the College has as its concern the main technical aspects of the profession, together with courses, educational conferences and seminars aimed at more general management. The duration of the courses may range from six weeks to two or three days. Many are aimed at overseas students, whilst others are run in-house by companies, and most recently a course aimed at completing the studies for Associateship of the Institute by means of one year's full-time academic study has been designed.

Insurance, is, as it has always been, an international affair, and it is no surprise, therefore, to find that the British insurance industry, as a result of the efforts of the industry and of Lloyd's in particular, is one of the biggest contributors to the overseas earnings of British invisible exports.

It is to be expected, therefore, that this international element permeates almost every aspect of the formal teaching for the professional and related examinations. Much of the teaching centres round risk management, and covers marine and aviation underwriting; product liability, personal injury, engineering insurance and reinsurance. The curriculum appears sound, well conceived and comprehensive in the teaching of international affairs – and quite indispensable as a guide to current practice and the circumstances in which the industry operates.

And yet, it is by no means coincidental that this industry, above almost all others, looks in its leadership less to specialisms, which of course it must have, and more to a general proficiency in insurance practice. Graduate entry consequently remains at a lower level than in many professional areas; and there is little sign that the 9000 Fellows of this Institute receive much advancement in their careers as a result of academic diligence and competence.

Insurance remains basically a 'pragmatic' industry. This may be because so much of the commercial success, at least at home, has rested on successful selling of life, accident, and pension policies. It may also be because, in the increasing diversity of the international sector, the unexpected almost always tends to happen, and the ability to cope with the unexpected demands above all commercial flair and flexibility, and some cultural empathy – particularly in the countries which seem most prone to natural and technological disasters.

The point is summarised very neatly in the guidance to recruits issued by the Legal & General:

You need a clear logical mind, able to grasp customers' needs and convert them into practical solutions. You need a fast and enquiring mind – a minute can make the difference between millions of pounds lost or made. You need an analytical mind that can interpret figures and draw conclusions.'

The same approach shows clearly in the list of sample questions circulated by Lloyd's in early 1987 to personnel managers of broking firms and chairmen of underwriting agencies. The questions, empirical yet pointed and testing, are relevant to the day-to-day practice of Lloyd's and cover a surprisingly wide field.

The message to recruits and younger employees is clear. We welcome you to our industry, says the employer, whether as a direct entrant from school, with good leaving records, or as a graduate of above average achievement. We are not particularly concerned with the disciplines you studied, but we would like you to be at home with figures, and able to write clear and well-argued accounts of your investigations and conclusions. If you can demonstrate your ability to learn languages, so much the better, particularly if you are aiming to work overseas.

In general though, the recruiters are less concerned with academic records, or with the present state of knowledge of new entrants, as with the ability to be able to get on with people, to present themselves well, to be willing to learn and submit to examinations in the main technical aspects of the profession and above all to be at home in dealing with the nitty-gritty of life, accident and pension assurance. In international business it might also demand the ability to tackle the horrendous insurance consequences of earthquakes in Mexico, hurricanes in South East England, technical failures in equipment in hospitals, in chemical plants in India and elsewhere, in nuclear eastablishments in the UK and the USSR, or in marine and aviation disasters in any country of the world.

To the short-term opportunist this may have little attraction. But is so happens that the longer-term requirements are particularly well adapted to the better products of the UK schools and universities, and the recruitment prospects, therefore, seem on the whole brighter than in some of the more volatile areas of industry and commerce.

The tourism industries

Our account of the UK provision in education and training for these industries forms part of Chapter 7, pages 179–189.

Transportation – the movement of people and freight and the conveying of information

A field as diffuse as this can have no single pattern of education or training whether in the movement of goods, people and services or in administration procedures.

It is, of course, possible to identify watersheds in development, both past and future, which have particular educational implications. These include containerisation of sea freight; the growth of ferry based road-rail transport in north-west Europe; the single Community market scheduled for 1992 with all that could mean for the simplification of international trade procedures; information transfer at unheard of speeds and in unprecedented volume, through the introduction of optical fibres and other technical developments; and finally, the Channel tunnel with its possibilities for striking a new balance between road-sea and rail transport throughout the length and breadth of Europe. To these special developments have to be added the continuous technological developments in equipment, in traffic control, in freight handling and in port and terminal facilities, together with an increased volume, particularly by air, which threatens continually to outstrip handling resources.

In the general development of its activities, the transport industry makes many of the same demands on its human resources as we have found in other professional areas. The need is for a continuous flow of well educated, numerate, mobile and highly flexible recruits to the industry, capable of operating on a worldwide basis with a combination of professional expertise, of character resilience and increasingly of the skills of international diplomacy. The perils of international law and convention following the increase in 'flagging' devices, particularly in the Gulf War; the frightening disasters in the sea and in the air; and the handling of the brittle state of industrial relations (both at home and abroad) are all part of the day-to-day problems of transport staff. It is perhaps a tribute to the industry's modes of recruitment and of training and particularly to the strengths of our national traditions that, whatever the disciplines and standards of the transport industry, there remains, as we have seen, extremely strong demand throughout the world for British personnel and in particular for sea-faring officers in overseas-registered ships.

The professional disciplines and standards of the transport industry are the prime responsibility of the Chartered Institute of Transport created significantly enough immediately after the First World War in 1919. It maintains the closest contacts with Government Departments, with the Chamber of Shipping, with the International Chamber of Commerce and with the relevant trades unions. The Institute conducts examinations in transport management leading to chartered professional status. It carries the general responsibilities of a major professional body for curricula development and for training with the help of academic establishments, training boards and with the Institute of Export, the Export Credit Guarantee Department (ECGD), with SITPRO and with the British Overseas Trade Board.

In higher education there are first degrees in traffic planning, management, technology and engineering, primarily at the technological universities such as Aston, Loughborough and UWIST, together with a degree in air transport engineering at the City University. The City University Business School, through its International Centre for Shipping, Travel and Finance, also offers an MSc degree which it describes as 'the only all-round approach' to these fields of study. CNAA degrees are mounted at Huddersfield Polytechnic and Napier College in Scotland. The colleges of maritime studies such as Warsash (now part of Southampton Institute of Higher Education) make a significant contribution to the technical training of merchant navy officers. Finally, the very active Transport Studies Group at the Polytechnic of Central London have for many years been a major centre for post-graduate work in transportation and have recently completed (as we have seen in Chapter 6) a major study of 'Freight Transport in the European Community' sponsored jointly by the Department of Transport and the Chartered Institute of Transport.

Business education – the wider context

The professional institutes described above and the academic establishments with which they work so closely are themselves the centre of a very much broader network of societies and associations which are at work in the same general field of education and training.

They include research institutes, learned societies, trade associations and chambers of commerce (including the International Chamber of Commerce) in addition to the training and research activities of individual firms. Prominent are the Royal Society of Arts, Manufactures and Commerce, the City and Guilds of London Institute, the Industrial Society, the Institute of Personnel Management, the British Institute of Management, the Institute of Directors, the Institutes of Export and Marketing, the Institute of Linguists and the London Chamber of Commerce Examinations Board. They all in turn draw support from Government Departments and para-governmental organisations, from local authorities, and from overseas from the USA and from Europe, and with an increasing contribution from the European Commission in Brussels.

As a result of these activities there has been established in the UK after years of uphill struggle and often far removed from the glamour of the newer business schools and the international academic institutions, a comprehensive structure of business and professional education which is difficult to match in any country of the world either in numbers or in quality and variety of education and training.

It is within this total context of business and professional education that much of the groundwork has already been constructed for major advances in the country's commercial and industrial efficiency. The culminating point of this activity is in management education and training, an aspect to which we shall now turn our attention.

Management in the UK – history and development

'A formal education, specifically for management, hardly existed in the United Kingdom before the war, apart from courses leading to the qualifications of professional bodies'. This introduction by Professor Harold Rose to his study of 'Management Education in the 70s' (NEDO 1970) is true enough, though subject to some major reservations. It is, moreover, particularly relevant in the context of invisible exports and the service industries, for it is in these particular areas that managerial concepts nurtured by the professional associations began to emerge almost as a by-product of their technical expertise.

Training for top ranks of management is, in fact, a concept of very considerable antiquity. Historically it took root first in the armed services, in government and in higher administration; and the thinking which it reflects still, as we have seen, forms a most significant element in the French educational philosophy.

In the United Kingdom the first Services Staff College was founded in

1801. It appears, however, to have met with a cool reception not least because the Duke of Wellington was not convinced that academic education was of any particular value to the soldier. However, the errors and failures of the Crimean War seemed to have persuaded a powerful lobby of the need for soldiers, 'whose boldness should be reinforced by knowledge'. This reinforcement of the basic character requirements of the senior officer (provided now in the main through initial selection) by formal training in administration, strategy and military technology remains to this day the basis for advancement to the higher ranks of the armed services. It was an attitude strongly endorsed by Field Marshall Montgomery who wrote, 'It is my belief that good generals are made rather than born; no officer will reach the higher ranks without very long study. The conduct of war is a life study'.

It is, therefore, appropriate that one of the first major institutes of management development founded in the UK after the war was labelled the Administrative Staff College. It now operates as the Management College, Henley, and, through its association with Brunel University, it has added to its distinguished record of teaching mature executives, extensive degree and doctorate courses in management and allied subjects. Through its associated company it has also pioneered many aspects of 'Distance Learning', but in many ways it remains one of the few colleges in the UK with this broad approach to training in administration and top management, a tradition which it took over and helped to transform some 40 years ago.

The formation and growth of the Staff College at Henley, and the even more spectacular developments which followed the successful fund-raising activities of the newly-formed Foundation for Management Education, and particularly the establishment of the two 'Franks' type business schools in Manchester and London, have all but obscured the continuous and very solid progress made over many years elsewhere in the United Kingdom, particularly in technical colleges, colleges of commerce and institutes of higher education. Post-graduate management courses were offered, for instance as long ago as 1930, by the Faculty of Technology of Manchester University and by the London School of Economics and Political Science. At the undergraduate level, Birmingham University introduced a full-time commerce degree at the turn of the century, whilst pioneering work along the same lines was taking place at Regent Street Polytechnic (later the Polytechnic of Central London). In Scotland the Royal Technical College of Glasgow, founded in 1879, and now the University of Strathclyde, has a long and honoured tradition as a centre of technical learning.

It is clear, therefore, that when Colonel Urwick proposed his 'National Scheme for Management Studies' in 1920 he had behind him a long history of academic progress in commercial and technical schools, in polytechnics and, to a much lesser extent, in universities. He was also drawing on more than a century's history of educational development in professional associations and institutes, and rightly saw in their encouragement and harmonisation a challenge both to general and specific management education.

It is true that in the post-war years the emphasis in management thinking switched from commerce and trading to manufacturing and production. This is reflected both in the subjects taught in the management schools and departments, and particularly in the case studies.

Moreover, attracted by the glamour and repute of the American graduate business schools such as Harvard and MIT, their British counterparts began to raise their academic sights as they sought to establish and maintain their position in the league of international business schools.

As their standards rose higher and higher, international academic acceptance began to take priority over domestic compatibility and the commercial credibility of their teaching within the context of UK industry. Numbers both at the graduate schools and in the business studies departments of universities, polytechnics and colleges grew in size at a remarkable rate. Indeed, the business studies degrees of the Council for National Academic Awards became one of the very largest of all the disciplines taught within higher education.

The growth, which was paralleled at a number of technological universities such as Bath, Aston and City, was accompanied by the development of combined curricula in which business studies and/or management formed a significant element; whilst new types of international degree and diploma courses emerged (as at the European Business School), embracing one or more European country and often with multiple qualifications awarded by the participating institutions.

There was, however, a more worrying aspect to this tale of academic growth and success. It was a danger of which Lord Franks himself warned with great force and clarity and which was discussed in great detail some 15 years later in a special issue of *The Business Graduate* (Autumn 1979). The danger was that in pursuit of academic excellence, management education as a whole might tend to lose touch with its customers and with their individual educational needs. In granting elite status to a few and relatively untried institutions, it had the effect, whether consciously or not, of down-grading and indeed demoralising the many institutions both inside and outside the academic world which had sought to keep alive over many years the concepts of management excellence within industry and commerce and, particularly, within the professions. The dangers, in fact, proved all too true. The gap widened between management education at the top and the rest of the field, with long-term effects on the internal development of management education as a whole.

The activity, it is true, grew both in range of subjects and in numbers both of institutions and of participants. But the initial glamour began to fade, and with it there developed a mounting anxiety as to whether this major investment in management education, both of money and of resources, was achieving a proper return in terms of managerial efficiency and company profits.

Once again the administrators, the educators and the customers turned in upon themselves and looked sharply at what was going on both at home and overseas. The two major reports which emerged, the 'Constable' and the 'Handy' Reports, are of major significance, not least from the point of view of the present book in that they confirm the vital interrelationships of professional and management education and the need to make more explicit this interplay in courses and seminars, particularly in the field of international commerce and the tradeable services. It is to those aspects that the remainder of this chapter is directed.

Management education – the changing needs of a knowledge-based economy

We have described above management education as the culminating point of business education and training. This is no less true for international trade and commerce than it is for manufacturing industry.

The educational demands respectively of trade and industry are, however, very different from each other; and it is felt, certainly amongst a number of commercial companies, that these differences are not adequately recognised in current management teaching.

Consequently, as we have already described in this chapter particularly with regard to banking, there is a growing feeling within companies that many open management courses are only partially relevant to the immediate needs of their firm, whilst (with a few exceptions) the general balance in content of the teaching appears inadequately to reflect the sharp shift in emphasis that has taken place in the business world from manufacturing and production to commerce, invisible exports and the international trading services.

The critics have a powerful case. Management, they argue, has, it is true, its own professionalism and with some justification may be taught as an integrated set of disciplines in the business schools and management departments and institutes. On the other hand, in their own particular commercial fields a great deal of what needs to be taught, at least on the managerial level, is in fact the product of specific professional disciplines. And it is the application of these particular skills, grounded as they are in specialist expertise, that constitutes in many areas the real key to management effectiveness.

It is in this dilemma that lies the basic problem of current management education, as is depicted very clearly in two reports referred to above, which were published almost simultaneously in 1987. It is in the solution of this dilemma that the key may well lie to the reorientation and regeneration of British management.

This is, perhaps, no place to discuss the detailed findings of the two reports, if only because they range over very much wider fields than the theme of this book. The reports were sponsored between them by some of the leading industrial and economic organisations in the country and they undoubtedly embody a rigorous and scholarly analysis of their subject. The Handy Report, in particular, presents valuable comparisons of education, training and development in the USA, West Germany, France, Japan and the UK, and a number of the findings are reflected in Chapter 10 of this book. Unfortunately, the comparisons are by no means flattering to the current situation in the UK.

We have, however, one major reservation on both reports, viewed from the standpoint of our own particular interest in international trade and commerce. Reference is made in the report to the influence of the professions in the UK, especially accountants. There is also a somewhat derisory reference to the total number of accountants in the UK – some 120 000 professionally qualified in their field, compared with 4000 in West Germany, 20 000 in France and 6000 in Japan. It is by no means easy to defend this heavy disproportion of accountants and, indeed, of some other professions in the UK compared with the bias in other countries towards qualified engineers, information technologists and specialists in sales and marketing.

It is also true, as demonstrated in both reports (and as we ourselves have discussed in Chapter 10), that there is a higher average level of educational achievement than in this country amongst managers in France, Germany and particularly Japan. They include a surprising number of doctorates in engineering, law, economics and commerce held by business directors and senior executives in Germany.

Where, however, the reports can be faulted is in their failure to explore further the possibility that within the very large number of *professionally* qualified men and women in the UK there is inherent a very significant management potential.

These young professionals are very different from what they used to be. Firstly, a high proportion are graduates, drawn from all disciplines, many with good class degrees, with business studies as a favoured (but by no means exclusive) first degree subject. The legal profession, for instance, is now based on 100 per cent graduate entry. Chartered accountants, both in England and Scotland, are some 90 per cent graduates, whilst even in the less academic slanted professions, such as insurance, the changing nature of the work calls for an increasing reliance not only on accountants and actuaries, but also on a knowledge of international affairs, of environmental sciences and of technology, of marketing and of languages.

Secondly, the deployment of professionally qualified accountants, lawyers and bankers within their firms no longer has to be exclusively in their own specialised field. On the contrary, they are often to be found at the heart of the company's business – in international finance and banking, in risk management, in company merger and takeover activities, in overseas development and in management consultancy. It is for this reason that we have much sympathy with the vision of Professor Handy in which he looks forward to a more complete synthesis between professional and management training.

It is true, as we have said, that professional training often includes elements of management as part of the qualifying syllabus. But there is a great deal of management theory and practice that is excluded from purely professional training and which, as in many cases, could be more appropriately taught within a management school or on specially tailored courses planned in conjunction with professional associations and with individual firms. The rapid developments at Henley and in certain City institutions, such as the City University Business School and the City of London Polytechnic, are, together with parallel progress in the banks, finance houses and consultants, illustrations of the very strong prevailing trend that has now set in.

There is, indeed, room for a new type of business management diploma or post-graduate degree (MBA) taken either immediately after qualification or, preferably, following some work experience. The courses could be either full-time or part-time, shorter perhaps than many of the existing MBA programmes, more limited and concentrated in content and more sharply focused on particular areas of application.

There are, undoubtedly, difficulties in the way of this type of development – attitudes of the older managers; resistance of the younger ones to extending their periods of education; suspicions of the educational establishment about the academic viability of the courses; and the shortage of teachers. There is above all a need for much greater flexibility on the part of professional institutes who will be required to accept major changes in both syllabus and teaching methods, and who need to take a totally new look at qualifying regulations and standards of training.

But the rewards for success are very great. Taken together with the broader curriculum, which will hopefully be introduced into the schools, it could ensure a considerable flow of professionally educated young men and women, who are in every way equipped to match their counterparts in other countries of the world, and who are ready to make their full contribution to modern international business. Moreover, in spite of this extended length of the educational cycle, they would still be set to enter the world of the fully qualified professionals and managers at an age (say in the late 20s) which is in every way comparable with the new generation of managers abroad, particularly in Germany.

Notes and references

1 General reports and reviews – vocational and higher education

'Higher Education – Meeting the challenge', (Cmd.114) HMSO, April 1987.

Competence and competition – training and education in the Federal Republic of Germany, the United States and Japan, (IMS for NEDC and MSC), August 1984.

'Professional bodies – Their qualifications and NCVQ'. Consultative paper 1987 (*see also* Nigel Croft, *The Director*, November 1987).

Review of vocational qualifications in England and Wales. Report of Working party MSC/DE.

'Working together in education and training' – (Cmd.9829), HMSO, July 1986.

British Accreditation Council for Independent Further and Higher Education – current list of accredited institutes and recognised sectoral bodies – January 1987.

Validation awards, courses etc. Publications and handbooks of BTEC, CNAA, colleges and institutes of higher education, polytechnics and universities.

2 Professional education

Stock Exchange and the City:

Discussions have been held with The Stock Exchange and the City University Business School on their Stock Exchange programme; with Henley Distance Learning Ltd on their programme for training and the examinations for the securities industry; and with the City Polytechnic on their many programmes on City affairs, including their part-time evening certificate on The Stock Exchange. We have also attended a most useful seminar organised by the Chairman and senior officers of The Stock Exchange, outlining their preparations for the 'Big Bang'.

Accounting:

We are grateful for the help received from Ruth Eisenberg, Under-Secretary for Education and Training at the Institute of Chartered Accountants.

The following two publications of the Institute are particularly interesting:

The pattern of student education and training – Digest of Statistics 1986.

Consultative paper on effective education and training for the 21st century, August 1986.

Regulations and details of curricula and qualifying examinations are published individually by each of the accounting institutes.

Finance

The broader field of finance forms a major part of the MBA studies at universities, polytechnics and business schools. There are also a number of courses with specialisms in international finance and financial management. Amongst these is the course at Strathclyde Business School on industrial management and accounting; the international options at the City University courses; the honours degree at Leeds Polytechnic in European finance and accounting which they run in association with *Hochschule* Bremen. Leeds University specialises in financial management in developing countries, whilst Ulster offers international trade and finance as an option within their BSc honours degree in finance, banking and commerce.

Details of all these courses and many others are contained within the published prospectuses and curricula of the individual institutions.

Banking

We have had a number of discussions with Mr Eric Glover, Director-General of the Chartered Institute of Banking, but the views expressed are entirely our own. We have also had made available to us the management development programme of Barclays Bank, and the graduate development courses on international banking of Midland Bank. On each of these programmes we were able to carry out a small piece of field research amongst the participants. We would like to thank Lorraine Watkins-Mathys of Buckinghamshire College of Higher Education for her work on this research. We also visited the Barclays Bank Training Centre at East Grinstead.

Details of the main relevant examinations of the Institute of Bankers are contained in the following publications:

'Banking Diplomas'
'International Banking Diplomas'
'Financial Studies Diploma'
A publication of the National Westminster Bank entitled   'Nobody's in better shape' (1986) is a useful introduction to the educational philosophy of the bank.

A useful additional reference is 'Big Bang brief', *The Economist,* August 1986, and two articles by David Lascelles in the *Financial Times* 'Taking the tough line – the Road to Tokyo' (March 1986) and 'New York to Tokyo' (April 1985).

Insurance

Chartered Insurance Institute (CII):
Annual report
Training pack – publications, examinations and postal tuition
Examination Handbook, 1987
Handbook on the Certificate of Proficiency, 1987

College of Insurance – Prospectus for one-year CII Associateship Diploma Course

Insurance Industry Training Council – *Training guide for the insurance industry*

Lloyds – Introductory test

Legal & General, *Join us under the Umbrella* – recruitment and training book.

Transportation

Chartered Institute of Transport Handbook (1987–88) and the Professional qualifying examinations and membership regulations (1987–88)
'Freight Transport for the Community'

Mike Browne *et al*, *Making the most of UK opportunities*, Transport Studies Group PLC, March 1987.

Export Managers and Freight Forwarders Handbook (1987)

SITPRO – Simplification of International Trade Procedures Board – annual reports, publications, audio-visual modules.

The City University have recently announced an MSc in shipping trade and finance aimed at giving a global view of the business and claiming to be the only all-round approach available.

3   Management education

H. J. B. Taylor, *The Administrative Staff College at home and overseas* – Lyon, Grant and Green, 1968. An interesting account of the early history of management education in the UK.

Harold Rose, *Management education of the 1970s*, NEDC 1970, – a significant review of the field and one of the first post-war surveys to be carried out in the UK.

The Barclays Bank report on export development in France, Germany and the United Kingdom. *Factors for international success*, June 1979 (seminal report on international management).

John Constable and Roger McCormick, *The making of British managers*, BIM/CBI, April 1979.

Charles Handy et al, *The making of managers* – a report on management education training and development in the USA, West Germany, France and the UK, for MSC/NEDC, BIM, April 1987.

Peter Moore, 'Positioning business schools in the UK', *Lloyds Banks Review*, April 1986.

R. Whitley, et al *'Masters of business – Business schools and business graduates in Britain and France'*, Tavistock Publications, London, 1987.

Bob Reid, 'Management education – charter flight', *THES* 25 March 1988.

PART IV

Issues, challenges and conclusions

12 Some major issues: invisibles and a balanced economy

Manufacturing versus services?

In the years since the Second World War Britain has faced two persistent economic problems. The first has been the relatively slow growth of the economy as a whole and of manufacturing in particular. This has shown up both in a lower level of output per head than in any of Britain's North European economic partners (and indeed than in most of the world's other advanced industrial countries) and in a marked loss of share in world trade. The second problem has been a long-term history of balance of payment difficulties. The massive surpluses generated by North Sea Oil production in the 1980s proved to be short-lived and exceptional. Yet the strength of the pound sterling that initially accompanied these surpluses was a major factor in accentuating the decline in British manufacturing, which had hitherto been a decline only in relation to the buoyant performance of other advanced industrial countries. Despite a sustained and latterly spectacular recovery over several years, manufacturing output had (by the end of 1987) still not returned to the levels of the peak year 1974 [1]. As we observed in the first chapter, this pattern is not to be found in any other major industrialised country. Moreover, as we also saw, Britain now imports substantially more manufactures than she exports. Annual increases in exports by volume and by value have failed to match the British hunger for imported goods. The dramatic fall in the price of oil in 1986 immediately exposed the underlying weakness in the balance of payments, for it had still been possible previously to take comfort in an overall visible surplus that included oil revenues.

It was these circumstances that sparked off the debate on manufacturing versus services in the mid-1980s. Services have been growing as a source of employment in almost all advanced countries, not just Britain. In the United States, for example, more people have worked in service industries than in manufacturing since the late 1950s. In fact, by 1985 less than 20 per cent worked in that sector, whereas the services accounted for some 60 per cent. And even in the 1950s the contribution of manufacturing to GNP was similarly little more than 20 per cent compared to nearly 40 per cent by services. While these trends emerged somewhat later in West Germany and the Benelux countries and an absolute fall in manufacturing employment did not occur in France, Belgium or Italy till after the mid-1970s, a clearly discernible structural change is to be observed among all advanced countries [2]. Professor Dorothy Riddle has calculated that, while even in low income countries some 40 per cent of GDP derives from the services sector, this percentage rises consistently through categories of development to some 66 per cent in advanced industrialised countries [3].

This universal phenomenon was named 'post-industrialism' as early as 1973 by Professor Daniel Bell of Harvard. Since then the concepts of 'post-industrial society' and 'deindustrialisation' have become common currency and there has been fierce debate in academic circles about their validity and significance for the future [4]. In Britain these discussions entered the public arena after Select Committees of the House of Commons (in 1984) [5] and of the House of Lords (1985) [6] conducted investigations into something new in the history of modern Britain, the failure of manufactured exports to match the value of imports. The Aldington Report (as the House of Lords Report became known after the Committee's chairman Lord Aldington), was seemingly stung, in its conclusions, into an eloquent plea for the continued vital importance of British manufacturing by the complacent evidence of the Treasury. This evidence showed essential confidence about the future, with views based on the assumption that deficits in manufacturing trade marked a simple and natural adjustment to the surpluses generated by oil and invisible exports, while the exchange rate acted as the agent of balance in the international market [6]. This view, which is, it might be said, reminiscent of eighteenth-century theories of the invisible hand, could hardly satisfy manufacturers. Lord Weinstock vehemently protested that he would not wish to see the country reduced to a land of beefeaters, a 'curiosity' dependent for its prosperity on income from tourism.

In 1986 the chairman of ICI, John Harvey-Jones, joined the fray with the Dimbleby Lecture, 'Does Industry Matter?' [8] arguing that Britain's decline was exceptional, not typical of some general post-industrial age, while manufacturing industry still accounted for over £50bn worth of exports per year, 25 per cent more than exports of banking, insurance and oil together. He was also able to point to the 1985 Bank of England article (to which we have referred in Chapter 1) which showed that Britain's share of world trade in services was actually falling, and at a similar rate to that of manufacturing. In the same year of 1986, The Royal Society of Arts launched a nation-wide campaign, Industry Year, in an attempt to arrest British industrial decline by a concerted attack on social and educational attitudes negative to industry.

This book has looked in some detail at the many, highly diverse activities that constitute Britain's *international* services industry, the sectors that make Britain the world's second largest net exporter of tradeable services. We must now ask, in the broader context of Britain's and indeed Europe's economy, how these services relate to manufacturing – whether in any real sense they could replace manufacturing and in what ways they are dependent on manufacturing.

Perhaps the first point to be made is that the term 'deindustrialisation' is itself a misnomer. True, heavy industries everywhere in the advanced world have shrunk in size as newly industrialised countries have added to competition. The shipping market, to take one major example, has stagnated, driving shipbuilding into a profound crisis, while newer materials such as plastics have partially replaced iron and steel production, to take another. Total manufacturing production has, however, only fallen in Britain, except for a period after the 1979 oil rise when a number of Western countries were affected. In the United States manufacturing output has risen, if not at the same rate as the services, yet surpassing 1979 levels by 1983, while industrial employment has remained roughly static. In Japan average growth of output slowed in the decade 1973–84 from 12.8 per cent average per annum in 1960–73 to 4.3 per cent [9]. What we are seeing in advanced industrial countries is not a process of general deindustrialisation such as might be imagined when looking at the devastated industrial landscapes of some northern British textile towns or the acres of empty factories in the Black Country. We are seeing rather a shift in emphasis, in employment and in speed of growth away from manufacturing towards the services, a process which is particularly remarkable in Britain because of her former historical reliance on heavy industry and her slow rate of adaptation to change. However, this statement requires further refinement. It is only parts of manufacturing that are in decline in Britain, while even those declared uncompetitive as recently as the 1984 House of Commons Report, cars and textiles, are showing signs of recovery. Moreover, high technology industry is growing, both in the UK and abroad, especially computer-related industries with software at the forefront.

Nor is the concept of the post-industrial society necessarily a very helpful one. Bell adopted it since he saw a parallel in the apparent waning of manufacturing as a source of employment and as a proportionate contributor to GNP with the earlier waning of mining and, before that, agriculture. But to suggest that we live in a post-agricultural age would be equally misleading. The United States remains the world's largest single agricultural producer. The EC grows more food than it can possibly consume. What we are witnessing is a continued increase in output of both agricultural and manufacturing but with fewer employed in those sectors as mechanisation and automation become the order of the day. It may be fair to speak of modern economies as service economies, but they are still industrial and agricultural also.

Are such modern economies *based* on services? This is an almost philosophical question. One of the reasons for the shift of employment out of manufacturing into services (which it is at present impossible accurately to plot because of our inadequate methods of gathering statistics) is that industry has engaged in a process of hiving off or 'externalising' services that were vital to its activity but previously hidden statistically because they were carried out in-house. No manufacturer could remain in business without research and development, without marketing and market research, without advertising and naturally without transport.

As competition has sharpened, especially in the years following the second oil recession, companies have increasingly tended to contract out such services. Specialist firms can in many cases supply a more global view and greater expertise thanks to specialisation, while their employees are not on the manufacturer's payroll. Moreover, if their services are unsatisfactory, others can be given the contract instead. We have followed this trend particularly in the area of distribution and express freight. It is competition that has led to the remarkable growth of international accountancy firms in the area of financial management and corporate consultancy, as we also saw in an earlier chapter. The development of British legal partnerships in Europe and the Far East has followed a similar pattern and was initiated by the internationalisation of trade and industry.

The internationalisation of industrial ownership within Europe and between Europe, North America and above all Japan, has also led to a growth in those services without which business cannot exist at all, financial services. As we look at the impressive growth of the City, which now contributes 14 per cent of UK national output, it is easy to forget that export loans, investment abroad whether direct or in stocks and shares, related activities in mergers and acquisitions, and even trade in currency have as their bed-rock the manufacturing process – producing, exporting, sustaining the economy which is itself the foundation for the currency. Advances in banking processes through equipment such as ATMs and automated clearing both domestic and international rely on computing hardware and telecommunications. In the technical revolution gripping telecommunications through optical fibre and digital technology, purchase of new equipment is centrally important and national procurement policies are in the forefront of political debate in the EC and elsewhere. Similarly, the new methods of securities trading that replaced The Stock Exchange floor would not be possible without highly sophisticated computing equipment, which requires frequent updating. Nor can it be denied that insurance and reinsurance are tied into a chain that leads back to manufacturing from insurance on the lives and households of those engaged in, or otherwise connected with industry, through car insurance to the insurance of aircraft, ships, factories, powerplants and even indemnities on the products themselves.

Beyond the financial sector, much of that diverse area, consultancies, derives directly from manufacturing or construction. Most obvious in this context is the overseas work of engineers, but also that of management consultants whose expertise could hardly exist without a substantial and sophisticated domestic corporate base. We have observed the intimate and quantifiable link between the sale of construction consultancy and of equipment and materials in Chapter 8. Overseas earnings from licences and patents are derived from the sale of products manufactured abroad. Indeed royalties derived from publications and from music are so closely bound up with the sale of books, cassettes and so forth that one cannot estimate the source of these royalties without reference to visible trade in the sector.

In short, it emerges from our sectoral analyses that the issue is not 'manufacturing versus services'. The two are inextricably linked in Britain and in all modern economies, while it is not incontestably true that services have directly 'replaced' manufacturing jobs or output when to an extent what we have seen is an externalisation of services not simply fresh growth. Indeed in a provocatively entitled volume, *Manufacturing Matters: The Myth of a Post-Industrial Economy*, Stephen Cohen and John Zysman have recently argued that the whole concept of the service-based economy is false. They calculated that as many as half US service jobs are linked to manufacturing and would disappear if imports were to replace domestic production [10].

Similarly we may ask what would happen to, say, British jobs in tourism if the American economy were to be transformed in this way or if manufacturing were to decline in output in Japan, West Germany or France. Would tourists still continue to visit Britain in their present numbers? Indeed, if the United States is to pull out of its precarious economic situation at the end of the Reagan Administration boom, it will have to place a renewed emphasis on exporting industry much as has occurred in the UK since 1985. Retrenchment in US citizens' disposable income would almost certainly have a negative effect on a whole range of UK service industries, not just tourism but also in the securities sector as well as manufacturing.

The question with which we are confronted is not, then, whether UK service industries can replace manufacturing in some post-industrial era. It is rather to what extent do the services, over and above their foundation in industry, generate their own growth by servicing one another – banks lending money to advertising companies, companies in The Stock Exchange buying and selling shares of services companies, management consultants advising financial conglomerates on organisation and manpower, financial information services using satellite communications to provide currency dealers with 24-hour marketing data, to give a few simple examples? For this is the reality of the economies that are replacing the manufacturing-led economies of earlier this century. They remain manufacturing-based but are becoming increasingly knowledge-intensive *service led*.

At the heart of the modern economic process is the growing reliance of all sectors on the rapid transmission of information – which, in a circular manner relies on manufactures – computers, satellites, optical fibres, facsimile machines and so on, as we show in Chapter 6. Closely related to this is a further question – if the British manufacturing base remains smaller than that of her competitors with a similar population (which is almost inevitable in the medium term at least, because the starting point is so low as we saw in Chapter 1) can UK international service industries, banks, insurers, consultants find an alternative bedrock of manufacturing in other countries? Our sectoral investigations strongly suggest that this could be the case in some sectors. British banks, but above all British insurance, accountancy/management consultancy and law firms are beginning to take advantage of a new domestic market, the European market with its 320 million inhabitants, the world's largest single market under a capitalist system. The European Commission's intention to create a complete internal market, including a market in services, by 1992 is surely of fundamental significance in this context. For, while British manufacturing was slow in reacting to the challenge of European Community membership and indeed almost impotent in some sectors to resist imports from West Germany and France, some British international services, if not all, are in the forefront of new developments on the one hand and possess for historical reasons more international experience and wider networks than many European competitors on the other. We return to this theme when considering the competitiveness of the City later in the chapter. For the moment, however, we turn to the vexed question of employment.

Patterns of employment and the changing demands on people

Sectoral changes

Superimposed upon the shift towards employment in services in Britain but equally severely, or almost equally severely, in the Benelux countries, West Germany and France, has been the emergence of high unemployment. Initially this was a direct response to the recession of 1974 and to the far graver industrial crisis of 1979–82. But subsequently competition and the need to raise productivity, which was particularly urgent (and indeed chronically necessary) in Britain, led to the continued shedding of surplus manpower and increasing reliance on new labour-efficient manufacturing technologies. Only in the service industries did employment continue to grow. For, whereas employment in UK engineering, for example, fell by 23.6 per cent from 1979–85 to a total of 2.5 m, it rose in the combined distribution and financial sectors by 11.9 per cent to 6.1 m. One of the largest scale studies ever carried out (based on interviews with 450 employers, questionnaires sent to 2830 employers and discussions with 26 trade associations) estimated in 1987 that these trends would continue [11]. It forecast that production industries and agriculture would further reduce their workforce by 8 per cent or 665 000 jobs in the period 1985–90. Thanks to its method of gathering evidence, the survey was able to account for half of the decline through a key phenomenon we have already identified, that of activities subcontracted out to service industries. The total estimated job increase in these industries could be 540 000 or 3.6 per cent, rather less than the fall in manufacturing jobs. It was therefore concluded that total employment, notwithstanding the continued expansion of services, could fall in the UK until 1990. Subsequent official statistics, however, suggest that manufacturing has proved more buoyant than the forecast believed and employment in that sector, through 1987 and into 1988, continued to rise.

Within the services themselves employment growth may be uneven. Transport employment, particularly in shipping, is likely to fall further, while financial and leisure services could show vigorous growth (of some 6.2 per cent and 11 per cent respectively). Now these figures make no distinction between services for the domestic market and international services. Indeed, it would be very difficult to make such a calculation since it would involve matching proportions of staff in companies with the proportions of the company's international business, a process that would be difficult in manufacturing let alone in services. Nor does the forecast separate out, for example, growth in leisure services based on domestic demand and that stimulated by overseas visitors. Nevertheless, it is certain that in British tourism the engine of growth has been the influx of foreign visitors rather than an increase in domestically based tourism. In the financial sector, too, there is evidence that overseas trade is a significant source of increased employment, for the introduction of new technology has enabled banks to cope with rapidly increasing volumes of domestic transactions without increasing staff. Indeed one of the most authoritative surveys yet carried out established that banks across Europe, and in the United States, expect their staff to remain constant over the next decade [12]. Extra recruitment in marketing, securities trading and systems development would be offset by falls in those areas where technology could be most effective, in the domestic branches network, basic bank operations and accounting (a process we have discussed from the educational perspective in the last chapter). The City on the other hand had been, until the end of 1987, a centre of growth hardly matched elsewhere, with foreign banks in the UK alone being responsible for 54 000 jobs including an increase from 1985–86 of some 11 000 (or 26 per cent) [13] and a number of overseas financial houses such as Nomura expecting to continue rapid expansion. We should expect this to continue as the City spreads into huge new developments in the Docklands and as the City's own airport, light railway and riverboat system come into full operation.

Admittedly the stock market crash of 1987 will almost certainly continue to involve retrenchment and may well offset some of these gains. But international banks and security houses are not the only major sources of recruitment: the British and American accountancy and consultancy partnerships based in London are today, as we saw, the largest recruiters of graduates in the UK. And as we witnessed particularly in the great manufacturing shakeout of the 1980–82 recession, severe competition and new trading circumstances lead to increased business in corporate consultancy.

Geographical factors

One of the charges frequently laid at the door of the City is that it does not assist employment in other parts of Britain and it has to be admitted that London is a magnet for all international service industries including that most ubiquitous of all, tourism. But the new technology, the possibility, for example, of instantaneous screen trading in any on-line location is altering or at least modifying that trend in the financial sector. Edinburgh has historically been a major centre for life assurance and pension funds. Since the late eighteenth century, Edinburgh had a reputation for shrewd fund investment, a reputation that was substantially boosted by nineteenth-century investments of money raised by jute exports, for example, in railways worldwide. Today, nine major life assurance companies have their headquarters in Edinburgh, and they, together with eleven independent investment managers, all members of Scottish Financial Enterprise, manage some £53 bn of international investment funds. As in the City, foreign interest in establishing in Edinburgh is growing. In 1986 Ivory and Sime Ltd set up a joint venture with Sumitomo Trust and Banking to form a consortium charged with the European investment of Japanese funds, and in 1986 a Glasgow fund manager teamed up with Yamaichi. In the first 6 months of 1987 premiums for the Scottish life offices were up by between 36 per cent and 54 per cent; 675 new jobs in this sector were created in Scotland in the same period [14]. Indeed, the Scottish Development Agency calculates that the financial sector in Scotland provides 90 000 jobs directly and 45 000 indirectly and the fear that 'Big Bang' would draw employment down to London has proved groundless.

In this case, then, historical tradition has provided, as in the City of

London, a critical mass of expertise which then evolves its own business dynamic. But the flexibility of location provided by computerised trading has enabled other centres to spring up with no previous history. A prime example is Poole in Dorset, where a pleasant country location, close to the Continent of Europe and London, is attracting an increasing number of financial houses including new office complexes for Chase Manhattan and for Barclays. We can, then, envisage the evolution of an international financial services network in the UK that has its principal centre in the City with further specialist centres in Scotland and the provinces. That Belfast might become such a centre for accountancy, for example, is a real possibility that is being pursued by a group of senior accountancy partners in that city.

Furthermore, just as the development of the City as the European financial centre in the 1960s and 1970s was based on its off-shore activities in the Eurocurrency and Eurobond markets rather than because of domestic strength, the Channel Islands and the Isle of Man are developing as off-shore centres from the UK. Jersey and Guernsey have over £4 bn invested in mutual funds, 45 banks are present in Jersey, 36 in Guernsey, and forex and discount markets are growing vigorously. Of £36 bn on deposit, some £16.4 bn are in non-sterling currencies. Indeed it is argued in the Isle of Man that, with just £2 bn deposited, it alone of the off-shore island banking centres has room for expansion [15].

Types of employment

What kinds of jobs are being created? Above all, what qualities do they require if growth and competitiveness are to be sustained? We considered these issues in relation to some major sectoral activities in the last chapter. A more comprehensive assessment has been undertaken by the Institute of Manpower Studies in three investigations, the OSG survey already mentioned above, a separate survey of the financial sector and a third extended survey of all the service sectors [16]. The conclusions emerging from all of them are broadly similar and correspond closely to those reached by the ILO in Geneva. Across the spectrum of employment, by 1990, part-time work will rise from some 20 per cent to 25 per cent of the total, while the majority of new jobs will be for women, who find part-time arrangements compatible with other domestic arrangements. At the same time the types of work available will become more demanding, more knowledge-intensive and requiring broader human and entrepreneurial skills both at senior and at the support level.

Specialists in programming and systems analysis will be in continued demand, while senior management will also increasingly need assistance from professionals in marketing, operational research and statistics. Managers will, however, be the key figures, possessing good human relations skills with the ability to work across disciplines and to evaluate and apply information technology. In short the shift in employment numbers towards the services will be characterised, according to these most extensive investigations, by the need for an ever more qualified, broadly skilled and professional full-time workforce, accompanied by the establishment of a growing number of non-career part-timers.

These findings match those of a large scale investigation into one single major sector but spanning most of Europe. Arthur Andersen & Co., were asked to look at the development of employment in banking in the next decade. They consulted 600 senior bankers and other experts and set up a panel of 25 selected bankers and analysts for detailed discussions [17]. The panel listed nine major factors for success in the 1990s, corroborating the findings from the 600 questionnaires. They are worth quoting in order of importance since they may be considered to apply across the whole spectrum of international service activities under consideration in this book:

1   Quality of management
2   Marketing
3   Quality of management information
4   Implementation of advanced technology
5   Innovative product/service development
6   Competitive cost base
7   Risk management
8   Emphasis on strategic planning
9   Capital adequacy

The human factor was identified as the most critical. Highlighting that conclusion, the report stresses that for the future it will be vital to recruit on ability rather than background, to put personnel policies in the centre of a bank's strategic planning, to improve training and transpose it from the old on-the-job basis to a more formal footing – and to recruit for top management generalists rather than specialists. Creative thinking and leadership are the qualities that will count.

Our own investigations bear out these views, as we already indicated in the detailed sectoral analyses of education and training in the last chapter. In our interviews with international bodies, professional institutes, trade associations, companies, professional partnerships and educational establishments across the range of international services (listed in Appendix 1) and located in Britain, the Federal Republic of Germany, Brussels, Switzerland and Hong Kong, a striking consensus emerged on the qualities and types of people that will be needed in the future.

The opportunities for minimally qualified, single skill or single activity people are declining. Increasingly, those who are being sought and, (in the Federal Republic of Germany particularly) trained, are people who can work directly with customers, informing them of the products and services available, 'selling' the company, eliciting information about their needs. Thus, what had rather been the task of the head of a branch or group is moving down more generally into the workforce. This requires good communication skills and the ability to understand and solve simple problems. The new employees must of course be computer-literate and confident in making decisions.

The middle structures of all companies will need strengthening and will require in addition to these same qualities the ability to manage teams effectively, under increasingly competitive, fast-moving and therefore more stressful circumstances.

Senior management will be the key to success. Here leadership qualities in the context of team-work and collegiality are likely to be central. Managerial decisions will need to be made rapidly but will have to carry weight with the middle management team. Top managers will have to understand sufficient of marketing to adopt effective policies for projecting the company, as well as having the ability to shape financial policy.

And for success in the international transactions that characterise all the sectors with which we are concerned, whether it be banking, management consultancy, or road haulage, a familiarity and empathy with the business cultures of trading partners will be ever more essential. This is best achieved through knowledge of foreign languages to provide access to the sets of values of individual business cultures. The quality that has to be derived from that knowledge and through extensive overseas experience is the ability to adapt to and master other ways of thinking and doing things organisationally, in a word, the quality of 'interculturality'.

The educational infrastructure.

These requirements come up against traditional strengths and weaknesses in the UK educational and employment recruitment traditions. We saw in chapter 10 a major contrast between the education open to the clerical support and lower management areas in Britain on the one hand and in Germany and Japan on the other. Both the latter countries have systems that are directed towards producing substantial numbers of thoroughly trained young people for the lower and middle echelons, whether through the German dual system of in-house apprenticeship and vocational colleges or the Japanese mass university and college approach. The UK, in counterdistinction, has historically concentrated on producing an elite, formerly recruited, especially in the financial sector, from public and grammar schools and latterly from the universities and polytechnics. There has been little emphasis in the entire system, thanks to the British imperial heritage, of training in foreign languages or cultures except for the minority who wished to continue in the educational sector as teachers or lecturers. Nor has there been any equivalent in numbers of the vast output of managers qualified with an MBA in the United States. We have not even been alone in cultivating an elite. We have already noted the importance of the *grandes écoles* in France and of senior management and engineers in West Germany with doctorates, but neither of those countries concentrated so exclusively on the elitist approach.

Yet the UK system also has great strengths. Our respondents in the financial sectors, for example, were agreed that they were able to recruit good people at trainee level. They seek open-minded, outward-going personalities, young people with ideas and the ability to work across a range of activities involving differing methodologies. The great majority of recruiters whom we met looked less at the specific discipline studied than at general personal ability. We experienced no criticism of university arts courses in Britain. On the contrary the powers of analysis and self-expression that such graduates had developed were welcome irrespective of whether their subject had been archaeology or economics. That is not to say that students of economics and business studies are not popular for their numeracy and their awareness of business (and that applies especially to the business studies students). Indeed they form the greatest single source of recruitment in accountancy as we saw. But perhaps the greatest strength of the business studies students is less their specific knowledge of accountancy or corporate structures than their exposure to the wide range of disciplines involved in management. For, as it was established in the major investigations by the Institute of Manpower Studies and Arthur Andersen & Co., there is an increasing premium on management with a broad vision, flexibility and a generalist rather than a specialist background.

This relates closely to the other major UK advantage at the graduate level, the age of graduation. A bright young graduate of 22 who still has formative intellectual years ahead in which to work in the company and to obtain professional qualifications is a very different employment prospect from the single-subject 29-year-old graduating from a German university. True, top German management in the financial sector is drawn from legal and economics specialists with proven academic track records. But principal recruitment remains in good measure from among the school-leaver apprentices because companies are deterred by the age of average university graduates. The UK advantage of age is equally applicable in the case of young scientists and technologists recruited into insurance and especially insurance broking and reinsurance – or for that matter marketing or accountancy. There is time for retraining on a solid if not highly specialised base of science or engineering.

There are, then, grounds for optimism that the British higher education system, including most importantly the arts departments, is producing the kind of people who have management potential for the international service industries. At present, formal training in management is largely provided in-house alongside professional training. But we observed a trend in banking, at least, for the professional training to be given less emphasis than the kind of management training that will further the marketing needs of an industry facing even keener competition both domestically and abroad. We certainly foresee the day when the pressure on graduate trainees in the international service industries to take specially designed MBAs or perhaps Diplomas in Business Administration of the type advocated by Constable and McCormick will be as great as in manufacturing and as common for advancement as passing professional institute examinations. Indeed, we do not entirely share the view of the Handy Report (Chapter 11, p. 312) that the uniquely large British output of accountants is a negative factor. The enormous growth of national and international consultancy work of all kinds in the accountancy sector suggests the value and general industrial and commercial applicability of that training.

Of course this is no reason for not raising the training requirements of management substantially and widely. Nevertheless, we conclude that for the time being when the UK international service industries are relatively competitive, greater fears are being expressed about the development of people suitable for the increasing demands of the lower and middle echelons, the technical and professional support staff on which management must rely frequently for its information, in its interface with the public, and for all back-up activities. The only industry that has been putting a major emphasis on this group, and that is thanks to its wide-ranging job structure, is tourism, as we saw. And that faces the permanent problem of an abnormally high rate of personnel turnover.

The international competition I – knowledge-based services

In the late 1980s, despite a buoyancy in manufacturing hardly experienced since the last war, the deficit in Britain's visible trade persists and worsens. Month after month, we read that 'invisibles' have 'come to the rescue' of the balance of payments. In 1987, the total visible deficit reached some £9.8 bn, but earnings from invisibles excluding government transfers almost reached £13 bn. At the same time, reductions in unemployment also derive primarily from the services sector, and we have argued that tourism and the financial sector are the mainstay of that growth. We have rejected the argument that manufacturing and services can easily be separated from, or set against, one another as 'alternatives' for future prosperity. Nevertheless, Britain together with

France and the United States are among the few states that enjoy a net surplus in services trading. But, as we saw in Chapter 1, Britain's share in world services is slipping as the world market grows and especially as Japan and other Far Eastern centres such as Singapore and Hong Kong expand their service activities. The strength of Britain's position lies in the very low import ratio, leading to a high net income, as the British Invisible Exports Council has vigorously argued. But this net surplus does not apply to all sectors. Tourism is of great national significance as a countrywide source of employment, yet as a net earner of foreign currency it tends to fluctuate between small surpluses and deficits thanks to its vulnerability to political and economic factors (such as terrorism and changes in the dollar exchange rate). Transport and most sadly shipping, which was still in substantial surplus in the mid 1970s, has shown even greater vulnerability to changes in the British trading policy pattern and to world market conditions. It is financial services and on a smaller scale consultancies and trade in knowledge that are the principal sources of net income. We must now ask whether this pre-eminence can be maintained?

Britain's trade in knowledge-based services shares one feature with all the advanced industrial countries and another with the United States and the Commonwealth. The first, common characteristic is the dependence on innovative research and an effective system of education, especially at the higher and post-experience levels. Whether we are speaking of engineering consultancy, medical services and advice, patents and royalties or educational services at home or abroad, Britain can only offer the rest of the world services that they will wish to buy if it remains in the forefront of technology and science and maintains the highest standards in higher education. Precisely the same conditions apply to all the advanced industrial countries with whom Britain competes. But the more sophisticated and specialised knowledge becomes across the entire scientific and technical spectrum the less feasible is it for any single country to be in the vanguard of all areas. This simple fact is compounded by a government policy which is committed to holding down real public expenditure in higher education and civil research and which looks to industry as the source for future growth in funds. The introduction of full fees for overseas higher education students in 1980 diverted students from traditional sources away from Britain to other attractive alternatives, the United States, Canada and Australia. All three are now of key importance in the training of undergraduates and postgraduates from Hong Kong, Singapore and Malaysia. It is a matter of grave concern to which the Overseas Students Trust has consistently drawn attention.

In research the University Grants Committee is systematically trying to maximise the output from the limited resources at its disposal by rationalising the numbers of departments engaged in particular sciences

and technologies to create larger centres with identified research specialisms and is introducing the concept of national and regional research
and equipment centres. These are wise responses to an increasingly
difficult situation. But if we are realistic we have to accept that because of
the inevitable proportionate increase in research costs and the impos-
sibility of retaining leadership in all fields when confronted by the
immense research power of countries like the United States and Japan,
the scope for continued real growth in trade in knowledge-based
activities may be restricted.

If there is to be growth it will have to happen not in competition with
our European partners but in conjunction with them. The European
Community as a whole has a potential research strength more than
equal to the world industrial leaders Japan and the United States. Here
lies the great future importance of the Community's research initiatives
such as ESPRIT in the information technology field and its encouragement of student mobility between European institutions of higher
education in the ERASMUS programme and between such institutions
and industrial companies in the COMETT programme. It is perhaps
through endeavours of this kind that the outlines of a new trading
future may be discerned – one in which we do not look at the
performance of individual European countries but at that of the Community.

But the one characteristic and great advantage in trade in knowledge-
based services that Britain possesses which is not shared by her
European partners is the English language. While English may be of
deceptive value when British industry seeks to sell manufactures into
foreign markets of another language and culture, it is undeniably
helpful when selling intellectual goods – technical education, books,
films, and television programmes. English provides such products with
worldwide mobility. Moreover, as a universally acceptable second
language, English is immensely useful in overseas project work on
which a multiplicity of nationalities may be engaged. And, in a number
of fields, where the rapid and unambiguous transfer of information is
vital, English has become the language of the activity. This is as true of
securities and currency trading as it is of air navigation. The global use of
English as a lingua franca also preserves a worldwide interest in British
culture as a major source of that language, and here the role of the
British Council cannot be underestimated. It is extraordinary that
successive governments have sought to cut back on British Council
expenditure, when the possession of the English language and culture is
one of the few remaining natural or comparative advantages left to
Britain and is a source of both political goodwill, and, through related
service industries such as publishing and education, a source of great
economic benefit too.

The British do not hold a monopoly over English however. Increasing numbers of students prefer to obtain an English-based education in North America or Australia. As an exporter of film and television the United States is considerably ahead of Britain. Moreover, patents, fees and royalties in the technological and entertainment fields are today the major source of invisible income to the United States. Nevertheless, the United Kingdom is a major force in all these sectors and with the exception of income from overseas students, Britain is second in world ranking only to the United States.

The international competition II – the financial sector

Competition, both in the educational and scientific publications area and in film and television is, then, keen and any damage to the infrastructure that produces them will take a long-term toll. But Britain's most substantial source of invisible exports is the financial sector – based on the City and the country's other related financial centres.

In some ways, the success of the City confounds all ordinary expectations. To the observer in the late 1950s or early 1960s it would have seemed unlikely that the City could become what is arguably not only the financial centre of Europe but that of the world. The British economy was not performing with the same vitality as that of West Germany, the United States, or France. Sterling could no longer be considered the world's trading currency. The dollar reigned supreme. The scope for international banking and overseas investment was restricted by exchange controls. The Stock Exchange was hemmed in by its single capacity structure and strict membership rules. But, as we have argued, the City was able to rise to pre-eminence because these restrictions applied only to domestic and domestically based activities. By almost an accident of history, financial transactions involving other currencies and carried out on behalf of other nationals were virtually uncontrolled. The City made its mark in the Eurocurrency and Eurobond markets where it acted as a giant off-shore centre, not only for similarly restricted European players but particularly for American banks constrained at home by the compartmentalisation deriving from the Glass–Steagall Act. The abolition of exchange controls in 1979 and 'Big Bang' in 1986 opened up the domestic market to that off-shore centre and allowed overseas concerns to participate directly in domestic securities and gilts trading. With four hundred foreign banks represented in London, a gross foreign currency turnover twice as large as that of New York, and the incorporation of The London Stock Exchange with ISRO (the organisation of the London Eurobond traders), the City has achieved a critical mass of activity and expertise that is not equalled anywhere else in the world.

However, much of that pre-eminence has been achieved not by British banks and securities houses but by foreign entrants. Mercury International (based on the merchant bank S G Warburg) is the only British company to feature regularly in the top ten Eurobond traders, where the leading players include Crédit Suisse–First Boston, Deutsche Bank and Morgan Guaranty, and latterly the great Japanese houses, Nomura, Daiwa, Nikko and Yamaichi. Indeed, a veritable symbol of the City's status was Deutsche Bank's decision in 1984 to move its DM Eurobond dealing team from Frankfurt to London, recognising that London had become the centre for secondary trading in such bonds if not for original issues. If we look at trading in newer instruments, we find different top players – in European commercial paper in 1986, for example, the leaders were Citicorp Investment Bank, Merrill Lynch Capital Markets, followed by Crédit Suisse–First Boston, The Swiss Bank Corporation Investments and Morgan Guaranty with Warburgs in seventh position and County Natwest Capital Markets in tenth. In note issuance facilities Citicorp again dominated (in 1985), this time followed by Chase Investment Bank and Morgan Guaranty and the Bank of Tokyo with Barclays Bank Group in seventh position.

In the pre-'Big Bang' scramble, overseas banks and investment houses moved into The Stock Exchange in a big way. There are now, as we saw in Chapter 3, twelve European bank members in The Exchange and a number of US banks, including Citicorp and Chase Manhattan. Nevertheless, views that there could not be room for as many market-makers either in equities or gilts have proved correct – and that even in the unprecedentedly long, sustained bull equities market that lasted until the autumn of 1987. Of the American houses, Shearson Lehman and Chemical Bank had both laid off staff before the October Crash. Of the UK companies, Greenwell Montagu had already pulled out of equities in March 1987, Lloyds out of gilts in June, to be joined by Morgan Grenfell and Kleinwort Benson who have both reduced their gilts trading staff [19]. There was, however, no drastic shakeout after the Crash: companies have generally adapted a wait-and-see attitude. Conglomerates have tightened their management strategies and pushed forward in niches rather than on all fronts.

If the financial houses of any single nation were dominant in London's international securities markets until the late 1980s, it was those from the United States. But that is changing. By the mid-1980s Japan had already become the world's largest creditor nation. Consistent and vast surpluses on visible trade gave Japan an investment power second to none. A tradition of private saving boosted by the buoyancy of industry and the strength of the Yen have allowed Japanese banks to become the world's largest measured by assets. By 1987 the world's top five banks were Japanese, forcing Citicorp into sixth place.

The search by Japanese savers for higher returns has made them turn increasingly to securities. At the same time the rigid compartmentalisation of the Japanese financial sector into banks (which are sub-divided into further rigid categories), securities houses and investment managers has driven Japanese financial institutions to seek freedom overseas. The major purchasers of US Treasury Bonds, and thus the financiers of the US budgetary deficits of recent years are the Japanese. Their interest in Eurobonds and European securities is likewise growing as Japanese life insurance companies are allowed to invest up to 25 per cent of their funds abroad. In 1961 only six Japanese banks had an overseas presence. By 1986 there were 450 Japanese bank subsidiaries, branches and agencies overseas. In 1985 Japanese international lending worldwide surpassed that of US banks, and together (at 26 per cent and 23.4 per cent respectively) accounted for half the world's lending [22]. In London in 1985 Japanese institutions had a 31 per cent share of international lending compared to 23 per cent ten years before, and while the British share was 19 per cent (21 per cent in 1975), the American banks' had fallen sharply from 38 per cent to 16 per cent. Indeed London has become the focus-point for Japanese overseas financial activities. Some 39 per cent of all their international assets were held in the UK in 1985. Even in overseas sterling loans they hold 20 per cent of the market, after an average annual increase of over 60 per cent since 1980! Japanese Euroyen issues are the fastest growing sector of the Euromarket, London is the world centre for these issues and the Euroyen is one of the four most popular Eurobond issues [23]. And, not surprisingly, while the world's largest banks in asset terms are Japanese, the world's largest securities house is also Japanese – the Nomura Securities Co.

Backed by the formidable research capacity of the Nomura Research Institute, Nomura has 28 offices in 26 financial centres. While London had been its European centre since 1964, the company has established a network of offices co-ordinated from London in eight European centres including Amsterdam, Brussels, Frankfurt and Paris. With only two employees in London in 1964, there is now a staff of some 350 of which only 54 are Japanese. In November 1986 a milestone was reached; Nomura was granted a licence by the British Government to commence banking activities under the name Nomura International Finance, linking in with its own banks in Amsterdam, Frankfurt, Zurich, Geneva and Lugano. Managing Director of the new company is an American, Dr Andreas Prindl, who has long experience of banking for Morgan Guaranty in both London and Tokyo. Nomura has now been joined as 'a licensed deposit-taker' by Daiwa, while Nikko and Yamaichi are expected to follow on the basis of reciprocity in Tokyo.

The strategy of the Japanese finance houses has not been to rush into The Stock Exchange at vast expense but to bide their time from a position of enormous asset and investment strength. There is a clear parallel between their techniques in exporting and in finance. In the former they have been prepared to accept long years of modest profits or even losses in order to consolidate an invulnerable market position. In that time they learned to refine their products and finally surpass those they found in the European and American marketplace. Andreas Prindl envisages a similar strategy for Nomura as a bank, seeking not to make the company a big bank overnight but to ensure that Nomura (which at home is not allowed to undertake banking activities) will not be short of skills 'when the battle for supremacy in the global market place really gets under way.' [24]

A deregulating world

The final deregulating of the domestic stock market in London in 1986 gave London an extra dimension to its international standing and confirmed the City as the European time-zone centre for trading.

But deregulation is not the prerogative of London. In an attempt to recapture business similar processes have been occurring, albeit less dramatically in Frankfurt, Paris, Amsterdam, Zurich and Tokyo. How do these centres compare with London?

In the Federal Republic, financial institutions have four great advantages: one of the world's strongest industrial bases with substantial export – and therefore investment – surpluses, a currency that is stronger than the dollar, a century of experience in universal banking covering securities dealing as well as bank lending, and one of the world's most thorough and structured apprenticeship schemes. And, while the Bundesbank has not exercised control in capital movements since the 1950s, in the 1980s it gradually permitted a full range of new financial instruments including zero coupons and floating rate notes. Foreign banks were, furthermore, permitted to lead-manage DM denominated Eurobonds. But the Federal German Government has stubbornly refused to scrap a stamp duty on stock market transactions, while more significantly the market is divided between eight regional centres with a link-up of compatible electronic trading systems only recently achieved. Furthermore, the stock market capitalisation of West German industry, though increasing as the banks try to persuade firms to issue equity rather than continuing with traditional bank borrowing, was by 1985 only 24 per cent of GDP compared to 65 per cent in the UK and 60 per cent in Japan. It is not, therefore, a coincidence that Deutsche Bank now runs its secondary trading activity in DM Eurobonds in London and, as the leading Eurobond dealer, has its significant international presence in London rather than Frankfurt.

The real rivalry is between Frankfurt, Paris and Zurich as the Continental European financial centre. In France the range of financial instruments has gradually been extended, commencing with long-term certificates of deposit in 1985, followed by commercial paper (called *billets de trésorerie* to avoid confusion with trade bills known as *papier commercial*) and a range of hedging instruments including financial futures. Indeed the financial futures long bond in 1986 outstripped in numbers of contracts London's gilts contracts by the autumn of that year. At the same time the monopoly of membership of the Bourse by the *agents de change* will be removed by 1992. In the meantime outside investors are able to buy up to 30 per cent of the *agents'* capital in 1988, up to 49 per cent in 1989, and 100 per cent in 1990. Turnover on the Bourse has risen tenfold over the last five years and there is a major institutional market in shares outside the Bourse traded through the Reuters' screen system. But, as in the case of the Federal Republic, there are still drawbacks for international players. The level of domestic market capitalisation is only 13 per cent, fixed commissions, though low, have not been eliminated, and the *agents de change* have not been quick to build up their capital base, to update their dealing systems, or to show interest in being bought up. It is the banks rather that possess the vision and the drive – with three banks in the world's top ten, and a highly developed electronic banking system using home computer terminals and 'smart' cards (cards fitted with electronic chips). With their progressive entry into the Bourse, Paris may well come to rival Frankfurt. Privatisation of the Banque Nationale de Paris, Crédit Lyonnais and Société Générale together with Paribas and Suez should add further to the momentum that is being built up [25].

Amsterdam [26], too, established a range of financial instruments and relaxed issuing and borrowing procedures in a deregulative move on 1st January 1986. Commissions have been successively reduced since 1984 and, assisted by the new membership of the Exchange by the three top Japanese securities houses, Nomura, Daiwa and Yamaichi, the Exchange has begun listings of Japanese stock. The European Options Exchange in Amsterdam has, (*see* Chapter 3), twice the turnover of London. Furthermore, it has link-ups in gold and silver options with Montreal, Vancouver and Sydney and in sterling/dollar options with Montreal. But in the Netherlands, too, there are difficulties. The attempt to create a true European trade in options has failed. The last foreign stock option, Belgium's Petrofina, left in 1986. The domestic securities trade is hampered by the persistence of a traditional preference by companies for bank loans rather than equity issues and the uptake of the array of new instruments has been slow. Moreover, it is estimated that trade in some 20 per cent of Dutch international stocks takes place not in Amsterdam but in London.

Like Amsterdam and Paris, Zurich, too, has been prompted by the drastic changes in London to modernise its portfolio of instruments and to update its dealing systems. In 1985 trading turnover had already risen by some 46.5 per cent. This figure should be enhanced by the introduction of continuous trading in blue-chip Swiss shares, a new index, an improved floor reporting system, a computer assisted trading system (CATS) for bonds and OTC stocks that is linked up with

Geneva and Basel and, from January 1988, the beginning of trade in options. But despite these changes it will be difficult for the Swiss exchanges to supplant any of the other major European financial centres.

London, together with Britain's other financial centres now linked through SEAQ, would appear to occupy a position of unassailable dominance. Building on twenty years of experience as the world's major centre for Eurobonds, the Eurocurrency markets and foreign exchange trading, London is the least government-regulated financial trading place in the world. True, the complex internal regulatory system seems daunting – but nonetheless necessary if the cancer of insider dealing is to be controlled and essential confidence is to be maintained, without which business could vanish. No other centre also possesses the same world role in insurance, insurance broking and, through that unique institution, Lloyd's of London, underwriting. Nor is it rivalled, despite their troubled past, in its possession of the world's major commodity markets.

To this depth of interrelated activity must be added three further advantages. First, there is the possession of English, which, as we argued above, makes London and other British centres a place that presents the fewest linguistic problems to non-English speaking players and is of course the language shared with the United States. Second, English law has proved itself an acceptable basis for international transactions, largely because of its attention to explicit detail rather than general conceptual statement. Third, the British-American system of accountancy has established itself as the universal approach for international companies and for newly industrialised countries, especially in the buoyant Far East.

With the dust of 'Big Bang' having settled, it is possible to obtain a clearer picture of relative success. The two UK clearing banks that are emerging as world forces are Natwest and Barclays. Natwest is now the second most profitable bank in the world after Citicorp. With County Natwest as its investment wing (and lead manager in the British Airports Authority flotation), Natwest is proving a highly successful conglomerate of world class. Its great British rival is Barclays, which together with Barclays de Zoete Wedd shares Natwest's global ambitions and has historically the largest overseas network of any British bank. Moreover, it suffered less in its securities activities from the October crash than County Natwest. Of the British merchant banks in their transition from traditional merchant banking to investment banking S G Warburg has had the greatest international impact followed by Schroders and Kleinwort Benson. But London's significance is boosted above all by the activities of foreign financial houses. Over 54 000, we noted, are already employed by foreign banks alone. While the giant Japanese banks may be regarded as competition to British domestic financial houses, their expansion into London as their European centre, helps consolidate London's dominant position in Europe.

Moreover, of the world's major global trading centres, compared with Tokyo and Hong Kong in the Far East and New York in North America, London is the most international. Admittedly, Tokyo, under pressure from the United States and Europe, has relaxed many of its tightest restrictions: foreign firms can issue and lead-manage Euroyen bonds, they can make yen loans to other than Japanese residents, licences are gradually being issued on a reciprocal basis to foreign investment banks in Japan, foreign banks may sell and deal in Japanese government bonds and foreign firms are gradually being admitted to membership of The Tokyo Stock Exchange [27]. But the principal overseas interest in Tokyo remains to obtain access to the giant domestic Japanese market rather than to deal there in either international bonds or equities.

Nor should we underestimate the barriers that result from considerable linguistic and cultural differences in both directions. That is one reason why the big Japanese banks and security houses are so active in Europe and New York. It is not simply governed by the need to invest vast and increasing domestic sums or simply to participate in the world's other financial trading centres. It is to gain the expertise that will be necessary eventually for Tokyo to move forward, not only as a vital leg in global trading (though in competition with Hong Kong) but as a Far Eastern centre for true international securities trading. In the meantime, freed from the structural restrictions at home, Japanese banks and security houses are more than happy to embark on expansion in London and a network of other European centres. This leaves London, for the while, as not only Europe's greatest financial centre, but arguably the world's greatest.

Liberalisation and the stability of the world's financial system

'Financial distress can be more readily contained if, like the bulkheads of a ship, the risks incurred within one sector of the financial services industry can be prevented from overflowing into other sectors. But with the trend towards global integration of the financial services industry, shock waves can be transmitted not only from bank to bank and from country to country but from the securities markets to banks and vice versa. Therefore, there is increasing potential for a self feeding and large scale crisis engulfing both banks and the securities markets internationally. Of course, the danger is particularly relevant in the UK in the aftermath of the Big Bang.' Richard Dale 1986 [28].

One of the persistent themes of this book has been liberalisation: discussions towards the liberalisation of trade in services worldwide in the Uruguay Round of GATT, the sequence of concrete steps taken in the EC to complete the internal market by 1992, the progressive liberalisation of the world's money markets and stock exchanges, (exemplified by 'Big Bang') and specific national deregulation measures such as the breaking of British Telecom's monopoly in the UK. The fundamental arguments behind these moves are that increased competition leads to better service, to a cheaper service, to more choice and to economic growth through creating larger international markets. These are particularly powerful arguments within the European Community which sees itself competing more effectively with the USA and Japan on the basis of a single, unified domestic market of 320 millions. Specifically in the financial sector the UK and the City have embraced radical deregulation to provide a competitive lead over more restricted markets.

We must now consider whether liberalisation in financial trading is an unblemished good. We have seen from the dubious consequences of the deregulation of air transport in the USA that leaving business open to market forces can result in volatility, inconsistency of prices, and, ironically, through the formation of a small number of all-powerful carriers, to a reduction in competition and even service.

We have discussed in what ways, in the narrower perspective of the UK, the international service industries can supplement manufacturing as a source of employment and provide vital support for the balance of payments. It has emerged that, in net income from overseas, the financial sector is of key importance. Yet there were many authorities long before the Crash of 1987 who feared that today's instantaneous global trading in capital and currency and the restructuring of financial institutions of the kind we witnessed before 'Big Bang' in London, could be endangering the very stability of the world's financial system [29].

Might this be the Achilles' heel of the City's supremacy – not the share of business captured by foreign banks and security houses, not competition from New York or Tokyo, Frankfurt or Zurich, but an inherent volatility of the system itself? Money, we saw, is like water, life-giving but highly mobile, liable to move suddenly in vast quantities, able to seep around the tightest barriers. Money also has to be believed in; there has to be confidence both in a currency and in a borrower – hence the original meaning of the term 'credit'. 'Big Bang' removed in the UK the time-honoured bulkheads between securities traders and brokers and between them and the banks, designed to stop cross-infection spreading from the securities area to banking. Indeed the City's financial conglomerates combine within their groups all major financial services and dealing activities.

These are some of the worries. The formation of conglomerates, active in a range of activities, makes it possible for failure in one part to affect another. The former Chairman of the Federal Reserve Bank, Paul Volcker stated before Congress in 1986: 'Experience clearly indicates that ... when a subsidiary or even a related enterprise of a bank holding company experiences financial problems strength will be drawn from other parts of the organisation (including bank subsidiaries) to protect the reputation of the entire organisation.' This is all the more worrying when we consider that the conglomerates, thanks to the opening up of world securities trading, may straddle chains of countries. For the internationalisation of capital which we have described not only spreads benefits but, through global trading of international equities and bonds on all the major stock exchanges, also opens the way to sudden worldwide losses of confidence or contagion.

The range and sophistication of the new financial instruments also have benefits to customers that can be matched by dangers. Born essentially of competition there are fears, expressed for example by the Cross Commission [30], that the products are being underpriced and are not therefore sound business. But worse is the fear that their complexity is leading to a progressive loss of transparency in the capital markets (we have to remember that some of these bonds have a life of thirty years) and will lead both to an incremental difficulty in management of the market and to Central Banks being unable to keep track of or control monetary policy.

At the same time, more and more weight is being thrown on to manipulating interest rates and through them exchange rates as a central instrument for controlling disequilibrium in the domestic balance of payments [31]. But the dependence on the manipulation of exchange rates can have effects on manufacturing which, as we experienced in the UK 1980–82, can be both devastating and outside industry's influence. Moreover, sterling, though not belonging to the European Monetary System (EMS), is more rapidly exposed to volatility than the currencies of EC states that do belong.

But perhaps the greatest current concern is the status of the US dollar exchange rate. The massive US trade and budgetary deficits continued throughout 1987 and into 1988 (to the benefit of goods and capital exporting countries such as Japan, the Federal Republic and Britain), while the dollar drifted and then fell with little immediate effect on those deficits. The Group of Seven calculated in September 1987 that if trends continued, US indebtedness would have reached $1600 bn by 1995, a burden that the IMF believed the markets would not accept. The Group therefore pledged itself to aim for exchange rate stabilisation. The resolution came too late, however.

The dramatic demonstration that these were not empty fears came initially just one month later in October 1987. The Stock Market crash appeared to have been sparked off by announcements that the huge US trade deficit in September 1987 had hardly recovered from its all-time record deficit the month before. This finally shook the confidence of one of the longest bull markets on record. In a single day, October 19th, now known as Black Monday, the London FTSE 100 index fell some 250 points on top of a similar fall that had commenced the week before. The international repercussions throughout the global market were immediate. The Dow Jones Index in New York, which had already been sagging, fell some 500 points. The Hong Kong Exchange had to be closed. A huge rescue operation had to be mounted to save the Hong Kong Futures Exchange from irretrievable collapse. On Tuesday October 20th the Nikke Dow Index in Tokyo fell from nearly 26 000 to 22 000, an unprecedented fall. When Hong Kong reopened on October 26th it fell 1120 points or nearly one-third of the market's value. Thereafter all markets continued to be highly volatile, each nervously awaiting results from the others. In just weeks over 25 per cent was wiped off the value of London's equity markets.

The damage was not confined to the stock markets for their crash infected foreign currency trading. It was hardly surprising since the underlying cause was not only inflated stock values in a bull market that had persisted too long. It was the American economy that was the source of the problem and by the middle of the second week of the Crash in late October the dollar was falling rapidly. For all the fevered purchases of American currency by the Japanese Central Bank, it rapidly broke through the magic barrier of 1 dollar to 140 yen to plunge by the end of the year to a low of 122 yen.

After Black Monday attention focussed on the US budget deficit rather than on the trade deficit. When agreement was reached after four weary weeks to trim some $30 bn off the deficit in the fiscal year 1988 and $46 bn in 1989, the market seemed to think that this was too little too late. Wall Street started to fall again. But this renewed loss of confidence was itself fuelled by the unimpeded fall in the value of the dollar, which resulted from fears about the trade deficit. The fall in the dollar then spread fears that inflation might increase, while the personal loss of capital suffered by the vast US equity-owning public created the spectre of recession. Together these doubts induced a further slide in the New York Stock Exchange in early December 1987.

What has to concern us here is the mechanism underlying these events. For the first time since deregulation became the order of the day and global trading became a reality, the related negative possibility of instantaneous global infection also became reality. The advantages of worldwide diversification of portfolios turned into the disadvantage of worldwide selling as the markets appeared unjustifiably bloated and oversubscribed. Moreover, in the United States, particularly, the initial stampede to sell was started by automatically programmed computer dealing systems. It occurred with a minimum of human intervention.

Exacerbating this unstable situation in the world's stock and currency markets is the near insolvency of the Latin American debtor countries. Latin American debts, which effectively ended a decade-long regime of syndicated bank loans as the major mode of international funding, has still left the world's major banks in considerable difficulties (*see* Chapter 3). Despite active provisionary policies (writing-off parts of the debt), the big UK banks, for example, would still be severely shaken if interest-servicing and capital repayment arrangements with any of the major Latin American debtors such as Mexico or Brazil were finally to break down entirely. In fact, much of the Midland Bank's difficulty, which laid it open in 1987 to predator approaches even from quarters such as the giant British advertising group Saatchi & Saatchi (prior to the Hong Kong Bank's acquisition of 14 per cent ownership), resulted from its California subsidiary bank's exposure to Latin American debt – a clear example of international cross-infection. A US recession induced, for example, by tax measures designed to control the budgetary deficit would, however, choke off a critical proportion of Latin American exports and make it virtually impossible for those countries to repay either interest or capital.

What can be done to contain these risks now that liberalisation is with us? The extensive self-regulatory system established in the UK is seen by some as blunting the competitive edge of the City. At the same time it is largely directed against internal abuses such as insider-dealing and towards protecting the client. Certainly, it provides a framework for maintaining prudential control. But the issue is whether systems of national control are adequate to control what are international markets of a *de facto* or quasi off-shore nature. Positive signs of international monetary collaboration are the agreements reached by the Bank of England and the US Federal Banking Regulatory Authorities early in 1987 on minimum capital ratios and on the inclusion in the supervision of banks their (increasingly popular) off-balance operations [32]. Agreements have also been reached on similar prudential measures within the European Community. These are very important steps forward. There is also a major role here for the Basel Committee on Banking Regulations and Supervisory Practices, which has been working out a multilateral, institutional framework for supervisors facing an increasingly complex and impenetrable scene [33].

But in the final analysis there is a tight-rope to be walked between control and a free-for-all [34]. The City owes its present dominant world position to the lack of control exercised over the Euromarkets in the 1960s and 1970s and then to the deregulation of the domestic market in the middle 1980s. Off-shore banking and securities trading outside the strict compartments of US and Japanese systems have been its strength and thus one of the strengths of the UK's trading economy. Too much control could frighten business away. Foreign financial houses already account for the bulk of international lending and Eurobond trading in London, and it would be no more difficult for them to move to Frankfurt than it was for Deutsche Bank to move its team to London in 1983. The Government reimposition of a compartmentalised system or some new form of exchange control therefore seems remote at the moment. Moreover, the sheer mass of expertise and the diversity of the services offered in London and the UK, which we have surveyed, suggest a dynamic, self-generation of strength that would be hard to imagine being reversed. This is a source of prosperity that is unrivalled in any other sector of the British economy.

What must be ensured through all possible international channels is that the risk of the world's whole financial system becoming infected by contamination from just a single part is contained. The events of October 1987 show just how rapidly a global collapse can occur and that the global securities market is difficult to isolate from currency markets and stability in these markets depends equally on achieving a new balance in the world's monetary system. We return to this in our Conclusions.

As the UK economy comes increasingly to rely on the earnings, gross and net, of the financial sector, it may, then, find itself as exposed here as it had been in the days when British manufacturing was ailing. Such fears have already helped to enhance a new prestige for manufacturing industry in its recovery since the mid-1980s. Nothing illustrates more clearly the UK's need for a balanced economy based on the twin strengths of manufacturing and a large diversity of services.

Notes and references

1   By Autumn 1987 output had approached that of 1979 immediately prior to the 1980–81 slump, according to CSO statistics, and was growing at an estimated annual rate of 5.5%. Reports in the *Financial Times*, September 1987.

2   For a valuable comparison and typology of deindustrialisation *see* Pascal Petit, *Slow Growth and the Service Economy*, Francis Pinter, London, 1986, esp. Chap. 3. pp. 49–80.

3   Dorothy I. Riddle, 'The Role of the Service Sector in Economic Development. Similarities and Differences by Development Category', in Orio Giarini (ed.) *The Emerging Service Economy*, Pergamon, Oxford, 1987, pp. 88–90.

4   *See*, for example, the famous collection of essays edited by Blackaby, *Deindustrialisation*, Proceedings of a National Institute of Economic and Social Research Conference, 1978. In the recent debate, Dorothy Riddle, for example, (in the essay quoted in reference 3 above, pp. 100–101) states, 'The growth and dynamism of the service sector, is a vital key to economic growth. While economies can, if necessary, import agricultural and manufactured goods, all economies need a certain basic services infrastructure in place in order to function at all … It makes little sense to continue defining economic growth in terms of 'industrialisation' – i.e. manufacturing sector growth – when the manufacturing sector plays only a support role (in the sense of providing equipment and supplies for other economic activities)'. Pascal Petit on the other hand (*see* reference 2 above, pp. 118–119) argues that neither earnings from direct investment abroad nor from financial investment nor from trade in

services can be seen to offer 'scope for the creation of a new, autonomous demand capable of helping the old industrialised countries to guarantee the long-term financing of the imports necessary to their growth'.

5   *The Growth in the Imbalance of Trade in Manufactured Goods between the UK and Existing and Prospective Members of the EEC*, 2nd Report from the Trade and Industry Committee, House of Commons, HMSO, 1984.

6   *Report from the Select Committee on Overseas Trade*, House of Lords, HMSO, 3 vols., 1985.

7   For the discussion with the Treasury *see* vol II, pp. 125 ff., esp. pp. 135–147. 'We will supply the changing of the guard, we will supply the Beefeaters around the Tower of London. We will become a curiosity. I do not think that is what Britain is about; I think it is rubbish'. House of Lords Report vol. II, p. 474.

8   Sir John Harvey-Jones, 'Does Industry Matter?', The 1986 Dimbleby Lecture, *The Listener*, 10 April 1986.

9   *See* Petit, p. 50.

10   Stephen Cohen and John Zsyman, *Manufacturing Matters: The Myth of a Post-Industrial Economy*, Basic Books, 1987.

11   *UK Occupation and Employment Trends to 1990*. An employer-based study of the trends and their underlying causes. (For the Occupations Study Group) by The Institute of Manpower Studies, June 1986.

12   *The Decade of Change – Banking in Europe – The Next Ten Years*. Arthur Andersen & Co., Lafferty Publications, London, February 1982, p. 11.

13   *The Banker*, November 1987.

14   *Enterprise News, The Journal of the Scottish Financial Community*, July/August, 1987, September/October 1987.

15   Edward Owen, 'Channel Islands, Foreign Exchange deals on the rise', Ian Hamilton Fazey, 'Isle of Man. A respectable Satellite' in *World Banking, Financial Times*, May 23 1986.

16   Amin Rajan, *New Technology and Employment in Insurance, Banking and Building Societies; Recent Experience and Future Impact*, Special Report, Institute of Manpower Studies Series, Gower, Aldershot, 1984. Amin Rajan, *Services – The Second Industrial Revolution? Business and job outlook for UK growth industries*, An employment-based study by the Institute of Manpower Studies for the Occupations Study Group, Buttersworths, London, 1987.

17   *See* reference 12 above.

18   Andrew Shegog, 'The Year of Living Cautiously', *Euromoney Supplement – Financial Innovations*, January 1987, pp. 10–13.

19   Hugo Dixon, 'Twilight of the Silly Season', *Financial Times*, September 16 1987.

20   For this and other detailed information *see* Felicity Marsh's valuable report, *Japan's Next Export Success – The Financial Services Industry*, Crawford's and

Economist Publications, London, 1986. Also useful is Hamish McRae's, *Japan's Role in the Emerging Global Securities Market*, Occasional Papers 17, Group of Thirty, New York, 1985.

21 *The Banker*, August 1987.

22 *Bank of England Quarterly Bulletin*, September 1986.

23 *See* Marsh, ref. 21, pp. 91 ff.

24 Both in an interview with one of us (NR) and an interview with *Banking World*, November 1986, p. 29.

25 *See* the articles by George Graham 'The capital markets, underpinned by public deficit', *French Banking, Finance and Investment, Financial Times*, December 19 1986. 'France's Big Bang', A late run for the winning post' *Financial Times*, April 7 1987. 'Not quite a Big Bang for the Bourse', April 11 1987. *See also* Caroline J. Gall, *The Big Bang: A lesson for the Paris Bourse?'* Unpublished dissertation. Buckinghamshire College of Higher Education, 1987, pp. 49 ff. 53.

26 *See Financial Times* survey, *The Netherlands, Banking and Finance and Investment*, especially Laura Raun, 'Caution prevails over liberalisation', Jeffrey Brown, 'Capital Markets. Slow response to new financial instruments', Laura Raun, 'European Options Market. A bag of projects waiting in the wings', Adrian Dicks, 'Amsterdam Stock Exchange. Striving for a place among giants', *Financial Times*, July 16 1986.

27 *See* McRae, ref. 21 above, pp. 17 ff.

28 Richard Dale, 'How safe is the Banking System?'. *Hume Occasional Paper 4*, The David Hume Institute, Glencorse, 1986.

29 *See* Dale, p. 9. The view is shared e.g. by Lambreto Dini, 'Towards a European Integrated Financial Market', *Banca Nazionale del Lavoro Quarterly Review*, December 1986, p. 392.

30 Group of Ten, Central Bank Governors' Study Group, (Chairman Sam Y. Cross). *Recent Innovations in International Banking*, Bank for International Settlements, Basel, 1986.

31 *See* the interesting article by Michael Prouse, 'Financial Deregulation. The Perils of Innovation', *Financial Times*, December 10 1986.

32 'Convergence of capital adequacy in the UK and US', and 'Agreed proposal of the United States Federal Banking Supervisory Authorities and the Bank of England on primary capital and capital adequacy assessment', in *Bank of England Quarterly Bulletin*, February 1987, pp. 85–86 and 87–93.

33 *See* Rinaldo Pecchioli, 'Keeping the Banks Safe and Sound: Trends in Prudential Supervision', *The OECD Observer*, November 1986, pp. 33; 35.

34 Compare the succinct account given by the Chairman of Barclays Bank, John Quinton to the US House of Representatives Sub-Committee on Telecommunications and Finance, 5 August 1987, 'The Global Securities Market regulatory implications', Barclays (London), 1987.

Conclusions

The cerebral revolution

The advanced industrial economies have moved into a new phase of development. The UK decisively entered this phase as it emerged from the recession of 1981. The new age is characterised and led by an emphasis on knowledge-based and information-intensive industries both in the manufacturing and service sectors. Successful and competitive manufacturing is increasingly reliant on the newest technology, and not only for automating production processes. Products themselves have to be in the forefront of technical and design development to compete on European and worldwide markets. The UK, a country with restricted natural resources and a small domestic market relative to Japan or the United States, is vitally dependent on success in exports. Moreover, since 1983, revenue from exported manufactures has failed to match expenditure on imports by increasingly large margins. For all these reasons the international service industries are playing an ever more prominent role in the economy.

As competition sharpens and companies seek greater efficiency they turn increasingly to outside services for expert assistance in marketing, distribution, and management systems. Growth requires capital and the finance houses are evolving ever more sophisticated instruments for supplying it. Mergers, acquisitions and joint ventures are daily events as companies in both industry and commerce seek to expand domestically and overseas. All these developments are reliant on the rapid transmission of information through computer networks, optical fibre cables, or via satellites. The services themselves in their pre-eminent role whether finance, transport, or consultancies of all kinds rely ever more heavily on the latest computing hardware, telecommunications systems and above all the knowledge and information fed through them. It is this cerebral revolution which is the governing force in the new economic phase rather than a shift from industry to services in some post-industrial or deindustrialised age. The relationship between technology, manufacturing, and international services is far too intimate for us to speak sensibly of the UK simplistically as a services economy.

In the Introduction we identified four trends affecting the future of the international service industries; fundamental technological change, deregulation and liberalisation of the markets and of trade in services, intensifying international competition – and a decisive emphasis in industry and commerce on information and knowledge transfer. The cerebral revolution may be said to subsume all these trends. They are its constituent characteristics.

This book has traced some of the manifestations of the cerebral revolution in our knowledge and information-led society in many, if not all, of the sectors of the UK's international service industries. Its starting point was the vital part played by these services as exports, invisible exports. Increasingly they are needed not only as a vital support and stimulus for manufacturing industry but as products that can themselves be sold into overseas markets or purchased in the UK by overseas concerns and individuals, particularly as tourists.

Britain's historical strength in international services

This reliance, in the context of the balance of payments, is only new in the sense that previously manufacturing was in trade surplus also. But at that time (and until the mid-1970s) fuel was a major UK import. Historically the UK has been a major supplier and source of international services for over two centuries. As would be expected of the world's first industrialised nation, and long before that a major maritime trading country, the UK was traditionally pre-eminent in shipping. Alongside that, and almost naturally, there grew international expertise and dominance in shipping information, in insurance and reinsurance. By the end of the nineteenth century Britain was also the world's largest exporter of capital and the home of the world's international trading currency, sterling.

Today, when that dominant position in industrial production has long since gone, we have to ask whether the UK's historical lead as a supplier of international services is doomed to follow the same path as manufacturing. True, it is quite possible that 1981 saw an all-time low in the fortunes of manufacturing industry relative to competitors. Certainly, the firmness and speed of the industrial recovery into the late 1980s is encouraging. But the question still has to be asked, as indeed it was by the Bank of England in 1985.

Recapturing traditional markets

Historical trends can, however, be reversed and not necessarily by specific design. The City's return to a position where it can claim to be the world's financial centre and is certainly Europe's began, as we saw,

1960s onwards. The City was, then, given two major impetuses through deregulation which went further than in any other centre: initially, the abolition of exchange controls in 1979 which was deliberate, then the deregulation of The Stock Exchange, which began almost fortuitously and only gradually assumed the deliberate design of 'Big Bang'. Of course, the City had major factors in its favour; its geographical position in the middle time-zone between the Far East and the USA and within the European Community; its possession of a unique critical mass of expertise in all aspects of world commerce; and last, yet certainly not least, its possession of the world's international language, English.

Nor are banking and trade in capital the only UK service sectors that had been historically significant and have also regained or confidently held their world ranking. The common characteristic of these other successful services is that, like most strongly growing economic activities, they are knowledge-intensive. They include fine art auctioning, legal services, financial information services, real estate sales, accountancy, insurance, insurance broking and Lloyd's activities.

Successful new services

But perhaps the most positive sign for the UK is less the maintenance or revival of old established international service industries than the good performance of new services, the concomitants of the 'cerebral revolution'. Here we have identified activities that fall into three broad groups: corporate and specialist consultancies, television and entertainment products, and in the realm of high technology computing software, telecommunications and global information services.

Factors in success

We may identify, then, three central factors in the UK's success. First, natural and historical advantage: geographical and time-zone location, a long maritime trading and industrial tradition, and possession of the English language together with other cultural advantages such as an inherently flexible legal system and an internationally accepted accountancy system. Second, changes in the system. These include changes in the rules such as the deregulation of The Stock Exchange, the breakdown of barriers between the compartments of the financial sector and the consequent injection of capital into professional partnerships, and change induced by technology such as the appearance of 24-hour global securities trading and highly sophisticated financial information services. Third, the emergence of the quality of people as the determinant factor in activities so heavily dependent on knowledge and information.

Vulnerabilities

We have also observed, however, the vulnerability of many of the UK's international service industries to external forces outside their control. We have already noted the exposure of shipping and international haulage to changing trends in trading patterns as the UK's trade turns away from deep-sea destinations (and oil imports from the Middle East or Nigeria decline) towards the European Community, while British exports fail to match imports from Europe. We also saw that British construction and engineering has suffered from the decline in world oil prices and the OPEC countries' consequent cut-back on infrastructure investment.

Insurance, the UK's largest source of net overseas earnings, has always found itself subject to business cycles, though unlike other trade cycles these seem to depend on the degree of competition and therefore premium-cutting rather than the economic state of the overseas markets themselves.

The UK tourist industry, to take a very different example, is dependent for its success on the disposable income of overseas visitors or potential overseas visitors. This is rapidly affected by adverse changes in exchange rates such as the depreciation of the US dollar as well as the circumstances of the visitors' domestic economies.

Indeed, if there were one single major factor to which international service industries are exposed, it is exchange rate fluctuations, and especially in the currencies of the key trading partners. For overseas investments, an element in the invisibles balance that we have not attempted to consider except in the context of capital market developments, changes in the relative value of dollar, yen or DM receipts can outweigh compensating changes in interest rates. And, of course, depreciation in the US dollar in particular as the key international currency can drastically affect the value of all consultancy fees and royalties expressed in dollars.

But such fluctuations are themselves reflections of disparities (perceived or real) in the economic performance of the world's leading economies. It was such a disparity, manifested in the United States' dual trading and budgetary deficits together with the dangerously high surpluses of West Germany and particularly Japan that triggered off the October 1987 stock market crash. The exposure of the booming international securities trade in London to such a violent market reaction need hardly be stressed. Nor can it be denied, as we argued in the last chapter, that the existence of global 24-hour trading in securities with its reliance, especially in the United States, on computer-led trading decision-making, helped to make that crash hyper-rapid and for a time seemingly uncontrollable.

Keys to the future I – stabilising a liberalised global monetary system

The key to the future, therefore, lies in two directions, one more promising than the other. The first, less promising element, is the ability to manage the new global, deregulated markets and to stabilise the world's monetary system. It is not yet clear, in the light of the events of late 1987, that stability, internationalisation and deregulation are compatible.

Much of the thrust of this investigation has been prompted by concern about Britain's external trading performance. However, the performance in any country's current account is today only one, albeit vital, factor affecting international monetary balances. Capital movements have to be considered at least as important. The vast increases in international liquidity that resulted from the oil price rises of 1973 and 1979 and the recycling of the consequent income to the oil-producing states, coupled with the existence of an already major off-shore eurocurrency market have diminished the relative impact of trade fluctuations on national balances and exchange rates. In the early 1980s Western banks found ready customers for the capital deriving from oil surpluses in the Third World, particularly Latin America. Their subsequent inability to repay interest and capital has substantially added to uncertainty in the world's monetary system as potential defaulting threatened the very existence of exposed banks. This new level of global instability has been reinforced, it must now be said, following the 1987 crash, by the sustained liberalisation of the world's securities markets which we have plotted in Chapters 3 and 12. True, the classical pattern of trade surpluses (such as those of the UK in the early 1980s and of Japan in the mid to late 1980s) offsetting trade deficits through capital investment (especially in the United States) has continued.

But short-term capital speculation in both currency and securities helped first to fuel the bull market of 1986–87 and then to prick the bubble.

What steps can be undertaken to reduce this inherent volatility? We noted some positive measures in the last chapter: UK-US and EC agreements on prudential banking measures concerning asset : debt ratios and off-balance trading. The Basel Committee's proposal for tighter international supervisory requirements in banking will create a system that can be policed more effectively. The elaborate self-regulation of the UK financial sector is another substantial advance in this context.

All these measures are primarily designed to restrict malpractice and to protect the investor. But they cannot have a direct influence on international monetary relations themselves. To enter a full discussion, at this point, of how the international monetary system may be seen to operate and might be managed is, of course, beyond the scope of our investigation, but such is the importance of stability to the UK's financial sector and therefore its invisible earnings (quite apart from the all-enhancing effect on the welfare of the economy and visible trade), that we should highlight the areas in which international co-operation is gravely needed.

In a recent study Professor W M Scammell has usefully illuminated what he sees as three key issues that should ideally be resolved if stability of the international system is to be achieved. They are:

1 the need for an international money stock for clearing international imbalances;
2 an effective method of adjustment between currencies;
3 (closely related to adjustment) a stabilising exchange rate system.

He concludes that the first is more easily satisfied when there is a flexible exchange rate which eases the demand for international liquidity. A key currency is still required, however, and the US dollar can no longer achieve this with any consistency.

On the second issue he is pessimistic in that the size of speculative capital flows now defies the ability of any single country to control its exchange rate.

On the third issue he proposes a hybrid of fixed and free-floating rates using bands or target zones.

It must be evident from our own analysis and from Scammell's views that we can no longer speak of a strictly controllable international monetary system. If there is any rationality behind the capital flows that threaten to upset an orderly system it must lie in the market's assessment of individual economies. If there is to be any protection for national currencies from sudden change, it must be through linkage with other currencies. And finally if there is to be any co-ordination between national economic policies and between currency exchange rates formal collaborative mechanisms must exist.

The stabilising role of the US dollar is fading as the disequilibrium between its budgetary and trade performance and that of Japan and European countries grows. Yet Japan's ability and experience to assume the role of key currency and world leader are not yet apparent.

In this vacuum, the significance of the European Community as a powerful group of economies in the process of harmonisation by 1992 is very apparent. Its internal attempt to stabilise exchange rates through the European Monetary System seems exemplary, and the emergence of a European currency, the ECU, which is less subject to volatility than any individual national currency is a development of great promise.

It therefore seems essential for the health of the UK's invisible sector, both from the narrower perspective of this book's preoccupation and for the UK's and Europe's economies more generally, that the mantle of leadership in international monetary affairs be assumed by the European Community. For that to happen it seems necessary for the pound to join the EMS and for the use of the ECU to be promoted as Europe's domestic and international trading currency. Fears for damage to sovereignty may make the prospect of a single European currency more remote. Co-ordination between the Community, the United States and Japan has to continue to be sought at both macroeconomic and monetary levels through organisations such as the Group of Ten and through a regular programme of summit meetings.

Keys to the future II – education and training

The other key is an unerring emphasis on education and training – for children still of school age, for young adults in further and higher education and in continuing, post-experience education.

An adequate supply of good calibre people is the most fundamental domestic requirement for the invisibles sector to prosper. Without that no company strategy will be effective. The UK's record since the 1950s was good in university science research and in the production of young, flexible, arts graduates well suited for the international service industries. Business studies and their ethos have also had a positive effect on a generation of graduates emanating especially from the polytechnics. But the record is poor when it comes to the low esteem on the part of the general public (and of many of the pupils themselves) in which education is held. This has had a deleterious effect on the achievement of the middle and lower range of pupils. The participation rate in higher education has been disappointing compared with the UK's competitors in the European Community, North America and Japan. Indeed, if we look at 16- to 20-year-olds, we find only one-fifth in education in Britain, whereas four-fifths are still being educated in Japan.

Worse still, it has to be said that the achievement of the secondary schools and the examinations system has been profoundly disappointing in producing so few leavers qualified to levels of general education comparable with those reached by a majority in West Germany or Japan. This has left some service industries, alongside manufacturing industry, with a lack of well-qualified, lower and middle level management and technicians. What, in our judgement, saved the City services has been the old established system of professional training requirements through the institutes, significantly enhanced in the last fifteen years by graduate entry to the professions. Though we have had reason to criticise the old-fashioned approach of some of these institutes, and their failure to adapt to the new graduate clientele, nonetheless they have instilled a sense of professional rigour that has stood banking, insurance, accountancy and the law in good stead. The need now is for a review of these syllabuses and their approaches in response to rapid change in the industries and to their growing international commitment. In tourism, perhaps the service industry with historically the closest similarity to manufacturing in respect of training requirements, there has been a major and concerted effort to raise the level and coverage of training across the country, led by a number of pioneers in higher education. In some of the City professions and especially banking we see a nascent trend towards insistence on management and marketing skills to supplement technical understanding. It is in this professional context that we welcome the proposals by the Handy and Constable Reports for a more universal system of and requirement for management qualifications.

The importance of international experience in education

It is also the rapidly growing importance of the international dimension (global and trans-European) in the service industries that demands change. Far too few courses, whether in the sciences or arts, involve any overseas industrial or commercial experience or attachment to overseas educational establishments. Knowledge of and a first hand contact with the domestic UK scene alone no longer suffices. Only modern language and area studies departments have adopted a consistent commitment to internationalism. Sadly, many teachers in higher education still fail to see how the educational experience for a young European, as all young Britons are, should include exposure to the cultures and languages of partner states. If measures are not taken, for example, through full involvement in the EC's ERASMUS and COMETT schemes for the mobility of students between European universities and between industry and universities, then the UK will be as ill-prepared for the completion of the internal market in 1992 as it was for entry to the Common Market in 1973. It was manufacturing that suffered then. But the most significant and substantial innovation in the new, complete Market, will be the freedom of services. It would be tragic if the UK were not prepared in this, an area of previous success. Here, the wonderful advantage of possessing English as a mother tongue, has had a negative effect, blinding the British to the need to become thoroughly at home in the foreign business cultures and languages of the UK's new European home market. For Europe is linguistically and culturally less a Common Market than a 'Diverse Market'. Yet at the same time it is a sleeping giant that must assume a leadership role in the world's monetary, technological and economic systems.

Conclusions – historical advantage and commitment to educational change and the promotion of Europe

In conclusion, in the midst of the revolution that is occurring as her economy shifts to a basis in knowledge and information, the UK enjoys several advantages – membership of the European Community, the world's largest internal market, while still speaking as its mother tongue the world's lingua franca; historically unique commercial institutions such as Lloyd's of London, a network of banks and insurance companies with long international experience, a legacy of successful markets in foreign exchange, fine art, real estate and others; a location in the world's middle trading time-zone; and what can still claim to be one of the world's liveliest and most diverse higher education systems.

Success will depend on the ability of the authorities to stabilise a world financial system that is more market driven than for over a century and with far greater immediate international enmeshment than in history. This is an area of great challenge, calling for insight, wisdom and statesmanship of a high order.

Success will further depend on a radical improvement in the curricula of schools and in the performance of average and below average pupils. Unfortunately, what may be needed is not only a change in system but a transformation in motivation and attitude towards the value of education.

There will have to be an expansion of higher education through wider access for young people and a major commitment to constant industrial and commercial revival through continuing management education fused with the long traditions of professional training in the international service industries. This is the outstanding example of how one central service industry, education itself, can stimulate growth and competitiveness in other service – and manufacturing – industries.

Finally, the UK must seize the opportunity of membership in the western world's largest economic union to play a leadership role in what may be a dangerously imbalanced world economic and financial order.

Reference

1 W. M. Scammell, *The Stability of the International Monetary System*, Macmillan Education, Basingstoke, 1987. Readers will also find valuable detailed discussion of this topic in *Threats to International Financial Stability*, Richard Portes and Alexander K. Swoboda (eds), CUP, Cambridge, 1987, (for the International Center for Monetary and Banking Studies and the Center for Economic Policy Research).

Appendix 1
Organisations, institutes, companies, etc. consulted by the authors

Government, semi-government and other national bodies
BBC
British Accreditation Council for Independent Further and Higher Education
British Council (Frankie de Freitas, Geoffrey Penzer and Dr James King)
British Embassy, Bonn (Ms C. Pestel, Mr A. F. Hatful, Ms R. M. Marsden, Mr J. W. Forbes-Meyler)
British Invisible Exports Council (Mr William Clarke and Mr Richard Mason)
British Overseas Trade Board (Mr Martin Roberts)
British Tourist Authority and English Tourist Board (Julia Watson, Len Lickorish and Martin Sandbach (Frankfurt))
Bundesinstitut für Berufsbildung, Bonn (Dr W. Kau)
Bundesministerium für Bildung und Wissenschaft, Bonn (Dr Müller-Solger)
Bundesministerium für Wirtschaft, Bonn (Dr J. Grünwald)
Central Statistical Office
Department of Education and Science
Department of Employment
Department of Trade and Industry (Alistair Hunter)
Deutsche Zentrale für Tourismus, Frankfurt (Dr Roth)
Deutsche Industrie-und Handelstag, Bonn (Herr D. Klauser)
Exports Credits Guarantee Department
Hamburg City Government (Herr R. Weiner)
HM Consulate General, Düsseldorf (J. D. N. Hartland-Swann)
HM Consulate General, Hamburg (Alec Goldsmith, Michael Dibben)
IBA
Liberalisation of Trade in Services Committee — LOTIS (Julian Arkell)
Manpower Services Commission (Lord Young and Sylvia Burns)
Port of Hamburg Authority (Herr Lübke)
Super Channel (Richard Hooper)
UK Permanent Representative to the European Communities (Gordon Thompson, Stewart Connolly, Stephen O'Leary)

International organisations
The European Commission (J. Vignon, Office of President, Peter Troberg DG XV, Frederik Sorensen DG VII)
General Agreement on Tariffs and Trade (GATT) — UK Commission, Ambassador Jaramillo

International Labour Office (ILO), Geneva (Mrs Medva Sarfat, Mr von Muralt, Mr Anton Faymann)

The Organisation for European Co-operation and Development (OECD) (John Drew, and members of the UK Commission)

United Nations Conference on Trade and Development (UNCTAD) (Richard Kronenmacher, Murray Gibbs, P. S. Randhawa)

Professional institutes and trade associations etc.

Advertising Association

Association of British Insurers (Tony Baker)

Association of British Travel Agents

Association of Insurance and Risk Managers in Industry and Commerce (R. G. Miller)

British Consultants Bureau (Francis Baden-Powell, Sir Andrew Derbyshire, RMJM)

British Health Education Council (Michael Williams)

British Water International

Bundesverband der Deutschen Industrie, Cologne (Herr von Wolff-Metternich)

Chartered Institute of Arbitrators

Chartered Institute of Bankers (Eric Glover)

Chartered Institute of Insurance (Pat Saxton)

Chartered Institute of Transport

Computer Services Association (Doug Eyeions)

Deutscher Transportversicherungsverband, Hamburg (Dr K. Groth)

Export Group for the Constructional Industries (Peter McGregor)

General Council of British Shipping (Peter le Cheminant)

Hamburg Chamber of Commerce (Herrn H. O. Dworek, Schirmer, Wiemer; Dr Schöne, Dr F. Timmermann)

Hong Kong Chamber of Commerce (J. MacGregor)

Hotel and Catering Training Board

Hotel Catering and Institutional Management Association (Elizabeth Gadsby)

Institute of Chartered Accountants in England and Wales (Ruth Eisenberg)

Institute of Risk Management

International Chamber of Commerce (Giles Wyburd)

The Law Society (Babette Brown)

Scottish Development Agency (Alan Henderson, Jim Williamson)

Scottish Financial Enterprise (Professor Jack Shaw)

Vienna Chamber of Commerce

Banks and other commercial institutions

Albingia Versicherungsgruppe, Hamburg (Dr Plath)

Alexander Howden Group (Margaret Cavanna)

Allianz, A. G. Holding, Munich (Dr Seyfried, Dr Eli)

Bank für Gemeinwirtschaft, Frankfurt (Dr Dettweiler)

Barclays Bank, London (Dr T. Soper), Hamburg (Herr T. A. Wischeropp) Brussels (M. R. L. Obert de Thieusies)

Baring Brothers (Sir John Baring)

Berenberg Bank, Hamburg (Herr C. Budelmann)

Commerzbank, Frankfurt, Glashütten (Herr Kayser, Dr H. W. Detrez)

County National Westminster Bank (Charles Villiers)
Deutsche Bank, Hamburg (Herr Herbert Wiedemann, Thomas Leut)
Deutsche Bundesbank, Frankfurt (Dr Senf)
Deutsche Westminster Bank, Frankfurt (Frank Leeson)
Dresdner Bank, Hamburg (Dr W. Sohl)
European Asian Bank, Hamburg (Herr Ranft)
Frankfurt Stock Exchange (Dr Hamke)
Hamburg Stock Exchange
Hamburgische Landesbank (Herr U. W. Kuske)
Hermes Kreditversicherungs AG, Hamburg (Dr S. Busch)
Hong Kong Bank, Hong Kong (Keith Witson) Hamburg (Herr Lemmerich)
Jardines, Hong Kong, (Martin Barrow)
Legal and General Insurance Co. (Colin Harris)
Lloyds Bank
Lloyd's of London (P. H. Reed, A. O'Dowde)
Midland Bank
Münchener Rück, Munich (Herr R. Küppers)
Nomura International Finance (Dr Andreas Prindl)
Nord-Hypo Bank, Hamburg (Herr Kohler, Dr Müller)
Schröder, Münchmayer, Hengst & Co., Frankfurt (Herr W. Hutmann)
Schroders (Mr G. von Mallinckrodt, Philip Robinson)
Schroders Asia Ltd., Hong Kong (Mr Hurst)
Sedgwick Group (R. Alexander)
Standard Chartered Bank, Hong Kong (Mr Wrangham)
The Stock Exchange (J. Lynton Jones, Sue Proctor)
Trade Policy Research Centre
Vereins und Westbank, Hamburg (Herr G. Tschunke)

Private firms and individuals
Abela Manufacturing (Chris Grater)
Belmont European Community Law Office, Brussels (Stanley Crossick)
Börsenzeitung, Frankfurt (Dr Schanz)
British Telecom (Martin Glazebrook)
Bruce, Peter (*The Financial Times*, Frankfurt/Bonn)
Carr, Jonathan (*The Financial Times*, Frankfurt)
Christie's (Joe Floyd and David Allison)
Clifford Chance, Brussels (Mr Ulick G. Bourke)
Coopers & Lybrand (Jane Sadler)
Deloitte, Haskins & Sells (Peter Flamanck)
Deutsch-Afrika Linien, Hamburg (Herr R. Brennecke)
Greenwell Montagu Research (Jonathan Walker)
Hamburg-Südamerikanische Dampfschiffsgesellschaft, Hamburg (Herr Robert Baack)
Hamilton, Adrian
Hamilton, J. Dundas
House of Lords — Lord Ezra (Aldington Report)
Horwath & Horwath (Jonathan Bodlender)
Johnson, Stokes and Masters, Hong Kong (Robin Peard)
Knight, Frank & Rutley

Lebuhn und Puchta, Hamburg (Dr Karl Puchta)
Lovell, White and King
Peat Marwick & McLintock, Guildford (Michael Stevens)
Reuters
Sotheby's International Realty
Sotheby's (Professor Wilton Ely)
Touche Ross (Jackie Watson)

Educational and research establishments
Bankakademie, Frankfurt (Dr Reinboth)
Banking Information Service (Brian Stevens)
Berufschule, Pinneberg, Schleswig-Holstein (Herr Helmut Witt)
Brighton Polytechnic
City of London Polytechnic (Peter Bond)
City Polytechnic, Hong Kong (Peter McPetridge)
City University (Shiv Mathur)
Deutsche Aussenhandels- und Verkehrsschule, Bremen (Dr. V. Weddige)
Dorset Institute of Higher Education
Glasgow University
Hong Kong University (Professors Brimer, Cheung, Tricker; Dr Chen, Dr Wong, Ms Linda Bauer)
Institute of Shipping Economics and Logistics, Bremen
International Management Institute, Geneva (IMI)
Leeds University
London Business School (John Stopford)
Manchester Business School
Manchester Polytechnic
Polytechnic of Central London (Mike Brown, David Gretton – Transport Studies Group)
Sheffield Polytechnic
Strathclyde University
University of Hamburg (Professor G. Dose, Professor C. H. Redicker)
University of Surrey
University of the Federal German Armed Forces, Hamburg (Professor Hans Reimann)
University of Ulster (W. A. Clarke)
Vienna Hotel Module and Training School
Wirtschaftsakademie, Hamburg (Dr H. O. Dworek)

Appendix 2
Glossary of abbreviations

ABI	Association of British Insurers
ABTA	Association of British Travel Agents
ADP	Automatic Data Processing
ADR	American Depository Receipts
AFBD	Association of Futures Brokers and Dealers
AFE	Agricultural Futures Exchange
AIB	Associate of the Institute of Bankers
AIBD	Association of International Bond Dealers
AIRMIC	Association of Insurance and Risk Managers in Industry and Commerce
ARIEL	Automated Real Time Investment Exchange Ltd.
AS	Advanced Supplementary Level of Education
ATM	Automated Teller Machine
BAA	British Airports Authority
BCB	British Consultants Bureau
BEP	Brevet d'enseignement professionel
BHEC	British Health Education Council
BHTS	British Home Tourism Survey
BIEC	British Invisible Export Council
BIFEX	British International Freight Futures Exchange
BII	British Institute of Innkeeping
BM	Business Monitor
BOTB	British Overseas Trade Board
BPS	British Phonographic Society
BRA	British Robotisation Association
BSB	British Satellite Broadcasting
BTA	British Tourist Authority
BTEC	Business and Technician Education Council
BTn	Baccalauréat de Technicien
BTS	Brevet de Technicien Supérieur
CAP	Certificat d'Aptitude Professionel
CATS	Computer Assisted Trading System
CBI	Confederation of British Industry
CBOE	Chicago Board Options Exchange
CCAB	Central Council for Accounting Bodies
CCC	Customer Co-operation Council

CD	Certificates of Deposit
CEBI	Confédération Européennee des Bureaux des Ingénieurs
CEDIC	International Confederation of Consulting Engineers
CHAPS	Clearing House Automated Payments System
CII	Chartered Institute of Insurance
CIT	Chartered Institute of Transport
CMEA	Council for Mutual Assistance (Comecon)
CNAA	Council for National Academic Awards
COMETT	Community Action Programme in Education and Training for Technology
COTAM	Certificate for Travel Agency Management
COTAC	Certificate of Travel Agency Competence
CP	Commercial Paper
CSA	Computing Services Association
CSE	Certificate of Secondary Education
CSO	Central Statistical Office
DAC	Development Aid Committee (of the OECD)
DES	Department of Education and Science
DOE	Department of Employment
DSc	Doctor of Science
DTI	Department of Trade and Industry (Department for Enterprise)
EC-EEC	European (Economic) Community
ECGD	Export Credit Guarantee Department
ECU	European Currency Unit
EDF	European Development Fund
EDI	Electronic Data Interchange
EFTPOS	Electronic Funds Transfer at Point of Sale
EGCI	Export Group for the Constructional Industries
EIC	European International Contractors
EMS	European Monetary System
ENR	Engineering News Record
EOE	European Options Exchange
ERASMUS	European Action Scheme for the Mobility of University Students
ESPRIT	European Strategic Programme for Research and Development in Information Technology
ESU	English Speaking Union
ETB	English Tourist Board
FCO	Foreign and Commonwealth Office
FIDIC	Féderation International des Ingénieur–Conseils
FIEC	Féderation International Européenne de la Construction
FIMBRA	Financial Intermediaries, Managers and Brokers Regulatory Association
FOREX	Foreign Exchange Market
FOX	London Futures and Options Exchange
FRA	Forward Rate Agreement
FRN	Floating Rate Note

FT	Financial Times
FTSE	Financial Times Stock Exchange Index
GATT	General Agreement on Tariffs and Trade
GCBS	General Council of British Shipping
GCE	General Certificate of Education
GCSE	General Certificate of Secondary Education
GDP	Gross Domestic Product
GEISCO	General Electric Information Services
GEMMs	Gilt-Edged Market Makers
GNP	Gross National Product
GNS	Group for Negotiations on Services (GATT)
HCIMA	Hotel, Catering and Institutional Management Association
HNC	Higher National Certificate
HND	Higher National Diploma
IATA	International Air Transport Association
IBRD	International Bank for Reconstruction and Development
ICAO	International Civil Aviation Organisation
IDA	International Development Association
IDB	Inter-Dealer Brokers
IEA	International Association for the Evaluation of Educational Achievement
IET	Interest Equalisation Tax
ILO	International Labour Office
IMF	International Monetary Fund
IMRO	Investment Management Regulatory Organisation
IMS	Institute of Manpower Studies (Sussex University)
IPE	International Petroleum Exchange
IPS	International Passenger Survey (DTI)
ISDNs	Integrated Services Digital Networks
ISRO	International Securities Regulatory Organisation
IT	Information Technology
ITC	International Tin Council
ITT	Institute of Travel and Tourism
LAUTRO	Life Assurance and Unit Trust Regulatory Organisation
LCE	London Commodities Exchange
LDCs	Lesser Developed Countries
LIBOR	London Inter-Bank Offered Rate
LIFFE	London International Financial Futures Exchange
LME	London Metal Exchange
LOTIS	Liberalisation of Trade in Services Committee
MBA	Master of Business Administration
MFN	Most Favoured Nations
MIT	Massachusetts Institute of Technology
MSC	Manpower Services Commission
MSc	Master of Science

NASDAQ	National Association of Securities Dealers Automated Quotations
NCVQ	National Council for Vocational Qualifications
NICs	Newly Industrialised Countries
NISER	National Institute of Social and Economic Research
OCL	Overseas Containers Ltd.
ODA	Overseas Development Association
OECD	Organisation for European Co-operation and Development
OEEC	Organisation for European Economic Development
OPEC	Organisation of Petroleum Exporting Countries
OTC	Over-the-Counter (trading)
PDM	Physical Distribution Management
PEP	Personal Equity Plans
Quotron	[American view data network]
RIE	Recognised Investment Exchange
RPBs	Recognised Professional Bodies
RUF	Revolving Underwriting Facility
SCOTVEC	Scottish Vocational Education Council
SEAQ	Stock Exchange Automatic Quotations
SEMBs	Stock Exchange Money Brokers
SIB	Securities and Investment Board
SITPRO	Simplification of International Trade Procedures Board
SNIF	Short-term Note Issuance Facility
SROs	Self-regulating Organisations
STOLPORT	Short Take-off and Landing Port
SWIFT	Society for Worldwide Inter-bank Financial Telecommunication
TELEKURS	[German view data network]
TOPIC	[UK Stock Exchange View Data Network]
TRIARCH	Trading Information Architecture
TSA	The Securities Association
TVEI	Technical and Vocational Education Initiative
UCC	Universal Copyright Convention
UNCTAD	United Nations Conference on Trade and Development
USM	Unlisted Securities Market
UWIST	University of Wales Institute of Science and Technology
VAN	Value Added Network
WIPO	World Intellectual Property Organisation
WTO	World Tourism Organisation
YTS	Youth Training Scheme

Index

Page numbers in bold type refer to the list of references at the end of each chapter.

Abela Manufacturing Services Ltd, 240
ABTA, *see* Association of British Travel
  Agents
Accountancy, 87–92, 312, 313, 322, 351
  education and training for, 291–5
  and overseas trade, 293–4
  and tourism consultancy, 239–40
ADRs (American Depository Receipts), 66
Africa
  books exported to, 251–2
Agricultural Futures Exchange (AFE), 120
Agriculture, 12, 24, 321
AIBD (Association of International Bond
  Dealers), 78
Air transport, 16, 139, 152–61
  Baltic Exchange, 126
  insurance, 109
  liberalisation of, 35, 40, 154–7, 161, 341
AIRMIC (Association of Insurance and
  Risk Managers in Industry and
  Commerce), 100, 304
Airports, 158–61
Aldington Report, 320
Alexander Howden, 105, 107, 110
Allianz (Insurance Co.), 96, 101
Alvey Research Fund, 258
Amsterdam
  airport, 160, 161
  financial markets, 338
Andersen (Arthur) & Co, 88, 90, 91, 328,
  330
Anstis, Liz, **260**
Archer, Bryan, 188
ARIEL (Automated Real Time Investment
  Exchange Limited), 66
Arkell, Julian, **41**, **223**
Armed services training colleges, 308–9
Art trade, 127–9
AS level examination, 281
Asian Development Bank, 232, 233
Assersohn, Roy, **112**

Association of British Travel Agents
  (ABTA), 184, 185
Association of Consulting Engineers, 204
AT & T, 162–3
ATM, 56, 57, 74
Auctions, 119, 127–9
Auditing, 88–90
Automated Real Time Investment
  Exchange Limited (ARIEL), 66

BAA (British Airports Authority), 159,
  160
Baden Powell, Francis, **223**
Baker & McKenzie, 238–9
Balance of payments
  and chartered surveyors, 133
  difficulties, 319
  and invisible earnings, 13–14
  and overseas students, 227–8
  royalties and performing rights, 253–4
  and tourism, 171, 172–3, 191
Baltic Exchange (British Mercantile and
  Shipping Exchange), 125–6
Banking services, 11, 15, 322
  and deregulation, 64–5, 70–2
  education and training for, 296–303
  employment in, 12, 13, 325–6, 328
  and the European Community, 39
  for export, 83–7
  and financial information services, 92
  and financial markets, 47–82
  and foreign exchange, 122
  and international competition, 339–40
  OECD Codes of Practice on, 28
  output, 12
Bannock, Graham, **41**
Baring, Sir John, **111**
Basel Committee, 352
Belgium, 20
  property development in Brussels, 132
Bell, Daniel, **21**, 320, 321

Bell Education Trust, 232
Benko, Robert P., **260**
BHEC, *see* British Health Education
    Council
BIEC (British Invisible Exports Council),
    14, 20, **22**, 33, 133, 170, 173, 194, 236,
    332
BIFEX (Baltic International Freight
    Futures Exchange), 120
Big Bang, 65–74, 89, 269, 300, 341
Bill of exchange in export credit
    insurance, 84, 85, 86
Bodlender, Jonathan, 260
Bohdanowicz, Janet, **111**
Book trade, 249–52
Boshoff, Leon, 107
Bretton Woods Agreement, 50, 54
British & Commonwealth Shipping, 141
British Airports Authority (BAA), 159,
    160
British Airways, 139, 152–3
British Consultants Bureau (BCB), 198–9,
    201, 202, 207
British Council, 231, 232, 233, 234, 333
British Health Education Council (BHEC),
    234, **259**
British Invisible Exports Council, *see* BIEC
British Medical Association, 234
British Midland Airways, 157
British Overseas Trade Board, 307
British Robot Association (BRA), 268
BSB (British Satellite Broadcasting), 249
British Telecom, 163
British Tourist Authority (BTA), 171
Brokers
    foreign exchange market, 122–3
    Stock Exchange, 49–50, 66, 67
Brown, Kevin, **167**, **168**
Browne, Mike, **168**
Brussels – property development, 132
BSB (British Satellite Broadcasting), 249
BTA (British Tourist Authority), 171
BTEC (Business and Technician Education
    Council), 182, 271, 287–8
Buckley, Peter, **195**
Building societies, 50, 51, 74–6
    and ATMs, 56
    and deregulation, 65
    and the European Community, 39–40
'Bull and Bear' issues, 62
Bullion market, 114–16
Bunker, Nick, **112**, **113**
Bush, Janet, **135**
Business education, 307–8
Business services – employment in, 12

Byrne, Jim, 300

Cabotage, 40, 143, 150
Cairncross, Francis, **80**, **134**
Cameron-Webb, Peter, 107–8
CAP (Common Agricultural Policy), 30
Carr, Jonathan, **112**
Catering industry *see* Hotel and catering
    industry
CBOE (Chicago Board Options
    Exchange), 57
CEBI (Confédération Européenne des
    Bureaux des Ingénieurs), 199
CEDIC (European Confederation of
    Consulting Engineers), 199
Cellular telephone system, 165
Central Council for the Accounting
    Bodies (CCAB), 291–2
Cerebral revolution, 348–9
    and education, 265–85
Channel Islands, 327
Channel Tunnel, 144, 147–9, 150, 158,
    306
Channon, Derek F., **80**, **195**
CHAPS (Clearing House Automated
    Payments System), 56
Charter airlines, 153–4, 157
Chartered Accountants *see* Accountancy
Chartered Institute of Bankers, 296–7,
    298, 300
Chartered Institute of Insurance, 304
Chartered Institute of Transport, 307
Chartered surveyors, 130–32
Christie's (auction house), 127, 129
Citicorp, 56, 58, 59, 61, 70, 110, 122, 335
City and Guilds Institute of London, 182,
    184, 185
City of London
    airport, 157, 159–60
    banking services
        employment in, 13
    City University Business School, 307,
        313
    education and training for, 288–91
    employment growth in, 325–6
    financial institutions, 15–16, 55–6,
        349–50
    and international competition, 334–5,
        339–40
    polytechnic, 313
    see also London
Civil Aviation Authority, 153
Civil engineering, 196–8, 200
Clarke, William M., **134**
Cleaning services, 12

Clearing banks, 339
  and deregulation, 71
  export credit insurance, 83–4, 86, 87
  and the new technology, 56
Clearing House Automated Payments
    System (CHAPS), 56
Cliffe, Mark, **134**
Clifford Chance, 236, 238
CNAA, *see* Council for National
    Academic Awards
Cockfield, Lord, 39
Codes of Practice – on trade
    liberalisation, 25–6, 26–9, 34, 102
Coggan, Philip, **135**
Cohen, Stephen, 323, **346**
Colleges
  banking courses, 296
  management training, 308–10
  overseas students, 226, 227, 229
  sixth-form, 287
  tourism courses, 186–7, 188–9
  see also Polytechnics; Universities
Commercial Paper (CP), 60, 61, 64, 335
COMETT programme, 333, 355
Commodities market, 94
  London Commodities Exchange,
    118–19, 120
Common Market *see* European
    Community
Compact discs (CDs), 254–5
Compartmentalisation of financial
    activities, 47–52, 344–5
Competition
  in the financial sector, 334–40
  in knowledge-based services, 331–4
  overseas projects, 215–16
  and tourism, 193–4
Comprehensive schools, 279–280, 282–3,
    286
Computers
  software market, 255–8
  see also New technology
Computing Services Association (CSA),
    255, 257
Conferences, 179, 189, 190, 194
Constable Report, 311, **316**, 355
Construction industry, 11, 196–224
Consultancy, 17–18
  accountancy, 89–92
  corporate, 89–92, 350
  design and construction, 201–3
  engineering, 196, 197–9
  markets, 210–12
  medical, 234
  telecommunications, 166

tourism, 225, 239–40
Container trade, 141, 144
Contracting
  construction industry, 200–1
  management, 205–6
Cooper, James, **168**
Coopers & Lybrand, 88, 89, 90, 293
Copyright, Design and Patent Bill (1987),
    240, 243–4, 252
Cornelius, Andrew, **167**
Corporate consultancy, 89–92, 350
Council for Invisible Exports, 33
Council for National Academic Awards
    (CNAA), 182, 288, 303, 310
Cross Commission, 342
Crossick, Stanley, **113**
CSA, *see* Computing Services Association
CSE (Certificate of Secondary Education),
    281
Currency restrictions, 192
Customs Co-operation Council (CCC),
    193

Dale, Richard, **80**, **347**
Deindustrialisation and the British
    economy, 3–10, 320, 321
Derbyshire, Sir Andrew, 207, **223**
Developing countries (Third World
    Countries)
  and consultancy, 197–8, 203–4, 209,
    211–12, 214, 220, 223
  loans to, 54–5
  telecommunications, 166
  water consultancy, 206–7
  see also Latin America
Development of Tourism Act (1969), 171,
    172
Dickinson, Gerald M., **112–13**
Dickson, Tim, **168**
Distance learning
  Stock Exchange examinations, 291
  in tourism, 183–4, 185–6
Dixon, Hugh, **346**
Dixon, Peter, 108
Donne, Michael, **168**, **169**
Drew, John, **42**
Du Cann, Sir Edward, **167**
Durham, Michael, **285**
Duty-free sales
  at airports, 159
  restrictions, in France, 192

Earnings
  consultancy, 210
  insurance, 95, 96, 97

legal services overseas, 236–7
overseas engineering projects, 199
overseas intellectual property trade,
  241–2
tourism, 174–5
Eastern Europe – robotisation, 268
ECGD, *see* Export Credit Guarantee
  Department
EGCI (Export Group for the Construction
  Industries), 201, 210
ECU (European Currency Unit), 38, 353
EDI (Electronic Data Interchange), 95
Edinburgh, 326
Education, 354–5, 356
  and the cerebral revolution, 265–85
  engineering, 198
  in France, Germany and Japan, 270–84
  post-school
    international comparison, 281–2
    in the UK, 286–36, 329–31, 354–5
  professional, 288–307, 354–5
  and tourism, 179–89
  trade in, 225–33
  see also under individual professions, e.g.
    Accountancy
Education Act (1976), 279–80
Education Reform Bill (1987), 266, 280,
  282–4
Edwards, John, **82**
EFTPOS (Electronic Funds Transfer at
  Point of Sale), 39, 56
Emery Worldwide, 158
Employment, 324–31
  in banking, 12, 13, 325–6, 328
  in Britain, 9–10
  in computer software, 257
  in financial services, 71
  futures market, 120–1
  geographical factors, 326–7
  and the new technology, 266–70
  sectoral changes, 324–6
  in service industries, 11–13, 38, 324–6
  shipping crews, 141–2
  in tourism, 12, 171, 177–80, 190, 191,
    194
EMS (European Monetary System), 38,
  342, 353, 354
Engineering consultancy, 17–18, 196–224
Engineering News Record, 210, 211, 212
English language, 333–4, 339, 350, 355
EOE (European Options Exchange), 63
Equities, investment in, 51
Equities 2000 system, 94
ERASMUS programme, 333, 355
Ernst & Whinney, 88, 89, 90

Estate agencies, 75
ETB (English Tourist Board), 171, 178
Eurobond market, 40, 53–4, 59–60, 61,
  66, 76, 79, 93–5
  and deregulation, 65, 66, 67, 69, 73, 334
  and export credit insurance, 85
  and foreign exchange, 122
  and international competition, 334, 335,
    336
Eurocurrency market, 53, 122, 334
Europe
  air transport, 152–8
  airports, 160–1
  consultancy markets, 211
  ports, 145
  property development, 131–2
European Community (EC), 341, 353–4
  air transport, 154, 155–6, 157–8, 161
  completion of Internal Market (1992),
    36, 38–41, 258, 324, 355
  and construction projects, 209
  and cross-border insurance, 40–1,
    102–4
  and international travel, 192
  and the legal profession, 237–8
  and manufactures export, 95
  property development, 131
  and research, 333
  and road haulage, 149–50
  shipping, 143
  students from, 233
  and telecommunications, 161, 163–5, 166
  and trade liberalisation, 25, 29, 30,
    35–41, **43**, 216
  visitors from, 174
European Currency Unit (ECU), 38, 353,
  354
European Development Fund (EDF), 220
European Monetary System (EMS), 38,
  342, 353, 354
European Options Exchange (EOE), 63,
  338
European Payments Union, 25
Evergreen shipping line, 144, 146
Examinations
  in France, 270–1
  Stock Exchange, 290–1
  in the UK, 280–1
Exchange controls, abolition of, 34, 54–5,
  66, 122, 334
Exchange Options Development Group,
  63
Exhibitions, 179, 189–91, 194
Expenditure
  by overseas students, 18, 227–8

by overseas visitors, 175, 176
trade fair and conference visitors, 189
Export Credit Guarantee Department
    (ECGD), 83, 84–5, 86, 217–18, 219,
    307
Export credit insurance, 83–7
Export Group for the Construction
    Industries (EGCI), 201, 210
Export houses, 133
Export prospects – construction and
    engineering, 207–16
Eyeions, Douglas, **261**

Federal Republic of Germany (West
    Germany)
  accountancy, 87, 88, 312
  age of graduates, 302, 330
  banking, 302–3
  book trade, 250
  computer software industry, 258
  and cross-border insurance, 40–1,
      102–4
  economy, 3, 4, 6, 7, 9, 20
  education and training in, 266, 271–6,
      279, 329, 330
  financial markets, 62, 76, 337
  insurance, 96
  legal services, 238
  management employment, 329
  music market, 253
  property development, 132
  service employment, 12
  shipping, 140
  visitors from, 189
Felixstowe, 146
Ferry services, 143–4
FIDIC (Fédération Internationale des
    Ingénieurs Conseils), 199, 201, 204–5,
    212
Fidler, Stephen, **81**
Films, 35
  earnings from royalties, 242
  exports of, 246–9, **260–1**
  OECD Codes of Practice on, 28
  sale of rights, 18
Financial control, 90
Financial services, 14, 47–82, 83–113,
    323–4, 349–50
  co-ordinated export policies, 214–15
  and deregulation, 65–74
  education and training for, 296–303
  export credit insurance, 83–7
  foreign exchange market, 121–4
  geographical location, 326–7

and international competition, 334–40
and liberalisation, 39–40, 340–5
OECD Codes of Practice on, 28
regulation of, 76–9
stabilising, 352–4, 356
and technological development, 268–9
see also Accountancy; Banking;
    Insurance
Financial Services Act (1986), 34, 73, 76,
    77–9, 89, 108, 117, 294
Finsinger, Jörg, **113**
Fire insurance, 98
Fisher, Andrew, **167**
Fisher, Sir Henry, 107
Floating exchange rates, 34, 54–5, 79
Floating rate note (FRN), 61–2
Food industry, 11
Foreign exchange market in London,
    121–4
Foreign languages
  and accountancy, 294, 295
  and banking, 299
  and legal training, 296
  and management employment, 329
  see also English language
Foreign trade – OECD Codes of Practice
    on, 27
Forfaiting in export financing, 85–6
Forward exchange contract, 86
Forward Rate Agreements (FRAs), 63
Forwards in foreign exchange dealings,
    123
FOX (London Futures and Options
    Exchange), 120–1
France
  accountants, 87, 88, 312
  banks, 58
  computer software industry, 258
  economy, 4, 5, 6, 7, 20
  education and training in, 266, 270–1,
      279, 330
  financial markets, 76, 337–8
  insurance, 101
  legal services, 238
  rail network, 147
  shipping, 140
  telecommunications, 162
  tourism, 192
Franks, Lord, 310
Freeports, 145
Freight markets, 158, 322
  Baltic Exchange, 125–6
  in the United States, 151
Freightliners, 146
FRN (Floating rate note), 61–2

Funding – overseas projects, 200–1, 220–3
Futures market, 62–3, 116, 117–18, 119–21, 123

GATT (General Agreement on Tariffs and Trade), 21, 25, 29–30, 31–5, 36, 41, **42**
  and intellectual property, 245–6
  Uruguay Round, 31, 38, 41, 42, 102, 192, 193, 207, 241, 246
Gatwick Airport, 159, 160
GCSE (General Certificate of Secondary Education), 281, 283
GEISCO (General Electric Information Services), 95
Germany *see* Federal Republic of Germany
Gibbs, Murray, **43**
Gilt-Edged Market-Makers (GEMMS), 68
Glass-Steagall Act (1933), 48, 58, 334
Gold market, 114–16
Goodman, Harry, **195**
Graduates, age of, 302, 330
Graham, George, **347**
Grammar schools, 279–80, 281, 286, 329
Gretton, David, **168**

Halifax Building Society, 74, 75–6
Hamburg freeport, 145
Hamilton, Adrian, **80**, **81**
Hamilton, J. Dundas, **80**
Hammond, Elizabeth, **113**
Handy Report, 311, 312, 316, 331, 355
Harrison, I. S., **223**
Harvey-Jones, Sir John, 320, **346**
Hastings, Catherine, **111**
Hastings, Philip, **168**
Haulage industry *see* Road haulage
HCIMA (Hotel, Catering and Institutional Management Association), 184
Health-Care – trade in, 225, 233–5, **259**
Heath, C. E., 110
Heath, Cuthbert, 105
Heath, Edward, 67
Heathrow Airport, 158, 159, 160
High technology *see* New technology
Hills, J., **80**
Hindley, Brian, **41**, **42**
Hodgson, Godfrey, **113**
Hogg, Nicholas, **134**
Hong Kong – legal services, 238–9
Hooper, Richard, **261**

Hotel, Catering and Institutional Management Association (HCIMA), 184
Hotel and catering industry
  education and training, 179–89
  employment in, 12, 177–8
  investment in, 176, 177
Hotel and Catering Industry Training Board, 182, 183–4
Hozier, Henry, 127
Human resources and accountancy, 91

ICL (International Computers Ltd), 258
IET (Interest Equalisation Tax), 52–3
Income *see* Earnings
Independent schools, 280, 281, 282
Indonesia, 232
Industrial Training Act (1964), 183
Information technology
  and accountancy, 90–1
  consultancy on, 90–1
  and the European Community, 39
  see also New technology
Insider dealing, 48, 334
Instinet (Institutional Networks Corporation), 57
Institute of Chartered Accountants, 291, 294–5
Insurance, 95–111, 322–3, 351
  broking, 104–11
  companies, 15, 51, 95–8
  education and training for, 303–6
  export credit insurance, 83–7
  freedom in cross-border, 40–1, 102–4
  OECD Codes of Practice on, 27
  trade barriers, 35, 102–4
  see also Lloyd's of London
Integrated Services Digital Networks (ISDNs), 164
Intellectual property, trade in, 225, 240–55, **260**, 333
Inter-Dealer Brokers (IDBS), 68
Interest Equalisation Tax (1963), 51
International Bank for Reconstruction and Development (IBRD), 219
International Civil Aviation Organisation (ICAO), 193
International Development Association (IDA), 219
International Finance Corporation, 219
International Labour Office (ILO), 31, 265, 267, 268
International Monetary Fund (IMF), **193**

International organizations – tourism, 192–3
International Petroleum Exchange (IPE), 120
International Realty Company, 130
International Securities Regulatory Organisation (ISRO), 73, 334
International Tin Council (ITC), 117
Investment
  income, 14
  in tourism, 176–7
IPE (International Petroleum Exchange), 120
ISDNs (Integrated Services Digital Networks), 164
ISRO (International Securities Regulatory Organisation), 73, 334
Italy
  economy, 3, 4, 5, 6, 7
  service employment, 12

Japan
  accountancy, 87, 312
  age of graduates, 302
  banks, 58, 70
  economy, 3, 4, 5, 6, 7, 9, 20
  education and training in, 266, 276–9, 329, 354
  financial markets, 48, 62, 77, 79, 335–6, 336–7, 338, 340
  manufacturing output, 321
  music market, 253
  property development, 131
  robotisation, 268
  telecommunications, 162, 166
  and trade liberalisation, 26, 34
Jaramillo, Felipe, 32, 42
Jobbers (Stock Exchange), 49–50, 66, 67
Johnson, Lyndon B., 53
Johnson Stokes and Masters, 238
'Just in Time' manufacturing, 150–1, 158

Katz, Ronald, 168
Kennacott, 118
Kerr, Ian M., 80
Knight, Frank & Rutley, 131
Knowledge-based services see Specialist skills and knowledge
Kronenmacher, Richard, 43

Land transport, 16, 40, 147–51
Landau, Sue, 111
Language see English language; Foreign languages

Lascelles, David, 64, 81, 82, 135
Latin America – debts, 33, 54–5, 59, 60, 343–4
Laverick, Patrick, 189, 260
Law
  and accountancy, 88
  on intellectual property, 240–1, 243–4
  recruitment and training, 295–6
  trade in legal services, 225, 235–9, 259
LDCs (less developed countries) construction contracts, 213–14
Legal services see Law
Leisure sector, 11, 12, 17
  employment in, 177, 178–9, 325
  investment in, 176
  see also Tourism
Lewis, Tony, 261
Liberalisation
  air services, 35, 40, 154–7, 161
  financial services, 39–40, 340–5
  trade, 21, 23–43
  and consultancy, 207
Liberalisation of Trade in Services (LOTIS), 216, 268
LIBOR (London Interbank Offered Rate), 61
Licenses, income from, 242, 243, 323
Life assurance, 99, 326, 336
LIFFE (London International Financial Futures Exchange), 63, 78, 119, 123
Link (ATM network), 74
Linklaters and Paines (L & P), 239
Lipman, Geoffrey, 167
Liston, David, 284
Liverpool freeport, 145
Llewellyn, D. T., 80
Lloyd's Loading List, 126
Lloyd's List, 126
Lloyd's of London, 55–6, 79, 100, 101, 104–9, 109–10, 111, 304, 339
  and export credit insurance, 85
  history, 98–9
  recruitment, 305
Lloyd's Register of Shipping, 55–6, 126–7, 146
Lloyd's Shipping Index, 12
London
  and the art trade, 128–9
  conferences, 190
  and the Eurobond market, 53, 54
  foreign exchange market, 121–4
  international service industries, 326
  and tourism, 175, 176, 191, 193
  see also City of London

London Commodities Exchange, 118–19, 120
London Futures and Options Exchange (FOX), 120–1
London Interbank Offered Rate (LIBOR), 61
London International Financial Futures Exchange, see LIFFE
London Metal Exchange (LME), 116–18, 119, 120
LOTIS (Liberalisation of Trade in Services), 216, 268
Luton Airport, 159
Luxembourg, 20
Luxembourg Compromise, 38, 155–6

Macmillan, Harold, 3
Man, Isle of, 327
Management
  education and training for, 308–14
  employment, 327–9
Management consultancy, 91
Management contracting, 205–6
Managing agents at Lloyd's, 105, 107
Manchester
  airport, 160
  G-Mex complex, 176–7
Manpower Services Commission (MSC), 182, 267, 284, 287
Manufacturing economy, 348
  decline of, 3–10, 319–20, 349
  exports, and new technology, 95
  and service industries, 10–11, 319–24, 341, 345
Marine insurance see Shipping
Marshall Aid, 25, 30, 52
Mason, Richard, 41
Matrix network (building societies), 74
MBA (Master of Business Administration) courses, 299, 300–1, 313, 330, 331
McGregor, Peter, 223
McRae, Hamish, 80, 134, 346–7
Medical equipment, exports of, 234–5
Medical students, 233–4
Merchant banks, 339
  and compartmentalisation, 48–9, 51–2
  and deregulation, 70–1, 71–2
  and export credit insurance, 85–6, 86, 87
Merchant shipping, decline in, 140, 142, 147
Mercury Communications Ltd, 163
Metals market, 116–18, 120
Meyer, F. V., 7, 21
Miller, Peter, 108, 109

Miller, Roger, 100, 112
Mitchell, Charles, 60
Monopoly and intellectual property, 245–6
Montgomery, Field Marshall, 309
Moore, John, 113, 166
Moore, Peter, 316
Morrell, James, 194
Mullock, David, 259
Murdoch, Rupert, 249
Music trade, 252–5

NASDAQ dealing system, 57, 65, 67, 69, 290
National Association of Securities Dealers, 57
National Council for Vocational Qualifications (NCVQ), 287
National technological schools, 287
Neill Report, 104, 108
Netherlands, 20
  Amsterdam airport, 160, 161
  financial markets, 76, 338
New technology
  and employment, 266–70, 326
  and financial services, 55–7, 289
  and Lloyd's, 109
  see also Information technology; Telecommunications
New York Insurance Exchange, 109
New York Stock Exchange, 65, 67, 290
Nicoll, Alexander, 81
NICs (newly-industrialised countries)
  construction contracts, 213–14
Nobes, Christopher, 111
Nomura Securities Co, 336–7, 338
Non-trariff barriers – GATT negotiations on, 33–5
Norway, 4, 9
  shipping, 140
Note issuance facility (NIF), 64
Nott, John, 66

O'Brien, Una, 258
OCL (Overseas Containers Ltd), 144
OECD (Organisation for Economic Co-operation and Development), 21, 25, 26–9, 30, 31, 42, 216
  Codes of Practice, 26–9, 34, 102
  Development Aid Committee (DAC), 222
OEEC (Organisation for European Economic Co-operation), 25–6, 30, 42
Oil prices – effects of increases, 54, 140, 211, 352

Oil tanker market, 140
Open account method in export credit
    insurance, 84
Open College, 182, 186
Open learning in tourism, 183–4
Open management courses, 311
Optical fibre technology, 161, 162
Options market, 63, 86, 117–18, 119–21,
    123, 338
Organizations, international tourism,
    192–3
Ostrey, Sylvia, 42
OTC (over the counter) trading, 57
Over-the-counter selling in tourism,
    184–5
Overseas Students Trust, 226, 228, 230,
    332
Overseas visitors, 174–6; see also
    Students, overseas
Owen, Edward, 346

P & O, 143–4, 146
Parker, Gordon, 146
Parkinson, Cecil, 67
Part-time work, 327
Patents, 242, 243, 244, 245, 323
Pavaux, Jacques, 168
Payment in export credit insurance, 84–7
Pearson, Clare, 81
Pearson, Malcolm, 106–7
Pearson, Richard, 22, 285
Peat Marwick McLintock, 88, 89, 90, 91,
    293, 294
Pecchioli, Rinaldo, 347
Peisley, Tony, 167
Performing rights, 254
Personal qualities
    and accounting, 293
    for management employment, 328–9,
        350
Petit, Pascal, 345
Pfeiffer, John, 285
Pharmaceutical companies, 234
Physical distribution management (PDM),
    150
Pisters, Marcel, 166, 168
Pitcher, George, 82
Pollock, Eric, 167
Polytechnics
    banking courses, 296
    City of London, 313
    law degrees, 296
    overseas students, 230–1
    tourism courses, 187, 188
Portes, Richard, 356

Ports, 144–7
Post-industrialism, 320–1
Postal services, 18
Prais, S. J., 284
Prest, Michael, 134
Price Waterhouse, 88, 293
Prindl, A., 79
Prindl, Andreas, 336, 337
Private sector
    balance of payments, 14
    invisible earnings, 18–19
Privatisation
    consultancy on, 89–90
    and overseas contracting, 203
Professional associations
    engineering consultancy, 198–9
    and financial markets, 78
    in the tourist industry, 184–5
    see also under individual associations, e.g.
        Institute of Chartered Accountants
Professional education, 288–307, 354–5
Property
    real estate, 130–32
    intellectual, 225, 240–55, 260, 333
Property rights, international and the
    international trading system, 244–5
Protectionism, 31, 34
    and the European Community, 36–7
    and financial markets, 51, 52
Prouse, Michael, 347
Publishing – exports of books, 249–52

Queen Elizabeth II Conference Centre,
    176, 190

Rada, Juan F., 111, 169
Railways, 147–9
Rajan, A., 22, 195, 267, 284, 285, 346
Randhawa, P. S., 43
Ray, George F., 22
Real estate, 130–33
Recognised Investment Exchanges (RIEs),
    78
Recognised Professional Bodies (RPBs), 78
Recruitment
    accountancy, 292–3, 294
    banking, 298–9
    futures market, 120–1
    insurance, 305–6
    law, 295–6
    Stock Exchange, 289–90
    tourist industry, 181
Registrar of Friendly Societies, 50, 75
Reid, Bob, 316
Reinsurance companies, 100, 109

Restrictive Trade Practices Act (1956), 66
Reuters, 69, 76, 92–5, 124
Revolving Underwriting Facility (RUF), 64
Rich Inc., 94–5
Riddle, Dorothy, 267–8, 320, **345–6**
RIEs (Recognised Investment Exchanges),
    78
Rimmington, Mike, **195**
Road haulage, 40, 139, 148, 149–51
Robotisation, 268
Rose, Harold, 308, **316**
Rothschild, Jacob, 69
Royalties, trade in, 241–2, 243, 249–52,
    253–4, 323
RPBs (Recognised Professional Bodies), 78
RUF (Revolving Underwriting Facility), 64

Samuels, Alex, **82**
Sasse affair, 107
Satellite technology, 39, 162–3, 249
Savonita affair, 106–7
Saxon, Pat, 101
Scammell, W. M., 353, **356**
Schleicher, Julius, 104
Schooling
    in Germany, 272–4
    in Japan, 277–9
    in the UK, 279–84, 286–7
Scotland
    accountancy training, 295
    banking recruitment, 299
    financial services, 15, 326
    legal training, 295–6
    life assurance societies, 99, 326
    management training, 309
    schools, 286
SCOTVEC (Scottish Vocational
    Educational Council), 182
SEAQ, *see* Stock Exchange Automated
    Quotation System
Securities and Investments Board (SIB),
    77, 79, 120, 290
Securities market, 49, 57, 58, 66–7, 335–6
Securitisation of banking and capital
    markets, 58–61
Self-Regulating Organisations (SROs),
    77–8, 79, 289
SEMBS (Stock Exchange Money Brokers),
    68
Service industries, 348, 355
    employment in, 11–13, 38, 324–6
    and the European Community, 35–41
    GATT negotiations on, 31, 32–3
    growth of, 8, 10–13, 267

liberalisation of trade in, 35–41, 216–17
and manufacturing, 10–11, 319–24, 341,
    345
successful, 350–1
vulnerabilities of, 351–2
in West Germany, 274
Sheffield Polytechnic, 181
Shegog, Andrew, **81**, **346**
Sherwood Forest Development Complex,
    177
Shipping, 16, 20, 139, 140–7
    Baltic Exchange, 125–6
    decline in market, 321, 325
    developments in, 306–7
    flags of convenience, 35, 141–2, 307
    insurance, 98, 99, 100, 109
    Lloyd's Register, 55–6, 126–7, 146
    ports, 144–7
Short-term Note Issuance Facility (SNIF),
    64
SIB, *see* Securities and Investments Board
Singapore, 232
Singh, Ajit, **21**
SITPRO (Simplification of Internal Trade
    Procedures Board), 83, 307
Siwek, Stephen S., **260**
Sky (satellite channel), 249
Small Business Expansion Scheme, 72
Smeaton, John, **196**
Smithsonian Agreement, 54
SNIF (Short-term Note Issuance Facility),
    64
Society of Civil Engineers, 196
Soft commodities market, 116, 118–19,
    121
Software, computing, 255–8
Sotheby's, 127, 129, 130
Southampton, 145
Sowton, Elizabeth, **112**
Spain and the Air Transport package, 40,
    155–6
Specialist skills and knowledge, 255–61,
    348
    international competition for, 331–4
Spot transactions in foreign exchange
    dealings, 123
SROs, *see* Self-Regulating Organisations
Staines, R., **134**
Stansted Airport, 159
Steedman, Hilary, 270
Step-down bonds, 62
Step-up bonds, 62
Stock Exchange, 322
    and compartmentalisation, 49–50, 51

and deregulation, 65–74
education and training for, 288–91
and international competition, 334, 335
and options, 63
origins of, 55–6
Stock Exchange Automated Quotation
    System (SEAQ), 68–9, 72, 339
Stock Exchange Money Brokers (SEMBS),
    68
Stock Market crash (1987), 269, 326,
    342–3, 351–2
STOLPORT (London City Airport), 157,
    159–60
Students, overseas, 226–31, **258**, 332
    expenditure, 18, 227–8
    medical, 233–4
Super Channel, 249
Surveyors, chartered, 130–32
Swaps in financial markets, 63–4, 123–4,
    218
Sweden – shipping, 140
SWIFT (Society of Worldwide Interbank
    Financial Telecommunications), 92
Switzerland
    banks, 70
    Zurich, 121–2, 338–9
Swoboda, Alexander K., **356**

Tapp, Julian, **113**
Tariff reform and GATT, 29–30, 31, 33–5
Taubmann, Alfred, 129
Taxation
    and the European Community, 37
    and financial markets, 51
Taylor, H. J. B., **316**
Technological change see New technology
Telecommunications, 18, 35, 39, 161–6,
    322
Telefax, 57
Telerate, 94
Television
    earnings from royalties, 242
    exports of programmes, 246–9, **260–1**
    sale of rights, 18
Telex, invention of, 56
Thames Water Authority, 207
Third Market, 72
Third World countries, see Developing
    countries
Thomas, David, **169**, **261**
Thomas, W. A., **80**
Thomson, David, **113**
Tin market, 116–17, 119
'Tom and Jerry' bonds, 62

Touche Ross, 88, 89–90
Tourism, 16–17, 170–95, 320, 323, 325,
    331, 332, 351, 355
    and the balance of payments, 19
    definition, 172–3
    education and training in, 179–89
    employment in, 12, 171, 177–80, 190,
        191, **194**
    future of, 191–4
    overseas consultancy, 225, 239–40, **260**
    statistics, 173–8
    and transport, 139
Tourist Authorities Information Centres,
    179
Trade barriers, 24–5
    in insurance, 102–4
    see also Liberalisation
Trade fairs, 179, 189–91
Training
    engineering, 198
    for the professions, 288–307
    and tourism, 179–89, 191
    see also Education
Transport, 16–17, 139–61
    development and training, 306–7
    employment in, 177, 179, 325
    and the European Community, 40
    OECD Codes of Practice on, 27
    vulnerability of, 139
    see also Air transport; Land transport;
        Shipping
Travel industry
    barriers to international travel, 192, 193
    employment in, 177, 179
Travel agencies, 184–5
Treasury management, 90
TRIARCH (Trading Information
    Architecture), 95
TSB (Trustee Savings Bank), 72
Turkey, 232
Turner, Brian, **195**
Turnkey contracts, 204–5, 215
TVEI (Technical and Vocational Education
    Initiative), 204–5, 215

UNCTAD (United Nations Conference on
    Trade and Development), 25, 29,
    30–1, 36, 41, **43**, 268
    and consultancy, 207
    and intellectual property, 241, 246
Unemployment, 324, 351
United States
    air transport
        deregulation of, 156

and the art trade, 127
banks, 58, 70
books exported to, 251, 252
commodities market, 118
computing software, 255
and consultancy, 202, 211
deindustrialisation, 8, 9
economy, 3, 4, 5, 6, 7
and the Euromarkets, 52–3
financial markets, 47–8, 57, 58, 60, 61,
    76–7, 79
freight services, 151
government bond services, 94
insurance broking, 109–10
as insurance market, 96
manufacturing output, 321
music market, 253
real estate market, 130
robotisation, 268
service employment, 12
service sector, 319
Stock Exchange examinations, 291
and the stock market crash (1987),
    342–3
telecommunications market, 162–3, 166
and trade liberalisation, 34, 35
visitors from, 171, 172, 174, 189, 192
Universal Copyright Convention (UCC),
    245
Universities
  banking degrees, 298–9
  engineering courses, 198
  law degrees, 296
  management training, 309, 310
  overseas students, 227, 229, 230
  tourism courses, 187–8
  in West Germany, 275
University Grants Committee, 332–3
Urwick, Colonel, 309–10
USM (Unlisted Securities Market), 72, 73
USSR (Union of Soviet Socialist
    Republics)
  book trade, 250
  robotisation, 268

VANS (Value-added network services),
    165
Villiers, C., **80**
Visitors, overseas, 174–6
Vocational training in France, Germany
    and Japan, 270–84
Volcker, Paul, 341–2

Volk, B., **166**, **167**
Voluntary Foreign Credit Restraint
    Programme (1965), 53

Wagner, Karin, **284**
Wales – grammar schools, 286
Warburg (S G) & Co, 53, 69, 70–1, 76,
    339
Water supply, technology and
    management overseas consultancy,
    206–7
Waters, Richard, **111**
Weinstock, Lord, 320
West Germany *see* Federal Republic of
    Germany
Western Europe
  book trade, 251
  robotisation, 268
Wheatcroft, Stephen, **167**
Whitley, Thomas, **316**
Wilkinson, Philip, 298
Williams, Elaine, **112**
Williams, Gareth, **258**
Williams, P., **258**
Wilson, Harold, 5
Wilton-Ely, John, **134**
Wolmar, Clive, **111**
Women – employment, 267, 327
Woodhall, Maureen, **258**
World Bank
  educational contracts, 232, 233
  overseas contracts, 203, 204, 205, 213,
      218, 219–21
World Intellectual Property Organisation
    (WIPO), 245
World Tourism Organisation (WTO),
    192–3
Wriston, Walter, 56

Yorkshire
  conference centres, 190
Young, Charles B., **81**
YTS (Youth Training Scheme), 271, 287
Yugoslavia, 26, 192

Zeebrugge disaster (1987), 143–4
Zero coupon bonds, 62, 64
Zurich
  financial markets, 338–9
  foreign exchange markets, 121–2
Zysman, John, 323, **346**